# Big Data Analytics for Cultural Heritage

# Big Data Analytics for Cultural Heritage

Editors

**Manolis Wallace**
**Vassilis Poulopoulos**
**Angeliki Antoniou**
**Martín López-Nores**

MDPI • Basel • Beijing • Wuhan • Barcelona • Belgrade • Manchester • Tokyo • Cluj • Tianjin

*Editors*
Manolis Wallace
University of Peloponnese
Greece

Vassilis Poulopoulos
University of Peloponnese
Greece

Angeliki Antoniou
University of Peloponnese
Greece

Martín López-Nores
University of Vigo
Spain


*Editorial Office*
MDPI
St. Alban-Anlage 66
4052 Basel, Switzerland

This is a reprint of articles from the Special Issue published online in the open access journal *Big Data and Cognitive Computing* (ISSN 2504-2289) (available at: https://www.mdpi.com/journal/BDCC/special_issues/data_heritage).

For citation purposes, cite each article independently as indicated on the article page online and as indicated below:

LastName, A.A.; LastName, B.B.; LastName, C.C. Article Title. *Journal Name* **Year**, *Volume Number*, Page Range.

**ISBN 978-3-0365-6326-8 (Hbk)**
**ISBN 978-3-0365-6327-5 (PDF)**

© 2023 by the authors. Articles in this book are Open Access and distributed under the Creative Commons Attribution (CC BY) license, which allows users to download, copy and build upon published articles, as long as the author and publisher are properly credited, which ensures maximum dissemination and a wider impact of our publications.

The book as a whole is distributed by MDPI under the terms and conditions of the Creative Commons license CC BY-NC-ND.

# Contents

**About the Editors** . . . . . . . . . . . . . . . . . . . . . . . . . . . . . . . . . . . . . . . . . . . . . . . . . . . . . . . . . . . . **vii**

**Manolis Wallace, Vassilis Poulopoulos, Angeliki Antoniou and Martín López-Nores**
An Overview of Big Data Analytics for Cultural Heritage
Reprinted from: *Big Data Cogn. Comput.* **2023**, 7, 14, doi:10.3390/bdcc7010014 . . . . . . . . . . . . 1

**Costas Vassilakis, Konstantinos Kotis, Dimitris Spiliotopoulos, Dionisis Margaris, Vlasios Kasapakis, Christos-Nikolaos Anagnostopoulos, et al.**
A Semantic Mixed Reality Framework for Shared Cultural Experiences Ecosystems
Reprinted from: *Big Data Cogn. Comput.* **2020**, 4, 6, doi:10.3390/bdcc4020006 . . . . . . . . . . . . 3

**Kimon Deligiannis, Paraskevi Raftopoulou, Christos Tryfonopoulos, Nikos Platis and Costas Vassilakis**
Hydria: An Online Data Lake for Multi-Faceted Analytics in the Cultural Heritage Domain
Reprinted from: *Big Data Cogn. Comput.* **2020**, 4, 7, doi:10.3390/bdcc4020007 . . . . . . . . . . . . 25

**Dimitris Spiliotopoulos, Dionisis Margaris and Costas Vassilakis**
Data-Assisted Persona Construction Using Social Media Data
Reprinted from: *Big Data Cogn. Comput.* **2020**, 4, 21, doi:10.3390/bdcc4030021 . . . . . . . . . . . 53

**Markos Konstantakis, Georgios Alexandridis and George Caridakis**
A Personalized Heritage-Oriented Recommender System Based on Extended Cultural Tourist Typologies
Reprinted from: *Big Data Cogn. Comput.* **2020**, 4, 12, doi:10.3390/bdcc4020012 . . . . . . . . . . . 67

**Markos Konstantakis, Yannis Christodoulou, John Aliprantis and George Caridakis**
ACUX Recommender: A Mobile Recommendation System for Multi-Profile Cultural Visitors Based on Visiting Preferences Classification
Reprinted from: *Big Data Cogn. Comput.* **2022**, 6, 144, doi:10.3390/bdcc6040144 . . . . . . . . . . 85

**Ioannis C. Drivas, Damianos P. Sakas, Georgios A. Giannakopoulos and Daphne Kyriaki-Manessi**
Big Data Analytics for Search Engine Optimization
Reprinted from: *Big Data Cogn. Comput.* **2020**, 4, 5, doi:10.3390/bdcc4020005 . . . . . . . . . . . . 97

**Irene Vargianniti and Kostas Karpouzis**
Using Big and Open Data to Generate Content for an Educational Game to Increase Student Performance and Interest
Reprinted from: *Big Data Cogn. Comput.* **2020**, 4, 30, doi:10.3390/bdcc4040030 . . . . . . . . . . . 119

**Georgios Drakopoulos, Yorghos Voutos and Phivos Mylonas**
Annotation-Assisted Clustering of Player Profiles in Cultural Games: A Case for Tensor Analytics in Julia
Reprinted from: *Big Data Cogn. Comput.* **2020**, 4, 39, doi:10.3390/bdcc4040039 . . . . . . . . . . . 139

**Jordi Morales-i-Gras, Julen Orbegozo-Terradillos, Ainara Larrondo-Ureta and Simón Peña-Fernández**
Networks and Stories. Analyzing the Transmission of the Feminist Intangible Cultural Heritage on Twitter
Reprinted from: *Big Data Cogn. Comput.* **2021**, 5, 69, doi:10.3390/bdcc5040069 . . . . . . . . . . . 163

**Vassilis Poulopoulos and Manolis Wallace**
Digital Technologies and the Role of Data in Cultural Heritage: The Past, the Present, and the Future
Reprinted from: *Big Data Cogn. Comput.* **2022**, *6*, 73, doi:10.3390/bdcc6030073 . . . . . . . . . . . **181**

# About the Editors

**Manolis Wallace**

Manolis Wallace, Associate Professor—Manolis Wallace is an associate professor of the Department of Informatics and Telecommunications of the University of Peloponnese. Previously, he was with the Athens Campus of the University of Indianapolis, where he served as the chair of the Department of Computer Science, as well as at the Foundation of the Hellenic World, where he served as a project coordinator. He now continues to work at the University of the Peloponnese, where he leads the Knowledge and Uncertainty Research Laboratory (ΓAB LAB).

**Vassilis Poulopoulos**

Vassilis Poulopoulos, Assistant Professor—Vassilis Poulopoulos is an assistant professor at the Department of Digital Systems of the University of Peloponnese. His fields of interest include big data analytics and cultural informatics. He has participated as a researcher in various national and European projects and has several publications in the aforementioned fields. As a member of the Knowledge and Uncertainty Research Laboratory (ΓAB LAB), he is engaged in building closer connections between the local community of Peloponnese and the university.

**Angeliki Antoniou**

Angeliki Antoniou, Assistant Professor—Dr Angeliki Antoniou is currently an Assistant Professor at the Department of Archival, Library & Information Studies, University of West Attica (Greece), an honorary research staff member at the Department of Information Studies, University College London (UCL, UK) and an external researcher at the Athena Research & Innovation Center (Athens, Greece). She received a degree in Preschool Education from the University of Athens (Greece), and Bachelor of Science in Social with Clinical Psychology from the University of Kent at Canterbury (UK). She has also obtained a Master of Science in Human Computer Interaction with Ergonomics (2001) from the University College London (UK) and a PhD from the Department of Computer Science and Technology (University of Peloponnese). She serves as a PC member and a referee in national and international conferences and international journals. Furthermore, she has participated both as a researcher and a coordinator in various national and European projects.

**Martín López-Nores**

Martín López-Nores teaches in the area of Telematics engineering at the University of Vigo, Spain. He has co-authored more than 150 publications in international forums and has been a project evaluator for national and international calls. He has been principal investigator in projects with companies and consortia at the European level, including the 7th Framework Program of the European Union and the H2020 program. His interests include communications services in mobile networks, the semantic web in the cultural heritage domain, and new technologies applied to the diagnosis and treatment of cognitive and communication disorders.

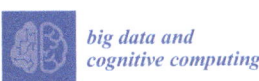

*Editorial*

# An Overview of Big Data Analytics for Cultural Heritage

Manolis Wallace [1,*], Vassilis Poulopoulos [1], Angeliki Antoniou [2] and Martín López-Nores [3]

[1] ΓAB LAB—Knowledge and Uncertainty Research Laboratory, Campus of the University of Peloponnese, 221 31 Tripoli, Greece
[2] Department of Archival, Library & Information Studies, University of West Attica, 122 43 Egaleo, Greece
[3] atlanTTic Research Centre for Information and Communication Technologies, Department of Telematics Engineering, University of Vigo, 36310 Vigo, Spain
* Correspondence: wallace@uop.gr

Cultural heritage is a domain that produces vast amounts of data, but it is also where the meaning of the data is crucially important, particularly to the extent that it refers to people's opinions, perceptions, and interpretations of their past and their present, or to people's feelings, preferences, and attitudes. As such, it was a natural development that big data analytics found its role in the field and produced some efficient tools and methodologies.

In this Special Issue, we have focused on the methods and tools of big data analytics that have been specifically developed for the domain of cultural heritage, as well as on experiences from the adaptation and/or application of general-purpose solutions to the domain.

Of course, one cannot overlook the fact that big data analytics and cultural heritage are domains that stem from fundamentally distinct sciences. This means that very few people possess suitable backgrounds in order to successfully tackle their combination. As a response to this, in [1], we see an early theoretical basis that brings us closer to shared cultural experiences in mixed reality systems and, in [2], we see a data lake for multi-faceted data analytics in cultural heritage. Both works place emphasis on providing powerful and ready-to-use solutions that do not require a strong IT background, making the proposed technologies more realistically available and applicable to the cultural domain.

The way each one of us experiences culture is a deeply personal matter. Therefore, the need for personalization cannot be ignored in our domain. On the other hand, rich information upon which to base personalization choices is rarely available in most cultural experience scenarios. Standardized visitor types are a common solution to this. In [3], we see how these types can be constructed and classified automatically via social media data while, in [4], we see how they can then be used to generate personalized recommendations for locations to visit and activities to engage in. The work in [5] further develops on this, allowing for the combination of standardized profiles.

These works focus on how to best serve those who are already familiar with and interested in a cultural knowledge base, site, or collection. However, how do we extend this knowledge to the general public in the first place? In [6], we see a novel search engine optimization approach that aims to improve the visibility of cultural collections on the Web, thus promoting the domain's marketability and sustainability.

Culture is a broad topic that is connected to almost every aspect of our lives; in many cases, it is connected to aspects which the primary focus of is anything but cultural. In [7], we see how cultural data can be used to stimulate student interest and promote learning performance, while in [8], we learn about the use of computer games in heritage preservation; the latter work is also related to the aforementioned issue of personalization.

Let us not forget that culture is not just about the past. Who we are, how we think, and how we interact in the modern world are manifestations of modern culture. In [9], we see how a discussion on feminism can be tracked and analyzed, in an approach that can be directly applied to other concepts which are frequently debated online.

**Citation:** Wallace, M.; Poulopoulos, V.; Antoniou, A.; López-Nores, M. An Overview of Big Data Analytics for Cultural Heritage. *Big Data Cogn. Comput.* **2023**, *7*, 14. https://doi.org/10.3390/bdcc7010014

Received: 21 December 2022
Accepted: 10 January 2023
Published: 13 January 2023

**Copyright:** © 2023 by the authors. Licensee MDPI, Basel, Switzerland. This article is an open access article distributed under the terms and conditions of the Creative Commons Attribution (CC BY) license (https://creativecommons.org/licenses/by/4.0/).

Finally, in [10], we take a broader look at the past, present, and future of the domain, discussing how technology drives and redefines the way we perceive and interact with culture.

Over the course of the last three years, while working on this Special Issue, we have witnessed great developments in big data analytics. The cultural applications of big data analytics have also been maturing and evolving rapidly and there is a clear potential for more fascinating developments in the times to come. For this reason, we are extending our editorial journey by launching the second volume of the Special Issue where we are aiming to explore the more recent developments in the field [11].

**Conflicts of Interest:** The authors declare no conflict of interest.

**References**

1. Vassilakis, C.; Kotis, K.; Spiliotopoulos, D.; Margaris, D.; Kasapakis, V.; Anagnostopoulos, C.-N.; Santipantakis, G.; Vouros, G.A.; Kotsilieris, T.; Petukhova, V.; et al. A Semantic Mixed Reality Framework for Shared Cultural Experiences Ecosystems. *Big Data Cogn. Comput.* **2020**, *4*, 6. [CrossRef]
2. Deligiannis, K.; Raftopoulou, P.; Tryfonopoulos, C.; Platis, N.; Vassilakis, C. Hydria: An Online Data Lake for Multi-Faceted Analytics in the Cultural Heritage Domain. *Big Data Cogn. Comput.* **2020**, *4*, 7. [CrossRef]
3. Spiliotopoulos, D.; Margaris, D.; Vassilakis, C. Data-Assisted Persona Construction Using Social Media Data. *Big Data Cogn. Comput.* **2020**, *4*, 21. [CrossRef]
4. Konstantakis, M.; Alexandridis, G.; Caridakis, G. A Personalized Heritage-Oriented Recommender System Based on Extended Cultural Tourist Typologies. *Big Data Cogn. Comput.* **2020**, *4*, 12. [CrossRef]
5. Konstantakis, M.; Christodoulou, Y.; Aliprantis, J.; Caridakis, G. ACUX Recommender: A Mobile Recommendation System for Multi-Profile Cultural Visitors Based on Visiting Preferences Classification. *Big Data Cogn. Comput.* **2022**, *6*, 144. [CrossRef]
6. Drivas, I.C.; Sakas, D.P.; Giannakopoulos, G.A.; Kyriaki-Manessi, D. Big Data Analytics for Search Engine Optimization. *Big Data Cogn. Comput.* **2020**, *4*, 5. [CrossRef]
7. Vargianniti, I.; Karpouzis, K. Using Big and Open Data to Generate Content for an Educational Game to Increase Student Performance and Interest. *Big Data Cogn. Comput.* **2020**, *4*, 30. [CrossRef]
8. Drakopoulos, G.; Voutos, Y.; Mylonas, P. Annotation-Assisted Clustering of Player Profiles in Cultural Games: A Case for Tensor Analytics in Julia. *Big Data Cogn. Comput.* **2020**, *4*, 39. [CrossRef]
9. Morales-i-Gras, J.; Orbegozo-Terradillos, J.; Larrondo-Ureta, A.; Peña-Fernández, S. Networks and Stories. Analyzing the Transmission of the Feminist Intangible Cultural Heritage on Twitter. *Big Data Cogn. Comput.* **2021**, *5*, 69. [CrossRef]
10. Poulopoulos, V.; Wallace, M. Digital Technologies and the Role of Data in Cultural Heritage: The Past, the Present, and the Future. *Big Data Cogn. Comput.* **2022**, *6*, 73. [CrossRef]
11. Wallace, M.; Poulopoulos, V.; Antoniou, A.; López-Nores, M. Special Issue "Big Data Analytics for Cultural Heritage, Volume II". *Big Data Cogn. Comput.* **2023**, *in preparation*. Available online: https://www.mdpi.com/journal/BDCC/special_issues/6CLOF63BOQ (accessed on 1 December 2022).

**Disclaimer/Publisher's Note:** The statements, opinions and data contained in all publications are solely those of the individual author(s) and contributor(s) and not of MDPI and/or the editor(s). MDPI and/or the editor(s) disclaim responsibility for any injury to people or property resulting from any ideas, methods, instructions or products referred to in the content.

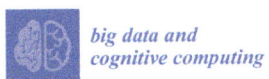 

Article

# A Semantic Mixed Reality Framework for Shared Cultural Experiences Ecosystems

Costas Vassilakis [1,*], Konstantinos Kotis [2], Dimitris Spiliotopoulos [1], Dionisis Margaris [3], Vlasios Kasapakis [2], Christos-Nikolaos Anagnostopoulos [2], Georgios Santipantakis [4], George A. Vouros [4], Theodore Kotsilieris [5], Volha Petukhova [6], Andrei Malchanau [6], Ioanna Lykourentzou [7], Kaj Michael Helin [8], Artem Revenko [9], Nenad Gligoric [10] and Boris Pokric [11]

[1] Department of Informatics and Telecommunications, University of the Peloponnese, 22100 Tripolis, Greece; dspiliot@uop.gr
[2] Department of Cultural Technology and Communication, University of the Aegean, 81100 Mitilene, Greece; kotis@aegean.gr (K.K.); v.kasapakis@aegean.gr (V.K.); canag@aegean.gr (C.-N.A.)
[3] Department of Informatics and Telecommunications, University of Athens, 15772 Athens, Greece; margaris@di.uoa.gr
[4] Department of Digital Systems, University of Piraeus, 18534 Piraeus, Greece; gsant@unipi.gr (G.S.); georgev@unipi.gr (G.A.V.)
[5] Department of Business Administration, University of the Peloponnese, 24100 Kalamata, Greece; tkots@us.uop.gr
[6] Spoken Language Group, Saarland University, 66123 Saarland, Germany; v.petukhova@lsv.uni-saarland.de (V.P.); andrei.malchanau@lsv.uni-saarland.de (A.M.)
[7] Department of Information and Computing Sciences, Utrecht University, 3584 CC Utrecht, The Netherlands; i.lykourentzou@uu.nl
[8] Department of Human Factors, Virtual and Augmented Reality, VTT Technical Research Centre of Finland Ltd., 02044 Espoo, Finland; kaj.helin@vtt.fi
[9] Semantic Web Company, 1070 Vienna, Austria; artreven@gmail.com
[10] DNETLabs, DunavNet, 21000 Novi Sad, Serbia; nenad.gligoric@dunavnet.eu
[11] ARVRtech, WC1N 3AX London, UK; boris.pokric@arvrtech.eu
* Correspondence: costas@uop.gr; Tel.: +30-2710-372-203

Received: 19 March 2020; Accepted: 14 April 2020; Published: 20 April 2020

**Abstract:** This paper presents SemMR, a semantic framework for modelling interactions between human and non-human entities and managing reusable and optimized cultural experiences, towards a shared cultural experience ecosystem that might seamlessly accommodate mixed reality experiences. The SemMR framework synthesizes and integrates interaction data into semantically rich reusable structures and facilitates the interaction between different types of entities in a symbiotic way, within a large, virtual, and fully experiential open world, promoting experience sharing at the user level, as well as data/application interoperability and low-effort implementation at the software engineering level. The proposed semantic framework introduces methods for low-effort implementation and the deployment of open and reusable cultural content, applications, and tools, around the concept of cultural experience as a semantic trajectory or simply, experience as a trajectory (eX-trajectory). The methods facilitate the collection and analysis of data regarding the behaviour of users and their interaction with other users and the environment, towards optimizing eX-trajectories via reconfiguration. The SemMR framework supports the synthesis, enhancement, and recommendation of highly complex reconfigurable eX-trajectories, while using semantically integrated disparate and heterogeneous related data. Overall, this work aims to semantically manage interactions and experiences through the eX-trajectory concept, towards delivering enriched cultural experiences.

**Keywords:** intelligent interaction; semantics; usability; mixed reality; cultural experience

## 1. Introduction

Cultural applications are increasingly used for the development and delivery of cultural experiences to users. To this end, research and development activities have targeted the design and implementation of applications and related systems to support all of the phases of the creation and operation of cultural applications, including content creation and organization, application development [1], application operation within venues [2,3], and in broad Internet of Things (IoT) environments [4–6].

Insofar, however, each cultural application is designed, implemented, and deployed separately, increasing the associated development costs (content development, code creation and testing, infrastructure deployment, and maintenance), while, at the same time, limiting the opportunities for sharing and reusing cultural experiences to the level of recommending isolated points of interests (PoIs) or coarse-grained routes [7–9]. The impact of these challenges is more pronounced in augmented, virtual, and mixed reality (AR/VR/MR) systems, for which content development, code implementation and deployment infrastructure are more complex and demanding. In addition, the range of the required hardware and software systems [10] poses further data integration and reuse issues.

The SemMR semantic framework proposes an integrated multi-technology and multi-entity approach towards addressing these challenges and supports current, as well as future, interactive technologies that are of low effort and cost, being accessible to all businesses. In particular, SemMR is inclusive towards technologies that are based on MR (including AR/VR). The main ingredients of the SemMR approach are the use of semantic technology for the utilization/integration of data and information discovered on Web sources, the cloud of Linked Open Data (LOD), and the IoT. Through this approach, the SemMR framework promotes experience sharing at user level, as well as data/application interoperability and low-effort implementation at the software engineering level. The framework is based on the notion of a shared cultural experience ecosystem (SCEE) in order to enable and support the management of enhanced user experience in the cultural domain. IoT is the key factor of future interaction [11] and the prominent source of the immense amounts of semantically linked data/information. In order to do so, the user behaviour must drive and be driven by the semantically integrated data/information/knowledge, thus creating a new world of seamless and immersive MR interaction between the real-world entities and the virtual entities. When specialized in the domain of MR, the SCEE ecosystem is denoted in this paper as MR-SCEE.

SemMR is based on two main concepts; the concept of the shared cultural experience ecosystem (SCEE) and the concept of the cultural experience as a semantic trajectory (eX-trajectory):

1. The eX-trajectory notion in SemMR is used for the representation of the mapping of a semantic trajectory to an MR experience. A trajectory concerns segments of connected traces/points that represent the movement of entities. A semantic trajectory is a trajectory that has been annotated with additional information that is related to those segments, usually to add knowledge related to moving entities in time and space and their experiences within those dimensions. Such experiences may involve multiple episodes or scenes within the segments of traces, where interconnected and interacting entities are moving and acting in the MR world, following spatiotemporal paths of special application-specific interests, exhibiting diverse behaviours (virtual or real).
2. SCEE is the eX-trajectory ecosystem within the SemMR semantic framework, generating, semantically integrating, and managing open and reusable cultural heritage content (cultural heritge experiences, data, and information), cultural applications, and methods. Multiple entities (human and non-human) may interact with each other at different time and space, thus creating a multi-dimensional space of shared cultural user experiences. The SemMR ecosystem maintains the shared eX-trajectories, where the length of each eX-trajectory (cultural experience) might vary. The SCEE is the enabler for advanced interaction and sharing, since expert and non-expert users may interactively author new experiences. On the other hand, along the user

interaction timeline, those experiences may dynamically intersect and interchange, resulting to unseen, but relevant, eX-trajectories.

SemMR is a semantic framework for modelling interactions between human and non-human entities and managing reusable and optimized eX-trajectories. It comprises of methods for: (1) creating and managing open, reusable, and optimized eX-trajectory content, applications and tools, (2) tracking, monitoring, and analysing user behaviour during interactions with the environment and with other entities, (3) optimizing (via reconfiguration) eX-trajectories at runtime or at development time, and (4) synthesizing eX-trajectories into new, but still reconfigurable, eX-trajectories, which are augmented by exploiting semantically integrated related data/information that is sourced from diverse and heterogeneous resources.

The contribution of this paper is outlined in the following three points:

1. The specification of the SemMR framework for enabling low-effort multi-entity interactions towards creating and managing reusable and optimized eX-trajectories.
2. The system architecture for implementing and realizing the SemMR framework.
3. The simulated performance evaluation for the deployment of the SemMR in an international cultural site.

The structure of the paper is outlined, as follows: Section 2 presents the related work. Section 3 details the proposed eX-trajectory concept. Section 4 introduces the SCEE, while Section 5 presents the system architecture for SemMR. Section 6 presents the instantiated implementation of SemMR for cultural experiences and Section 7 presents the user behaviour modelling. Section 8 presents the evaluation on the scalability of the proposed framework for a sizable cultural site, an archaeological museum, and, finally, Section 9 discusses the proposed framework and outlines future work.

## 2. Related Work

As cultural application development and use proliferates, researchers have developed a number of approaches that underpin and facilitate different parts of the cultural application lifecycle. Amato et al. [12] present SNOPS, a system that consolidates participatory sensing, IoT platforms, and recommendation systems under an instantiation of the Service-Oriented Architecture, targeting the collection of information from data sources, which are then exploited for the formulation of context-aware recommendations for users. The context of the recommendations is represented as an upper-level ontology, which encompasses classes for modelling users, objects/places of interest, time intervals, activities (either explicitly modelled or deduced), environmental conditions, and devices (both user access devices and sensors). Chianese et al. [2] describe the design and implementation of a system that is able to leverage cultural spaces into smart cultural environments following the concept of Single Smart Spaces ($S^3$), which result in enhanced user experience. The system that is proposed in [2] retrieves (a) data from sensors that perceive the real world, (b) information from structured and unstructured data sources, and (c) knowledge from users moving into the smart cultural environment, and processes the input to deliver knowledge to users to facilitate a number of tasks, including navigation and information finding. The concept of $S^3$ is also adopted in [12,13], where a context-aware framework for cultural heritage applications is presented. The framework presented in [12,13] captures contextual information under a Context Dimension Tree, which represents six dimensions of the contextual information: users interacting with the system; items within the smart space; activities performed on items; situations within which activities are carried out; locations of activities; and, times when activities were performed. From this information, the system continuously learns usage patterns and propagates the resulting knowledge to users.

The exhiSTORY approach [14,15] integrates IoT and semantic technologies, together with clustering and personalization techniques to leverage exhibits within cultural venues to smart, self-organizing exhibits that cooperate with each other and provide visitors with comprehensible, rich, diverse, personalized, and highly stimulating experiences. In more detail, within the exhiSTORY approach, each exhibit maintains an amount of self-descriptive data and semantic information, and communicates with both (a) neighbouring exhibits and (b) the smart space, to create multiple meaningful collections of items. Each collection tells a story about a specific subject. Subsequently, personalization technologies are employed to select the most prominent stories to be told to visitors, after consulting their profiles.

In the following paragraphs, we elaborate on the research work and technologies related to the main axes of the SemMR framework, namely (i) semantic data management, (ii) virtual entities and IoT, (iii) user profiling, and (iv) mixed reality.

### 2.1. Semantic Data Management: Link Discovery and Data Integration

Link discovery (LD) is the process of identifying relations (links) between data/information objects of different provenance (i.e., that that have been retrieved from different sources). The identified relations are then used to support several tasks, including data/information integration and deduplication. In the case of spatial datasets, the goal of LD is to identify pairs of spatial objects for which a given set of relations is satisfied. Existing works in this area have mainly targeted the discovery of topological relations (intersects, contains, crosses, meets, etc.) between spatial objects, while the recent work on maskLink [16] has been employed for discovering proximity relations, as well as in trajectory reconstruction and semantic enriching of trajectory segments.

RADON [17] is a recent topological relation discovery approach for relations between data sources of areas and it can discover efficiently multiple relations while using space tiling. Smeros and Koubarakis [18] studied link discovery on spatiotemporal RDF data by examining several topological relations that are defined on polygons. Finally, the maskLink approach [16,19] tackles both topological and proximity relations. It has been implemented in a flexible framework, which includes features, such as:

1. streaming and archival data access,
2. efficient blocking technique for LineString geometries (minimizing the computational overhead produced by MBRs of such geometries), and
3. a suite of generic and "ready-to-use" functions that can be exploited for domain-agnostic trajectory enrichment, demonstrated for the support of complex event recognition [20].

Going beyond the state-of-the-art methods in LD and data integration, SemMR develops LD algorithms for discovering spatiotemporal relations (as well as other well-defined semantic relations) between the eX-trajectories, supporting the meaningful exploitation of similar and related trajectories.

### 2.2. Virtual Entities: IoT Management and Trustful Interactions

The interaction with objects in MR worlds requires sensing from physical space, or even sensing of user parameters to be able to provide high value user experience. To achieve this, a full IoT infrastructure for collecting important data for VR/AR space reconstruction, as well as device virtualization, device management, and trustful interaction must be provided. In device virtualization, there are several commercial IoT-related products that aim to aggregate all of the data that IoT can generate in cloud storage and then expose them to developers through RESTful interfaces and libraries for enhanced service creation. However, these initiatives remain bound to an information-centric view, where the main value of the things is more on the information they can generate and less on the possibility to include augmented AR/VR interaction with an object and between users, offering services and actuation on it.

In IoT management paradigm, trust-related issues need also be addressed, for instance, ways to manage trust between entities without the existence of a central authority. These issues may be addressed while using clear and simple semantics. As trust management mechanisms have been widely studied in various research fields [21], it is now commonly accepted that the seamless integration of trust management mechanisms in IoT is needed [22,23]. The recommendation and standardization of a well-defined trust negotiation language supporting the semantic interoperability of IoT context is a challenging and open IoT-trust modelling and management topic [24,25].

SemMR delivers an integrated framework for: (a) capturing and virtualizing human and non-human (mobile and smart) entities (users, smart rooms, smart phones, smart bands, smart tags, etc.) and their interconnections, supporting their automated identification and recognition, and their open (re)use by cultural experience authoring environments, and (b) modelling and computing trust for the interaction of the virtualized entities, based on principles, such as friendship, ownership, collaboration, as well as on contextual information, such as environmental conditions that are sensed by the smart tag.

*2.3. User Profiling*

SemMR uses profiling methods to adapt user interfaces and interactions to the specific characteristics of users, particularly their age, gender and cultural background, their physical and cognitive abilities, their level of engagement, and their preferences. Consequently, it is necessary to model the user profiles at different levels: their intrinsic characteristics (physical characteristics, identity, age, disabilities, behaviour, emotional state, skills, etc.), their physical environment (location), their social environment (job position, tasks), and their needs and preferences. User profiles can be explicitly built by inquiring the users for direct information, or implicitly by deducing their profile from their interaction with the system. Implicit and explicit profiles are complementary aspects. It is important to keep in mind that user profiles change over time and that, in that context, a dynamic user profile is fundamental for successful personalisation. Other works utilise the user personality traits to deduce work leadership profiles and construct harmonious and effective teams [26].

User profile creation and maintenance can be supported through a multitude of mainstream methods. Fine-grained tracking of facial expressions and body movement on the visible spectrum can be achieved using hardware, such as Intel®RealSense, 3D Kinect and eye-trackers (e.g., Tobii Glasses). Moreover, biometric signals can be recorded and tracked while using sensors, such as NeXus EXG and Blood Volume Pulse. These allow for multimodal interaction, a very natural social form of interaction that has been shown to improve human learning and the treatment of medical conditions. Learning and user experience and acceptance may be enhanced by immersive interactive environments [27]. Learning might be reinforced by multi-sensory approaches that may be used for the personalisation of the assessment and reflection phases for improved user experience.

User profiles may be associated with, or abstracted to, user behaviour models. There are several paradigms for user behaviour modelling and action planning for domains of varying complexity with most prominent concerning Finite State Machines (FSM), Agent-Based Modelling approaches, Social Force models and Activity-Based Models [28]. In FSM, each user action leads to a new state. Simple algebraic structures relate internal states to input and output sequences offering a general model of user behaviour. FSMs were successfully used to model human-robot interactions and dialogue behaviour [29,30]. Agent-based systems are developed for simulating (virtual) human behaviour in a variety of disciplines, from knowledge building in collaborative online communities, like wikis [31,32] to task assignment in crowd work environments [33–35] to the way people select which exhibits to see in the physical space of a museum [36]. Users are represented as intentional rational agents. An agent model includes perception, beliefs, desires, planning/reasoning, commitment, intentions, and acting, and represents a comprehensive model of user behaviour simulation.

Social or behavioural forces specify the degree of behavioural change (e.g., changes in acceleration or in direction), as reaction to external forces that are exerted by the environment or other agents. These forces have a stimulating or repelling effect on the motivation of humans to perform certain activities [37].

SemMR models adaptive user and system behaviour in dynamic non-sequential interactions. For this, cognitive models that produce detailed simulations of human (multi-)task performance are designed in order to implement simulated artificial agents to play a role in a multi-agent (multi-entity) setting.

## 2.4. Mixed Reality

MR refers to environments where real world and virtual world objects are presented together in a single display. The two most common methods for creating such MR environments are AR and Augmented Virtuality (AV). AV blends elements from the real world to the Virtual Environment (VE), while AR works by superimposing computer-generated objects upon the Real Environment (RE). Virtual Reality (VR) is an alternative approach that constructs and displays entirely synthetic worlds that may simulate the physical properties of the real world, where users can be totally immersed in [38,39]. In most AR applications, the RE is streamed through the camera feed of a device, such as a smartphone or a camera-equipped Head Mounted Display (HMD), with the virtual objects being superimposed on the RE by either using computer vision with fiducial markers, or sensors, to properly adjust their position and rotation. However, recently, marker-less AR received significant attention and it is now widely used in popular AR applications development platforms.

Nowadays, most of the popular VR and AV application development platforms utilize sophisticated sensors to support room-scale applications, allowing for hand presence in the virtual world and full body motion support [40], along with wireless support. Eye tracking is also exploited in some high-end HMD platforms to provide better experience in AV.

Wireless HMDs feature high quality inside-out tracking, allowing for developers to seamlessly blend real and virtual environment in AV and AR applications. Finally, state-of-the art technology enables brain activity and eye movement detection, which allows for user behaviour tracking for real time personalization and enhancement of user experience in MR applications.

SemMR enhances MR development systems/platforms by (a) integrating a graphical drag-n-drop code-free authoring environment for synthesizing open and reusable MR experiences, (b) recommendation methods for automatically suggesting related external data/info to be attached to MR content for enhancing it, and for automatically suggesting new eX-trajectories to support the reconfiguration of existing (towards optimization), (c) focusing on IoT to allow for seamless and 'live' interaction of interconnected trustworthy deployed entities (human and non-human ones), (d) properly understanding human behaviour and cognition while experiencing MR worlds, (e) semantically integrating external heterogeneous and disparate information in order to enrich the content of the MR experiences, improving their quality and, thus, the quality of the user experience, and (f) appropriate models and methods for the reuse of connections between virtual and real objects, in more than one MR world, enlarging, this way, the MR environment

## 3. Experience as a Trajectory (eX-trajectory)

A movement track represents the ability to capture the movement of an object or entity moving in a geographical space over some period of time. This temporal sequence of the spatiotemporal positions is represented as pairs of 'instant' and 'point'. Additional data (depending on the capabilities of the movement recording device) may also be recorded, e.g., the instant speed or stillness, acceleration, direction, and rotation. Such captured data are the raw data. In some applications, there is no interest in keeping and analysing continuous non-stop records of raw movement data. Instead, segments of interest may be selected, i.e., a specific movement track within a 'start' and 'stop' (Begin and End) point. Trajectories are the segments of an object movement track that are of interest for a given application. For instance, when considering an application that is required to track and analyse tourist movement and cultural activities in the city of Athens. For this (big) data recording example, the application identifies a trajectory for the whole track that is left by an individual tourist in Athens (e.g., 'inside Athens' trajectory), but also another trajectory tracking a specific daily cultural experience track of this individual (e.g., 'a tourist in Athens on a Sunday tour' or 'a tour in the Museum of Acropolis on Friday morning').

In some cases, the application processes require using contextual data or information to complement and augment raw data. For instance, to be able to interpret the trajectories of people in a city, additional information regarding the city (e.g., the map or the PoIs of the city) is required. Spatiotemporal data (coordinates) can be reverse geocoded and transformed into names/identities of PoIs (e.g., monuments, parks, or shop names) or names of streets and squares. For example, information about events of any nature, from football games to concerts and protest marches, enables traffic monitoring applications to distinguish among normal and exceptional traffic conditions, leveraging the interpretation of spatiotemporal data (positions). Adding information to raw trajectories is called semantic enrichment of trajectories. Such enrichment requires the process of complementing existing data with additional data/information, i.e., annotations. Additional data/information is connected either to parts of (segments, points) of a trajectory, or to the trajectory as a whole. In this context, a semantic trajectory is a trajectory that has been augmented with annotations that add context. In a tourist example, recording the movement pattern of a museum visitor (e.g., ant, grasshopper) [41] is a trajectory-level semantic annotation. On the other hand, marking the person's presence at a location, as a visit to a temporary modern art exhibition, is a semantic annotation at the location level.

*3.1. eX-Trajectory Modelling*

Trajectories are widely defined as the segments of the object's movement track that are of interest for a given application. Semantic trajectories are trajectories that have been enhanced with semantic annotations and/or one or more complementary segmentations. One might superimpose a structure of homogeneous segments that are meaningful for the particular application to enhance the knowledge captured by trajectories. These homogeneous segments are called episodes. Episodes are defined as a maximal subsequence of a trajectory, such that all of its spatiotemporal positions comply with a given predicate [42].

Existing semantic trajectory modelling and representation approaches impose limitations on the structure or the elements of trajectories. More specifically, they either:

1. represent relationships to other entities using plain textual annotations [43,44] instead of semantic links, considerably limiting the accuracy and exploitability of entity relationship information. On the other hand, the use of semantic links to model (a) the relationships between trajectories and other data or (b) the relationships between trajectories and semantic resources that are associated with the behaviour of moving objects would provide a fully-fledged, accurate, and exploitable representation of the same information;
2. impose restrictions on the components that can be used for structuring a trajectory, by only allowing a limited set of event types to be included [45]; and,
3. require that the ingredients/parts of trajectories adhere to several implicit or explicitly expressed rules [43,46,47].

For example, in some works, semantic trajectories are sequences of sub-trajectories [43], while, in others, they are sequences of episodes [46]. For the datAcron ontology [48], the representation of trajectories at multiple and interlinked levels of analysis is supported. In related works, a rich set of constructs for the representation of semantic trajectories is presented as sequences of episodes, each being associated with raw trajectory data and (optionally) with a spatiotemporal model of movement, although without a fine association between raw movement data and abstract models of movements [46]. In Bogorny et al. [43], semantic trajectories are defined as lists of sub-trajectories, and each sub-trajectory as a list of points. Events and episodes are connected to specific resources at specific levels of analysis: events that are mostly related to the environment are only connected to points [43], while episodes concern things occurring at trajectory-level and they can be linked to specific models of movement [46].

*3.2. eX-Trajectory Management and Analytics*

A trajectory behaviour is defined as a set of specific characteristics that can be used to identify a particular connection or link to a moving object or to a set of moving objects. The behaviour is defined by a predicate that expresses whether a given trajectory (or a given set of trajectories) shows the corresponding behaviour [42]. For instance,

1. a "Tourist" behaviour might concern a daily trajectory that shows the Tourist behaviour, if (a) its departure (Begin) point P1 is a place of type "Accommodation", (b) it makes at least one stop at a place of type "Museum" or "Tourist Attraction", (c) it makes one stop at a place of type "Eating Place", and (d) its arrival (End) point is in the same P1 place as its departure point.
2. A "Meet" behaviour might concern a set of trajectories that show the specific (meet) behaviour, if every trajectory of the set roughly ends at the same space (point) and at the same time (instant).

A trajectory can be characterized by several behaviours. For instance, a trajectory can show both a "Speeding" and a "Tourist" behaviour and simultaneously be part of a group of trajectories showing the "Meet" behaviour. For each behaviour, the predicate relies on different characteristics. The trajectories of tourists visiting a city may be analysed for (a) creating tourist profiles and recommending personalized itineraries and services, (b) the flow regulation of visitors and tourist either within cultural venues or at city level, etc. Processes that analyse trajectories to identify similarities and dissimilarities among them (including a feature-based comparison between trajectories), classify the trajectories into types based on their similarity, and extract the salient features that differentiate one trajectory group from another underpin all of this. A set of distinguishing features (called patterns or behaviours) forms a summary description of the group of trajectories.

Several systems for trajectory data management and analysis exist. SpatialHadoop [49] and Simba [50] enable distributed spatial analytics based on the MapReduce paradigm. Nevertheless, they do not exploit the characteristics of trajectory data for efficient data management and analytics. A cloud-based system by Bao et al. [51] and Elite [52] provide distributed solutions for big trajectory data. They utilize specific partitioning strategies in distributed environments in order to support data retrieval. Other systems that offer distributed storage and computing also exist. SnappyData [53] integrates Apache Spark and Apache Geode to support efficient streaming, transactions, and interactive analytics. Although these systems provide solutions that enhance Spark and eliminate inefficiencies of heterogeneous systems, they do not provide flexible operations and optimizations for trajectory data analytics. A recent related work on UlTraMan [54] adopts a flexible framework that supports customizable data formats, partitioning strategies, index structures, processing methods, and analysis techniques, which offer better support to realize optimizations and complex analytics. UlTraMan also adopts a unified engine that supports efficient trajectory data management and analytics.

## 4. Results Mapping Cultural Experiences to Semantic Trajectories

SemMR integrates key technologies, such as semantic and IoT technologies, for user interaction, in order to advance cultural experiences within a new shared cultural experience ecosystem (Figure 1), accommodating provisions for supporting MR-based interaction.

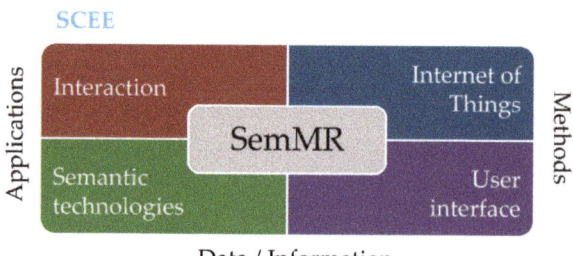

**Figure 1.** The shared cultural experience ecosystem (SCEE).

The key concept in SemMR is the handling of real-world information as part of virtual entities (VE) that change and evolve, either individually or as part of related groups. The VEs are in collaboration to create experiences and they may interact with human experiencers or with each other in scenarios or stories. Such interaction (that can be seen as a dialogue between multiple types of entities, human, and virtual) might be dynamically shape when trajectories of previous and recently authored experiences coincide or become relevant. Multiple users may interact with multiple entities at different times, thus creating a shared experience user space in cultural or other domains. The SemMR ecosystem maintains the shared experiences that are complete, allowing for variable length (number of visiting points of interest/events/activities and their duration). User behaviour is monitored by employing interaction metrics and sensor data from wearables, such as smart bands, on the users. Through the analysis, the shared experiences are reconfigured and then presented to the SemMR entities for selection and interaction. The SCEE is the enabler for advanced interaction and experience sharing, since experts may author interactive experiences that may intersect and interchange in a dynamic fashion during the interaction, offering new relevant cultural interaction potential to the users.

## 5. System Architecture

Based on the SemMR framework, this section elaborates on the architectural design of a SemMR-based system, which constitutes its first realization/instantiation. The proposed system in Figure 2 is considered to be a sample instantiation of the framework, without only limiting SemMR to the proposed architectural design that is presented in this paper. However, the architectural design presented below is based on one-to-one mapping of its components (methods and tools) to the concept that is specified in SemMR.

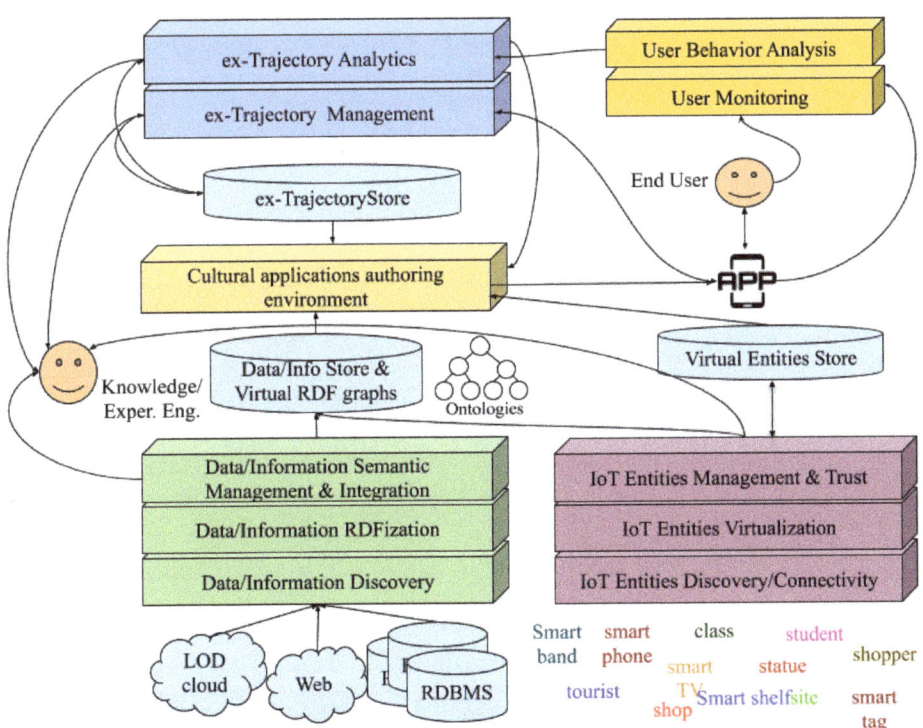

**Figure 2.** Proposed system design architecture based on SemMR framework.

The main components of the proposed SemMR-based system are the following:

1. eX-trajectory management and analytics,
2. management of IoT/VEs,
3. management of semantic data and information,
4. monitoring and analysis of user behaviour, and
5. the cultural application authoring environment.

The functionality of each component is detailed in the following paragraphs.

*5.1. eX-Trajectory Management and Analytics*

This component is responsible for managing and analysing eX-trajectories while using methods for representing, storing, querying, linking, synthesizing, and enriching eX-trajectories. It identifies similarities between eX-trajectories, which are the types of relations between one or more eX-trajectories. It supports a multitude of analytic tasks for eX-trajectory behaviour, compilation of statistics, and advanced methods for mining co-movement pattern from eX-trajectories. It provides a number of services, by exploiting data from other architectural components and, more specifically: (a) it generates recommendations for the reconfiguration of eX-trajectories, utilizing user behaviour analytics data that are sourced from the user behaviour analysis component; (b) it supports the integration of VEs into eX-trajectories through the use of data that were obtained from the IoT/VE management component; and, (c) it enriches the eX-trajectory data and information by utilizing data that were sourced from the data/information management component.

*5.2. IoT/VEs Management*

This component is responsible for (a) promoting connectivity between human and non-human entities, (b) enabling abstract representation (virtualisation) of those entities using the semantics of the SemMR ontology, (c) managing VEs by offering services for the efficient storage and querying of data/information created by VEs in the context of their involvement in eX-trajectories, and (d) supporting trustful interactions in the context of cultural spaces, through the realization of a relevant trust model and the computation of trust between VEs.

*5.3. Semantic Data/Information Management*

This component facilitates: (a) search and discovery of disparate and heterogeneous domain-specific data and information related to eX-trajectories, (b) transformation of data to a common syntax and model (RDF) and data integration under a common view, based on the SemMR ontology as well as suitable domain-specific ontological models, and (c) the enhancement of eX-trajectories, through the computation of offering recommendations containing unified and integrated data and information; to this end, the semantic data/information management employs semantic matchmaking methods.

*5.4. User Behaviour Monitoring and Analysis*

This component is designed for facilitating (a) the tracking and monitoring of human entities during interaction, (b) analysing user behaviour to identify confusion, boredom, uncertainty, frustration, etc., (c) examining the user affective mental state and preferences to reach decisions regarding intervening actions that must be taken, including offering of comments, the generation of recommendations for path changing, (d) identification and presentation of additional content, (e) augmenting the initial user profile, already present in SemMR by contributing physiological aspects that are derived from the monitor and analysis of user movement, and (f) realizing an integrated interactive interface, through which feedback might be provided.

## 5.5. The Cultural Authoring Environment

This component is responsible for authoring eX-trajectories and developing cultural apps with low effort. It provides the following: (a) a graphical drag-n-drop code-free authoring interface of eX-trajectories, (b) methods for synthesising open and reusable eX-trajectories, (c) methods for integrating VEs into eX-trajectories, and (d) methods for enhancing eX-trajectories through semantic enrichment. This environment allows for the creation of domain-specific cultural applications that are delivered to the intended audience for immediate use. The cultural authoring environment interfaces with the MR devices and, in general, the infrastructure that is required for the MR application delivery and makes these interfaces available to developers as objects and APIs for a higher level of abstraction. In this fashion, the MR application development is disassociated from the idiosyncrasies and peculiarities of the hardware and, therefore, can be more efficiently developed and with better portability.

In the heart of SemMR, there is a triple store for storing and querying integrated data in Resource Description Framework (RDF) data model [55] and the SemMR ontology encoded in the OWL W3C ontology language [56]. The SemMR ontology is designed to encompass representations for eX-trajectories, VEs, and all additional domain-specific data and information that is required, i.e.,

- data regarding the human movement, behaviour and interactions; these may include raw data sourced from sensors through the user monitoring module, or results of the analysis of these data, as determined by the user behaviour analysis module, and
- data sourced from the Web/LOD/RDBMS, which will be utilized for the semantic enrichment of eX-trajectories.

The design of concepts and properties in the SemMR ontology regarding semantic trajectories is based on the definitions provided by the datAcron ontology for the representation of semantic trajectories of moving objects [48] and the semantic trajectories design patterns provided by Zhang et al. [57].

The SemMR ontology development process will follow a collaborative workflow, such as the one specified in the HCOME methodology [58], while using the collaborative ontology engineering tool WebProtégé and discussion threads via e-mail and Google docs/groups. In the architecture diagram that is illustrated in Figure 2, three stores are depicted as a conceptual approach to the organization of the SemMR data/information management; however, this is not necessarily the case for implementing three different physical stores.

Figure 3 depicts the SemMR key offerings and supported technologies.

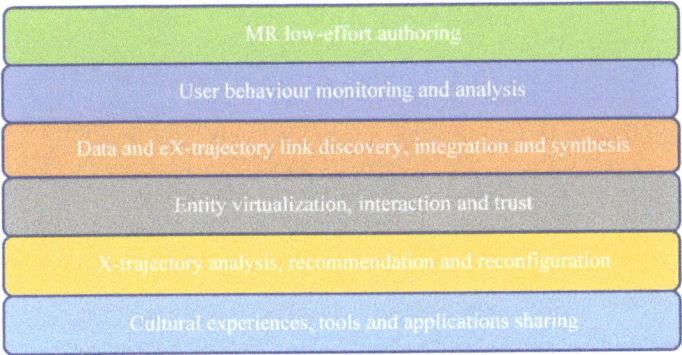

**Figure 3.** SemMR key technologies.

## 6. SemMR Example Ontological Specifications

In the following subsections, we present the cultural heritage domain considerations and the ontology specifications that implement the semantic trajectory for the domain semantics.

### 6.1. Cultural Heritage Domain

The CrossCult ontology (IRI: http://kb.crosscult.eu/) organizes cultural object semantics in multiple layers, aiming to underpin the representation of connections between cultural heritage data. The CrossCult ontology extends the basic CRM modelling of CH data semantics, by accommodating the modelling of users (of applications) and visitors (of venues), as well as venues (sites, buildings, rooms, etc.). Furthermore, it defines semantics such as interest and review (subclasses of *E73 Information Object* in CRM). Moreover, the CrossCult ontology reuses elements from the namespaces of FOAF (e.g., for modelling persons, their activities and relationships between persons), Dublin-Core (to describe periods of time and specialised datatypes), and SKOS (to model relationships between concepts), as well as DBpedia (primarily for enriching instances of the Upper-level ontology with links to DBpedia concepts) to offer a more comprehensive coverage of concepts of interest.

A modelling choice of CrossCult ontology, adopted in the SemMR ontology modelling, is the reuse of the specialised CIDOC CRM [59] classes, such as *E22.Physical Man Made Object* and *E24.Physical Man Made Thing*, which provide a unified view to a wide range of concepts. Artefacts, paintings, museum exhibits, monuments, are modelled as instances of those CRM classes. This design choice also enables the use of standard semantics for modelling spatial, temporal, geometrical, and other semantic relationships.

Figure 4 depicts a description of an exhibit (PoI), while Figure 5 illustrates the exhibit (PoI) modelling within SemMR. The CrossCult definition of a *Visit* (and related classes i.e., *Visitor* and *VisitingStyle*) in its *User-Model* namespace has a central role in the representation of the knowledge in SemMR.

In the example that is depicted in Figure 6, we illustrate how individual routes followed by users are linked with a particular visiting style (e.g., ant, grasshopper, butterfly, etc. [36]). Note that a relationship between users and visiting styles is also accommodated at the user profile level, indicating which visiting style a user typically follows. However, it is possible to represent differentiations from the typical user behaviour, occurring at the individual route level, as shown in the example. The visiting style of each individual visit is determined by analysing the user traces against the locations of the exhibits.

> Marble statuette of goddess Demeter enthroned. The goddess wears polos and her hair is shaped in tentacles. She bears a reaching to the feet sleeved chiton and a cloak covering the lower part of her body. The goddess removes the garment from her face with her left hand. She holds an apple on her right hand, on the level of her shoulder. Originated from Vlahokerasia and dated to the 4th century B.C. Dimensions: Height 0.40m, width 0.19m. Location: Room 15, 1st floor.

**Figure 4.** Textual description of an exhibit (PoI).

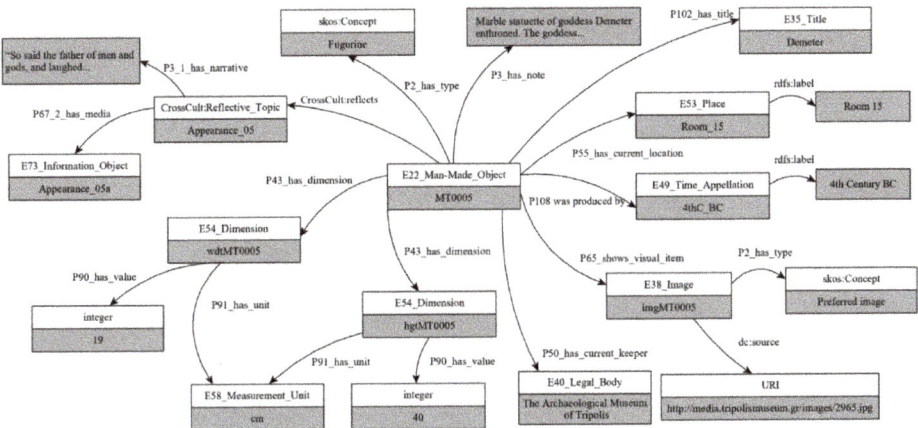

**Figure 5.** Informational model for an exhibit (point of interest) in the SemMR ontology.

```
<EquivalentClasses>
    <Class IRI="http://www.crosscult.eu/UserModel#Visitor"/>
    <ObjectIntersectionOf>
        <Class IRI="http://xmlns.com/foaf/0.1/Person"/>
        <ObjectSomeValuesFrom>
            <ObjectProperty IRI="http://erlangen-crm.org/160714/P14i_performed"/>
            <Class IRI="http://www.crosscult.eu/UserModel#Visit"/>
        </ObjectSomeValuesFrom>
    </ObjectIntersectionOf>
</EquivalentClasses>
<SubClassOf>
    <Class IRI="http://www.crosscult.eu/UserModel#Visit"/>
    <Class IRI="http://erlangen-crm.org/160714/E7_Activity"/>
</SubClassOf>
<ObjectPropertyDomain>
    <ObjectProperty IRI="http://www.crosscult.eu/UserModel#hasVisitingStyle"/>
    <Class IRI="http://www.crosscult.eu/UserModel#Route"/>
</ObjectPropertyDomain>
<ObjectPropertyRange>
    <ObjectProperty IRI="http://www.crosscult.eu/UserModel#hasVisitingStyle"/>
    <Class IRI="http://www.crosscult.eu/UserModel#VisitingStyle"/>
</ObjectPropertyRange>
```

**Figure 6.** Linking of visitors, visits, and visiting styles.

*6.2. Semantic Trajectories*

Motivated by real-life needs in critical domains, such as aviation and maritime, the datAcron ontology provides a coherent and generic representation of semantic trajectories for moving objects [48]. It reuses the ontologies: DUL, SimpleFeature, NASA Sweet, and SSN. A semantic trajectory consists of a sequence of temporally non-overlapping trajectory parts, as shown in the ontology definitions in OWL syntax depicted in Figure 7; each of these parts may be either (a) a semantic node, (b) a raw position obtained from some sensing device, or (c) a trajectory segment. Each trajectory part can be associated with spatiotemporal information regarding its occurrence; in this context, the point or region of the trajectory part occurrence can be expressed via a specific geometry, while the temporal dimension of the trajectory part occurrence can be expressed through a time instant or interval.

Similar to the above definitions, but in a more simplified and generic way, the semantic trajectory design pattern [60] presented in the OWL snapshots that are depicted in Figure 8, defines a semantic trajectory as a number of segments and fixes (synonym to points in other vocabularies). According to OWL, it defines a number of interfaces to incorporate additional geographic information, domain knowledge, and device data.

```xml
<owl:Class rdf:about="http://www.datacron-project.eu/datAcron#Trajectory">
    <rdfs:subClassOf rdf:resource="
    http://www.ontologydesignpatterns.org/ont/dul/DUL.owl#Region"/>
</owl:Class>
<owl:Class rdf:about="http://www.datacron-project.eu/datAcron#TrajectoryPart">
    <rdfs:subClassOf rdf:resource="
    http://www.ontologydesignpatterns.org/ont/dul/DUL.owl#Region"/>
    <dc:creator>datAcron-project</dc:creator>
    <rdfs:comment>A Node, a raw position or a segment of a trajectory</rdfs:comment>
</owl:Class>
<owl:ObjectProperty rdf:about="http://www.datacron-project.eu/datAcron#comprises">
    <rdfs:subPropertyOf rdf:resource="http://www.datacron-project.eu/datAcron#hasPart"/>
    <rdfs:domain rdf:resource="http://www.datacron-project.eu/datAcron#TrajectoryPart"/>
    <rdfs:range rdf:resource="http://www.datacron-project.eu/datAcron#TrajectoryPart"/>
</owl:ObjectProperty>
<owl:Class rdf:about="http://www.datacron-project.eu/datAcron#Segment">
    <rdfs:subClassOf rdf:resource="http://www.datacron-project.eu/datAcron#TrajectoryPart"/>
    <dc:creator>datAcron-project</dc:creator>
    <rdfs:comment>A trajectory part</rdfs:comment>
</owl:Class>
```

**Figure 7.** Semantic trajectory definition according to datAcron ontology.

```xml
<owl:Class rdf:about="http://descartes-core.org/ontologies/trajectory/#SemanticTrajectory">
    <rdfs:subClassOf>
        <owl:Restriction>
            <owl:onProperty rdf:resource="
            http://descartes-core.org/ontologies/trajectory/#hasSegment"/>
            <owl:someValuesFrom rdf:resource="
            http://descartes-core.org/ontologies/trajectory/#Segment"/>
        </owl:Restriction>
    </rdfs:subClassOf>
</owl:Class>
<owl:Class rdf:about="http://descartes-core.org/ontologies/trajectory/#Fix">
    <rdfs:subClassOf>
        <owl:Restriction>
            <owl:onProperty>
                <rdf:Description>
                    <owl:inverseOf rdf:resource="
                    http://descartes-core.org/ontologies/trajectory/#hasFix"/>
                </rdf:Description>
            </owl:onProperty>
            <owl:someValuesFrom rdf:resource="
            http://descartes-core.org/ontologies/trajectory/#SemanticTrajectory"/>
        </owl:Restriction>
    </rdfs:subClassOf>
</owl:Class>
```

**Figure 8.** Definition of a semantic trajectory as a number of segments and fixes.

In SemMR, we link/connect any of the two semantic trajectories representation to the CrossCult ontology, in order to be able to formally represent the eX-trajectory, as defined in this work. To do so, we propose a number of simple design patterns in the SemMR namespace, as described below. In the description of the design patterns, the ontologies listed in Table 1 are used; Table 1 also lists the mapping between the prefixes used in the examples and the full ontology IRIs:

1. Define new concept: eXtrajectory as subClassOftraj:SemanticTrajectory

$$eXtrajectory \sqsubseteq SemanticTrajectory \quad (1)$$

2. Link/connect *traj:SemanticTrajectory* to *cros:Visit* (which represents a specific visit by a particular user) via an object property (*:visitMade*)

$$eXtrajectory \sqsubseteq \exists visitMade.Visit \quad (2)$$

3. Link/connect *traj:SemanticTrajectory* to *crm:E28_Conceptual_Object*, to allow the explicit representation of the semantics that are associated with a trajectory. Similarly, *traj:Segment* and *traj:Fix* are linked/connected to *crm:E28_Conceptual_Object*, to allow for the representation

of semantics that are associated with trajectory segments and individual points. Under this arrangement, all representational levels of eX-trajectories may bear relationships to semantics. However, it should be noted that the semantics appearing at the highest level, used in any context, are the ones conveying the actual meaning of the trajectory more accurately, overriding the lower-level ones. For instance, an eX-trajectory *exTr0001* may be comprised of the segments "visit to a museum" (associated with cultural semantics), "launch at a restaurant" (associated with food service and local cuisine semantics), and "shopping at a flea market" (associated with street market and local products semantics). However, the eX-trajectory *exTr0001* might be associated with tourist behaviour semantics, modelling the overall behaviour, and not the lower level details of the constituent parts.

4. Link/connect *cros: Visit* to *crm:E28_Conceptual_Object*, to allow for the explicit representation of the semantics targeted by a particular user visit. This is required, since different users may be following a specific semantic eX-trajectory (which is linked to the *cros:Visit object*), focusing on the diverse semantics of the eX-trajectory. For instance, a visitor may follow the "Acropolis of Athens" eX-trajectory focusing on the ritual aspects of monuments, while another visitor may follow the same eX-trajectory, focusing on the architectural aspects of monuments. By capturing the point of view of each individual user, more elaborate analytics can be produced, and more accurate matching can be performed, leading to better recommendations.

Table 1. Ontologies used for the framework evaluation.

| Prefix | IRI | Ontology |
| --- | --- | --- |
| traj | http://descartes-core.org/ontologies/trajectory/ | Semantic trajectory design pattern |
| cros | http://kb.crosscult.eu/ | CrossCult |
| crm | http://erlangen-crm.org/160714/ | CIDOC/CRM |

## 7. User Behaviour Modelling

Modelling the adaptive user and system behaviour in dynamic non-sequential interactions is a core advantage of the SemMR framework. This is of key importance for a number of settings, including (a) cultural sites and cities with tourist attractions, since their visitors are free to roam and view the site points of interest in no particular order and (b) learning environments, where learners are able to choose between learning paths or access and use learning material in distinct sequences, collaborating with other learners or instructors. Towards this, cognitive models that produce detailed simulations of human (multi-) task performance were designed and used to implement simulated artificial agents in a multi-agent (multi-entity) setting. AI agents compute the most plausible task action(s), given their understanding of the context, actions of others, their preferences and goals, provide alternatives and plans, roll out possible outcomes, and, therefore, are able to adapt their behaviour to their partners. They also know why they select a certain action and can explain why the choices made lead to each specific outcome (explainable AI). Agents can be built while using rather limited real or simulated expert and/or interactive data: an agent is supplied with initial state-action templates encoding domain knowledge (as eX-trajectories enriched with VE and IoT information), the user's profile, and preferences. Over time, the agent learns from the collected interactive experiences. Suggestions and optimizations are performed by finding prior experiences (instances) that are the most frequently or most recently used and/or are most similar to the current situation (contextual parameters, user affective state, user's goals, and preferences), blending the instances together to the extent that they match the interactive state.

The advantage of the SemMR approach is that it requires far less experiences for the system to be able to interact with the user in a sensible way and that it incrementally improves as its set of instances increases in size. It also allows for utilizing experiences of others to guide and enrich the experiences for new users. Additionally, growing data from the eX-trajectories store, paired with increased computational power, can be used to apply modern powerful Artificial Neural Networks (ANNs) and Deep Learning (DL) approaches, which showed a significant impact on many AI and HCI applications [61,62]. Finally, the SemMR model accounts for real-time user interaction errors, which supports the modelling of dialogue repair in user understanding, and the integration of a memory and interest model, reflecting the individual and changing configurations of the user's mind.

## 8. Evaluation

We ran a set of simulation experiments with artificial users in order to evaluate the feasibility of the approach, the appropriateness of the recommended eX-trajectories, and the scalability of the proposed framework. In this set of experiments, eX-trajectory recommendations were formulated and served to (artificial) users with diverse profile characteristics. Subsequently, the suggestions were evaluated for suitability against the relevant user profiles. Furthermore, the simulation process entailed concurrent formulation of recommendations to measure the execution time that is required for different levels of concurrency and quantify the response time of the SemMR instantiation.

For these experiments we used two machines. The first one was equipped with 2x Intel Xeon 8-Core CPUs, 64GB of RAM, and 480GB SSD with a transfer rate of 550MBps; the total estimated cost of this machine is less than 1.5K Euros, refurbished. This machine hosted the proposed framework, as well as the SemMR instantiation (database and MR eX-trajectory services). It also managed the database items, exhibit locations and semantic descriptions (already pre-processed as VEs), user profiles and trajectories, new content from IoT links (already retrieved but not pre-processed), and recorded and analysed the user paths. The second machine created the pool of concurrent users-visitors. For each user/visitor, the respective trajectory was built, when compared to existing trajectories and synthesized new, suggested trajectories, randomly, between 2–5 trajectories and 4–7 suggestions for each user tour. The machines were connected through an 1Gbps local area network.

For the cultural experience validation, we simulated scenarios for the visitors of the Acropolis Museum in Athens, which contains nearly 4250 works of art and welcomes an average of 4.5K visitors per day (nearly 1.5M per year) and while assuming that less than half of them visit it at the same time.

The user profiles that were utilized in the validation experiment were synthetically generated and included the following aspects: age, music choices, game choices, art preferences, museum theme preferences, mood, visiting style, gender, place of origin, and a returning visitor indicator, following the results of the study presented in Alexandersson et al. [63]. Each user profile could be matched to one of the six personas (predetermined user stereotypes) identified for the Acropolis museum in [64], however the degree of similarity for the best match varied from an absolute match to 5/8 attributes (the "mood" and the "returning visitor indicator" were not part of the stereotype modelling, only appearing in the user profile). Similarly, the eX-trajectory database was synthetically populated. Descriptions of landmark exhibits were crafted according to the permanent collection descriptions offered in the museum's website and, subsequently, areas of the museum were also modelled while using information from the Acropolis Museum application in the Google Arts and Culture website complemented with information from in-situ visits. Both landmark exhibit and museum area descriptions were semantically tagged. The semantic tags included the thematic area of the objects (e.g., religion, everyday life, wars, death, mythology, etc.), the artefact era, and the type of the artefacts (statues, household objects, buildings, grave goods). Subsequently, eX-trajectories with varying duration and spatiotemporal patterns were created and inserted into the eX-trajectory database, observing the profiles of the users. For instance, visitors with ant-type visiting style move sequentially along the areas of the museum, increasing their speed when the theme of the museum area does not intersect with their theme preferences, while moving more slowly in areas having content they are interested in. On the other hand, grasshopper visitors only approach certain exhibits falling within their interests spending a significant amount of time in front of them, crossing empty spaces and moving at a fast pace in other cases [36]. Physical fatigue was also considered in the generation of spatiotemporal sequences, with the effect being more significant in spatiotemporal sequences that are associated with older persons, as asserted in [63]. Overall, 100 user profiles and 620 eX-trajectories were generated and inserted into the virtual entities and eX-trajectory data store.

The eX-trajectories that were generated by the system were parsed and evaluated for appropriateness to each user profile and visitor path. They were found to be in alignment with the user's visiting style, thematic preferences, and associated stereotype. For approximately 70% of the user/path combinations, 1–3 of the suggestions contained exhibits beyond the user profile thematic preferences, thus fostering novelty and serendipity [65]. As far as performance is concerned, Figure 9 indicates the overhead of formulating the eX-trajectory recommendations under varying degrees of concurrency.

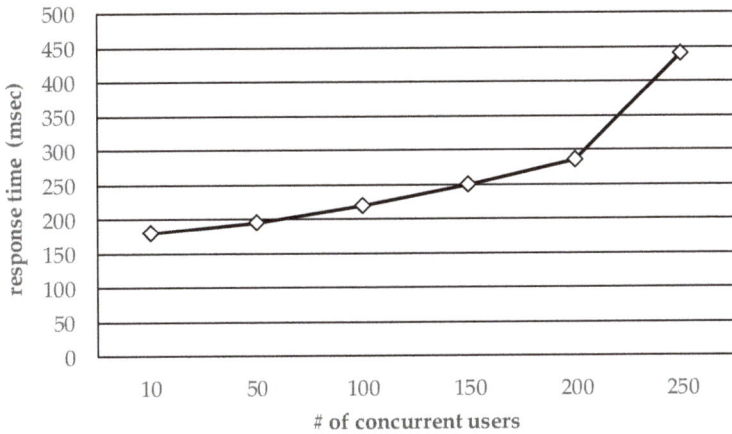

**Figure 9.** Trajectory proposals formulation time for varying degrees of concurrency.

In Figure 9, we can clearly see that the overhead per execution is small (approximately from 0.18 to 0.3 s, depending on the level of concurrency) and scales linearly with the number of concurrent executions (users). However, for concurrency levels that are higher than 200, the machine was saturated, and performance dropped rapidly, indicating that a second machine (of the same specifications, as the one used in our experiment) must be added.

Overall, the cost required for the machines hosting the SemMR framework is estimated to be less than 17K Euros, which is deemed to be reasonable and affordable, in order to fully support a museum of the size of the Acropolis Museum.

## 9. Discussion and Conclusions

This paper presented SemMR, a framework for creating a new ecosystem of shared and optimised cultural experiences, offering the potential to accommodate MR interaction. The SemMR approach employs semantic technology for the utilization/integration of data/information discovered on the current Web sources, the Linked Open Data (LOD) cloud, and the Internet of Things (IoT), promoting experience sharing at user level, as well as data/application interoperability and low-effort implementation at the software engineering level. Sustainability is demonstrated by the validation of the framework in real-world use cases involving both end-users, as well as paired technology integrators from industry that not only aim to deploy SemMR, but also to create the experiences per situation and lead the formative user studies for usability evaluation, focusing on the integration and long-term impact of the integrated technologies to the specifics of the application environment.

This paper presents the SemMR framework, along with the proposed architectural design for its implementation and the scalability metrics based on a use case instantiation. The presented work introduces methods and tools for multi-entity interactions between entities of different types, to create reusable and optimized cultural experiences with low effort, towards a shared cultural experience ecosystem. Specifically, the SemMR framework introduces methods and interfaces for code-free implementation and the deployment of shared and reusable MR content, applications, and tools, emphasizing the notion of the eX-trajectory. The SemMR instantiations (implementation) of the framework deliver high quality cultural experiences, facilitating the interaction between a variety of entity types that interact in a virtual and fully experiential world. In addition, SemMR proposes methods for tracking, monitoring, and analysing user behaviour and the user interaction with the environment and other users, towards optimizing MR experiences by recommending their reconfiguration in two modes, which is at run-time (dynamically) or at development time (statically).

In the current work presented in this paper, the following SemMR components have been implemented: the ontology and the data stores, the MR eX-trajectory services for the management and analytics of trajectories, and, partially, the methods for user monitoring and user behaviour analysis for the evaluation of the framework with the experimental use case.

For future work, the SemMR system implementation that includes all components presented in Figure 2 that correspond to all key technologies that are described in this paper will enable the system deployment to real users for formative evaluation. Such an endeavour is expected to create new content that might be evaluated by both users and experts, such as museum curators. For the latter, an open research challenge is the automatic selection of the most relevant content from external sources and its integration to the authored content, for a seamless, yet enhanced, cultural experience.

**Author Contributions:** Conceptualization, C.V. K.K. and D.S.; methodology, C.V., K.K., D.S., D.M., V.K., C.-N.A., G.S., G.A.V., T.K., V.P., A.M., I.L., K.M.H., A.R., N.G. and B.P.; software, K.K., D.M.; validation, D.M. and K.K; formal analysis, C.V., K.K., D.S., D.M., V.K., C.-N.A., G.S., G.A.V., T.K., V.P., A.M., I.L., K.M.H., A.R., N.G. and B.P.; investigation, X.X.; resources, X.X.; data curation, X.X.; writing—original draft preparation, C.V., K.K., D.S., D.M., V.K., C.-N.A., G.S., G.A.V., T.K., V.P., A.M., I.L., K.M.H., A.R., N.G. and B.P.; writing—review and editing, C.V., K.K., D.S. and D.M.; visualization, C.V., K.K., D.S., D.M., V.K., C.-N.A., G.S., G.A.V., T.K., V.P., A.M., I.L., K.M.H., A.R., N.G. and B.P.; supervision, C.V., K.K., D.S. and D.M. All authors have read and agree to the published version of the manuscript.

**Funding:** This research received no external funding.

**Conflicts of Interest:** The authors declare no conflict of interest.

## References

1. Fidas, C.; Sintoris, C.; Yiannoutsou, N.; Avouris, N. A survey on tools for end user authoring of mobile applications for cultural heritage. In Proceedings of the 2015 6th International Conference on Information, Intelligence, Systems and Applications (IISA), Corfu, Greece, 6–8 July 2015; pp. 1–5.
2. Chianese, A.; Piccialli, F.; Valente, I. Smart environments and Cultural Heritage: A novel approach to create intelligent cultural spaces. *J. Locat. Based Serv.* **2015**, *9*, 209–234. [CrossRef]
3. Vassilakis, C.; Antoniou, A.; Lepouras, G.; Wallace, M.; Lykourentzou, I.; Naudet, Y. Interconnecting Objects, Visitors, Sites and (Hi)Stories Across Cultural and Historical Concepts: The CrossCult Project. In *Digital Heritage. Progress in Cultural Heritage: Documentation, Preservation, and Protection*; Ioannides, M., Fink, E., Moropoulou, A., Hagedorn-Saupe, M., Fresa, A., Liestøl, G., Rajcic, V., Grussenmeyer, P., Eds.; Springer International Publishing: Cham, Switzerland, 2016; pp. 501–510.
4. Colace, F.; Santo, M.D.; Greco, L.; Lemma, S.; Lombardi, M.; Moscato, V.; Picariello, A. A Context-Aware Framework for Cultural Heritage Applications. In Proceedings of the 2014 Tenth International Conference on Signal-Image Technology and Internet-Based Systems, Marrakech, Morocco, 23–27 November 2014; pp. 469–476.
5. Maietti, F.; Di Giulio, R.; Piaia, E.; Medici, M.; Ferrari, F. Enhancing Heritage fruition through 3D semantic modelling and digital tools: The INCEPTION project. *IOP Conf. Ser. Mater. Sci. Eng.* **2018**, *364*, 12089. [CrossRef]

6. Maietti, F.; Medici, M.; Ferrari, F.; Ziri, A.E.; Bonsma, P. Digital Cultural Heritage: Semantic Enrichment and Modelling in BIM Environment. In *Digital Cultural Heritage, Proceedings of the Digital Cultural Heritage: Final Conference of the Marie Skłodowska-Curie Initial Training Network for Digital Cultural Heritage, ITN-DCH 2017, Olimje, Slovenia, 23–25 May 2017*; Ioannides, M., Ed.; Springer International Publishing: Cham, Switzerland, 2017; pp. 104–118.
7. Hashemi, S.H.; Kamps, J. Exploiting behavioral user models for point of interest recommendation in smart museums. *New Rev. Hypermedia Multimed.* **2018**, *24*, 228–261. [CrossRef]
8. Hashemi, S.H.; Kamps, J. Where to Go Next? In Proceedings of the 25th Conference on User Modeling, Adaptation and Personalization-UMAP '17, Bratislava, Slovakia, 9–12 July 2017; ACM Press: New York, NY, USA, 2017; pp. 50–58.
9. Sansonetti, G.; Gasparetti, F.; Micarelli, A.; Cena, F.; Gena, C. Enhancing cultural recommendations through social and linked open data. *User Modeling User-Adapt. Interact.* **2019**, *29*, 121–159. [CrossRef]
10. Martin, J. Top Six Augmented and Virtual Reality Technology Challenges. Available online: https://www.jabil.com/blog/top-augmented-and-virtual-reality-challenges.html (accessed on 5 April 2020).
11. Greenough, J.; Camhi, J. Here are IoT trends that will change the way businesses, governments, and consumers interact with the world. Available online: https://www.businessinsider.com/top-internet-of-things-trends-2016-1?nr_email_referer=1&utm_content=BISelect&utm_medium=email&utm_source=Sailthru&utm_campaign=BI%2520Select%2520Mondays%25202016-08-29&utm_term=Business%2520Insider%2520Select%2520-%2520Engaged%252C%2520Active%252C%2520Passive%252C%2520Disengaged (accessed on 5 April 2020).
12. Amato, F.; Chianese, A.; Moscato, V.; Picariello, A.; Sperli, G. SNOPS. In Proceedings of the Twelfth International Workshop on Web Information and Data Management-WIDM '12, Maui, HI, USA, 29 October–2 November 2012; ACM Press: New York, NY, USA, 2012; p. 49.
13. Chianese, A.; Piccialli, F. Designing a Smart Museum: When Cultural Heritage Joins IoT. In Proceedings of the 2014 Eighth International Conference on Next Generation Mobile Apps, Services and Technologies, Oxford, UK, 10–12 September 2014; pp. 300–306.
14. Poulopoulos, V.; Vassilakis, C.; Antoniou, A.; Wallace, M.; Lepouras, G.; Nores, M.L. ExhiSTORY: IoT in the service of Cultural Heritage. In Proceedings of the 2018 Global Information Infrastructure and Networking Symposium (GIIS), Thessaloniki, Greece, 23–25 October 2018; pp. 1–4.
15. Vassilakis, C.; Poulopoulos, V.; Antoniou, A.; Wallace, M.; Lepouras, G.; Nores, M.L. exhiSTORY: Smart exhibits that tell their own stories. *Future Gener. Comput. Syst.* **2018**, *81*, 542–556. [CrossRef]
16. Santipantakis, G.; Doulkeridis, C.; Vouros, G.; Vlachou, A. MaskLink: Efficient Link Discovery for Spatial Relations via Masking Areas. *arXiv* **2018**, arXiv:1803.01135.
17. Sherif, M.A.; Dreundefinedler, K.; Smeros, P.; Ngomo, A.-C.N. RADON—Rapid Discovery of Topological Relations. In Proceedings of the Thirty-First AAAI Conference on Artificial Intelligence, San Francisco, CA, USA, 4–9 February 2017; AAAI Press: Menlo Park, CA, USA, 2017; pp. 175–181.
18. Smeros, P.; Koubarakis, M. Discovering Spatial and Temporal Links among RDF Data. In Proceedings of the 9th Workshop on Linked Data on the Web, Montréal, QC, Canada, 12 April 2016; pp. 1–7.
19. Santipantakis, G.M.; Glenis, A.; Patroumpas, K.; Vlachou, A.; Doulkeridis, C.; Vouros, G.A.; Pelekis, N.; Theodoridis, Y. SPARTAN: Semantic integration of big spatio-temporal data from streaming and archival sources. *Future Gener. Comput. Syst.* **2018**. [CrossRef]
20. Santipantakis, G.M.; Vlachou, A.; Doulkeridis, C.; Artikis, A.; Kontopoulos, I.; Vouros, G.A. A Stream Reasoning System for Maritime Monitoring. In Proceedings of the 25th International Symposium on Temporal Representation and Reasoning (TIME 2018), Warsaw, Poland, 15–17 October 2018; Alechina, N., Nørvåg, K., Penczek, W., Eds.; Schloss Dagstuhl—Leibniz-Zentrum fuer Informatik: Dagstuhl, Germany, 2018; Volume 120, pp. 201–217.
21. Yan, Z.; Zhang, P.; Vasilakos, A.V. A survey on trust management for Internet of Things. *J. Netw. Comput. Appl.* **2014**, *42*, 120–134. [CrossRef]
22. Kolokotronis, N.; Brotsis, S.; Germanos, G.; Vassilakis, C.; Shiaeles, S. On Blockchain Architectures for Trust-Based Collaborative Intrusion Detection. In Proceedings of the 2019 IEEE World Congress on Services (SERVICES), Milan, Italy, 8–13 July 2019; Volume 2642–939X, pp. 21–28.
23. Kotis, K.; Athanasakis, I.; Vouros, G.A. Semantically enabling IoT trust to ensure and secure deployment of IoT entities. *Int. J. Internet Things Cyber-Assur.* **2018**, *1*, 3–21. [CrossRef]

24. Hossain, M.M.; Fotouhi, M.; Hasan, R. Towards an Analysis of Security Issues, Challenges, and Open Problems in the Internet of Things. In Proceedings of the 2015 IEEE World Congress on Services, New York, NY, USA, 27 June–2 July 2015; pp. 21–28.
25. Sicari, S.; Rizzardi, A.; Grieco, L.A.; Coen-Porisini, A. Security, privacy and trust in Internet of Things: The road ahead. *Comput. Netw.* **2015**, *76*, 146–164. [CrossRef]
26. Lykourentzou, I.; Antoniou, A.; Naudet, Y.; Dow, S.P. Personality Matters: Balancing for Personality Types Leads to Better Outcomes for Crowd Teams. In Proceedings of the 19th ACM Conference on Computer-Supported Cooperative Work & Social Computing-CSCW '16, San Francisco, CA, USA, 27 February–2 March 2016; ACM Press: New York, NY, USA, 2016; pp. 259–272.
27. Dede, C. Immersive Interfaces for Engagement and Learning. *Science* **2009**, *323*, 66–69. [CrossRef] [PubMed]
28. Kunze, M.; Weske, M. *Behavioural Models: From Modelling Finite Automata to Analysing Business Processes*; Springer: Cham, Switzerland, 2016; ISBN 978-3-319-44960-9.
29. Ghigi, F.; Torres, M.I. Decision Making Strategies for Finite-State Bi-automaton in Dialog Management. In *Natural Language Dialog Systems and Intelligent Assistants*; Lee, G.G., Kim, H.K., Jeong, M., Kim, J.-H., Eds.; Springer International Publishing: Cham, Switzerland, 2015; pp. 209–221. ISBN 978-3-319-19291-8.
30. Janošek, M.; Žáček, J. Modelling robot's behaviour using finite automata. *AIP Conf. Proc.* **2017**, *1863*, 70018.
31. Lykourentzou, I.; Vergados, D.J.; Naudet, Y. Improving Wiki Article Quality Through Crowd Coordination: A Resource Allocation Approach. *Int. J. Semant. Web Inf. Syst.* **2013**, *9*, 105–125. [CrossRef]
32. Lykourentzou, I.; Papadaki, K.; Vergados, D.J.; Polemi, D.; Loumos, V. CorpWiki: A self-regulating wiki to promote corporate collective intelligence through expert peer matching. *Inf. Sci. (N.Y.)* **2010**, *180*, 18–38. [CrossRef]
33. Basu Roy, S.; Lykourentzou, I.; Thirumuruganathan, S.; Amer-Yahia, S.; Das, G. Task assignment optimization in knowledge-intensive crowdsourcing. *VLDB J.* **2015**, *24*, 467–491. [CrossRef]
34. Lykourentzou, I.; Mtalaa, W.; Vergados, D.; Naudet, Y. Guiding wiki crowds through resource scheduling. In Proceedings of the 6th Multidisciplinary International Scheduling Conference: Theory and Applications, Ghent, Belgium, 27–30 August 2013; pp. 753–756.
35. Schmitz, H.; Lykourentzou, I. Online Sequencing of Non-Decomposable Macrotasks in Expert Crowdsourcing. *Trans. Soc. Comput.* **2018**, *1*. [CrossRef]
36. Lykourentzou, I.; Claude, X.; Naudet, Y.; Tobias, E.; Antoniou, A.; Lepouras, G.; Vassilakis, C. Improving museum visitors' Quality of Experience through intelligent recommendations: A visiting style-based approach. In Proceedings of the 9th International Conference on Intelligent Environments, Athens, Greece, 16–17 July 2013; Botía, J.A., Charitos, D., Eds.; IOS Press: Amsterdam, The Netherlands, 2013; pp. 507–518.
37. Adam, C.; Gaudou, B. BDI agents in social simulations: A survey. *Knowl. Eng. Rev.* **2016**, *31*, 207–238. [CrossRef]
38. Kasapakis, V.; Gavalas, D.; Dzardanova, E. Mixed Reality. In *Encyclopedia of Computer Graphics and Games*; Lee, N., Ed.; Springer International Publishing: Cham, Switzerland, 2018; pp. 1–4. ISBN 978-3-319-08234-9.
39. Milgram, P.; Kishino, F. A taxonomy of mixed reality visual displays. *IEICE Trans. Inf. Syst.* **1994**, *77*, 1321–1329.
40. Roth, D.; Lugrin, J.; Büser, J.; Bente, G.; Fuhrmann, A.; Latoschik, M.E. A simplified inverse kinematic approach for embodied VR applications. In Proceedings of the 2016 IEEE Virtual Reality (VR), Greenville, SC, USA, 19–23 March 2016; pp. 275–276.
41. Margaris, D.; Vassilakis, C. Improving Collaborative Filtering's Rating Prediction Quality by Considering Shifts in Rating Practices. In Proceedings of the 2017 IEEE 19th Conference on Business Informatics (CBI), Thessaloniki, Greece, 24–27 July 2017; Volume 1, pp. 158–166.
42. Parent, C.; Pelekis, N.; Theodoridis, Y.; Yan, Z.; Spaccapietra, S.; Renso, C.; Andrienko, G.; Andrienko, N.; Bogorny, V.; Damiani, M.L.; et al. Semantic trajectories modeling and analysis. *ACM Comput. Surv.* **2013**, *45*, 1–32. [CrossRef]
43. Bogorny, V.; Renso, C.; de Aquino, A.R.; de Lucca Siqueira, F.; Alvares, L.O. CONSTAnT—A Conceptual Data Model for Semantic Trajectories of Moving Objects. *Trans. GIS* **2014**, *18*, 66–88. [CrossRef]
44. Demidova, E.; Barbieri, N.; Dietze, S.; Funk, A.; Holzmann, H.; Maynard, D.; Papailiou, N.; Peters, W.; Risse, T.; Spiliotopoulos, D. Analysing and Enriching Focused Semantic Web Archives for Parliament Applications. *Future Internet* **2014**, *6*, 433–456. [CrossRef]

45. Baglioni, M.; Fernandes de Macêdo, J.A.; Renso, C.; Trasarti, R.; Wachowicz, M. Towards Semantic Interpretation of Movement Behavior. Available online: https://link.springer.com/chapter/10.1007/978-3-642-00318-9_14 (accessed on 5 April 2020).
46. Fileto, R.; May, C.; Renso, C.; Pelekis, N.; Klein, D.; Theodoridis, Y. The Baquara2 knowledge-based framework for semantic enrichment and analysis of movement data. *Data Knowl. Eng.* **2015**, *98*, 104–122. [CrossRef]
47. Nogueira, T.P.; Martin, H. Querying semantic trajectory episodes. In Proceedings of the 4th ACM SIGSPATIAL International Workshop on Mobile Geographic Information Systems-MobiGIS '15, Seattle, WA, USA, 3 November 2015; ACM Press: New York, NY, USA, 2015; pp. 23–30.
48. Santipantakis, G.M.; Vouros, G.A.; Doulkeridis, C.; Vlachou, A.; Andrienko, G.; Andrienko, N.; Fuchs, G.; Garcia, J.M.C.; Martinez, M.G. Specification of Semantic Trajectories Supporting Data Transformations for Analytics. In Proceedings of the 13th International Conference on Semantic Systems-Semantics2017, Amsterdam, The Netherlands, 11–14 September 2017; ACM Press: New York, NY, USA, 2017; pp. 17–24.
49. Eldawy, A.; Mokbel, M.F. SpatialHadoop: A MapReduce framework for spatial data. In Proceedings of the 2015 IEEE 31st International Conference on Data Engineering, Seoul, Korea, 13–16 April 2015; pp. 1352–1363.
50. Xie, D.; Li, F.; Yao, B.; Li, G.; Zhou, L.; Guo, M. Simba. In Proceedings of the 2016 International Conference on Management of Data-SIGMOD '16, San Francisco, CA, USA, 26 June–1 July 2016; ACM Press: New York, NY, USA, 2016; pp. 1071–1085.
51. Bao, J.; Li, R.; Yi, X.; Zheng, Y. Managing massive trajectories on the cloud. In Proceedings of the 24th ACM SIGSPATIAL International Conference on Advances in Geographic Information Systems-GIS '16, Burlingame, CA, USA, 31 October–3 November 2016; ACM Press: New York, NY, USA, 2016; pp. 1–10.
52. Xie, X.; Mei, B.; Chen, J.; Du, X.; Jensen, C.S. Elite: An elastic infrastructure for big spatiotemporal trajectories. *VLDB J.* **2016**, *25*, 473–493. [CrossRef]
53. Mozafari, B.; Ramnarayan, J.; Menon, S.; Mahajan, Y.; Chakraborty, S.; Bhanawat, H.; Bachhav, K. SnappyData: A Unified Cluster for Streaming, Transactions and Interactive Analytics. In Proceedings of the 8th Biennial Conference on Innovative Data Systems Research, Chaminade, CA, USA, 8–11 January 2017; pp. 1–8.
54. Ding, X.; Chen, L.; Gao, Y.; Jensen, C.S.; Bao, H. UlTraMan: A Unified Platform for Big Trajectory Data Management and Analytics. *Proc. VLDB Endow.* **2018**, *11*, 787–799. [CrossRef]
55. W3C. Resource Description Framework (RDF). Available online: https://www.w3.org/RDF/ (accessed on 12 August 2019).
56. W3C. Web Ontology Language (OWL). Available online: https://www.w3.org/OWL/ (accessed on 18 August 2019).
57. Zhang, W.; Wang, X.; Huang, Z. A System of Mining Semantic Trajectory Patterns from GPS Data of Real Users. *Symmetry* **2019**, *11*, 889. [CrossRef]
58. Kotis, K.; Vouros, G.A. Human-centered ontology engineering: The HCOME methodology. *Knowl. Inf. Syst.* **2006**, *10*, 109–131. [CrossRef]
59. International Committee for Documentation (CIDOC) of the International Council of Museums (ICOM). *ISO/TC 46/SC 4, ISO Standard 21127:2014: A Reference Ontology for the Interchange of Cultural Heritage Information*, 2nd ed.; International Organization for Standardization: Geneva, Switzerland, 2016; pp. 1–104.
60. Hu, Y.; Janowicz, K. The Semantic Trajectory Pattern. In *Ontology Engineering with Ontology Design Patterns*; Hitzler, P., Gangemi, A., Janowicz, K., Krisnadhi, A., Presutti, V., Eds.; IOS Press: Amsterdam, The Netherlands, 2016; pp. 321–327. ISBN 978-1-61499-676-7.
61. Antonakaki, D.; Spiliotopoulos, D.; Samaras, C.V.; Pratikakis, P.; Ioannidis, S.; Fragopoulou, P. Social media analysis during political turbulence. *PLoS ONE* **2017**, *12*. [CrossRef] [PubMed]
62. Spiliotopoulos, D.; Tzoannos, E.; Stavropoulou, P.; Kouroupetroglou, G.; Pino, A. Designing user interfaces for social media driven digital preservation and information retrieval. In Proceedings of the 13th International Conference on Computers Helping People with Special Needs, ICCHP 2012, Linz, Austria, 11–13 July 2012; Volume 7382 LNCS, pp. 581–584.
63. Alexandersson, J.; Aretoulaki, M.; Campbell, N.; Gardner, M.; Girenko, A.; Klakow, D.; Koryzis, D.; Petukhova, V.; Specht, M.; Spiliotopoulos, D.; et al. Metalogue: A Multiperspective Multimodal Dialogue System with Metacognitive Abilities for Highly Adaptive and Flexible Dialogue Management. In Proceedings of the 2014 International Conference on Intelligent Environments, Shanghai, China, 30 June–4 July 2014; pp. 365–368.

64. Antoniou, A.; Katifori, A.; Roussou, M.; Vayanou, M.; Karvounis, M.; Kyriakidi, M.; Pujol-Tost, L. Capturing the visitor profile for a personalized mobile museum experience: An indirect approach. In Proceedings of the 24th ACM Conference on User Modelling, Adaptation and Personalisation, Halifax, NS, Canada, 13–17 July 2016.
65. Shani, G.; Gunawardana, A. Evaluating Recommendation Systems. In *Recommender Systems Handbook*; Ricci, F., Rokach, L., Shapira, B., Kantor, P.B., Eds.; Springer: Boston, MA, USA, 2011; pp. 257–297. ISBN 978-0-387-85820-3.

© 2020 by the authors. Licensee MDPI, Basel, Switzerland. This article is an open access article distributed under the terms and conditions of the Creative Commons Attribution (CC BY) license (http://creativecommons.org/licenses/by/4.0/).

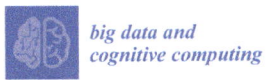 

Article

# Hydria: An Online Data Lake for Multi-Faceted Analytics in the Cultural Heritage Domain

Kimon Deligiannis, Paraskevi Raftopoulou, Christos Tryfonopoulos *, Nikos Platis and Costas Vassilakis

Department of Informatics & Telecommunications, University of the Peloponnese, GR22131 Tripolis, Greece; deligiannis@uop.gr (K.D.); praftop@uop.gr (P.R.); nplatis@uop.gr (N.P.); costas@uop.gr (C.V.)
* Correspondence: trifon@uop.gr, Tel.: +30-2710-230-175

Received: 29 March 2020; Accepted: 15 April 2020; Published: 23 April 2020

**Abstract:** Advancements in cultural informatics have significantly influenced the way we perceive, analyze, communicate and understand culture. New data sources, such as social media, digitized cultural content, and Internet of Things (IoT) devices, have allowed us to enrich and customize the cultural experience, but at the same time have created an avalanche of new data that needs to be stored and appropriately managed in order to be of value. Although data management plays a central role in driving forward the cultural heritage domain, the solutions applied so far are fragmented, physically distributed, require specialized IT knowledge to deploy, and entail significant IT experience to operate even for trivial tasks. In this work, we present Hydria, an online data lake that allows users without any IT background to harvest, store, organize, analyze and share heterogeneous, multi-faceted cultural heritage data. Hydria provides a zero-administration, zero-cost, integrated framework that enables researchers, museum curators and other stakeholders within the cultural heritage domain to easily (i) deploy data acquisition services (like social media scrapers, focused web crawlers, dataset imports, questionnaire forms), (ii) design and manage versatile customizable data stores, (iii) share whole datasets or horizontal/vertical data shards with other stakeholders, (iv) search, filter and analyze data via an expressive yet simple-to-use graphical query engine and visualization tools, and (v) perform user management and access control operations on the stored data. To the best of our knowledge, this is the first solution in the literature that focuses on collecting, managing, analyzing, and sharing diverse, multi-faceted data in the cultural heritage domain and targets users without an IT background.

**Keywords:** cultural heritage; big data management; data lake; data store; analytics and visualization; open source

## 1. Introduction

In the last few years Cultural Informatics (CI) has surfaced as a new promising domain that constitutes the socio-technological approach to understand, represent, communicate and re-invent cultures and cultural institutions [1]. CI may also be used in a disruptive fashion, aiming to change the way we understand and experience our cultural heritage [2], by enabling us, for example, to create personalized museum experiences [3,4], to discover facets and stories from new or existing cultural heritage data [5–7], or to create inter-linked cultural data repositories [8–11]. While performing these tasks, CI are creating an avalanche of data, produced by a vast number of related activities such as profiling of or feedback from museum and cultural venue visitors [12–15], social media activity (e.g., posts and comments) related to cultural events [16–23], papers and specialized conferences on the topic [24–27], and raw data on cultural objects such as artifact descriptions [28–31]. This data is typically fragmented and distributed among the different stakeholders, while the data management solutions that are involved vary greatly, ranging from simple spreadsheet files for the less tech savvy to typical data stores such as relational databases [32–34] or semantically richer knowledge bases [9,10,35,36].

From the above, we can conclude that data management is a key technological factor that drives the Cultural Heritage (CH) domain forward [35,37], but the data management solutions applied so far are fragmented, physically distributed, heterogeneous, non-aligned and require specialized IT knowledge to deploy and operate (e.g., [38–40]). Moreover, the asynchronous nature of the data acquisition process itself poses new challenges in the collection, organization, and processing of the relevant data [37]. Proposed solutions for data storage of cultural information (e.g., [9,10,35,41]) usually require significant computing infrastructure, which is not easy to obtain or maintain, and the constant support and active involvement of IT experts even for trivial tasks, like creating a graph from the given data, updating the produced statistics, or incorporating a new data source/set. Typically, reconfiguring an existing solution for reuse in another setup or setting one up from scratch for the specific cultural data management problem requires *(i)* time-consuming meetings between scientists of different disciplines trying to understand each other's needs and goals, and *(ii)* resource-consuming IT infrastructure that calls for outsourcing to IT specialists and regular maintenance/upgrades to keep up with technological requirements [42]. Due to these issues, a great number of stakeholders (such as small museums or humanities research groups) that lack the resources for infrastructure and/or computing expertise still rely on outdated approaches like *(i)* storing their data in spreadsheets or raw files, *(ii)* sharing their data with colleagues through email, cloud uploads of zip files, or even by snail mailing electronic copies in removable media, and *(iii)* analyzing the data via sub-standard tools and trial software. Such practices create, in turn, other concerns like data freshness/integrity issues due to versioning, issues with the significance of reported results due to data scarcity/fragmentation, and even ethical issues like unequal access to data and resources [43].

In this work, we present *Hydria*, a novel *free online data lake* meant for *acquiring, storing, organizing, analyzing* and *sharing* heterogeneous, multi-faceted cultural heritage data. Hydria and all the provided functionality (given in detail in the following sections) are fully developed by the authors by resorting to open source tools. The data lake architecture [44] adopted in the design of Hydria enables the direct incorporation of heterogeneous information that has been recorded in dispersed formats, while specialized processing engines ingest data without compromising the data structure, making it available for tasks such as visualization, mining, analytics and reporting. In this sense, the proposed system targets primarily the functional requirements posed by the cultural informatics domain, and enables researchers, curators and other stakeholders within the cultural informatics domain to easily acquire, manage and share data/knowledge within Hydria.

Thus, the Hydria system proposed in this paper is an innovative, integrated framework that enables users with *no prior IT knowledge* to *(i) setup and launch*, in an easy and transparent way, data acquisition services like topical focused crawlers, social media monitors, web scrapers and dataset imports, *(ii) collect* questionnaires and other types of user input data by resorting to several built-in and customizable data entry forms, *(iii) record, organize and manage* collected data by storing them in different data stores (called *data ponds* in the Hydria terminology), *(iv) share* whole data sets or horizontal/vertical data shards via a powerful publish/subscribe mechanism that notifies users when other data ponds store data of interest, *(v) search and analyze* data by using a powerful yet simple point-and-click mechanism that performs queries on the stored data and extracts the requested information in several formats/outputs such as histograms, pie charts, (heat) maps, (stacked) bars/columns, area charts and various file types (like CSV/TSV and raw), and *(vi)* perform basic and advanced *user management* tasks (such as manage users, assign user privileges and permissions, perform access control on data and data ponds). All services are designed for usage *by non-IT experts* and are configured/executed by resorting to step-by-step wizards, contain in-context explanations for the different system functions and provide online help with examples.

The contributions of this work are three-fold:

(i) We put forward Hydria, an *online, free, zero-administration* data lake that offers both fundamental and advanced user and data/knowledge management functionality for big cultural data management. To the best of our knowledge, this is the first system that focuses on collecting, managing, analyzing, and sharing diverse, multi-faceted data in the cultural heritage domain and allows users without an IT background to deploy, populate, and manage their own data stores within minutes, alleviating the need to rely on expensive custom-made solutions that require IT infrastructure and skills to maintain.

(ii) We present the *architectural solutions* behind the proposed system, discuss the individual module technologies and provide details on the module orchestration. We also describe several *novel services* that include automated data harvesting from the web and social media, integrated user input collection via standard and customizable data types, easy to perform data analysis and visualization, publish/subscribe functionality to facilitate sharing of different facets and data shards, and access control mechanisms.

(iii) We advocate the appropriateness of our approach for the cultural heritage domain and showcase different scenarios that highlight its usefulness for cultural data management.

From the argumentation presented above, it becomes clear that a free online system in the form of a *data lake* that is meant for *acquiring, storing, organizing, analyzing* and *sharing* heterogeneous, multi-faceted cultural heritage data would be a valuable asset to several different cultural heritage applications such as museum curation, user study management, bibliographical analysis, dataset management, and data integration. Moreover, such a system would be an invaluable source to many cultural informatics projects that either lack the resources or lack the IT expertise to design and deploy their own software and/or hardware infrastructure.

The rest of the paper is organized as follows. Section 2 discusses related work. Subsequently, Section 3 presents the overall system architecture and outlines the different modules as well as the respective services, while Section 4 provides an indicative case study during the Alpha testing phase of Hydria within the TripMentor project [45]. Section 5 presents various application scenarios in the cultural heritage domain and discusses how different stakeholders may benefit from using Hydria. Finally, Section 6 concludes this article and provides future research directions.

## 2. Related Work

In this section, we overview related research approaches that *(i)* are associated with the data acquisition and knowledge extraction for the cultural heritage domain based on social media, *(ii)* present the most prominent solutions in information systems meant for cultural heritage, and *(iii)* include museum and/or user recommendation information systems intended to improve visitors experience in cultural venues.

*2.1. Social Data Management in the Cultural Heritage Domain*

As an ever-growing number of social networks users constantly post opinions about cultural venues (by publishing reviews, describing their perceived experiences, using check-ins, subscribing to upcoming events, etc.), high volumes of data/content of great interest to cultural heritage applications is generated within popular social media platforms. The work presented in [16,17] aims to bridge the social media and cultural heritage domains and shows a way to stimulate history reflection by assembling games, social networks, history, and culture. In [20] the authors introduce the notion of the *prosumer*; the term refers to people that, besides consuming information, also produce new content when visiting cultural sites. A prominent paradigm in this line is the HeritageGO system proposed in [18]. HeritageGO tries to convert raw cultural heritage data coming from countries with a vast amount of cultural PoIs into meaningful digital information; towards this effort, the authors present social networks users as the main data harvesting lever and use metric quality models to filter the acquired data.

The approaches presented in [19–23] focus on improving cultural tourism and enhancing the visitors' experience by enriching the information concerning historical sites, monuments and other cultural PoIs with social media content, which is uploaded by social networks users and obtained using web mining techniques. To do so, identification methods that use geotagged multimedia data from social networks or location-aware services and sensors (e.g., GPS) attached on tourists' mobile devices have been implemented, while classification tools are used to rank the most relevant cultural heritage landmarks with respect to the user context (e.g., location) to render smart interactions among tourists and the cultural surrounding. The work presented in [46] proposes a Twitter big data-centric solution, which acknowledges a collection of Key Performance Indicators (KPIs) focusing on the quantity metric evaluation of cultural heritage sensitivity as interpreted by Twitter users, by merging natural language processing, semantic methodologies, location reports and time inspection.

Regarding the use of multimedia content in the cultural heritage domain, [47] is a prominent work; the authors describe the main aspects of multimedia social networks (MSNs), present the interactive system GIVAS, and highlight its importance to archeologists, cultural heritage researchers and tourists, as it consists a multimedia cooperative framework for managing, exploring, visualizing and sharing cultural heritage data. In [30], the author discusses how published multimedia data (especially videos) concerning cultural heritage venues and gathered from social media are of great importance to field consultants for generating 3D models (by using structure for motion methods).

PATCH [48] is a portable system able to harvest cultural heritage content from distributed and heterogeneous sources (such as social networks), to supply its users with profitable and personalized information and services based on their interests and their surroundings, and to provide data management, retrieval and analysis services. This system is the most conceptually and functionally similar work to the Hydria data lake; however PATCH was designed for the needs of a specific project and applied to a particular research study, while our work is an online, free, zero-administration data lake that offers both fundamental and advanced user and data/knowledge management functionality in the cultural heritage domain, able to be customized for the requirements of any cultural heritage project, and addresses all users, without requiring any IT background/skills.

*2.2. Information Systems for Cultural Heritage*

Information management in the cultural heritage domain concerns a cycle of organizational activity: the acquisition of cultural content from one or more sources, the storage and distribution of this data to those who need to evaluate it, and its final disposition through archiving. Over the years, many solutions aiming at the management, sharing and analysis of cultural heritage information have been proposed, while other investigations have tried to classify the variety of software tools and systems associated with the vast amount of data in the cultural heritage domain. The authors in [35] perform an itemized categorization of software tools and systems used in the cultural heritage area, associated with both spatial and temporal data. The contribution in [42] aims at exploring and classifying knowledge organization systems that are used in the cultural heritage field, while it applies extensive qualitative evaluation to the most prominent ones.

The work presented in [38] introduces the notion of *smart space* as a software development approach that enables creating service-oriented information systems for emerging computing environments for the Internet of Things (IoT), and considers the different principles to semantic-driven design of service-oriented information systems. In a similar spirit, [39] presents the ExhiSTORY infrastructure and discusses how sensors and the IoT can be used in cultural heritage sites so that exhibits communicate with the visitors towards generating rich, personalized, coherent, and highly stimulating experiences. In [49], a number of separate streams and current systems functionalities are examined through the usage of the European EU-CHIC framework, in order to achieve optimal suggestions for enhancing the management of cultural heritage data. The CHIS project [36] points at constructing an information system to assist operations that involve different user types in the cultural heritage domain, offering a scientific advancement that can improve personalized services in a business environment. The research in [50] focuses on mobile software development for cultural information educational purposes and presents how mobile device users can be well-informed about cultural heritage sites when they visit them.

On the basis of several studies carried out on cultural landscapes in a spatial-planning perspective, [51] discusses the potential and limits of Geographical Information Systems (GIS) for supporting the territorialization of multidisciplinary landscape analysis for the management of a site of the UNESCO world heritage list, and proposes an approach for a GIS responding to landscape-oriented studies. Two similar approaches that propose a 3D representation of cultural objects, in order to facilitate researchers in determining both the relationships between data and the spatial relationships between cultural information, are presented in [31,52].

Recommendation systems are very popular in many scientific domains; in the cultural heritage field, recommendation systems constitute powerful tools that may help users improve their experience in cultural venues/PoIs. The work in [53] proposes that guidelines and recommendations should be used in all cultural infrastructures in Poland, associated with technical perspectives of digitization (such as technical and structural metadata, rules series, parameters and formats). The work in [54] describes an info-mobility recommendation system, coined TAIS, that assists tourists while traveling. TAIS can interpret user actions, uncloak their preferences, and suggest cultural sites in respect to the users' current locations (while also providing possible transportation means). The approach in [40] concerns a (big data) architecture that is able to host applications that retrieve data of the cultural heritage field from distributed and heterogeneous repositories; the authors introduce an innovative user-focused recommendation method for cultural element proposal to be applied on top of the data management infrastructure. Finally, the work in [41] introduces a novel ontology-based user method, pointing at improving personalized suggestions and users' visit experience by learning their background and interests.

*2.3. Information Systems for Museums*

In recent decades, a great number of cultural institutions (e.g., museums or national archives) integrate information systems in order to catalogue and document their exhibits, disseminate cultural information from their web sites and/or deliver informal education to their audience. Moreover, many information systems applied in institutions use Virtual Reality (VR) and Augmented Reality (AR) technologies aiming at enhancing tourists' experiences. The Digital Diorama [55] is a Mixed Reality (MR) system applied to museums focusing on rendering more features than existing dioramas in museum exhibitions, by prefetching background information. The work in [56] aims to enrich visitors' experiences in museum exhibitions by introducing a multichannel information system. The work in [57] introduces a virtual informal education system for the well-known ancient illustration of "Qing-ming Festival by the Riverside", by using VR technology to generate a wide, captivating, and responsive virtual environment. The work in [58] elaborates on the installation and integration of information systems in museums, identifying four success factors for relevant projects, while stressing the fundamental differences between museums and commercial companies. The approach in [59] describes the formulation and the adaptation of an AR-based system tailored for museum supervision; this research aims to narrow the gap between man and machine by applying instinctive as well as user-friendly synergies in an omnipresent computing environment. In a similar direction, TOMS [60] is a collaborative semantic-based system developed to provide sharing services of a vast variety of cultural heritage multimedia content between national museums in Thailand.

Personalization systems emphasize on tailoring a service or a product in order to accommodate particular individual preferences; presently, many museums and cultural institutions adopt personalization systems in order to offer custom-fit guidance and thus improve visitors' experiences. The work in [13] proposes a multimedia information system that is able to support multiple display devices, is built on top of an application server hosting plentiful digital content, and is presented to visitors in respect to their particular requirements. In [14], the authors demonstrate Future Worlds, a knowledgable game-based environment for cooperative feasibility investigations in science museums that is able to dynamically identify and adjust visitors' specific preferences while touring in the exhibition. The approach in [15] puts forward a web intelligent virtual assistant-based service for virtual museum explorations that can advance suggestions in respect to the museum exhibits and tailored to user's choices. In a similar spirit, [61] discusses experimental results obtained towards personalizing a museum visit based on gaming, using an approach relying on users' cognitive style, social networks, and recommendations. In [62], the authors, trying to connect cultural heritage, games and social networks, design social network games to be used for accomplishing user profiling and supporting museum visits; the games are also presented in a generic framework in cultural heritage. Finally, in [3], the authors investigate the use of indirect profiling methods through a visitor quiz, in order to provide the visitor with specific museum content, identify key profiling issues, and discuss guidelines towards a generalized approach for the profiling needs of cultural institutions.

Other works adopt different technological approaches, such as location-aware or spatial methods, in order to provide particular tour guidelines to their visitors. In [63], the authors investigate the practical usage of GIS as a tool, while inspecting how museums can adapt GIS technologies in separate operating zones. The work in [64,65] demonstrates a similar approach of a 3D information system, developed to manage cultural heritage information, which provides information layers that link with the exterior environment of the artifacts, following a similar to the GIS solution, in order to allow relationships between individual items.

To the best of our knowledge, Hydria is the first system that focuses on collecting, managing, analyzing, and sharing diverse, multi-faceted data in the cultural heritage domain and allows users without an IT background to deploy, populate, and manage their own data stores within minutes, alleviating the need to rely on expensive custom-made solutions that require IT infrastructure and skills to maintain.

## 3. System Architecture

The *Hydria data lake* allows users to *(i)* harvest and/or import data from structured and semi-structured data sources, *(ii)* collect user input data by resorting to several built-in and customizable data entry forms, *(iii)* store and manage collected data by organizing them in different big data management data stores (called *data ponds* in the Hydria terminology), *(iv)* share whole data sets or horizontal/vertical data shards via a powerful publish/subscribe mechanism that notifies users when other data ponds store data of interest, *(v)* search, filter and analyze data by using a powerful yet simple point-and-click mechanism that performs queries on the stored data and extracts the requested information in several visual representations and outputs, and *(vi)* perform basic and advanced user management tasks on the stored data. In Hydria, data ponds are custom-made database collections that are used to conceptually group data within a specific cultural heritage application. Figure 1 provides a high-level view of the system architecture, of the different services and functionalities implemented, and their conceptual organization within the Hydria data lake. In what follows, we present in detail the different services and modules that comprise the Hydria ecosystem and briefly outline the functionality and added value of each module.

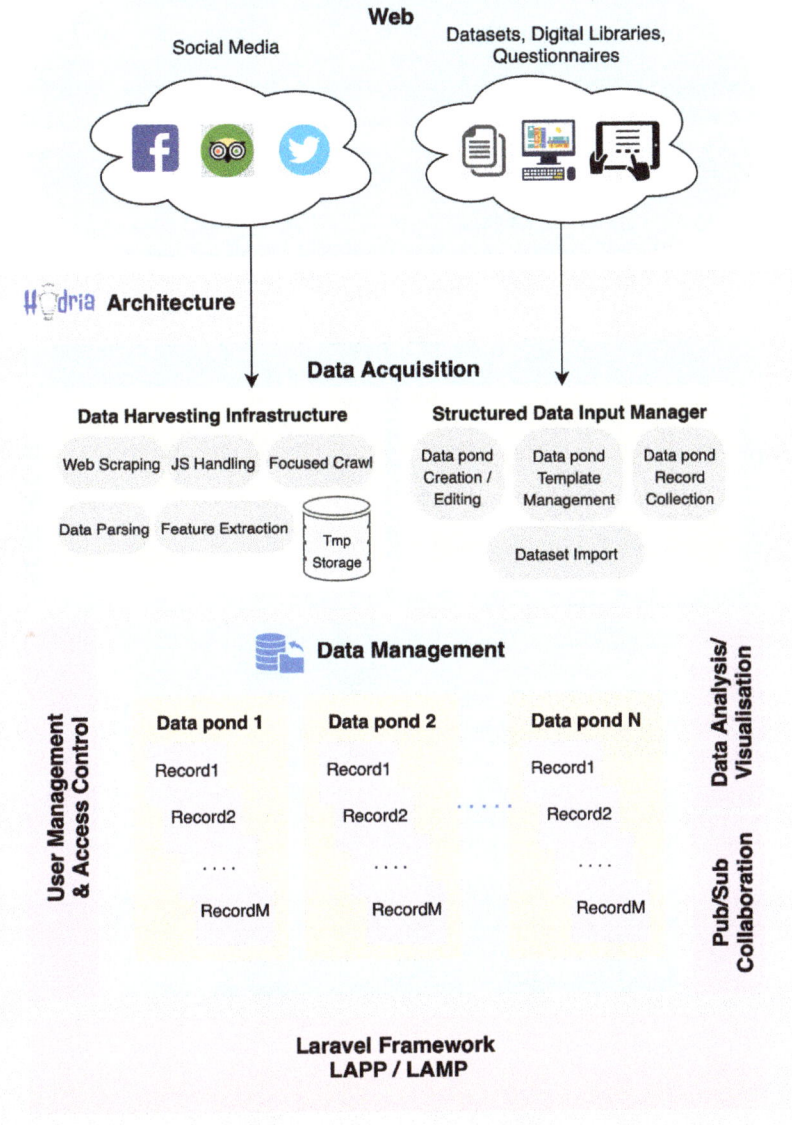

**Figure 1.** Hydria data lake architecture.

*3.1. The Data Acquisition Module*

Information of interest to many cultural heritage applications are present in many different websites ranging from online encyclopedias like Wikipedia [66], online digital libraries like Europeana [67] or DBLP [68], to portals and directories like governmental sites on culture (e.g., Odysseus [69], the portal of the Greek Ministry of Culture and Sports) and WikiCFP [70]. However, presently, a lot of data/content of great interest to cultural heritage applications may be also discovered within popular social media like Facebook, TripAdvisor or Twitter. A vast number of people (of any origin, language or educational profile) have accounts in (typically more than one) social media platforms, and use them to post their opinion about cultural heritage venues by publishing reviews, to describe their perceived experiences by uploading posts, to designate favorite destinations and provide useful points of interest (PoIs) by using "check-ins", or to keep up to date by subscribing to upcoming events hosted by different types of venues [71–73].

To cover this widespread need for data acquisition within the cultural heritage domain, Hydria provides a flexible yet powerful Data Acquisition module that is conceptually separated into two distinct submodules:

(i) The *Data Harvesting submodule*, which allows Hydria users to setup and deploy automated data collection crawlers and web scrapers (spiders) that are able to navigate the web and popular social media platforms, discover and harvest content of interest, and store the harvested data to the Hydria data lake. The Data Harvesting submodule is discussed in more detail in Section 3.1.1.

(ii) The *Structured Data Input submodule*, which allows Hydria users to import whole datasets into Hydria and collect user input data by exploiting several built-in and customizable data entry forms. The Structured Data Input submodule is elaborated on in Section 3.1.2.

3.1.1. The Data Harvesting Submodule

The Data Harvesting submodule implements several distinct services that may be invoked by Hydria users to initiate automated data collection. At the heart of this submodule lies the web scraping service that extends the basic components of the open source web scrapper Scrapy [74,75] for scraping social media content. Currently, the web scraping service supports two of the most popular social media platforms, Facebook and TripAdvisor, while support for more is under development. Setting up the web scraping service only involves providing the initial seed URLs from the aforementioned social media; the service automatically recognizes which social platform and what type of data (e.g., venues, PoIs, reviews) is targeted for data harvesting and launches the appropriate web scrapper instance. To tackle user privacy issues that may arise during spidering, the web scraping service provides no spidering options for individual users (i.e., one cannot scrape user pages) and supports only the collection of aggregate values and fields that are general enough so that no person may be identifiable by reasonable means. The data flow process is controlled by the scrapper execution engine that is responsible for the data flow between all components of the Hydria system and is summarized below:

1. The engine receives a *scrape* request, which is a custom-made class that is used to parse responses and extract scraped data, and pushes it to the scheduler for later use; then the engine expects to read scheduled tasks from the Scheduler, in order to process them further.
2. The scheduler performs scheduling on the available requests and returns to the engine the next request to be further processed (downloaded). Then, the engine forwards the request to the downloader through an appropriate message broker. When the page download is completed, the downloader creates a response and forwards it back to the engine via the message broker.
3. Once the engine gets the response, it moves it to the spider for processing through the message broker. When the spider processing is over, the scraped data are returned and *new* requests are sent to the engine via the message broker.
4. The engine initially passes the scraped data to the item pipeline, which is the software that is in charge of processing the data after they have been extracted by the spiders, then dispatches the processed request to the scheduler and subsequently awaits the next request to scrape.
5. The above steps are performed iteratively, until no more scheduled requests are available. Note that all the extracted items are temporarily pushed in a persistent local data store (one per initiated scraper).

This procedure can be applied straightforwardly on plain HTML pages that are received from the server; however, to enhance the user experience, practically all major social media sites employ JavaScript, making their content more interactive. This practice, however, poses challenges to the scraping procedure; to overcome these challenges, we have also developed a JavaScript handling service by adapting and integrating the Selenium library [76]. The Selenium library provides a useful tool for data harvesting and web scraping: the Selenium renderer uses a web browser engine to render a given URL and mimics human behavior on the web page. This allows the web scraping (and the crawling) service to interact with JavaScript functions that exist on the target website (e.g., infinite scrolling) and avoid unnecessary hold-ups in the spidering process. The JavaScript handling service uses the Google Chrome web driver for the Selenium renderer.

Apart from spidering popular structured social media platforms, the Data Harvesting submodule contains also a *focused crawl* service that is designed to perform *thematic* crawls on the clear web with the purpose to discover new resources that may contain cultural heritage data of interest. From the Hydria user side, setting up the focused crawling service only involves providing a relevant (to the task) query (e.g., "cultural heritage" or "archeological museum") that will be used to produce the initial crawl seeds. The underlying crawling infrastructure is based on the ACHE crawler [77], one of the most popular focused crawlers [78] available, which prioritizes URLs in the crawl frontier and categorizes the crawled pages as relevant or irrelevant using machine learning-based techniques. To direct the crawl towards topically relevant websites (i.e., websites with content relevant to cultural heritage) we use an SVM classifier, which is trained by resorting to an equal number of positive and negative examples of websites that are used as input to the *model builder* component of ACHE. Subsequently, the *seed finder* [79] component is used to aid the process of locating initial seeds for the focused crawl on the clear web; this is achieved by combining the pre-built classification model with the topic-related user-provided query discussed above. Since the crawled websites may be anything from blog posts to organizational web pages and do not have a predetermined structure (unlike the social media pages), the collected content is only parsed to remove HTML markup and is stored as raw text in the Hydria data lake.

Finally, the Data Harvesting submodule contains two auxiliary services (namely data parsing and feature extraction) that are used to extract textual content and features from the harvested websites.

3.1.2. The Structured Data Input Submodule

Apart from the crawling and web scraping functionality that were presented in the previous section, Hydria also supports structured data input via the relevant submodule. Structured data input supports several services that provide users with the necessary functionality to *(i)* import data from a structured CSV/XML/JSON formatted dataset, *(ii)* create (in a stand-alone data pond) a questionnaire-style form that may be used in surveys and the associated user answers, and *(iii)* reuse all or part of these questionnaires via the creation and management of templates. Each of the aforementioned services is associated with a data pond that is created to allow users to manage the stored data (more details about data pond creation and management are given in Section 3.2). To achieve this functionality, the Structured Data Input submodule implements several distinct services as follows.

The *Dataset Import service* is used to automatically load/store a structure dataset into a Hydria data pond; the service automatically matches the columns of a CSV/XML/JSON tagged file with the pre-specified data pond fields and for each data item (typically a row in the CSV file or element under the root of the XML/JSON document) a new record is created and stored in Hydria under the corresponding data pond. Notice that this service may be also used as a separate stand-alone step for importing harvested web/social media content that has undergone processing outside of Hydria; i.e., when the harvesting task is over, the user may select to process the downloaded content outside of Hydria and subsequently manually load the result of this intermediate processing into a separate data pond.

The rest of the available services target the creation of questionnaire-style forms that allow Hydria users to create and store data collection tasks that involve electronic input of end-users into structured forms (e.g., surveys, end-user evaluations, museum experience records, etc.). In order to facilitate data pond creation and reuse of common parts between constructed questionnaires, Hydria supports (via an appropriate template management service) the creation and use of *templates* that can be shared or reused between different data ponds. This functionality is native in Hydria and is tightly coupled with (i) the creation, maintenance and analysis of data ponds (described in detail in Section 3.2) and (ii) the access control mechanism for the different data ponds (described in detail in Section 3.5).

### 3.2. The Data Management Module

The Data Management module supervises the creation, editing, organization and management of the data ponds, and performs all necessary storage and retrieval operations to the database back-end (i.e., manages the stored data related with a specific data pond or a specific record). It supports a flexible, adaptive and intuitive way for designing and composing a data pond or a data pond template.

The Data Management module employs several different services that allow Hydria users to create and edit data ponds. Such activities are supported by an easy-to-use wizard mechanism that guides the Hydria user through the whole process. Building a new data pond/template involves defining a title and a description for it; subsequently the user specifies the different fields for the data pond (i.e., the attributes to be stored) by providing for each field its textual description and its type. According to the selected attribute type, hidden fields or dialogs appear for inserting more specific information about the attribute (e.g., if the attribute is of type *multiple choice*, the user has to fill up a list of values or select one of the existing template lists). The available data types that currently Hydria supports are as follows: title (this field is not fillable, although it is used to separate data pond sections), text, integer, decimal, date, multiple choice, picture drawing, image file, and complex data types.

*Complex data types* are a construct provided to allow for more efficient modelling of cases where a group of fields appear multiple times within a document, across different documents in the same data pond, or even across documents in different data ponds. Examples of such cases may be interpretations of cultural items (with each interpretation having an author, a summary, and extended analysis and supporting documents, and each cultural item being potentially subject to multiple interpretations), or company addresses (each address consists of a street name, a number, a city, a zip code and a country, and a single company may have multiple addresses). To introduce a complex data type, a user needs to provide the specification of a recurring attribute with more than one fields. Please note that the complex data type definition may be subsequently modified to change the attribute order and/or edit or delete a specific attribute by using the corresponding controls on the wizard; any changes are reflected to data ponds using the modified complex data type. The advantages of creating and using complex data types include better data modelling, increased flexibility in the design of data ponds with complex/recurring attributes, elevated knowledge capture capabilities and, consequently, the ability to formulate more expressive and semantically rich queries.

To ensure data consistency across data ponds and to enhance data integrity and input validation, Hydria natively supports the following two features:

(i) Hydria allows users to *share* data pond templates by supporting the reuse of all or a part of data pond fields (e.g., demographic data in questionnaires) across different data ponds. To promote this functionality, the data pond creation service prompts the user to consider reusing one of the available data pond templates before creating a new data pond.

(ii) Hydria provides users with the ability to *dynamically* create, store and edit drop-down lists of elements. To do so, the user specifies a unique name for the drop-down list and enters the list elements. Subsequently, when defining a multiple choice field (i.e., attribute), the user needs to set the data type to multiple choice and either select one of the stored drop-down lists from the pop-up window or dynamically create a new one that is thereafter stored along with the other drop-down lists for further (re)use.

Finally, notice that Hydria has no direct policy on how one stores or uses the stored data. This is particularly important in the case of evolving data(sets) where the user has many different options to store, monitor, or analyze data evolution. In particular, she has the option to create different data ponds for different snapshots of the data, use different fields to model data evolution within the data pond, or store solely the differences between various data snapshots.

*3.3. The Data Analysis Module*

The Data Analysis module supports search, filtering and analysis of the data stored in each data pond of the Hydria data lake. It provides a powerful yet easy-to-use data manipulation and query mechanism that allows users to formulate queries against the data ponds involving selection, projection, grouping and ordering operations through simple point-and-click interaction and without requiring any background knowledge of SQL (Figure 2). The provided mechanism also contains in-context explanations for the different data analysis elements and provides online help with examples. This functionality is targeted mainly towards users with limited relevant experience. Besides analyzing each data pond, the module also offers data extraction and visualization functionality in a variety of different formats such as histograms, pie charts, (heat) maps, (stacked) bars/columns, area/mekko/bubble charts, scatter plots, and various file types (like CSV/TSV and raw text). The implemented data visualization component involves a three-step process where the user *(i)* defines the type of the chart to be exported, *(ii)* specifies the base dataset by selecting the data pond and the data pond field(s) that will be used to create the chart, and *(iii)* may apply filtering conditions (restrictions) on the chosen dataset.

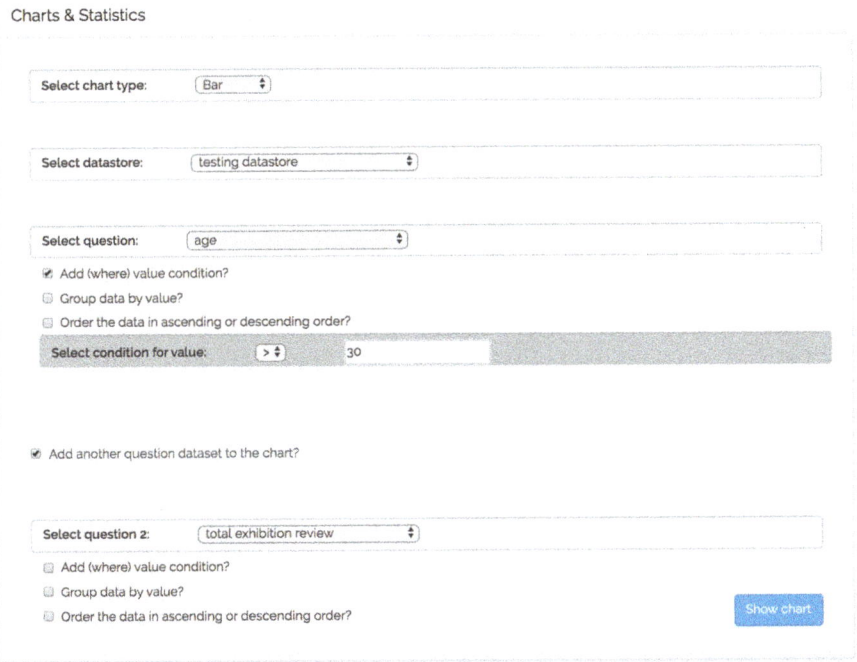

**Figure 2.** Filter and project records.

*3.4. The Publish/Subscribe Module*

The Publish/Subscribe module is essentially an efficient and easy-to-use collaboration tool that allows users to share their collected datasets (or parts of them), as well as to discover and access datasets of other users within the Hydria ecosystem. This tool is not intended for use by the Hydria system end-users (i.e., people participating in a Hydria survey, or museum visitors that provide feedback via a Hydria questionnaire), but rather targets other user categories like curators/super-users (see Section 3.5 for a detailed description of the Hydria user roles). Using this functionality involves the following two-step process:

1. A user may use the data pond search functionality to look for data ponds stored within the Hydria data lake that satisfy a given keyword query; after selecting one or more data ponds that are included in the result, she may send a subscription request to the owner of the specific data pond(s) asking for permission to access the data pond's schema definition, i.e., the list of attributes of the data pond, their descriptions and data types. If the owner of the data pond accepts the subscription request, the user is eligible to access the data pond's schema definition.
2. After examining the data pond schema, the user may decide to request access to specific attributes of the data pond at record level. In this case, she may select one or more attributes of the targeted data pond and send a follow-up subscription request to the owner of the data pond. Once the owner receives the new request, she is able to either deny, accept the request as is, or remove any of the attributes that should not be shared at record level, and confirm the sharing of the remaining ones.

When both stages have been completed, the user is able to access the subscribed records for preview, incorporate them into her own data ponds, or create charts and visualizations using the data analysis and visualization tool. Moreover, the subscribed user will be notified whenever new records that match her subscription are incorporated in the subscribed data pond.

### 3.5. The User Management Module

The User Management module is responsible for performing basic and advanced user management tasks, such as manage users in the Hydria community, assign user privileges and permissions, and perform access control on data ponds and the stored data within them. It supports the following three types of users:

(i) *System administrators*, who are able to access, create, edit, preview, delete and filter all the data ponds and records that are stored in the data lake; they are also capable of managing all types of Hydria users, as well as the user-role assignments.
(ii) *Power users*, who are typically curators in charge of one or more data ponds in the Hydria ecosystem. They are typically able to create new data ponds, initiate the collection of data from different online sources such as social media, the web, existing datasets, or end-users via questionnaires and surveys. They have access privileges in the data ponds that they create and in the records within these data ponds; they may analyze, filter and visualize the stored data, and collaborate with other power users in Hydria in the context of data sharing. A power user may also request to link specific end-users to new or existing data ponds.
(iii) *End-users*, who may participate in surveys and questionnaires issued by Hydria power users and view/edit their own data; an end-user is neither allowed to create new data ponds, nor to view data of other end-users within the same data pond. They may, however, use the analysis tools to perform limited analysis tasks on their own contributed data.

Figure 3 presents the UI for the creation of a new user from the administrator point of view in Hydria.

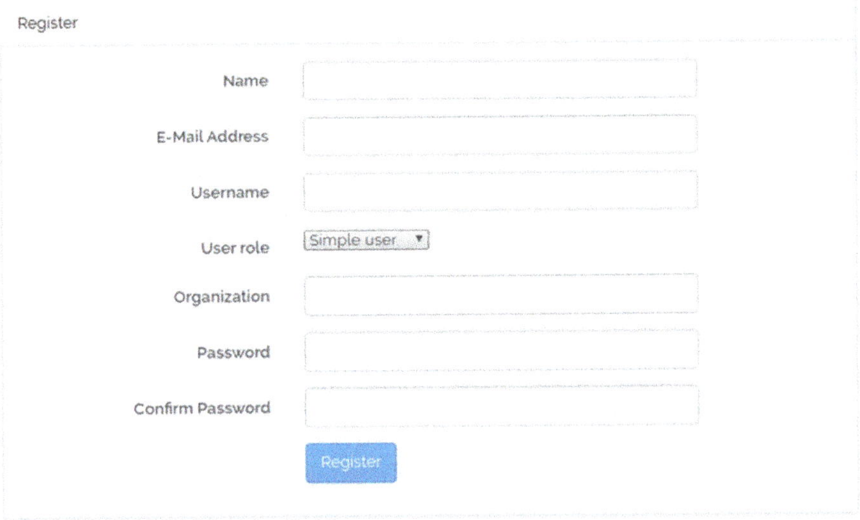

**Figure 3.** User creation form.

*3.6. Implementation Aspects*

Hydria has been entirely developed by open source software. The Data Acquisition module uses the Linux/Apache/MariaDB/PHP (LAMP) solution stack for temporary storage of the extracted data and was developed using Python tools [80]. The rest of the modules were built by using the Laravel Framework [81] and use the Linux/Apache/PostgreSQL/PHP (LAPP) solution stack as the back-end database infrastructure. Also, many of Hydria functionalities were developed using JavaScript/JQuery/AJAX.

## 4. The TripMentor Case Study

In the context of Alpha testing the Hydria platform, we made the system available to partners within the TripMentor project [45] that aims at creating a tourist guide for the region of Attica, Greece. The partners had varying levels of IT expertise, ranging from relatively experienced to very experienced, and were asked to use Hydria for collecting, storing, and managing data relevant to the project, by deploying the different services offered by Hydria and using the functionality provided. In the following, we report the results for this case study, as these were drawn from field observations as well as from the analysis of usage logs and collected data.

The TripMentor partners used Hydria to navigate within TripAdvisor [82] and Facebook [83] and detect content relevant to the tourism domain; the interest of focus was primarily points of interest (PoIs) located in the *Attica region in Greece*, due to the nature of the TripMentor project. The data retrieved was stored in the Hydria data lake, and the stakeholders involved used Hydria functionality to design the necessary data ponds, modify selected data records, mine and visualize information from the stored data, and export files for further analysis.

*4.1. Data Harvesting*

To crawl the web for content and data relevant to the TripMentor project, the integrated ACHE crawler was used within the Hydria environment. To set up the crawler, a number of relevant pages within the domain of interest were used as seed URLs; such URLs included tourist articles and blog posts related to cultural and tourist activities in the Attica region. To implement the page classification required by ACHE, different features of the page URL, title and content were exploited, which were determined after an examination of the patterns followed by the pages in different social networks. For instance, for the TripAdvisor spider the following features were used:

(i) The page URL was matched against the regular expression patterns `.*/attraction/.*` and `.*/attica/.*` (note that in Hydria regex expressions are case insensitive), using the `url_regex` classifier type, since the URLs of the PoIs in TripAdvisor start with the word *attraction* and contain the name of the region (*Attica*, in our case).
(ii) The page body was matched against the regular expression pattern `.*/greece/.*` using the `body_regex` classifier type, to ensure that the word *Attica* found in the URL actually refers to the Greek region (and not e.g., to the Attica city in the State of NY).

Similarly, for the Facebook crawlers patters from the seed URLs were exploited; for instance, to identify the activities available in the city of Athens, Greece (which is located in the Attica region), the seed URLs start with the string *Things-to-do-in-*, which is followed by the city name (Athens), and this is in turn followed by the name of the country (Greece).

Notably, a multitude of additional operators are available for more complex classification tasks, which include matching of the title (`title_regex` classifier type), combination of regular expression matches through the `AND` and `OR` operators, or using machine-learning-based text classifiers (SVM, Random Forest) using the `title_regex` classifier type.

Having collected the seed URLs, six distinct spiders were developed, in an effort to cover a wide spectrum of events and many different scopes; four of them targeted data harvesting from the Facebook platform, while the remaining two were deployed over TripAdvisor. Table 1 summarizes the outcome of the data harvesting process.

**Table 1.** TripMentor-related data ponds records after Hydria harvesting process.

| Data Ponds | Records |
|---|---|
| facebook_venues | 10,405 |
| facebook_posts | 139,880 |
| facebook_comments | 203,523 |
| facebook_events | 150 |
| tripadvisor_venues | 6869 |
| tripadvisor_user_reviews | 298,769 |

### 4.1.1. Facebook Spiders

In this section, we discuss the deployed Facebook spiders for the TripMentor case study and present some initial statistics and insights on how the Hydria social media spiders may be used within the cultural informatics context. Please note that the spiders and data ponds were setup and deployed by the TripMentor project partners; our statistics and observations are based on usage logs and the schema analyzes of the data ponds used to store the collected data.

The first spider, which constitutes the initial setup within Hydria, was deployed over Facebook and extracted a total number of 10,405 different PoIs in the Attica region; a time period of approximately 48 hours was needed to conclude the data harvesting operation, and the collected PoIs are categorized as shown in Table 2. For each of these venues, the spider retrieved and stored in a Hydria data pond the following fields from the related Facebook profile pages: the venue name, the venue unique ID as stored in the Facebook platform, the hours/days of the week that the venue is open to visitors, the venue website, the venue phone number, the registered email address, the physical address of the venue, the total number of check-ins for the venue (i.e., the visitor traffic), the average review score of the venue, the venue category, and the geographical coordinates (latitude and longitude) of the venue. Please note that all the collected data were about venues and cultural events, and no personal or user-specific data were harvested or stored.

Table 2. Different PoIs in the Attica region extracted by the first FB spider.

| Venue Category | # of PoIs |
|---|---|
| Arts and Entertainment | 2116 |
| Breakfast and Brunch Restaurants | 114 |
| Cafe | 2854 |
| Hotels | 778 |
| Landmarks | 614 |
| Museums | 210 |
| Parks and Outdoors | 712 |
| Restaurants | 3007 |

Having retrieved the PoIs unique IDs from the previous process, a new spider that generated the venues profile page URLs using the venue IDs was created and launched within Hydria for a subset of the collected PoIs (approximately 1.7 K PoIs). The spider was then deployed and collected around 140 K posts related to the targeted PoIs in a time frame of around 168 h (one week). All retrieved posts were stored in a separate data pond within Hydria, along with the following metadata: The post unique ID, the profile source of the post, the profile that shared this post, the upload date of the post, the post text, the total number of reactions and the number for each individual reaction type (e.g., likes), and the URL of the post. Notice that posts and the collected post sources refer to venues and cultural events and are not related to persons or personal data, while the collected reactions correspond to aggregate numbers and cannot be traced back to individual users. In particular, regarding the information on the profile that shared the post, only the id of the profile was collected and transformed using an one-way function, hence the data cannot be associated with the original profile; however maintaining the ability to determine whether two posts were posted by the same user profile.

By using the generated venue profile page URLs, another spider was setup and executed within the Hydria environment; it employed 587 seed URLs and was able to retrieve around 240 K user comments within a time frame of 168 h (one week). The collected data was also stored in a separate Hydria data pond and contained fields like: the date that the comment was posted, the total number of the reactions in each comment, the comment text, and the comment URL. Notice that the collected comments and the related metadata do not contain user information or personal data; no user IDs were collected and our logs show that all user references in the comment text were deleted by using the Hydria text cleaning (regex-based) functionality.

Next, profiles of venues that are known as major event organizers were used as initial seeds to bootstrap and launch an event harvesting spider that was able to extract a few hundred upcoming events and their relevant event cards. The seed URLs were identified by the TripMentor stakeholders by manually inspecting the collected venues and using tacit knowledge regarding the major event organizers in the region of Attica. Again, the harvested data were stored in a separate Hydria data pond, with the fields stored within this data pond including the event name and date(s), the physical address of the event, the number of people interested to visit this event, the URL of the event, the unique identifier of the PoI where this event was found, the unique identifier of the event, and the text description of the event. Please note that only aggregate numbers on the number of individuals interested in the event are harvested and no personally identifiable information is either collected or stored within Hydria.

4.1.2. TripAdvisor Spiders

In this section, we discuss the deployed TripAdvisor spiders for the TripMentor case study; this set of spiders is used to showcase the versatility and usefulness of the data harvesting component. As with the Facebook spiders, we had no control over the TripAdvisor spiders deployed and the data ponds created; all setup, deployment and data manipulation was done by the TripMentor project partners. The statistics and metadata presented in this work were drawn from usage logs and the data pond schemas.

The first spider was setup and deployed over TripAdvisor aiming to extract PoIs in the Attica region; after a runtime of around 48 h, it collected information about 7 K different PoIs, belonging in a vast variety of different categories (as identified by the respective TripAdvisor field) including monuments, museums, landmarks, natural reserve sites, parks and water parks, different types of restaurants, cafes, etc. For each one of the collected PoIs, the following fields were stored in the Hydria data pond: the venue name in different languages, the overall venue review score, the total number of venue reviews, the ranking of the PoI with respect to other PoIs of the same category in the same broader area (e.g., "4th out of 10 restaurants within the district"), the categories that this PoI appears in, the physical address of the PoI, the PoI phone number, and the TripAdvisor URL of the PoI.

Subsequently, a spider to collect the individual user reviews (without the associated user information) for the 7 K venues/PoIs that were previously harvested was created. After setup and deployment, the spider was able to extract around 300 K individual user reviews in a time frame of around 120 h (five days); the fields of each review that were detected and stored in the respective Hydria data pond are: the review title, the review text, the date of the review, and the review score (in the TripAdvisor bubble format). For the purpose of better understanding the user background, the spider also collected anonymized information about each user that posted a review. This data does not contain any personally identifiable information and was limited on purpose to the following general fields and aggregate metrics: the user country of origin, the total number of user votes (rounded to the nearest ten), the total number of TripAdvisor contributions (rounded to the nearest ten), general user tags (like "history lover"), and generalized age ranges of users. Notice that this information is common among a vast number of TripAdvisor users and cannot be used to personally identify an individual.

The spider examples presented above show only a fraction of the functionality that is available within Hydria. Apart from focused crawlers to crawl the Web for relevant pages and Facebook or TripAdvisor spiders to harvest data from the respective social media sites, Hydria also provides Twitter monitors. These monitors use the Twitter [84] search or stream API to perform keyword-based filtering of published tweets; all retrieved tweets may be subsequently stored in appropriately configured Hydria data ponds for further processing.

*4.2. Importing Datasets and Adding/Modifying Records*

Besides automated data harvesting, Hydria also offers a file import service (as described in Section 3.1.2) that allows users to easily import their own datasets into a Hydria data pond. In our case study, we asked partners from the TripMentor project to use the file import tool to incorporate a new CSV dataset into Hydria. One of the project partners responded and reported that they used Hydria to store a home-brewed list of tourism stakeholders (who could be interested in the project results) in a Hydria data pond. The imported dataset consisted of several hundreds of individual records of companies and stakeholders operating in the tourism sector alongside their contact information, and was shared with the rest of the TripMentor partners by defining the appropriate access rights.

Subsequently, other project partners were able to browse the created data pond with the tourism-related companies and add or modify records as needed by filling out the different data pond fields, tagging records with notes for the data pond curator, and save any desired changes in the specific data pond. Figure 4 gives an overview of the aforementioned data pond; at the top of the figure, controls providing access to all available data pond functionality are presented to the user. Figure 5 shows the add record tool where the user may insert individual records, providing data for a multitude of fields of different types (free text; number; drop-down lists; complex types; and an image field).

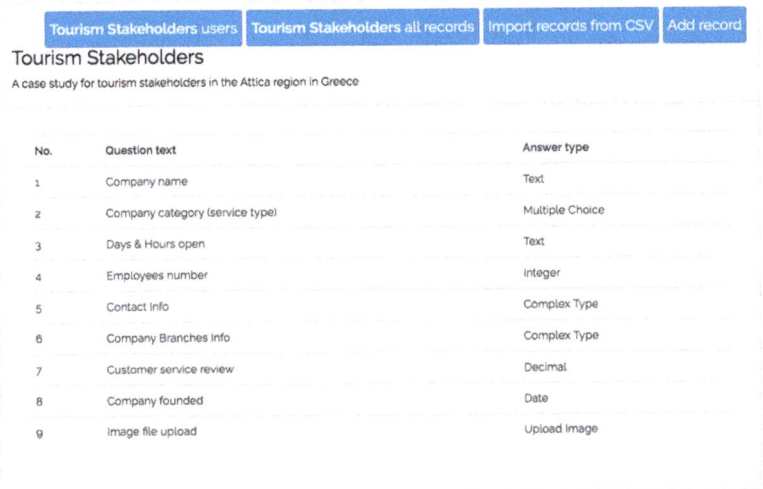

**Figure 4.** A data pond example.

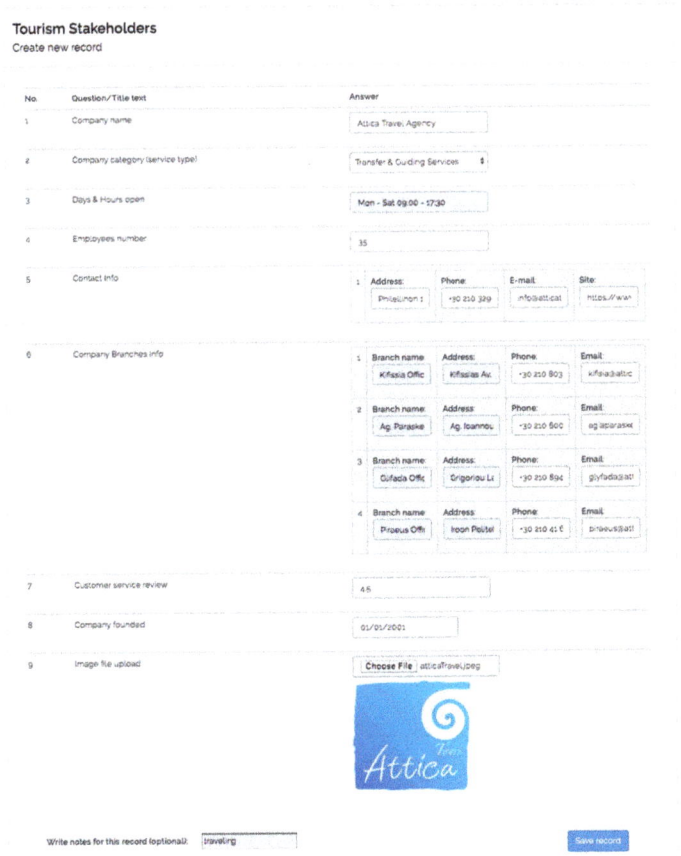

**Figure 5.** Manual record creation.

In this figure, we can observe the use of the complex data types feature, to design groups of input fields which may also be recurring. For example, in the aforementioned dataset the curator may select to use a complex data type to jointly represent longitude/latitude information (under the complex type named "coordinates"), or branch information (comprising fields "branch name", "address", "phone" and "email"). Additionally, the curator may use the latter complex type (branch information) as a recurring input field, to model contact information about a company that has multiple branches. Recurring input fields effectively model the master-detail relationships between parent and child objects (one-to-many relationships). In the future, we plan to support more complex data types, such as voice and video recording, time-series and streaming data.

### 4.3. Reusing Data Ponds and Data Pond Templates

To support the reuse of all or a part of a data pond (e.g., the contact details) between different data ponds, the notion of data pond templates is introduced in Hydria. When a curator creates a new or edits an existing data pond, Hydria prompts her to (re)use one of the available data pond templates; Figure 6 presents the editing of a data pond with seven different data type fields from the administrator's UI.

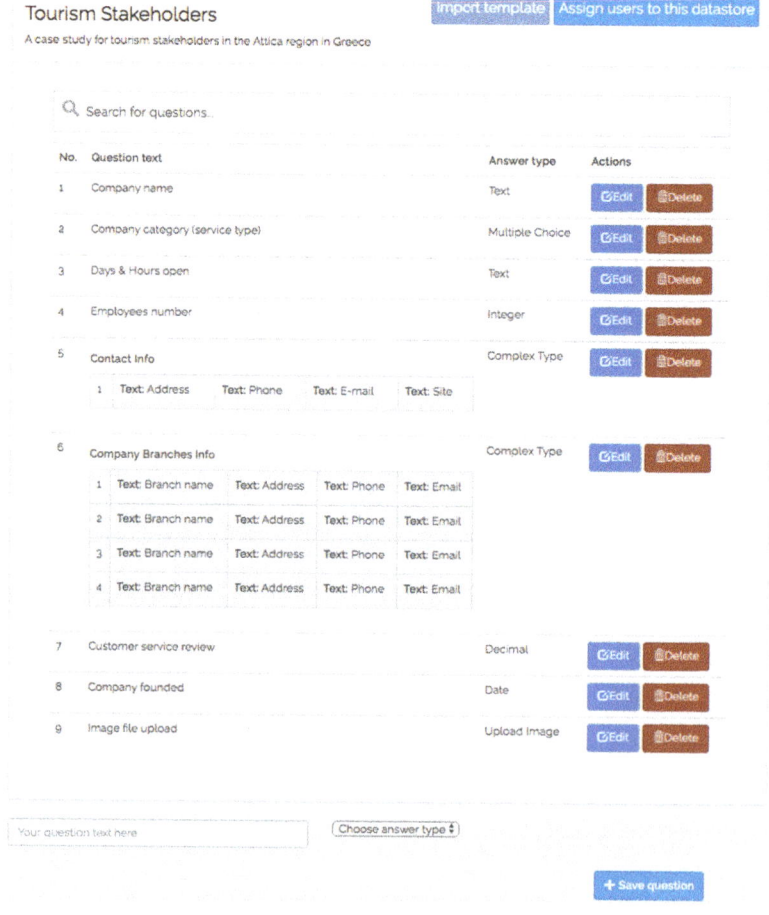

**Figure 6.** Data pond editing.

*4.4. Visualizing Information*

Having populated the Hydria data ponds with data concerning different TripMentor needs (e.g., PoIs and related information from Facebook and TripAdvisor spiders, and tourism stakeholder data), the TripMentor partners were able to search, analyze, filter and visualize the stored data by using the powerful yet easy-to-use Hydria data analysis module. The analyzed and visualized information is presented in Figure 7 and is entirely produced using tools provided within the Hydria environment (i.e., no external visualization modules were used to create the graphs shown).

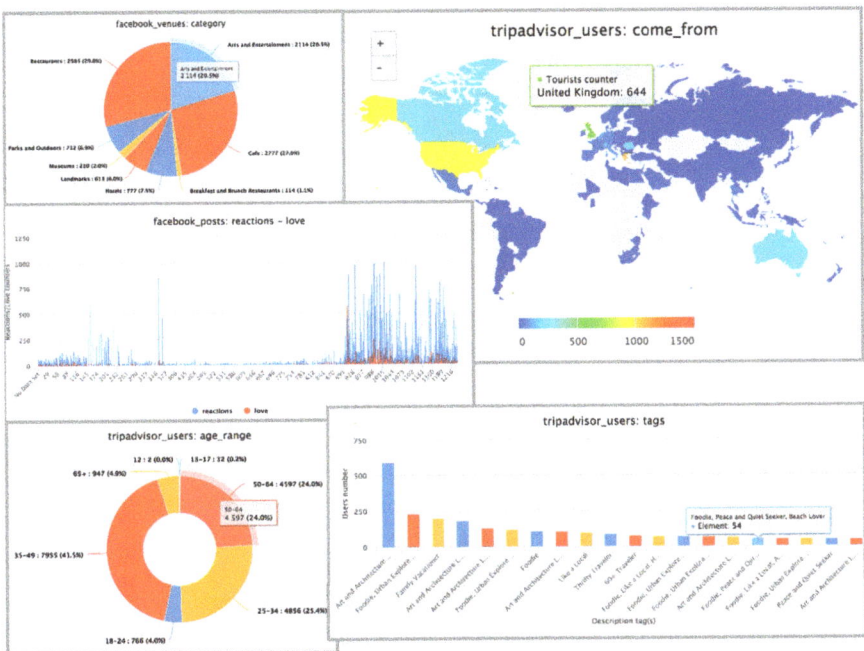

**Figure 7.** Graphs produced by the TripMentor data.

More specifically, the top left graph in Figure 7 presents a pie chart with the different PoIs in the Attica region grouped by venue category, while the graph in the center of Figure 7 provides a bar chart with the total number of Facebook reactions vs. the number of love reactions on posts created for the different venues in the Attica region. Both aforementioned graphs visualize the data harvested in the context of TripMentor from Facebook spidering. The rest of the graphs presented in Figure 7 visualize the data extracted from the TripAdvisor social network; the bottom left graph shows the age range of the users that checked in or commented about different cultural venues in the Attica region in a donut chart; the bottom right diagram presents a bar chart with the most popular (self-assigned) user tags of users who have visited at least one PoI in the Attica region in Greece; and the geo graph in the top-right corner of the figure presents the geographical location of origin (at country granularity) of the visitors of the PoIs within the respective data lake.

Notice that the visualizations in Figure 7 present only a meaningful sample (in the context of the examined case study) of the available data processing and visualization capabilities of Hydria; these capabilities extend to include numerous additional graph types (as enumerated in Section 3.3 above), export to different formats such as raw/CSV/TSV, and many more.

## 5. Indicative Application Scenarios for Hydria

In this section, we provide four distinct application scenarios that demonstrate the versatility of Hydria and highlight its usefulness in diverse cultural heritage setups.

### 5.1. Hydria for Curators

In this application scenario let us consider Auguste, a curator for a small regional museum who wants to collect data that include mentions of the museum he is responsible for from various online social networks, and perform simple sentiment analysis on these mentions to understand what the visitors like or dislike about the museum. Since the museum resources are not sufficient for maintaining an IT department or acquiring the necessary computational resources, Auguste resorts to manually skimming through scattered visitor reviews on various social media (e.g., Facebook, TripAdvisor, Google reviews) and regularly searching Twitter to get an overall feeling of the visitor opinions about his museum. Of course, as this is a constantly evolving process, he has to personally search for new useful reviews and take into account recent unexpected events (e.g., a power outage that disappointed many first time visitors) that may drive review scores adrift.

Clearly, Auguste would greatly benefit from an online, free, and powerful information system that would allow him to create and launch automated social media harvesting tools able to monitor popular social platforms and store content (e.g., posts, tweets, reviews) in a transparent way at an online, easily accessible data store. Such a system would allow him to access the stored data, perform the required opinion analysis, and easily visualize the results into different types of graphs to be used for press and media releases.

### 5.2. Hydria for Researchers

On another scenario, Nikki, member of a humanities research group, wants to perform an analysis of how particular events in European history are perceived by citizens of different European countries and record reflections of individuals on those events. This survey is part of a European effort and involves a large consortium of researchers of different disciplines; as Nikki's group is coordinating the survey, she is also responsible to set up the platform for the collection and processing of survey data. Nikki cannot use any of the popular survey creation tools as they do not support access control to the data and user management (each consortium partner should only have access to the data they collected, with the exception of the coordinator who should be able to access all data). She finally decides to contact an IT company and explain the needs and specificities of the survey. Subsequently, her group would need to buy and maintain a costly IT infrastructure onsite to host the developed solution and, possibly, hire an IT professional/company to keep both the system and the infrastructure up to date.

Clearly, Nikki and her group would benefit from accessing an online service that would allow her to create and deploy such a platform in a fast, free, and effortless way; this system would be a valuable tool *beyond anything currently supported*. After the platform creation, Nikki will be able to create and manage the users of the deployed platform and define access control policies. These users will then be able to login and either input questionnaire data, or directly provide the survey subjects with appropriate credentials that would identify the owner of the input. When the data collection phase is completed, the survey coordinator (i.e., Nikki's group) may use the available searching and filtering techniques to issue appropriate queries, export data of interest for analysis (e.g., to tools like SPSS), and visualize the findings of the analysis in an easy and intuitive way. Since Nikki's group is coordinating the survey, it has access to all inserted data, while other groups' access is restricted to the data policy enforced.

### 5.3. Hydria for Data Scientists

Sophia is a computer scientist working in an organization that provides support in the construction and maintenance of a collaborative home-brewed database for cultural heritage applications. In this context, Sophia is responsible for the curation of the database and the enrichment/integration with existing Web resources like DBpedia [85] and various online thesauri (e.g., the Getty Art & Architecture Thesaurus [86]) using both manual/crowdsourced and automatic techniques [87,88]. As this knowledge base is continuously evolving, monitoring its quality over time becomes an essential task. Having access to an appropriate information system that is able to support publish/subscribe functionality for alerting of possible events or data inputs of interest would allow Sophia and other data scientists to subscribe (with appropriate textual and attribute constraints) and get notified about (i) spurious and/or unusual input in the collaborative database, (ii) the creation/evolution of different schemas used to represent various data facets, and (iii) the trending of specific terms or attributes in the database. Such functionality would be an invaluable tool that would simplify database moderation, as Sophia would, for example, be notified about (i) an unusual database update action that mistakenly records the "Benaki Museum" in Attica, Wyoming, instead of Attica, Greece, (ii) a new published dataset on European History of Art containing appropriate metadata for exhibits located in museums that are already using the system for storing collection specific information, or (iii) a new research topic.

*5.4. Hydria for End Users*

Finally, Matteo is an under-graduate student from an Information Studies department writing his thesis in contextual reasoning for cultural heritage applications. Matteo is mainly interested in retrieving scientific publications on his topic of interest, following the work of prominent researchers in the area, and studying the evolution of the field over time. Due to the particularities of his research field (i.e., focused but interdisciplinary topic, heavy mathematical background), he regularly resorts to online resources—like the DBLP digital library [68] and WikiCFP [70] portal—to search for new relevant areas, to study and map the evolution of the field in terms of scientific papers and related venues (like conferences and workshops). To do so, it is required to periodically download relevant datasets from these sites (e.g., the raw DBLP data of all indexed papers), filter them to maintain only relevant information and store them for further processing (e.g., perform timeline analysis on the new available data). Even though searching for interesting/related works this week turned up nothing, a search next week may return new information or even new datasets. Clearly, an information system that is able to (i) easily integrate several online digital sources, (ii) incorporate new datasets, (iii) analyze and visualize the analysis results, and (iv) capture his long-term information need (using publish/subscribe functionality) would be a valuable tool that would allow Matteo to save both time and effort.

## 6. Conclusions and Outlook

We have presented Hydria, the first online, free, zero-administration platform that offers both fundamental and advanced user and data/knowledge management functionality for big cultural data and targets users with little or no IT background. Hydria enables the direct incorporation of heterogeneous data that has been recorded in dispersed formats, while specialized processing engines ingest data without compromising the data structure, making it available for tasks such as visualization, mining, analytics and reporting. Thus, a system in the form of a data lake meant for acquiring, storing, organizing, analyzing and sharing multi-faceted cultural heritage data constitutes a valuable asset to several different cultural heritage applications such as museum curation, user study management, bibliographical analysis, dataset management, and data integration.

In this work we discussed the architectural solutions behind the proposed system, outlined the individual module technologies and provided details on the module orchestration. We also described several novel services that include automated data harvesting from the web and social media, integrated user input collection via standard and customizable data types, easy to perform data analysis and visualizations, publish/subscribe functionality to facilitate sharing of different facets and data shards, and access control mechanisms. Finally, we advocated the appropriateness of our approach for the cultural heritage domain and showcased different scenarios that highlight Hydria's usefulness for cultural data management. We continuously develop new functionality to support more import/export formats and more sophisticated data types, perform user studies to improve usability and document additional user needs, incorporate more data analysis tools and simplify the data analysis procedure, and incorporate versatile data streams from sensors and IoT devices.

Currently, Hydria is running on a commodity server and is dealing mainly with the TripMentor project needs; however, the long-term plan is to release it as a free service to any interested parties. This entails tackling several important issues that include scaling, platform viability and impact measurements. Regarding scaling, we plan to reshape Hydria before releasing a free public version of the system; the intended reshaping includes modifying some system components to be cloud-native, so as to provide resource elasticity and exploit the benefits emanating from cluster computing infrastructures. Platform viability and maintenance after the end of the project is a typical issue in applied research; we plan to actively pursue new funding that will allow us to continue the development and extension of Hydria. Moreover, the open source ecosystem of tools used to build Hydria allows us to release it as an open source project to the development community to further aid project maintainability. Finally, appropriate impact measurements are an important direction that will drive and affect both the large-scale deployment and the viability of the platform. Hydria, as also usually happens with many research prototypes, is not directly involved in generating revenue, so impact measurements could involve KPIs such as user base, data quality, application versatility, release efficiency, and system reliability.

The work presented in this paper has several implications for both practitioners and researchers. At practical level, it introduces a tool that empowers its users to access, interrelate, analyze, share and visualize multi-faceted data harvested from structured or semi-structured sources, through an intuitive graphical interface, without the requirement of any IT skills. While the implemented system targets the cultural information domain, it can be straightforwardly adapted to any domain where data sourced from social networks and the linked open data (LOD) cloud need to be harvested, managed, analyzed and shared, such as the marketing, political and social analysis domains. The Hydria data lake may also contribute the data pond contents to the LOD cloud, reciprocating from social networks and the LOD cloud through the provision of unified and integrated datasets. The sharing mechanisms of the Hydria system can be leveraged to provide persistent identifiers and automatically register data ponds (or parts of them) that are characterized as "public" to searchable directories, adhering thus to the FAIR data principles [89].

Regarding the research dimension, the architectural paradigm of Hydria, which is a key factor to its success, can be adopted in other classes of systems that offer services to non-IT experts, such as scientific data analysis systems or business data analysis systems. The proliferation of systems based on the architecture of Hydria will accelerate the development cycle of analysis and visualization algorithms that are suitable for non-IT experts, since the extension of the prospective user base will facilitate gathering of relevant requirements and allow the collection of richer testing and evaluation feedback.

Another research direction for the Hydria platform is to extend cooperation between users beyond data sharing, to include expertise finding among the users of Hydria for advice seeking or joint execution of tasks requiring diverse areas of expertise (e.g., multidisciplinary tasks). To this end, algorithms for expert identification can be developed for the Hydria platform, or appropriate existing algorithms can be identified and tuned (e.g., [90–92]). Expert searches may also extend outside the scope an Hydria installation (or a federated Hydria installations network), through the interfacing of the Hydria platform to expert hiring and crowdworking platforms [93] as well as the adoption and customization of algorithms for the synchronization of these tasks [94]. In all cases, all types of modules developed for the Hydria system (e.g., analysis or visualization algorithms, or components supporting expert identification and cooperation between users), as well as knowledge about best practices, can be stored in shared and searchable repositories, providing a dynamic, evolving and self-sustained ecosystem for the Hydria platform.

**Author Contributions:** Conceptualization, K.D., P.R., C.T. and C.V.; Methodology, K.D., P.R., C.T. and C.V.; Software, K.D., P.R., C.T., N.P. and C.V.; Visualization, N.P., K.D.; Validation, K.D., P.R., C.T. and C.V.; Writing—Original draft, K.D., P.R., C.T., C.V.; Writing—Review & editing, K.D., P.R., C.T., N.P. and C.V. All authors have read and agree to the published version of the manuscript.

**Funding:** This research has been co-financed by European Union and Greek national funds through the Operational Programme "Competitiveness, Entrepreneurship and Innovation", under the call RESEARCH—CREATE—INNOVATE (project code: T1EDK-03874).

**Conflicts of Interest:** The authors declare no conflict of interest. The funders had no role in the design of the study; in the collection, analyzes, or interpretation of data; in the writing of the manuscript, or in the decision to publish the results.

## References

1. Kenteris, M.; Vafopoulos, M.N.; Gavalas, D. Cultural Informatics in Web Science: A Case of Exploiting Local Cultural Content. In Proceedings of the 12th Pan-Hellenic Conference on Informatics, Samos Island, Greece, 28–30 August 2008.
2. Salvatore, C.L. (Ed.) *Cultural Heritage Care and Management: Theory and Practice*; Rowman & Littlefield: London, UK, 2018.
3. Antoniou, A.; Katifori, A.; Roussou, M.; Vayanou, M.; Karvounis, M.; Kyriakidi, M.; Pujol-Tost, L. Capturing the Visitor Profile for a Personalized Mobile Museum Experience: An Indirect Approach. In Proceedings of the 24th ACM Conference on User Modeling, Adaptation and Personalisation (UMAP 2016), Halifax, NS, Canada, 13–17 July 2016.
4. Deladiennee, L.; Naudet, Y. A graph-based semantic recommender system for a reflective and personalised museum visit. In Proceedings of the 12th International Workshop on Semantic and Social Media Adaptation and Personalization (SMAP), Bratislava, Slovakia, 9–10 July 2017.
5. Bourlakos, I.; Wallace, M.; Antoniou, A.; Vassilakis, C.; Lepouras, G.; Karapanagiotou, A.V. Formalization and Visualization of the Narrative for Museum Guides. In Proceedings of the Semantic Keyword-Based Search on Structured Data Sources Conference (IKC), Gdansk, Poland, 11–12 September 2018; Springer: Cham, Switzerland, 2018; pp. 3–13.
6. Vassilakis, C.; Poulopoulos, V.; Antoniou, A.; Wallace, M.; Lepouras, G.; Nores, M.L. exhiSTORY: Smart exhibits that tell their own stories. In *Future Generation Computer Systems*; Elsevier: Amsterdam, The Netherlands, 2018; Volume 81, pp. 542–556.
7. Meghini, C.; Bartalesi, V.; Metilli, D.; Benedetti, F. A Software Architecture for Narratives. In Proceedings of theItalian Research Conference on Digital Libraries, Udine, Italy, 25–26 January 2018.
8. Bampatzia, S.; Bravo-Quezada, O.G.; Antoniou, A.; Nores, M.L.; Wallace, M.; Lepouras, G.; Vassilakis, C. The Use of Semantics in the CrossCult H2020 Project. In Proceedings of the Semantic Keyword-Based Search on Structured Data Sources Conference (IKC), Cluj-Napoca, Romania, 8–9 September 2016; Springer: Cham, Switzerland, 2016; Volume 10151, pp. 190–195.
9. Kyvernitou, I.; Bikakis, A. An Ontology for Gendered Content Representation of Cultural Heritage Artefacts. *Digit. Humanit. Q.* **2017**, *11*. Available online: https://discovery.ucl.ac.uk/id/eprint/10041951/ (accessed on 23 April 2020).
10. Vlachidis, A.; Bikakis, A.; Kyriaki-Manessi, D.; Triantafyllou, I.; Antoniou, A. The CrossCult Knowledge Base: A Co-inhabitant of Cultural Heritage Ontology and Vocabulary Classification. In Proceedings of the European Conference on Advances in Databases and Information Systems, Nicosia, Cyprus, 24–27 September 2017.
11. Bartalesi, V.; Meghini, C. Using an ontology for representing the knowledge on literary texts: The Dante Alighieri case study. *Semant. Web* **2017**, *8*, 385–394. [CrossRef]
12. Antoniou, A.; Lepouras, G. Modeling visitors' profiles: A study to investigate adaptation aspects for museum learning technologies. *J. Comput. Cult. Herit. (JOCCH)* **2010**, *3*, 1–19. [CrossRef]
13. Martin, J.; Trummer, C. Personalized Multimedia Information System for Museums and Exhibitions. In *Lecture Notes in Computer Science, Proccedings of the 1st International Conference on Intelligent Technologies for Interactive Entertainment (INTETAIN), Madonna di Campiglio, Italy, 30 November-2 December 2005*; Springer: Cham, Switzerland 2005; Volume 3814, pp. 332–335.

14. Rowe, J.P.; Lobene, E.V.; Mott, B.W.; Lester, J.C. Serious Games Go Informal: A Museum-Centric Perspective on Intelligent Game-Based Learning. In *Lecture Notes in Computer Science, Proceedings of the 12th International Conference on Intelligent Tutoring Systems (ITS), Honolulu, HI, USA, 5–9 June 2014*; Springer: Cham, Switzerland, 2014; Volume 8474, pp. 410–415.
15. Tavcar, A.; Antonya, C.; Butila, E. Recommender System for Virtual Assistant Supported Museum Tours. *Inform. (Slovenia)* **2016**, *40*, 279–284.
16. Vassilakis, C.; Antoniou, A.; Lepouras, G.; Poulopoulos, V.; Wallace, M.; Bampatzia, S.; Bourlakos, I. Stimulation of reflection and discussion in museum visits through the use of social media. *Soc. Netw. Anal. Min.* **2017**, *7*, 40. [CrossRef]
17. Bampatzia, S.; Antoniou, A.; Lepouras, G.; Vassilakis, C.; Wallace, M. Using social media to stimulate history reflection in cultural heritage. In Proceedings of the 11th International Workshop on Semantic and Social Media Adaptation and Personalization (SMAP), Thessaloniki, Greece, 20–21 October 2016; pp. 89–92.
18. Fontanella, F.; Molinara, M.; Gallozzi, A.; Cigola, M.; Senatore, L.J.; Florio, R.; Clini, P.; D'Amico, F.C. HeritageGO (HeGO): A Social Media Based Project for Cultural Heritage Valorization. In Proceedings of the 27th Conference on User Modeling, Adaptation and Personalization (UMAP), Larnaca, Cyprus, 4–17 July 2019; pp. 377–382.
19. Nguyen, T.T.; Camacho, D.; Jung, J.E. Identifying and ranking cultural heritage resources on geotagged social media for smart cultural tourism services. *Pers. Ubiquitous Comput.* **2017**, *21*, 267–279. [CrossRef]
20. Monti, L.; Delnevo, G.; Mirri, S.; Salomoni, P.; Callegati, F. Digital Invasions Within Cultural Heritage: Social Media and Crowdsourcing. In *Lecture Notes of the Institute for Computer Sciences, Social Informatics and Telecommunications Engineering, Proceedings of the 3rd International Conference on Smart Objects and Technologies for Social Good (GOODTECHS), Pisa, Italy, 29–30 November 2017*; Springer: Cham, Switzerland, 2017; Volume 233, pp. 102–111.
21. Nguyen, T.T.; Hwang, D.; Jung, J.J. Using Geotagged Resources on Social Media for Cultural Tourism: A Case Study on Cultural Heritage Tourism. In *Lecture Notes of the Institute for Computer Sciences, Social Informatics and Telecommunications Engineering, Proceedings of the 7th International Conference on Big Data Technologies and Applications (BDTA), Seoul, Korea, 17–18 November 2016*; Springer: Cham, Switzerland, 2016; Volume 194, pp. 64–72.
22. Liew, C.L. Participatory Cultural Heritage: A Tale of Two Institutions' Use of Social Media. *D-Lib Mag.* **2014**, *20*. Available online: http://www.dlib.org/dlib/march14/liew/03liew.html (accessed on 23 April 2020). [CrossRef]
23. Jensen, B. Instagram as cultural heritage: User participation, historical documentation, and curating in Museums and archives through social media. In Proceedings of the Digital Heritage International Congress, Marseille, France, 28 October–1 November 2013; pp. 311–314.
24. 7th International Euro-Mediterranean Conference (EuroMed), LNCS, Nicosia, Cyprus, 29 October–3 November 2018; Springer: Cham, Switzerland, 2018. Available online: https://wbc-rti.info/object/event/17918 (accessed on 23 April 2020).
25. 3rd Joint SIGHUM Workshop on Computational Linguistics for Cultural Heritage, Social Sciences, Humanities and Literature (LaTeCH), ACL, Minneapolis, MN, USA, June 2019. Available online: https://www.aclweb.org/anthology/volumes/W19-25/ (accessed on 23 April 2020).
26. 10th International Workshop on Human-Computer Interaction, Tourism and Cultural Heritage (HCITOCH), LNCS, Florence, Italy, 5–7 September 2019; Springer: Cham, Switzerland, 2019.
27. *Communications in Computer and Information Science, 1st International Conference on VR Technologies in Cultural Heritage (VRTCH), Brasov, Romania, 29–30 May 2018*; Springer: Cham, Switzerland, 2018; Volume 904. Available online: http://library.oapen.org/handle/20.500.12657/23304 (accessed on 23 April 2020).
28. Bai, D.; Messinger, D.W.; Howell, D. A pigment analysis tool for hyperspectral images of cultural heritage artifacts. In Proceedings of the Algorithms and Technologies for Multispectral, Hyperspectral, and Ultraspectral Imagery XXIII, Society of Photo-Optical Instrumentation Engineers (SPIE) Conference Series, Anaheim, CA, USA, 9–13 April 2017; Volume 10198.
29. Hoonjong.; Stoykova, E.; Berberova, N.; Park, J.; Nazarova, D.; Park, J.S.; Kim, Y.; Hong, S.; Ivanov, B.; Malinowski, N. Three-dimensional imaging of cultural heritage artifacts with holographic printers. In Proceedings of the 19th International Conference and School on Quantum Electronics: Laser Physics and Applications (ICSQE), Sozopol, Bulgaria, 26–30 September 2016; Volume 10226.

30. Themistocleous, K. Debate and Considerations on Using Videos for Cultural Heritage from Social Media for 3D Modelling. In Proceedings of the 6th International Conference on Progress in Cultural Heritage: Documentation, Preservation, and Protection (EuroMed), Nicosia, Cyprus, 31 October–5 November 2016; Volume 10058, pp. 513–520.
31. Torres, J.C.; López, L.; Romo, C.; Arroyo, G.; Cano, P.; Lamolda, F.; del Mar Villafranca, M. Using a Cultural Heritage Information System for the documentation of the restoration process. In Proceedings of the Digital Heritage International Congress, Marseille, France, 28 October–1 November 2013; pp. 249–256.
32. Nurminen, M.; Heimburger, A. Representation and Retrieval of Uncertain Temporal Information in Museum Databases. In Proceedings of the 21st European—Japanese Conference on Information Modelling and Knowledge Bases (EJC), Tallinn, Estonia, 6–10 June 2011; Volume 1. Available online: http://ebooks.iospress.nl/publication/6781 (accessed on 23 April 2020).
33. Chias, P.; Abad, T. Visualising Ancient Maps as Cultural Heritage: A Relational Database of the Spanish Ancient Cartography. In Proceedings of the 12th International Conference on Information Visualisation, London, UK, 9–11 July 2008; Volume 1.
34. Meyer, E.; Grussenmeyer, P.; Perrin, J.P.; Durand, A.; Drap, P. A web information system for the management and the dissemination of Cultural Heritage data. *J. Cult. Herit.* **2007**, *8*, 396–411. [CrossRef]
35. Jancsó, A.L.; Jonlet, B.; Hoffsummer, P.; Delye, E.; Billen, R. An Analytical Framework for Classifying Software Tools and Systems Dealing with Cultural Heritage Spatio-Temporal Information. In *Lecture Notes in Geoinformation and Cartography, Proceedings of Workshops and Posters at the 13th International Conference on Spatial Information Theory (COSIT); L'Aquila, Italy, 4–8 September* 2017; Springer: Cham, Switzerland, 2017; pp. 325–337.
36. Colace, F.; Santo, M.D.; Greco, L.; Chianese, A.; Moscato, V.; Picariello, A. CHIS: Cultural Heritage Information System. *IJKSR* **2013**, *4*, 18–26. [CrossRef]
37. Chinnov, A.; Kerschke, P.; Meske, C.; Stieglitz, S.; Trautmann, H. *An Overview of Topic Discovery in Twitter Communication through Social Media Analytics*; AMCIS: Morristown, NJ, USA, 2015.
38. Korzun, D.G. Designing Smart Space Based Information Systems: The Case Study of Services for IoT-Enabled Collaborative Work and Cultural Heritage Environments. In *Frontiers in Artificial Intelligence and Applications, Proceedings of the 12th International Baltic Conference on Databases and Information Systems (DB&IS), Riga, Latvia, 4–6 July 2016*; Arnicans, G., Arnicane, V., Borzovs, J., Niedrite, L., Eds.; IOS Press: Clifton, VA, USA, 2016; Volume 291, pp. 183–196.
39. Poulopoulos, V.; Vassilakis, C.; Antoniou, A.; Wallace, M.; Lepouras, G.; Nores, M.L. ExhiSTORY: IoT in the service of Cultural Heritage. In Proceedings of the IEEE Global Information Infrastructure and Networking Symposium (GIIS), Thessaloniki, Greece, 23–25 October 2018; pp. 1–4.
40. Su, X.; Sperlì, G.; Moscato, V.; Picariello, A.; Esposito, C.; Choi, C. An Edge Intelligence Empowered Recommender System Enabling Cultural Heritage Applications. *IEEE Trans. Ind. Inform.* **2019**, *15*, 4266–4275. [CrossRef]
41. Pandolfo, L.; Pulina, L.; Grosso, E. A User Model Ontology for Adaptive Systems in Cultural Tourism Domain. In *Frontiers in Artificial Intelligence and Applications, Proceedings of the 1st International Conference on Applications of Intelligent Systems (APPIS), Las Palmas de Gran Canaria, Spain, 10–12 January 2018*; Petkov, N., Strisciuglio, N., Travieso-González, C.M., Eds.; IOS Press: Clifton, VA, USA, 2018; Volume 310, pp. 212–219.
42. Díaz-Corona, D.; Lacasta, J.; Latre, M.Á.; Zarazaga-Soria, F.J.; Nogueras-Iso, J. Profiling of knowledge organisation systems for the annotation of Linked Data cultural resources. *Inf. Syst.* **2019**, *84*, 17–28. [CrossRef]
43. Larosiliere, G.D.; Carter, L.D.; Meske, C. How does the world connect? Exploring the global diffusion of social network sites. *J. Assoc. Inform. Sci. Technol. (JASIST)* **2017**, *68*, 1875–1885. [CrossRef]
44. Miloslavskaya, N.; Tolstoy, A. Big Data, Fast Data and Data Lake Concepts. *Procedia Comput. Sci.* **2016**, *88*, 300–305. [CrossRef]
45. TripMentor Project. Available online: https://www.researchgate.net/project/TripMentor (accessed on 1 April 2020).
46. Chianese, A.; Marulli, F.; Piccialli, F. Cultural Heritage and Social Pulse: A Semantic Approach for CH Sensitivity Discovery in Social Media Data. In Proceedings of the 10th International Conference on Semantic Computing (ICSC), IEEE Computer Society, Laguna Hills, CA, USA, 4–6 February 2016; pp. 459–464.

47. Moscato, V.; Picariello, A.; Subrahmanian, V.S. Multimedia Social Networks for Cultural Heritage Applications: The GIVAS Project. In *Data Management in Pervasive Systems*; Data-Centric Systems and Applications; Springer: Cham, Switzerland, 2015; pp. 169–182.
48. Colace, F.; Santo, M.D.; Moscato, V.; Picariello, A.; Schreiber, F.A.; Tanca, L. PATCH: A Portable Context-Aware ATlas for Browsing Cultural Heritage. In *Data Management in Pervasive Systems*; Data-Centric Systems and Applications; Springer: Cham, Switzerland, 2015; pp. 345–361.
49. Vodopivec, B.; Eppich, R.; Zarnic, R. Cultural Heritage Information Systems State of the Art and Perspectives. In *Lecture Notes in Computer Science, Proceedings of the 5th International Conference on Progress in Cultural Heritaage: Documentation, Preservation, and Protection (EuroMed), Limassol, Cyprus, 3–8 November 2014*; Springer: Cham, Switzerland, 2014; Volume 8740, pp. 146–155.
50. Alkhafaji, A.S.A.; Fallahkhair, S. Smart Ambient: Development of Mobile Location Based System to Support Informal Learning in the Cultural Heritage Domain. In Proceedings of the 14th International Conference on Advanced Learning Technologies (ICALT), IEEE Computer Society, Athens, Greece, 7–10 July 2014; pp. 774–776.
51. Cassatella, C.; Volpiano, M.; Seardo, B.M. Interpreting historic and cultural landscapes: Potentials and risks in Geographical Information Systems building for knowledge and management. In Proceedings of the Digital Heritage International Congress, IEEE, Marseille, France, 28 October–1 November 2013; pp. 107–110.
52. Torres, J.C.; López, L.; Romo, C.; Soler, F. An Information System to Analize Cultural Heritage Information. In *Lecture Notes in Computer Science, Proceedings of the 4th International Conference on Progress in Cultural Heritaage: Documentation, Preservation, and Protection (EuroMed), Limassol, Cyprus, 29 October–3 November 2012*; Springer: Cham, Switzerland, 2012; Volume 7616, pp. 809–816.
53. Ploszajski, G. Technical Metadata and Standards for Digitisation of Cultural Heritage in Poland. In *New Trends in Multimedia and Network Information Systems*; Frontiers in Artificial Intelligence and Applications; IOS Press: Amsterdam, The Netherlands, 2008; Volume 181, pp. 155–170.
54. Smirnov, A.V.; Kashevnik, A.M.; Ponomarev, A. Context-based infomobility system for cultural heritage recommendation: Tourist Assistant—TAIS. *Pers. Ubiquitous Comput.* **2017**, *21*, 297–311. [CrossRef]
55. Narumi, T.; Hayashi, O.; Kasada, K.; Yamazaki, M.; Tanikawa, T.; Hirose, M. Digital Diorama: AR Exhibition System to Convey Background Information for Museums. In *Lecture Notes in Computer Science, Proceedings of the International Conference on Virtual and Mixed Reality—New Trends, Orlando, FL, USA, 9–4 July 2011*; Shumaker, R., Ed.; Springer: Cham, Switzerland, 2011; Volume 6773, pp. 76–86.
56. Gentile, A.; Andolina, S.; Massara, A.; Pirrone, D.; Russo, G.; Santangelo, A.; Trumello, E.; Sorce, S. A Multichannel Information System to Build and Deliver Rich User-Experiences in Exhibits and Museums. In Proceedings of the International Conference on Broadband, Wireless Computing, Communication and Applications (BWCCA), IEEE Computer Society, Barcelona, Spain, 26–28 October 2011; pp. 57–64.
57. Chen, S.; Pan, Z.; Zhang, M. A Virtual Informal Learning System for Cultural Heritage. *Trans. Edutainment* **2012**, *7*, 180–187.
58. Wu, S. Systems integration of heterogeneous cultural heritage information systems in museums: A case study of the National Palace Museum. *Int. J. Digit. Libr.* **2016**, *17*, 287–304. [CrossRef]
59. Chen, C.; Chang, B.R.; Huang, P. Multimedia augmented reality information system for museum guidance. *Pers. Ubiquitous Comput.* **2014**, *18*, 315–322. [CrossRef]
60. Chanhom, W.; Anutariya, C. TOMS: A Linked Open Data System for Collaboration and Distribution of Cultural Heritage Artifact Collections of National Museums in Thailand. *New Gener. Comput.* **2019**, *37*, 479–498. [CrossRef]
61. Naudet, Y.; Antoniou, A.; Lykourentzou, I.; Tobias, E.; Rompa, J.; Lepouras, G. Museum personalization based on gaming and cognitive styles: The BLUE experiment. *Int. J. Virtual Communities Soc. Netw. (IJVCSN)* **2015**, *7*, 1–30. [CrossRef]
62. Bampatzia, S.; Bourlakos, I.; Antoniou, A.; Vassilakis, C.; Lepouras, G.; Wallace, M. Serious games: Valuable tools for cultural heritage. In Proceedings of the International Conference on Games and Learning Alliance, Utrecht, The Netherlands, 5–7 December 2016; Springer: Cham, Switzerland, 2016; pp. 331–341.
63. Dorter, G.; Davis, L. Bringing geographic information systems (GIS) into the museum world. In Proceedings of the Digital Heritage International Congress, IEEE, Marseille, France, 28 October–1 November 2013.
64. Soler, F.; Torres, J.C.; León, A.J.; Luzón, M.V. Design of cultural heritage information systems based on information layers. *JOCCH* **2013**, *6*, 1–17. [CrossRef]

65. Soler, F.; Torres, J.C.; León, A.J.; Luzón, M.V. Design of an Information System for Cultural Heritage. In Proceedings of the Spanish Computer Graphics Conference (CEIG), Eurographics Association, Jaén, Spain, 12–14 September 2012; pp. 113–122.
66. Wikipedia The Free Encyclopedia. Available online: https://www.wikipedia.org/ (accessed on 1 April 2020).
67. Europeana. Available online: https://www.europeana.eu/portal/en (accessed on 1 April 2020).
68. DBLP: Computer Science Bibliography. Available online: https://dblp.org/ (accessed on 1 April 2020).
69. Odysseus Ministry of Culture and Sports. Available online: http://odysseus.culture.gr/index_en.html (accessed on 1 April 2020).
70. WikiCFP A wiki for Calls For Papers. Available online: http://www.wikicfp.com/cfp/ (accessed on 1 April 2020).
71. Meske, C.; Junglas, I.A.; Schneider, J.; Jaakonmaki, R. How Social is Your Social Network? Toward A Measurement Model. In Proceedings of the 40th International Conference on Information Systems (ICIS), Munich, Germany, 15–18 December 2019.
72. Stieglitz, S.; Meske, C.; Ross, B.; Mirbabaie, M. Going Back in Time to Predict the Future—The Complex Role of the Data Collection Period in Social Media Analytics. *Inf. Syst. Fronti.* **2018**. [CrossRef]
73. von der Putten, A.M.R.; Hastall, M.; Köcher, S.; Meske, C.; Heinrich, T.; Labrenz, F.; Ocklenburg, S. "Likes" as social rewards: Their role in online social comparison and decisions to like other People's selfies. *Comput. Hum. Behav.* **2019**, *92*, 76–86. [CrossRef]
74. Myers, D.; McGuffee, J.W. Choosing scrapy. *J. Comput. Sci. Coll.* **2015**, *31*, 83–89.
75. Scrapy at a Glance. Available online: https://docs.scrapy.org/en/latest/intro/overview.html (accessed on 10 March 2020).
76. Chaulagain, R.S.; Pandey, S.; Basnet, S.R.; Shakya, S. Cloud based web scraping for big data applications. In Proceedings of the IEEE International Conference on Smart Cloud (SmartCloud), New York, NY, USA, 3–5 November 2017; pp. 138–143.
77. Santos, A.; Pham, K. GitHub—VIDA-NYU/ache. Available online: https://github.com/VIDA-NYU/ache (accessed on 1 April 2020).
78. Barbosa, L.; Freire, J. An adaptive crawler for locating hidden-web entry points. In Proceedings of the 16th International Conference on World Wide Web (WWW), Banff, AL, Canada, 8–12 May, 2007; pp. 441–450.
79. Vieira, K.; da Silva, L.B.A.S.; Freire, J.; Moura, E. Finding seeds to bootstrap focused crawlers. *World Wide Web (WWW)* **2016**, *19*, 449–474. Available online: https://link.springer.com/article/10.1007/s11280-015-0331-7 (accessed on 23 April 2020). [CrossRef]
80. Bonzanini, M. *Mastering Social Media Mining with Python*; Packt Publishing Ltd.: Birmingham, UK, 2016.
81. Stauffer, M. *Laravel: Up & Running: A Framework for Building Modern PHP Apps*; O'Reilly Media: Sebastopol, CA, USA, 2019.
82. TripAdvisor: Read Reviews, Compare Prices & Book. Available online: https://www.tripadvisor.com/ (accessed on 1 April 2020).
83. Facebook. Available online: https://www.facebook.com/ (accessed on 1 April 2020).
84. Twitter. Available online: https://twitter.com/ (accessed on 1 April 2020).
85. DBpedia Homepage. Available online: https://wiki.dbpedia.org/ (accessed on 1 April 2020).
86. Art & Architecture Thesaurus Online. Available online: https://www.getty.edu/research/tools/vocabularies/aat/index.html (accessed on 1 April 2020).
87. Marketakis, Y.; Minadakis, N.; Kondylakis, H.; Konsolaki, K.; Samaritakis, G.; Theodoridou, M.; Flouris, G.; Doerr, M. X3ML mapping framework for information integration in cultural heritage and beyond. *IJDL* **2017**, *18*, 301–319. [CrossRef]
88. Stavropoulos, T.G.; Kontopoulos, E.; Meroño-Peñuela, A.; Tachos, S.; Andreadis, S.; Kompatsiaris, Y. Cross-domain Semantic Drift Measurement in Ontologies Using the SemaDrift Tool and Metrics. In Proceedings of the MEPDaW & LDQ @ ESWC, Bologna, Italy, 29 May 2017.
89. Initiative, G.F. FAIR Principles. 2019. Available online: https://www.go-fair.org/fair-principles/ (accessed on 6 April 2020).
90. Bozzon, A.; Brambilla, M.; Ceri, S.; Silvestri, M.; Vesci, G. Choosing the Right Crowd: Expert Finding in Social Networks. In Proceedings of the 16th International Conference on Extending Database Technology (EDBT), Genoa, Italy, 18–22 March 2013; Association for Computing Machinery: New York, NY, USA, 2013; pp. 637–648. [CrossRef]

91. Lin, S.; Hong, W.; Wang, D.; Li, T. A survey on expert finding techniques. *J. Intell. Inf. Syst.* **2017**, *49*, 255–279. [CrossRef]
92. Nikzad–Khasmakhi, N.; Balafar, M.; Reza Feizi–Derakhshi, M. The state-of-the-art in expert recommendation systems. *Eng. Appl. Artif. Intell.* **2019**, *82*, 126–147. [CrossRef]
93. Lykourentzou, I.; Khan, V.J.; Papangelis, K.; Markopoulos, P. Macrotask Crowdsourcing: An Integrated Definition. In *Human—Computer Interaction Series*; Lykourentzou, I., Khan, V.J., Papangelis, K., Markopoulos, P., Eds.; Springer International Publishing: Cham, Switzerland, 2019; pp. 1–13. [CrossRef]
94. Schmitz, H.; Lykourentzou, I. Online Sequencing of Non-Decomposable Macrotasks in Expert Crowdsourcing. *Trans. Soc. Comput.* **2018**, *1*, 1–33. [CrossRef]

© 2020 by the authors. Licensee MDPI, Basel, Switzerland. This article is an open access article distributed under the terms and conditions of the Creative Commons Attribution (CC BY) license (http://creativecommons.org/licenses/by/4.0/).

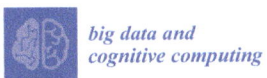 big data and cognitive computing

Article

# Data-Assisted Persona Construction Using Social Media Data

Dimitris Spiliotopoulos [1,*], Dionisis Margaris [2] and Costas Vassilakis [1]

1. Department of Informatics and Telecommunications, University of the Peloponnese, 22100 Tripolis, Greece; costas@uop.gr
2. Department of Informatics and Telecommunications, University of Athens, 15784 Athens, Greece; margaris@di.uoa.gr
* Correspondence: dspiliot@uop.gr; Tel.: +30-2710-372203

Received: 19 June 2020; Accepted: 14 August 2020; Published: 19 August 2020

**Abstract:** User experience design and subsequent usability evaluation can benefit from knowledge about user interaction, types, deployment settings and situations. Most of the time, the user type and generic requirements are given or can be obtained and used to model interaction during the design phase. The deployment settings and situations can be collected through the needfinding phase, either via user feedback or via the automatic analysis of existing data. Personas may be defined using the aforementioned information through user research analysis or data analysis. This work utilizes an approach to activate an accurate persona definition early in the design cycle, using topic detection to semantically enrich the data that are used to derive the persona details. This work uses Twitter data from a music event to extract information that can be used to assist persona creation. A user study in persona construction compares the topic modelling metadata to a traditional user collected data analysis for persona construction. The results show that the topic information-driven constructed personas are perceived as having better clarity, completeness and credibility. Additionally, the human users feel more attracted and similar to such personas. This work may be used to model personas and recommend suitable ones to designers of other products, such as advertisers, game designers and moviegoers.

**Keywords:** persona; user experience; user interface design; topic modelling; usability; personalization; cultural events

## 1. Introduction

Personas are constructs that represent user archetypes and have been used extensively in various stages of human-computer interaction design. Personas have traits that subsets of potential users exhibit [1]. The traits can be mapped to user requirements, usually not in a one-to-one manner but rather as abstracted characteristics that the user requirements can be derived or fine-tuned to. Personas may be useful in various stages of a design. For the requirements or needfinding phase, designers use them to formulate the requirements, and explain them to the design team by applying them to the personas. For the design phase, prototyping may be applied to personas for testing. For the evaluation, the product is applied to the personas in order to evaluate whether the expected goals are met and identify whether the needs were met and to what extent. For the deployment stage, personas may be applied accordingly, depending on the actual persona and product, from market share penetration evaluation to research objectives fulfilment to ethical and inclusiveness verification [2].

Personas can be integrated to use case models, resulting in revised or adapted use case models that describe more compact sets of use cases [3]. They may also be created and utilized as part of stories and scenarios [4] for enriching scenario or case-driven interaction design processes. On the other hand, other studies include recommendations toward separating scenarios and persona descriptions [5].

Designing personas well is an important aspect, since only a small number of personas may be created for them to be useful. Therefore, personas have to be concise enough to accurately express the design requirements, as well as conceptually abstract enough to provide the required coverage of the user types and requirements [6]. One of the major shortcomings of personas is that they can hardly account for change, especially fast change. Even the most well-constructed personas may become partially obsolete or inaccurate after a period of time, resulting in the need for additional effort, time and expense in order to repair inconsistencies and lost credibility [7].

Salminen et al. did an extensive study to evaluate how persona creation and utilization are affected by statistical online analytics using big data [8]. The critical points that were reported are the main challenges that this paper addresses and are as follows:

1. Creating personas is a costly and lengthy process,
2. Personas may be biased by their creators,
3. Personas may be non-verifiable and untrustworthy when they depend on the information used for their creation,
4. Personas may become inaccurate over time.

There are several approaches to data-driven persona construction, systems and methodologies for quantitatively generating personas using large amounts of online social media data [9]. However, data-generated personas were found to suffer from similar shortcomings to the traditional manually constructed personas. Coherency and consistency is an inherent problem and a challenge for persona designers when constructing and utilizing the elements of information in a meaningful and usable form [10].

Automatically generated personas address challenge 1 and 2 by utilizing web data to automatically create a number of personas, requiring minimal human involvement. However, they cannot address trustworthiness and inaccuracy over time. Designer-generated personas are costly and take time to create. Additionally, they may be biased by their creators. However, they generally address challenges 3 and 4 better than automatically created personas, since designers may pick sources and specific data that seem trustworthy, as well as selecting representative information that they deem to be as futureproof as possible. From the above information, it would be interesting to put an approach to the test that may address all challenges to a certain degree.

This work examines how traditional persona design may be assisted by persona metadata derived from fast-changing big data. Building on the identified shortcomings of the manual and the data-generated persona construction and their individual advantages, this paper proposes a hybrid approach that is simple enough to apply, yet contextual and analytical so as to provide useful insights.

The structure of the paper is outlined as follows: Section 2 presents the related work. Section 3 presents the motivation and rationale behind this work. Section 4 details the experimental setup and method. Section 5 presents the results of the user study experiments in persona construction, while Section 6 presents the evaluation of the cultural event persona construction. Section 7 discusses the paper's results and outlines future work.

## 2. Related Work

Personas are not constant. One of the major points of critique in the use of personas is that they become irrelevant or non-applicable very soon. Therefore, the designer needs to account for variations and update the personas. The change can be significant, even for six-month or yearly periods. An advantage of data-driven persona construction is that continuous time-stamped data may be used to account for persona variation over time [11]. The challenge for data-driven persona construction is to monitor and identify how change happens over time: the veracity, velocity and volume. Findings show that topical interests, as reflected by personas constructed using data from online sources, change by an average of over 20%, while only a third of the personas in those cases experience topical consistency [12]. This shows the necessity for a constant update of the personas in order to reflect the changes in topical interests. The frequency of the employed routine data analysis to achieve the updates reflects upon the design lifecycle [13].

Automatic Persona Generation is the implementation of a methodology for quantitatively generating data-driven personas from online social media data [14]. Personas may be generated automatically, in real time, using very rich social media data that include timestamps such as YouTube, eliminating most of the labor associated with persona construction [15]. On the other hand, personas that are built from user data may be incomplete or incomprehensible, and therefore unusable as they are, requiring the designer to barge in and fill in the blanks [16]. Therefore, the interpretation of the persona characteristics is designer-dependent and sometimes designer-biased.

Tapping into social web information is a challenging task, mainly due to reasons that are associated with the processing and analysis of social web data [17,18]. On the other hand, the personas themselves are created for various tasks; there are personas that are required for marketing, for social research and for educational designs, amongst others. There are personas that can cover all possible cases (elastic) or personas that are only useful for narrow or very specific cases. Christoforakos et al. examined marketing stakeholder personas for prototyping [19], while Schoch et al. created personas to understand social barriers and used them for prototyping a web app [20]. Ozkan et al. showed the importance of how designers or product owners, in their case the university faculty, regard the disconnection between them and users, in their case the students, using personas as a design technique for revamping a university school curriculum [21].

Personas may be influenced by their designers or by researchers who are making assertions about the expectations of other users. The designer team, as well as the example data and their size, form a dynamic mix that unknowingly assigns bias to the personas [22,23]. Salminen et al. examined data-generated personas under the assumption that bias may be affected by the age and gender of the persona as well as by the number of generated personas [24]. The study found that a small number of personas increased the bias, which would be a valid hypothesis since the bias-inducing parameters would be exaggerated in a small set of personas. In their study, female personas were found to be underrepresented for small persona sets. Therefore, algorithmic bias is present and a manual validation by experts is necessary.

The vast number of data may lead to personas that either summarize user requirements or contain overly precise information, making them have an insignificant impact [25]. Demographics are a textbook example for broad data that require proper taming so that they either do not result in unnecessary large number of personas or they are not spread thin and consumed by other persona attributes. A study using YouTube data from videos utilizing the full demographic classification showed that 2772 demographic-based personas would be generated using the existing demographic groupings for gender, age and origin [26]. An et al., (2018) used aggregated data to define customer behavior segments and created personas based on the demographics from those segments [27].

Co-creating personas benefits users so as to have them engage in accessible design, and it achieves a broader inclusion of demographics in the co-created personas [28]. Extending the use of personas outside user archetype modelling, personas can be used for roleplay simulation with real users for collaborative design [29]. In a recent study, interaction design across cultures could be aided using child-generated personas [30]. The study found that children could be more expressive, providing details based on enthusiasm, which in turn provided behavioral and activity-based thematic scenarios.

Depending on the generated number of personas, unsupervised learning methods, such as clustering or topic modelling, may be used to cluster the personas based on their attributes, thereby providing a means to go from raw data to understandable semantics. The actual attributes and the way they are presented to designers affects their perception of the personas. Salminen et al. determined that using actual numbers to describe attributes had a positive effect on the perception of the persona usefulness by users such as analysts but a significantly negative effect on the perception of the persona completeness by both analysts and market experts [31].

Transparency in data-driven generated personas is achieved by providing the sources of the information on the personas. Transparency affects credibility (decrease), completeness (increase) and clarity (increase). The persona gender also affects the perceived completeness of the persona by the user, but this was evident only for female personas [32].

Incomplete personas that may not contain certain types of information constitute an attempt by researchers to eliminate factors that induce bias and uncertainty. For example, "thin" personas that do not contain personalization samples such as a name and picture but retain demographic (gender, origin, age) and behavioral attributes are used for automated categorization methods, such as clustering to reduce the numbers of generated personas [33]. That way, persona sets are described by their clustered core objective information and avoid the causes of subjectiveness that the personal attributes would induce.

Another way to fine-tune or reduce persona sets is by traditional large scale online surveys and a quantitative analysis of the questionnaire information so as to revise the persona sets or even create additional personas that were not generated by the data-driven methods [34]. Xu and Lee identified persona types for online shopping communities using large scale surveys [35]. They analyzed the data in terms of social connections and characteristics, such as reading and posting behavior, which led, via clustering, to a limited number of personas as categories of users. Those "very thin" personas were described by their main representative social behavior characteristic and an accompanying descriptive sentence. An additional aspect that designers can keep in check is perceived likability. Studies show that, similar to designer bias, users and designers are affected by visual properties. To keep this effect from happening, pictures (stock, generated or otherwise, e.g., sketched) may be refrained from being used so that the acceptance of the persona by the users will not be affected by the likeability of the persona picture [36].

## 3. Motivation

Data-driven persona generation may utilize multiple analysis techniques as well as traditional methods for accurate persona construction. Kim et al. used a trend analysis as well as face-to-face interviews and online surveys to extract cybersecurity-attributed user characteristics [37]. They used this hybrid technique to compare the data from the three sources (trend analysis, face-to-face interviews and online surveys) in order to formulate the personas. Such a post-analysis was quite difficult, since the data collection from the sources was performed in parallel and the data were not cross-fed during or after the collection process. Therefore, the datasets had different granularity and coarseness values, as well as no automatic connections, which the users were then tasked to understand and correlate.

All the aforementioned identified issues related to the collection of data, analysis of the persona attributes, construction and use of personas result in problems that end users, designers, marketeers and researchers ultimately face [38,39]. Matthews et al. identified the main issues with personas with regard to users, finding them misleading and distracting as well as abstract and impersonal [40]. The authors argue that perhaps a more prudent approach to persona formulation would be to avoid persona attributes that mislead and distract the users. Furthermore, they deem this aspect as being more important than striving to create engaging personas.

From the above information, it is argued that automatically data-generated personas cannot fully replace the designers delving into the data and the insights and intuitions that they gain for the design requirements. Several studies also identify specific persona shortcomings that trigger mistrust, causing the designers to refrain from adopting them fully for their design approaches. Achieving a balance between data-generated personas and human intuition is the motivation of this work.

The hypothesis is that, based on the related literature, data-assisted persona construction may yield more accurate personas. The approach of this work is that, instead of collecting human knowledge from questionnaires and interviews and combining or fusing the knowledge with the data-generated personas, the designers can be assisted on a higher level with data-processed information related to persona construction. The information is stripped from any data or aspects that affect human decisions on a sentimental or likeness level, thereby shielding the designers from knowingly or unknowingly induced bias. This way, the design process is supported by the data analysis, while at the same time allowing the designers to utilize higher-level data knowledge in their traditional persona construction approach.

In the following subsections, we present the experimental approach to big data assisted persona construction, examining the effectiveness of an elaborate data analysis for the created personas, and comparing it with the traditional and frequently used data collection and analysis by human designers.

## 4. Experimental Setup and Method

In the following paragraphs, we elaborate on (i) the experimental design, (ii) the data-driven persona metadata-assisted designer user study and (iii) the evaluation of the persona designs using standard metrics.

### 4.1. Data

The data were collected from Twitter for the well-known live music event @rockamring from January to February 2020 (inclusive). The collection crawled the most frequent relevant hashtags, such as #rar2020 and #rockamring. The former was used for the topic modelling, and both were used for the pictures, videos and links. We used a pipelined process to clean up and validate the data [41]. Out of the posts collected, 1811 were used for topic modelling using the Latent Dirichlet Allocation (LDA) approach [42,43].

The topics were modelled as interesting based on LDA clusters, the tie strength of the context words from a sentiment analysis, and quantitative social sharing information from their associated Twitter posts [44]. User information, including gender, demographics and name/photo were excluded to avoid biasing the designers for or against specific information. Figure 1 shows the topics of interest as extracted for the aforementioned period.

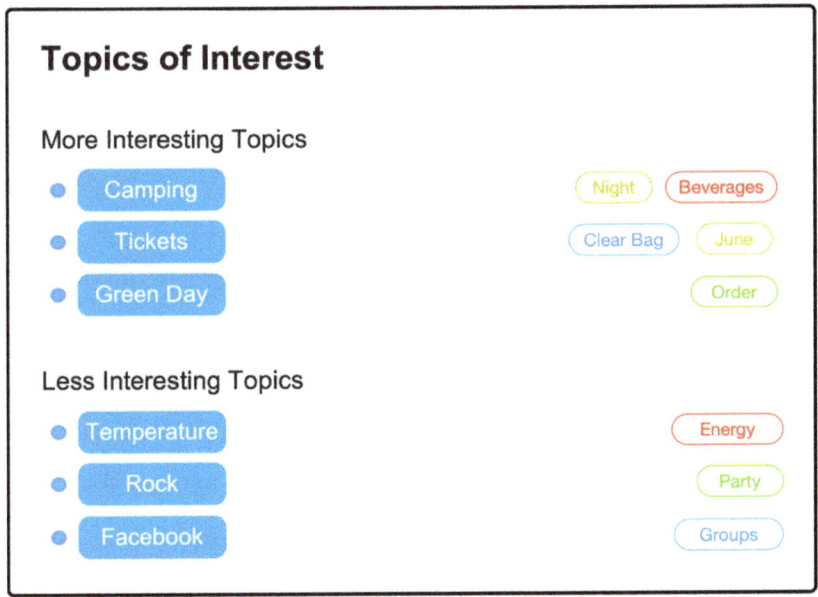

**Figure 1.** Topics presented to the designer participants. The main topics are on the left and related keywords are on the right. The keyword colors represent the identified sentiment (green: positive, yellow: neutral, red: negative, blue: no sentiment).

*4.2. Participants*

The user study and evaluation participants were recruited through the University forum and social networks. Thirty English speaking participants were selected, 57% male and 43% female. The average age of the participants was 22 years. All were undergraduate and graduate students, while 70% of them reported having taken an HCI-related course and all had previously participated in human studies. All reported familiarity with the use of social networks for obtaining information. All participants attended an informal lecture on personas and user design. Examples of personas and their use were provided during that session. After their familiarization, they were explained about the study specifics and given the tasks (Table 1).

**Table 1.** Persona construction and evaluation task breakdown.

| Group | Task | Sources |
|---|---|---|
| A | create personas using topic modelling from twitter data | topic information |
| B | create personas using any information deemed useful | Twitter, analytics tools |
| A + B | evaluate personas of two random participants, one from each group | persona perception scale, usability evaluation questionnaire |

The participants were randomly placed into two groups of 15 people each. The task was to construct thin personas, so photos, biographical information, personal status, quotes, work and background text were optional. The reason for this was to eliminate or minimize the potential bias for the persona peer evaluation. The participants were given a minimum of one hour and a maximum of two hours to construct personas for the selected music event. They were told to use an online translation app for the non-English content, knowing that the specific event had a large amount of German language content. The study facilitators recorded details of interest on paper during the sessions.

## 5. Persona Construction

All participants from both groups created personas in the allotted timeframe. Since the participant experience in creating personas varied, the time spent to finish the tasks could not reflect on the data usefulness for either group. A total of 159 personas were constructed by all participants. Table 2 shows the breakdown of the number of personas created per group and participant gender.

**Table 2.** Number of personas constructed per participant group (task) and gender.

| Group | All Participants | Male Participants | Female Participants |
|---|---|---|---|
| A | 4.4 (std: 1.18) | 4.38 (std: 1.19) | 4.43 (std: 1.27) |
| B | 6.2 (std: 1.37) | 6.67 (std: 1.00) | 5.50 (std: 1.64) |
| A + B | 5.3 (std: 1.56) | 5.59 (std: 1.58) | 4.92 (std: 1.50) |

Group A participants constructed 66 personas in total, while Group B participants constructed 93, which was 41% more. It is also evident that the female and male participants of Group A constructed about the same average number of personas, while in Group B, male participants constructed more than one additional persona than their female group partners did.

The task of the Group B participants was more demanding, since they were not provided with the topic analysis information and had to explore the data on their own. In order to do so, they utilized several online Twitter analytics tools, such as the Tweet Sentiment Visualizer (https://www.csc2.ncsu.edu/faculty/healey/tweet_viz/tweet_app/), which enables insight into sentiment, topics, timeline, connections, maps and timelines (Figure 2), and the Floom (https://floom.app/) app, which enables a quick look into the keywords mentioned in Twitter streams (Figure 3).

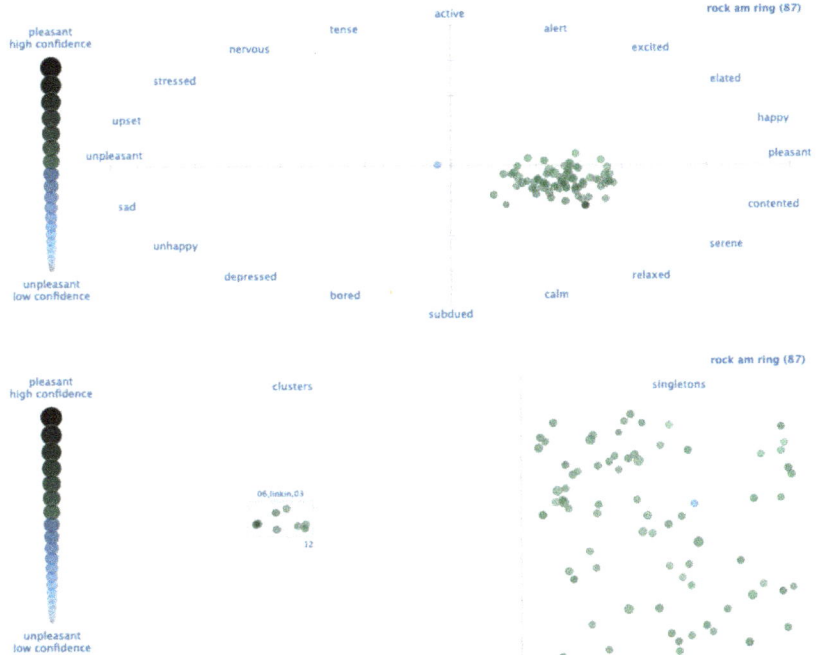

**Figure 2.** Looking into the data for persona construction: sentiment (**top**) and topics (**bottom**). The users select and view the sentiment for the entities of interest and the cluster information for a deeper view of how topics are semantically identified.

**Figure 3.** Standard keyword cloud for Twitter streams. The designer may use the keywords to search social media and the web for user comments that they can utilize for the persona construction.

The Group B participants also used Twitter and Facebook as a source. They utilized the information that was automatically generated to quickly access and verify the content and select representative posts and threads for useful information.

## 6. User Evaluation

The participants were asked to evaluate randomly assigned personas created by their peers. Each respondent evaluated two personas, for a total of 318 persona evaluations. The personas were assigned randomly, one from each group, for every evaluator. This work utilized the Persona Perception Scale, developed by Salminen et al. [45], for a user evaluation of social-media data-generated personas. This scale fully applies to our peer evaluation tasks, since it accounts for multiple aspects of interest. The exploratory nature of this work encouraged the use of a full scale for the facilitators to be able to observe possible subtle differences between the two groups.

Group A participants used our topic modelling tool to get the information for the personas (Figure 4). The topic analysis also provided trending information for both the topics and the keywords. Additionally, we utilized a customized model for the SentiStrength sentiment analysis tool, which included emotions [43]. The designers utilized the information for the present detailed topics, which included sentiment and trending information.

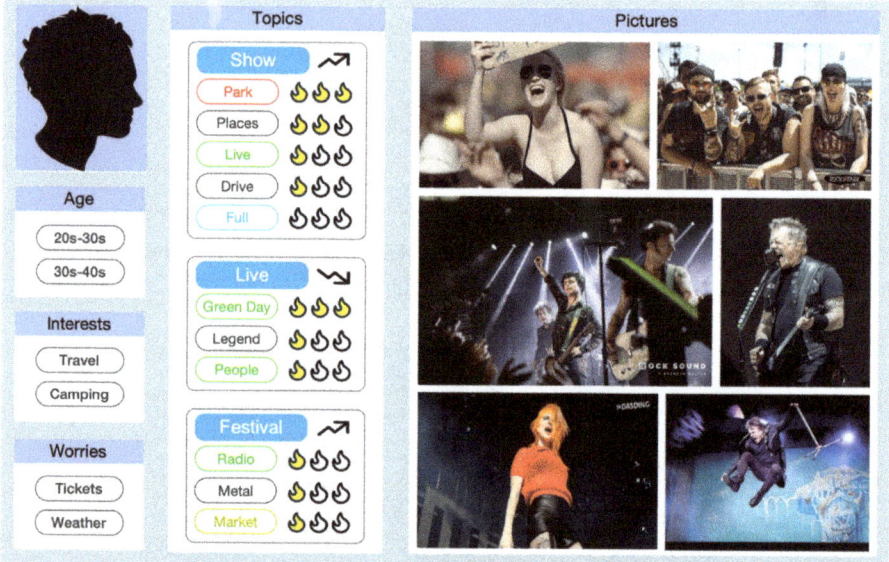

**Figure 4.** User-constructed topic modelling-assisted thin persona.

Group B participants used the output of the analysis tools as a guide for the validation and selection of the most prominent information to use for their persona construction (Figure 5). All sections of the persona were selectable, and the data options were editable. Observing the designers, they edited the age groups based on social media data, selected the number of keywords and validated their sentiment using at least two sources of information. Picture selection was a necessary process, since variations of the same pictures would originally lead to a few pictures overwhelming the selection. The users reported that the Group B personas exhibited a much greater variety of pictures.

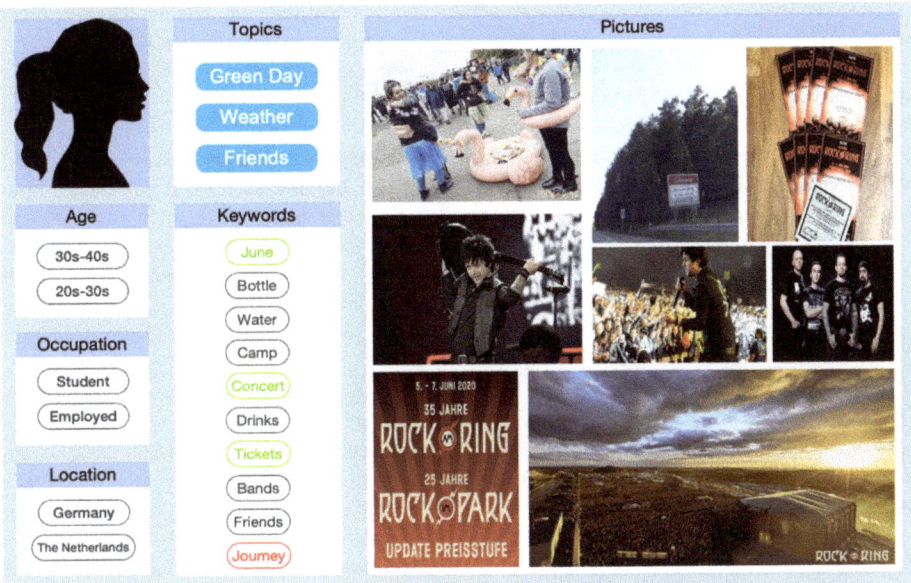

**Figure 5.** User-constructed meta-data-assisted thin persona.

Figure 6 depicts the average user evaluation responses per perceived persona aspect on a standardized Likert scale of 1–5.

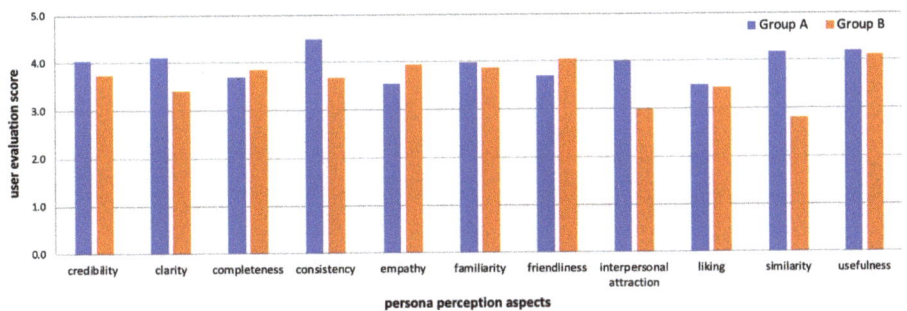

**Figure 6.** Persona perception user study results.

The Group A designers who utilized the advanced topic information scored higher on credibility, clarity and consistency, while Group B scored higher in completeness and empathy. This can be explained by the fact that Group A participants utilized already curated and streamlined topic information from the same source, while Group B participants accessed multiple sources that were also different per participant. The use of the same source information led to clearer and to more consistent results that were also perceived as more credible. On the other hand, the use of multiple sources led to a higher number of constructed personas, some of which contained more personal (or less general) information bits that were perceived as being more complete as a whole, as well as more sympathetic by the evaluators.

The two groups scored similarly for familiarity and liking, showing that the topic modelling accurately reflected on familiar terms and descriptions, and both approaches resulted in personas that were liked by the respondents. Personas constructed by Group B were perceived as marginally friendlier, which was also the result of the utilization of more personal information bits.

The major findings of this study were the responses on the interpersonal attraction (the level of attractiveness of the personas by the participants) and the similarity (the level of perceived similarity of the participants to the personas). The personas constructed by Group A participants scored much higher in the evaluation for both aforementioned aspects. This was not expected, nor was it hypothesized before the study. One possible explanation was that the clarity and consistency of the personas constructed using the topic modelling knowledge resulted in the users feeling more attracted and similar to the personas. Another possible explanation, mentioned by the evaluators during the post-study discussion, was that topic modelling clustered the data to more abstract notions, thereby flattening possible extreme or outlier data that could lead to unattractive personas. Even if the number of such personas would be very low, it might still affect their perceived attractiveness and feeling of similarity for the evaluators.

The participants also self-reported their acceptance and confidence for the personas they created. The rationale behind this metric is derived from the user experience evaluation, where the designs are evaluated by the end users and the designers use that feedback to self-reflect on their designs. In our case, the participants evaluated other personas but also their own on the bases of their acceptance to use their personas themselves and their confidence about their response. Figure 7 shows that the participants of Group B reported a much higher acceptance with a similarly high confidence. The participants of Group A reported a high acceptance of their own designs, which was, however, lower on average than that of the other group, with a very high confidence. Based on the literature, this is an expected result, and it is justified from the fact that the Group B participants were fully responsible for the data collection, analysis and persona design. Thus, they were confident that they did their best to design personas that they would use themselves. On the other hand, the participants of Group A used the already analyzed data to the best of their abilities, and they were confident that they produced very good results. However, they could not be sure that the data they had in their hands provided the maximum coverage of the requirements.

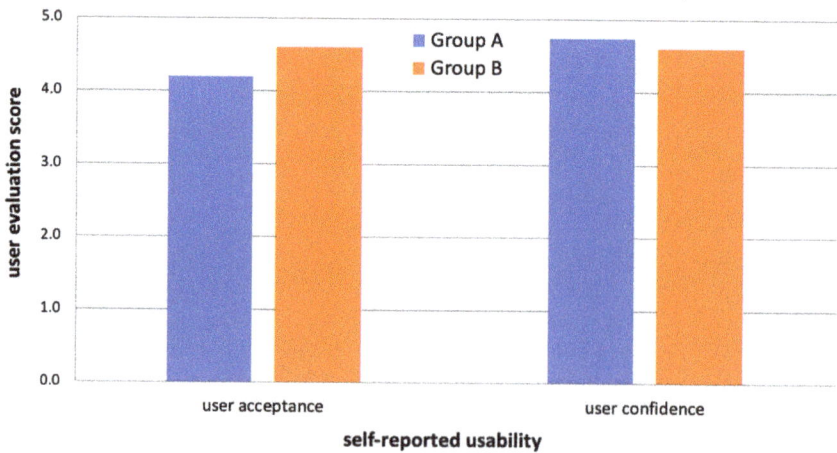

**Figure 7.** Participants' self-reported acceptance and confidence about their constructed personas.

## 7. Conclusions and Future Work

This paper presented a human study that aimed to examine the effect of big data utilization on persona construction. It followed the rationale, derived from earlier works, that automatically data-generated personas cannot fully replace the designer's immersion in actual data in terms of persona creation.

The findings showed that deep analysis and the use of data analytics, such as topic modelling, can lead to personas that are perceived as clear, consistent and complete. Furthermore, this persona design is perceived as very appealing to users and the personas as something that the users would feel quite similar to. This approach requires much less effort than traditional human-directed data analysis and may be especially helpful for limited scope personas, such as music events, thematic museums (e.g., war museum), as well as educational or medical applications.

Based on the findings of this work, an optimal approach to persona construction using big data analytics could be a combination of the two approaches that were examined, or even a triple combination of data-generated personas using data analytics and manual analysis for refinement. This work has basic limitations with regard to the target of the persona construction, namely a music event. This is a limited scope domain that was selected to demonstrate how data analytics may reveal aspects not easily discovered by designers, but how it may also allow for an extensive human study to be made possible by limiting the data and the scope of the experiments.

To evaluate the findings from this work against purely automatic data-generated personas, a comparative evaluation, including personas automatically generated using approaches such as the one by Salminen et al. [46], would be required. However, this was not applicable for our experiments because of the focus shift and the additional effort that this would require by the participants, as well as the complexity that the endeavor of such a non-standard evaluation between the three (automatic data-generated, topic modelling, user analysis) approaches would introduce. Moreover, there are already existing works that compare fully automatically generated personas with traditional ones, and which have yielded results that have been discussed in this paper [47].

This work has limitations that are bound by the tools, the data and the users. The tools and their use is a matter of personal expertise by the designers. The data that are used also comprise a designer choice (in this case, it was a cultural event), as do the sources. The tools were selected for their ease of use, since the users were familiar with them. As a process, the persona construction would not have been affected by using different or additional tools; however, the content and user decisions could have been. For example, tweaking the LDA parameters or having additional data for the analysis would possibly yield different results, and the users would have to work with those as their choices. However, an automatic persona construction would also have been affected by such parameters. The same core data sources have been used for all user groups in order to retain comparative fidelity.

To monitor changes, topic change information may be displayed, such as trending topics, a timeline view and clustering with regard to sentiment. This would allow designers to edit or amend their personas to account for major cases. Specific situations, such as the recent global COVID-19 pandemic, may lead to specific considerations regarding design thinking (for quarantine or online user experiences), introducing new potential users and methods for content delivery that requires a fast adaptation of user design. The persona design and update would be key for a user design's rapid adaptation to new situations and emerging requirements, by utilizing the information change from the main differences of the personas.

For future work, we are planning to include an analysis of textual information from existing social network users for the automatic adaptation of existing personas with regard to their content description for a fully-fledged persona construction [48,49]. Additionally, multiple sources, such as Facebook, could be utilized for automatic enrichment, since users reported that they found interesting information and expected it to be a valid resource for cultural event-based user content.

**Author Contributions:** Conceived, designed and performed the experiments; analyzed the data and wrote the paper, D.S., D.M. and C.V. All authors have read and agreed to the published version of the manuscript.

**Funding:** This research received no external funding.

**Conflicts of Interest:** The authors declare no conflict of interest.

**References**

1. Guo, A.; Ma, J. Archetype-Based Modeling of Persona for Comprehensive Personality Computing from Personal Big Data. *Sensors* **2018**, *18*, 684. [CrossRef] [PubMed]
2. Miaskiewicz, T.; Kozar, K.A. Personas and user-centered design: How can personas benefit product design processes? *Des. Stud.* **2011**, *32*, 417–430. [CrossRef]
3. Dittmar, A.; Forbrig, P. Integrating Personas and Use Case Models. In Proceedings of the Human-Computer Interaction—INTERACT 2019, Paphos, Cyprus, 2–6 September 2019; Lamas, D., Loizides, F., Nacke, L., Petrie, H., Winckler, M., Zaphiris, P., Eds.; Springer International Publishing: Cham, Switzerland, 2019; pp. 666–686.
4. Nielsen, L. Personas in Use. In *Personas—User Focused Design*; Nielsen, L., Ed.; Springer: London, UK, 2019; pp. 83–115, ISBN 978-1-4471-7427-1.
5. Nielsen, L. Making Your Personas Live. In *Personas—User Focused Design*; Nielsen, L., Ed.; Springer: London, UK, 2019; pp. 161–170, ISBN 978-1-4471-7427-1.
6. Pruitt, J.; Grudin, J. Personas: Practice and Theory. In Proceedings of the 2003 Conference on Designing for User Experiences—DUX '03, San Francisco, CA, USA, 6–7 June 2003; ACM Press: New York, NY, USA, 2003; pp. 1–15.
7. Salminen, J.; Jansen, B.J.; An, J.; Kwak, H.; Jung, S. Are personas done? Evaluating their usefulness in the age of digital analytics. *Pers. Stud.* **2018**, *4*, 47–65. [CrossRef]
8. Jansen, B.J.; Salminen, J.O.; Jung, S.-G. Data-Driven Personas for Enhanced User Understanding: Combining Empathy with Rationality for Better Insights to Analytics. *Data Inf. Manag.* **2020**, *4*, 1–17. [CrossRef]
9. Jung, S.G.; Salminen, J.; An, J.; Kwak, H.; Jansen, B.J. Automatically Conceptualizing Social Media Analytics Data via Personas. In Proceedings of the International AAAI Conference on Web and Social Media, Stanford, CA, USA, 15 June 2018.
10. Salminen, J.; Şengün, S.; Jung, S.; Jansen, B.J. Design Issues in Automatically Generated Persona Profiles: A Qualitative Analysis from 38 Think-Aloud Transcripts. In Proceedings of the 2019 Conference on Human Information Interaction and Retrieval, Glasgow, Scotland, UK, 10–14 March 2019; Association for Computing Machinery: New York, NY, USA, 2019; pp. 225–229.
11. Jung, S.; Salminen, J.; Jansen, B.J. Personas Changing Over Time: Analyzing Variations of Data-Driven Personas During a Two-Year Period. In Proceedings of the Extended Abstracts of the 2019 CHI Conference on Human Factors in Computing Systems, Glasgow, Scotland, UK, 4–9 May 2019; Association for Computing Machinery: New York, NY, USA, 2019.
12. Jansen, B.J.; Jung, S.; Salminen, J. Capturing the change in topical interests of personas over time. *Proc. Assoc. Inf. Sci. Technol.* **2019**, *56*, 127–136. [CrossRef]
13. Kouroupetroglou, G.; Spiliotopoulos, D. Usability methodologies for real-life voice user interfaces. *Int. J. Inf. Technol. Web Eng.* **2009**, *4*, 78–94. [CrossRef]
14. Jung, S.-G.; Salminen, J.; Jansen, B.J. Giving Faces to Data: Creating Data-Driven Personas from Personified Big Data. In Proceedings of the 25th International Conference on Intelligent User Interfaces Companion, Cagliari, Italy, 17–20 March 2020; Association for Computing Machinery: New York, NY, USA, 2020; pp. 132–133.
15. An, J.; Cho, H.; Kwak, H.; Hassen, M.Z.; Jansen, B.J. Towards Automatic Persona Generation Using Social Media. In Proceedings of the 2016 IEEE 4th International Conference on Future Internet of Things and Cloud Workshops (FiCloudW), Vienna, Austria, 22–24 August 2016; pp. 206–211.
16. Chang, Y.; Lim, Y.; Stolterman, E. Personas: From theory to practices. In Proceedings of the 5th Nordic conference on Human-computer interaction building bridges—NordiCHI '08, Lund, Sweden, 20–22 October 2008; ACM Press: New York, NY, USA, 2008; pp. 439–442.
17. Schefbech, G.; Spiliotopoulos, D.; Risse, T. The Recent Challenge in Web Archiving: Archiving the Social Web. In Proceedings of the International Council on Archives Congress, Brisbane, Australia, 20–25 August 2012; pp. 1–5.
18. Aivazoglou, M.; Roussos, A.O.; Margaris, D.; Vassilakis, C.; Ioannidis, S.; Polakis, J.; Spiliotopoulos, D. A fine-grained social network recommender system. *Soc. Netw. Anal. Min.* **2020**, *10*, 8. [CrossRef]

19. Christoforakos, L.; Tretter, S.; Diefenbach, S.; Bibi, S.-A.; Fröhner, M.; Kohler, K.; Madden, D.; Marx, T.; Pfeiffer, T.; Pfeiffer-Leßmann, N.; et al. Potential and Challenges of Prototyping in Product Development and Innovation. *i-com* **2019**, *18*, 179–187. [CrossRef]
20. Schoch, E.; Choi, A.M.L.A.; Lee, H.; Connor, S.; Rose, E.J. The Food Locker: An Innovative, User-Centered Approach to Address Food Insecurity on Campus. In Proceedings of the 37th ACM International Conference on the Design of Communication, Portland, OR, USA, 4–6 October 2019; Association for Computing Machinery: New York, NY, USA, 2019.
21. Ozkan, D.S.; Reeping, D.; McNair, L.D.; Martin, T.L.; Harrison, S.; Lester, L.; Knapp, B.; Wisnioski, M.; Patrick, A.; Baum, L. Using Personas as Curricular Design Tools: Engaging the Boundaries of Engineering Culture. In Proceedings of the 2019 IEEE Frontiers in Education Conference (FIE), Covington, KY, USA, 16–19 October 2019; pp. 1–7.
22. Niskanen, K.; Bosch, M.; Wils, K. Scientific Personas in Theory and Practice—Ways of Creating Scientific, Scholarly, and Artistic Identities. *Pers. Stud.* **2018**, *4*, 1–5. [CrossRef]
23. Bosch, M. Looking at Laboratory Life, Writing a Scientific Persona: Marianne van Herwerden's Travel Letters from the United States, 1920. *L'Homme* **2018**, *29*, 15–34. [CrossRef]
24. Salminen, J.; Jung, S.-G.; Jansen, B.J. Detecting Demographic Bias in Automatically Generated Personas. In Proceedings of the Extended Abstracts of the 2019 CHI Conference on Human Factors in Computing Systems, Glasgow, Scotland, UK, 4–9 May 2019; Association for Computing Machinery: New York, NY, USA, 2019.
25. Salminen, J.; Jung, S.; Jansen, B.J. The Future of Data-driven Personas: A Marriage of Online Analytics Numbers and Human Attributes. In Proceedings of the 21st International Conference on Enterprise Information Systems—Volume 1: ICEIS, Heraklion, Crete, Greece, 3–5 May 2019; SciTePress: Setúbal Municipality, Portugal, 2019; pp. 608–615.
26. Jung, S.-G.; An, J.; Kwak, H.; Ahmad, M.; Nielsen, L.; Jansen, B.J. Persona Generation from Aggregated Social Media Data. In Proceedings of the 2017 CHI Conference Extended Abstracts on Human Factors in Computing Systems, Denver, CO, USA, 6–11 May 2017; Association for Computing Machinery: New York, NY, USA, 2017; pp. 1748–1755.
27. An, J.; Kwak, H.; Jung, S.; Salminen, J.; Jansen, B.J. Customer segmentation using online platforms: Isolating behavioral and demographic segments for persona creation via aggregated user data. *Soc. Netw. Anal. Min.* **2018**, *8*, 54. [CrossRef]
28. Neate, T.; Bourazeri, A.; Roper, A.; Stumpf, S.; Wilson, S. Co-Created Personas: Engaging and Empowering Users with Diverse Needs Within the Design Process. In Proceedings of the 2019 CHI Conference on Human Factors in Computing Systems, Glasgow, Scotland, UK, 4–9 May 2019; Association for Computing Machinery: New York, NY, USA, 2019.
29. Li, B.; Segonds, F.; Mateev, C.; Lou, R.; Merienne, F. Design in context of use: An experiment with a multi-view and multi-representation system for collaborative design. *Comput. Ind.* **2018**, *103*, 28–37. [CrossRef]
30. Sim, G.; Shrivastava, A.; Horton, M.; Agarwal, S.; Haasini, P.S.; Kondeti, C.S.; McKnight, L. Child-Generated Personas to Aid Design Across Cultures. In Proceedings of the Human-Computer Interaction—INTERACT 2019, Paphos, Cyprus, 2–6 September 2019; Lamas, D., Loizides, F., Nacke, L., Petrie, H., Winckler, M., Zaphiris, P., Eds.; Springer International Publishing: Cham, Switzerland, 2019; pp. 112–131.
31. Salminen, J.; Liu, Y.-H.; Engün, S.; Santos, J.M.; Jung, S.; Jansen, B.J. The Effect of Numerical and Textual Information on Visual Engagement and Perceptions of AI-Driven Persona Interfaces. In Proceedings of the 25th International Conference on Intelligent User Interfaces, Cagliari, Italy, 17–20 March 2020; Association for Computing Machinery: New York, NY, USA, 2020; pp. 357–368.
32. Salminen, J.; Santos, J.M.; Jung, S.-G.; Eslami, M.; Jansen, B.J. Persona Transparency: Analyzing the Impact of Explanations on Perceptions of Data-Driven Personas. *Int. J. Hum. Comput. Interact.* **2019**, *36*, 788–800.
33. Jansen, B.J.; Jung, S.; Salminen, J. Creating Manageable Persona Sets from Large User Populations. In Proceedings of the Extended Abstracts of the 2019 CHI Conference on Human Factors in Computing Systems, Glasgow, Scotland, UK, 4–9 May 2019; Association for Computing Machinery: New York, NY, USA, 2019.
34. McGinn, J.; Kotamraju, N. Data-Driven Persona Development. In Proceedings of the Twenty-Sixth Annual CHI Conference on Human Factors in Computing Systems—CHI '08, Florence, Italy, 5–10 April 2008; ACM Press: New York, NY, USA, 2008; pp. 1521–1524.

35. Xu, Y.; Lee, M.J. Identifying Personas in Online Shopping Communities. *Multimodal Technol. Interact.* **2020**, *4*, 1–19.
36. Salminen, J.; Jung, S.-G.; Santos, J.M.; Jansen, B.J. Does a Smile Matter if the Person Is Not Real? The Effect of a Smile and Stock Photos on Persona Perceptions. *Int. J. Hum. Comput. Interact.* **2020**, *36*, 568–590.
37. Kim, E.; Yoon, J.; Kwon, J.; Liaw, T.; Agogino, A.M. From Innocent Irene to Parental Patrick: Framing User Characteristics and Personas to Design for Cybersecurity. *Proc. Des. Soc. Int. Conf. Eng. Des.* **2019**, *1*, 1773–1782. [CrossRef]
38. Margaris, D.; Kobusinska, A.; Spiliotopoulos, D.; Vassilakis, C. An Adaptive Social Network-Aware Collaborative Filtering Algorithm for Improved Rating Prediction Accuracy. *IEEE Access* **2020**, *8*, 68301–68310. [CrossRef]
39. Kizgin, H.; Dey, B.L.; Dwivedi, Y.K.; Hughes, L.; Jamal, A.; Jones, P.; Kronemann, B.; Laroche, M.; Peñaloza, L.; Richard, M.-O.; et al. The impact of social media on consumer acculturation: Current challenges, opportunities, and an agenda for research and practice. *Int. J. Inf. Manag.* **2020**, *51*, 102026. [CrossRef]
40. Matthews, T.; Judge, T.; Whittaker, S. How Do Designers and User Experience Professionals Actually Perceive and Use Personas? In Proceedings of the SIGCHI Conference on Human Factors in Computing Systems, Glasgow, Scotland, UK, 4–9 May 2019; Association for Computing Machinery: New York, NY, USA, 2012; pp. 1219–1228.
41. Risse, T.; Demidova, E.; Dietze, S.; Peters, W.; Papailiou, N.; Doka, K.; Stavrakas, Y.; Plachouras, V.; Senellart, P.; Carpentier, F.; et al. The ARCOMEM Architecture for Social- and Semantic-Driven Web Archiving. *Futur. Internet* **2014**, *6*, 688–716. [CrossRef]
42. Blei, D.M.; Ng, A.Y.; Jordan, M.I. Latent Dirichlet Allocation. *J. Mach. Learn. Res.* **2003**, *3*, 993–1022.
43. Antonakaki, D.; Spiliotopoulos, D.; Samaras, C.V.; Pratikakis, P.; Ioannidis, S.; Fragopoulou, P. Social media analysis during political turbulence. *PLoS ONE* **2017**, *12*, e0186836. [CrossRef] [PubMed]
44. Chorley, M.J.; Colombo, G.B.; Allen, S.M.; Whitaker, R.M. Human content filtering in Twitter: The influence of metadata. *Int. J. Hum. Comput. Stud.* **2015**, *74*, 32–40. [CrossRef]
45. Salminen, J.; Kwak, H.; Santos, J.M.; Jung, S.-G.; An, J.; Jansen, B.J. Persona Perception Scale: Developing and Validating an Instrument for Human-Like Representations of Data. In Proceedings of the Extended Abstracts of the 2018 CHI Conference on Human Factors in Computing Systems, Montreal, QC, Canada, 21–26 April 2018; Association for Computing Machinery: New York, NY, USA, 2018.
46. Salminen, J.; Sengun, S.; Kwak, H.; Jansen, B.; An, J.; Jung, S.-G.; Vieweg, S.; Harrell, D.F. Generating Cultural Personas from Social Data: A Perspective of Middle Eastern Users. In Proceedings of the 2017 5th International Conference on Future Internet of Things and Cloud Workshops (FiCloudW), Prague, Czech Republic, 21–23 August 2017; IEEE: New York, NY, USA, 2017; pp. 120–125.
47. Salminen, J.; Jansen, B.J.; An, J.; Kwak, H.; Jung, S.-G. Automatic Persona Generation for Online Content Creators: Conceptual Rationale and a Research Agenda. In *Personas—User Focused Design*; Nielsen, L., Ed.; Springer: London, UK, 2019; pp. 135–160, ISBN 978-1-4471-7427-1.
48. Margaris, D.; Vassilakis, C.; Spiliotopoulos, D. Handling uncertainty in social media textual information for improving venue recommendation formulation quality in social networks. *Soc. Netw. Anal. Min.* **2019**, *9*, 64. [CrossRef]
49. Margaris, D.; Vassilakis, C.; Spiliotopoulos, D. What makes a review a reliable rating in recommender systems? *Inf. Process. Manag.* **2020**, *57*, 102304. [CrossRef]

© 2020 by the authors. Licensee MDPI, Basel, Switzerland. This article is an open access article distributed under the terms and conditions of the Creative Commons Attribution (CC BY) license (http://creativecommons.org/licenses/by/4.0/).

Article

# A Personalized Heritage-Oriented Recommender System Based on Extended Cultural Tourist Typologies

Markos Konstantakis *, Georgios Alexandridis and George Caridakis

Intelligent Interaction Research Group, Cultural Technology Department, University of the Aegean, 81100 Mytilene, Greece; gealexandri@aegean.gr (G.A.); gcari@aegean.gr (G.C.)
* Correspondence: mkonstadakis@aegean.gr

Received: 25 April 2020; Accepted: 29 May 2020; Published: 4 June 2020

**Abstract:** Recent developments in digital technologies regarding the cultural heritage domain have driven technological trends in comfortable and convenient traveling, by offering interactive and personalized user experiences. The emergence of big data analytics, recommendation systems and personalization techniques have created a smart research field, augmenting cultural heritage visitor's experience. In this work, a novel, hybrid recommender system for cultural places is proposed, that combines user preference with cultural tourist typologies. Starting with the McKercher typology as a user classification research base, which extracts five categories of heritage tourists out of two variables (cultural centrality and depth of user experience) and using a questionnaire, an enriched cultural tourist typology is developed, where three additional variables governing cultural visitor types are also proposed (frequency of visits, visiting knowledge and duration of the visit). The extracted categories per user are fused in a robust collaborative filtering, matrix factorization-based recommendation algorithm as extra user features. The obtained results on reference data collected from eight cities exhibit an improvement in system performance, thereby indicating the robustness of the presented approach.

**Keywords:** cultural tourism; typology; personalization; user experience; recommender systems; collaborative filtering; hybrid matrix factorization

## 1. Introduction

In recent years, user adaptive systems have become popular in many application areas, including the cultural tourism domain, which is nowadays recognized as one of the most important forms of touristic traffic. The proliferation of user-adaptive *recommender systems* (RS) in this area is growing rapidly, since cultural tourism is an activity strongly related to the personal desires and interests of visitors [1]. The large number of resources and data available online have resulted in the fast dissemination of cultural information, but, on the other hand, they have also contributed to the problem of *information overload*; that is, the difficulty in identifying those resources best suited to each individual's needs.

Therefore, managing these voluminous resources with principles and techniques pertaining to big data analytics, in an effort to offer suitable and personalized support to visitors, constitutes one the most interesting challenges in this research field. In this sense, it is of vital importance to be able to segment cultural tourists, taking into account their whole cultural experiences. However, although cultural tourism shows remarkable growth and popularity, little research has been done to categorize cultural tourists by integrating both their cultural centrality (e.g., cultural motivation, importance of culture in the decision to visit) and depth/levels of cultural experience [2–4].

In light of the above, further interest in studying cultural tourism and its participants has been developed, as they exhibit their own distinct characteristics. It is an indisputable fact that experiencing cultural assets plays an important role in motivating a person's travel decisions. Nevertheless, cultural tourism destinations require a more precise categorization of their visitors and their underlying motivations, since not every person is motivated by the same reasons for learning, experimenting or self-exploring. Because of this assumption, that cultural tourists are not alike, most of the literature in cultural tourism follows a segmentation approach, giving emphasis in determining the typology of the cultural tourists [5]. Consequently, McKercher [6] developed a relevant typology by addressing two fundamental dimensions; *cultural centrality* and *depth of user experience*. The aforementioned typology provides a useful and functional framework for segmenting cultural tourists and has been further tested and employed in subsequent empirical studies [7,8].

Recommender systems are a key technology in addressing the concerns outlined above and assist travelers in making optimal decisions. In principle, a well-designed and effective RS can help a cultural visitor in exploring, comparing and choosing the most interesting destinations that fit his/hers preferences and needs. Most modern RS operate by modelling both potential visitors and destinations; that is, by studying past interactions of their users and the places they have visited, along with explicit preferences, usually expressed on a rating scale. In order to provide users with personalized recommendations, RS eventually select the most relevant destinations that match with the modelled user's profile. Therefore, user profiles are an important RS component, playing a key role in its effectiveness [9]. In this sense, any additional information relevant to each user's taste is expected to further improve the quality of the recommendations.

In this regard, the main goal of this work is the enhancement of the user profiles built by cultural RS through the incorporation into them of additional information regarding the cultural tourist type, as assessed by the McKercher's framework. More specifically, this work extends collaborative filtering matrix factorization algorithms, considered to be the state-of-the-art in RS, through the inclusion of the each user's cultural profile in the factorization process, as obtained by the aforementioned framework. To the best of our knowledge, our work is among the first to address cultural recommendations in this dimension, while the outcome of this study provides a better understanding in the areas of segmenting, profiling and recommending for cultural tourists. The rest of this paper is organized as follows; Section 2 presents a literature overview of cultural tourism, visitor profiles and recommender systems. Section 3 outlines the proposed methodology, while Section 4 presents the data used in the experiments. Section 5 discusses obtained results and finally, the work concludes in Section 6, where some general remarks are made and possible future directions are also considered.

## 2. Literature Review

Cultural tourism is a type of tourism particularly relevant to a destination's culture and more precisely with aspects such as the lifestyle, history, arts, architecture, religion, heritage and other related elements. Travellers who participate in this form of activity, by visiting cultural places and organizations are considered to be "cultural tourists"[10]. Of course, this definition is too broad; indeed, all tourists may be involved in cultural activities, in one way or another. For this reason, several studies examine the heterogeneous nature of cultural tourists, proposing various typologies and segmentations [11].

Niemczyk [12] considers cultural tourism as a type of travel from a person's area of residence during vacation, for a period of time not more than 12 months. This involves the individual being aware, to some extent of the place of visit, in which culture (the core element of the tourist experience) plays a significant role when planning the journey. A number of studies [13–15] indicate that cultural tourists tend to be better educated and older than the general travelling public. Additionally, they stay longer in a particular area, participate in travel activities more often than other categories of tourists and spend more money in the places they visit [13]. Women constitute an important part of this type of tourism [15], while cultural travellers are more likely to use a variety of sources to gather information when planning trips [14].

Specialized literature attempted to classify tourists on the basis of their chosen activities, motivations, lifestyles and depth of experience. Stylianou-Lambert [10] tried to explain the differences between cultural tourists in art museums, interviewing participants from Cyprus. De Simone [16] studied the relationship between tourist typologies and heritage tourist attitudes, based on demographics, travel behavior, experience and satisfaction. Nguyen [8] categorized heritage tourists in Vietnam, using a questionnaire survey with two basic variables; the importance of cultural tourism in the decision to visit a city and the depth of cultural experience. Also, Konstantakis [17,18] proposed two different methodologies; CURE and REPEAT. The former identifies and extracts cultural user personas by eliminating the requirement of explicit user input, while the latter processes implicit data from users' mobile devices and explicit data from users' answers into a questionnaire, in order categorize each visitor and assume the personalization level that fits his/her interests better.

Meanwhile, McKercher [11] developed a cultural tourist typology addressing two dimensions; the centrality of cultural tourism and the depth of cultural engagement, thus providing a useful and functional theoretical framework [4], which has been further tested [11] and employed in subsequent empirical studies. Taking into consideration the importance of cultural heritage in the final decision to visit a destination and the experience the user is seeking, McKercher distinguishes five types of tourists (Figure 1):

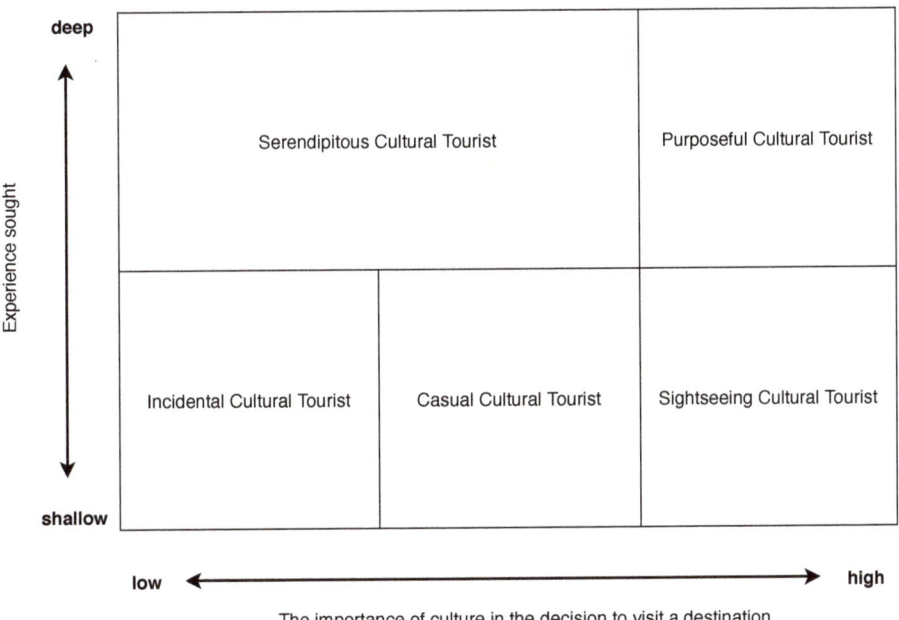

**Figure 1.** Cultural tourist types according to McKercher [11].

1. The **purposeful** cultural tourist, for whom the main purpose of visit is gaining knowledge of another place's culture. Learning the cultural heritage of a place is an important reason to visit a destination and this kind of approach creates a deep cultural experience.
2. The **incidental** cultural tourist, for whom culture does not play any role in the decision to visit a particular cultural destination and even though s/he might visit one, his/her participation in cultural events is minimal.

3. The **serendipitous** cultural tourist, for whom culture plays little or no role in the decision to visit a particular cultural destination, but if s/he finds himself/herself in one, his/her participation in cultural events is maximal, resulting in a deep cultural experience.
4. The **casual** cultural tourist, whose focus on cultural matters is of little importance when planning to travel, and even in the event of encountering cultural activities, their cognitive impact is rather shallow on him/her.
5. The **sightseeing** cultural tourist, who desires to gain knowledge about the culture of another place, but in reality his/her visit is of a rather loose nature, focused on entertainment [12].

Furthermore, Kantanen and Tikkanen [19] were based on McKercher's typology to examine the impact of cultural tourism on visitors' perception processes concerning cultural attractions. Finally, Vong [7] examined the cultural tourist typologies in Macau pertaining to an urban game, by employing McKercher's typology through a questionnaire survey in visiting tourists.

To date, only a handful of studies have attempted to examine cultural tourism experience and the technological impact from a holistic point of view. The integration of *information & communication technologies* (ICT) has benefited the promotion of cultural experiences. With the development of new technologies, modern types of tourist activities are growing, which are capable of transforming and augmenting cultural tourism experience in a higher level. These new augmented experiences are expected to increase user engagement, allowing technology to function either as a mediator or as the core experience itself [20].

A key element for the introduction of ICT in the cultural heritage domain is the perceived *user experience* (UX). Cultural institutions should consider that their visitors come from different backgrounds and have mixed expectations during their visits. Their engagement with the exhibits or ICT also varies. Therefore, it is of major importance to be able to understand and adapt the technology in order to offer a meaningful experience to visitors. Cultural spaces should adjust the use of traditional ways of presenting exhibits to a more relevant way, in line with technological changes, whether by using more effective digital media or interactive exhibits [21].

In this regard, RS are one of the principal ways of delivering personalized content to the visitors of a destination. RS are software systems that try to model their users' unique taste, based on the interactions the latter have with the places they visit [22]. This interaction is typically multimodal; it might be *explicit*, when a user actively evaluates a place s/he visits and/or *implicit*; when the interaction between a visitor and a place is deduced by the system itself. In the first case, user opinion might be expressed in a number of ways; e.g., through ratings on a predefined scale (like/dislike, 5-star system, etc.), through answered questionnaires or even through free-form text (comments, etc.). In the latter case, user preference is extracted from his/her actions; e.g., visiting/"checking-in" a place or taking photos. Of course, the former type of interaction is highly desired because it is more closely related to the actual taste of the visitor. However, it requires a high level of user engagement in order to be efficient, which, obviously, cannot be guaranteed for every potential user.

Recommender Systems can be incorporated in the cultural domain in a number of ways. Their most widespread application is probably in proposing places to visits, known as *points of interests* (POIs), in the form of a ranked list. POIs may range from geographical areas and cities to particular places within a city [23] or even specific locations within a cultural heritage site, such as an archeological site or a museum [24]. An extension of the aforementioned systems are RS that recommend *paths* or *travel routes*; in this case, the route is modelled as a sequence of spatially correlated POIs to be visited in a pre-defined order. Again, the route may involve a broad geographical area of POIs that are many kilometers apart, locations within a city [25] or even exhibits within a constrained heritage space (museum, cultural site) [26]. Apart from proposing spatially correlated POIs that are of interest to their users, path RS are also usually bounded by the route itself; in total duration and/or distance. Finally, cultural RS may also be used to suggest experiences, such as activities and events.

In this work, a cultural RS that produces a list of suggested POIs to visit is going to be outlined. The proposed system is going to model implicit user interactions, as this type of data are more robust and can be obtained in an unobtrusive manner, that does not affect the overall UX. In order to produce more efficient recommendations, users are going to be profiled according to their cultural persona type, based on additional variables (apart from centrality and depth of experience), such as frequency of visits, visiting knowledge and duration of the visit. The proposed cultural typology differs from the previous works and provides an enriched information system which, in turn, is going to be fused in the recommendation process, as it shall be described in more detail in the subsequent section.

## 3. Methodology

In this section, the various components of the proposed approach are discussed, starting with the cultural tourist typology (Section 3.1). Then, the proposed methodology of extracting user personas through questionnaires is outlined (Section 3.2). Finally, details about the implemented RS and the way user personas are incorporated in the recommendation processes are presented in Section 3.3.

*3.1. Cultural Tourist Typology*

A brief critical assessment of the various cultural tourist typologies reveals that the majority of them do not conform to the behaviors of today's travelers who, especially when it comes to young ages, organize and often experience their journey with a focus on new technologies and the online social media networks. Equally important is the fact that most typologies do not take into account the reality that travelers often "move" between different typologies, depending on their available time, income, health, family and other obligations. It is also regularly overlooked that decisions concerning a destination are the result of a compromise between the various members of the holiday team (relatives and/or friends).

A modern typology is therefore necessary, taking into account the complex modes of behavior encountered in the socio-economic realities, particularly for cultural travelers. In addition, since the experiences that make up each trip vary, special emphasis should be placed on the opportunities offered by cultural tourism for travelers to embrace different social roles or to enhance their social status and on the importance that tourists themselves attach to their journey in relation to the characteristics of their everyday lives. As it is practically impossible to devise a typology that would reflect the behavior of all travellers, it should be pointed out that, in general, interpretations occasionally proposed for travelers' motives lead to the conclusion that cultural tourism allows escaping from an existing situation or facilitating the search for another reality. For this reason, and after a thorough study of the relevant literature, this work adopts the McKercher typology [6] of cultural tourists, which is also supported by a number of studies outlined in Section 2.

*3.2. Proposed Methodology*

The difficulty in building a broadly accepted and valid methodology for determining the number of cultural tourists and the correlation they have with cultural heritage in order to create a RS, is one of the key challenges of this research. Moreover, the main objective is not to devise a new methodology, but to help make suitable suggestions instead, by using tools which are widely applied in academic and research studies, but are often neglected in the cultural management field [27]. However, prior to grouping cultural tourists, there must first be a systematic technique and a very basic questionnaire with information related to socio-demographic data, motivation and behavioral intentions. On the other hand, in order to determine the different types of users and the degree of their cultural attitude, a simple matrix can be created to relate the different variables (activities, duration of stay, purpose of travel etc.).

More specifically, for indoor cultural destinations, where entry and departure can be monitored, various types of tools and technologies (surveillance cameras, GPS and Bluetooth devices, sensors, beacons) can be employed, allowing the verification of the exact number of cultural visitors and the immediate observation of their effective behavior. Therefore, it is possible to determine the relationship these tourists have with the visited space; that is, the duration of their stay, the time spent in each room or area of the visiting cultural place, most attractive artifacts, attitude and interests [28]. However, for outdoor cultural destinations where there are no means of monitoring entry and departure, direct observation is difficult to implement. In such cases, the most suitable solution, despite its limitations, is the questionnaire.

Consequently, in this research, a questionnaire has been used for collecting data related to the issues raised above, from a sample of $N = 200$ respondents, chosen randomly after completing their visit to the new Acropolis Museum, between 18 February and 25 February 2020. Respondents were approached and asked by the researchers to fill in the questionnaire, providing information on their visits to heritage sites, as well as other relevant information regarding their trip, while interviewers stayed nearby to answer any possible questions the participants might have had. The questionnaire, available in Appendix A, was implemented with close-ended questions and the responses are summarized on Table 1. The questions pertained to three distinct aspects, as outlined below:

1. The tourists' **socio-demographic characteristics** (age, gender, level of education, occupation).
2. Information regarding the **visit to cultural heritage destinations**, such as previous visits, travel motivation, perception of the destination, activities they participated in during their visit, other places they plan to visit during their trip and their willingness to stay longer or to revisit the cultural destination.
3. Information regarding the two dimensions, **centrality** and **depth of user experience**, suggested by the model of cultural tourist classification of Section 2 and additional data for the three variables governing cultural visitor types, which have been proposed in our research for categorizing cultural heritage tourists (frequency of visits in a cultural destination—visiting knowledge of the cultural destination—duration of the visit during a cultural trip).

Table 1. Sample characteristics/Questionnaire responses.

| Variable | Category | Frequency (N) | Percentage (%) |
|---|---|---|---|
| **Socio-demographic characteristics** | | | |
| Age | 19–25 | 17 | 8.6 |
| | 26–35 | 53 | 26.4 |
| | 36–50 | 89 | 44.8 |
| | 51–64 | 37 | 18.4 |
| | 65+ | 4 | 1.8 |
| Education | primary | 1 | 0.6 |
| | secondary | 10 | 4.9 |
| | higher | 189 | 94.5 |
| Occupation | student | 19 | 9.4 |
| | employee | 160 | 79.9 |
| | unemployed | 21 | 10.7 |
| **Cultural dimensions/variables** | | | |
| Frequency of the visit in cultural destinations | 1–3 times | 111 | 55.8 |
| | 4–6 times | 55 | 27.6 |
| | 7 or more times | 34 | 16.6 |
| Duration of the visit during a cultural trip | <1 h | 4 | 2.0 |
| | >1 h | 36 | 18.4 |
| | 1–3 h | 141 | 70.6 |
| | 3 h and more | 19 | 9.8 |
| Visiting knowledge of the cultural destination | very low | 2 | 0.6 |
| | low | 9 | 4.3 |
| | medium | 42 | 21.0 |
| | high | 88 | 44.4 |
| | very high | 59 | 29.6 |

Based on the responses, *analysis of variance* (ANOVA) tests have been performed in order to evaluate the time spent in tourist activities among the McKercher's cohorts [4,7]. Our findings indicated that there were distinct differences between tourists with respect to their cultural profile and activity engagement. At the same time, further variables emerged outside of centrality and depth of experience, such as frequency of visits (first time—frequent—infrequent variable), long stay—day trippers and previous cultural space knowledge (no search—little search—very extensive search). Those variables, displayed on Table 2, are at the core of our efforts to create an enriched cultural tourism typology.

Table 2. Variables governing cultural visitor types.

| | Variable | Description |
|---|---|---|
| 1 | Centrality | how important cultural tourism is for the user to visit the site |
| 2 | Depth of user experience | level of involvement and real knowledge acquisition during the visit |
| 3 | Frequency of visits | how often s/he travels on average a year |
| 4 | Visiting knowledge | if s/he has prior knowledge of the visiting Area |
| 5 | Duration of the visit | time spent for an activity within the cultural tour |

Previous studies [29,30] have suggested the length of stay in a cultural destination is related to the activities tourists engage in. In our questionnaire, this variable is determined by the question *"How long did you stay in a cultural destination?"*, where respondents answered *"() Day(s) / () Night(s)"*. The analysis of the responses indicated that the average length of stay was 7.5 nights during a cultural visit. Based on this observation, the numeric responses have been collapsed into four categories: (i) *short stays* (1–4 days), (ii) *medium stays* (5–10 days), (iii) *long stays* (11–17 days) and finally, (iv) *exceptionally long stays* (over 17 days). Additionally, participants were asked how many different sites do they visit on average during a trip to a cultural destination (Appendix A). The responses to this question helped determine the depth of their cultural engagement and those two variables (length of stay, number of experiences) helped determine the degree of cultural centrality, according to Table 3.

Table 3. Degree of cultural centrality based on number of experiences and duration of visit.

| Centrality | Number of Experiences | | | |
|---|---|---|---|---|
| | Short Stay | Medium Stay | Long Stay | Exceptionally Long Stay |
| Low | 1 to 2 | 3 to 4 | 5 to 6 | 7 or more |
| Moderate | 3 to 4 | 5 to 6 | 7 to 8 | 9 or more |
| High | 5 to 6 | 7 to 8 | 9 to 10 | 11 or more |

According to McKercher's typology (Section 2), the *purposeful cultural tourists* are those for whom the cultural profile of a place played a strong reole in their decision to visit a destination, thus resulintg in a high cultural centrality and reception ( the highest ranking among other profiles and visitor types). Likewise, in *sightseeing cultural tourists*, culture played an important role in their travelling motivation, but in the end, their resulting cultural experience was of low depth. *Casual cultural tourists* exhibit a moderate level of cultural centrality and depth of experience. For the *serendipitous cultural tourists*, even though the cultural centrality had been limited at the beginning of their journey, they ended up visiting cultural destinations and gaining a fairly deep level of experience. Finally, the cultural centrality of *incidental cultural tourists* had been very limited and their cultural experience was moderate [12].

Relevant studies [4,6,7,12] indicate that purposeful and serendipitous cultural tourists conducted extensive research regarding the cultural space prior to arrival (visiting knowledge), compared to the other cultural group types. Casual tourists also seem to visit more destinations (high rate) than others types of tourists (frequency of visits). On the contrary, incidental tourists travel less than the other categories (low rate). Regarding the duration of the visit in a cultural destination, purposeful tourists indicated that they were willing to stay longer (high rate), while casual and incidental tourists had the lowest rate. Concerning general information on a cultural space, as a matter of fact, serendipitous and purposeful tourists conducted extensive information search about the destination prior to arrival (high rate), while the numbers in the other groups were less than 50% (medium and low rate). Considering the nature of the item measurement, a mean value in $[1,2]$ has been considered to be low, $(2,4)$ medium and $[4,5]$ high. These findings are summarized on Table 4 and on the Kiviat diagram of Figure 2.

**Table 4.** Cultural tourist rating.

|  | Centrality | Depth of User Experience | Frequency of Visits | Visiting Knowledge | Duration of the Visit |
| --- | --- | --- | --- | --- | --- |
| Purposeful | 4.5 | 4.5 | 3 | 4 | 4.5 |
| Sightseeing | 4 | 2 | 3 | 3 | 4 |
| Incidental | 2 | 3 | 1 | 1 | 2 |
| Serendipitous | 1 | 4 | 3 | 4.5 | 4 |
| Casual | 3.5 | 3 | 4 | 2 | 2 |

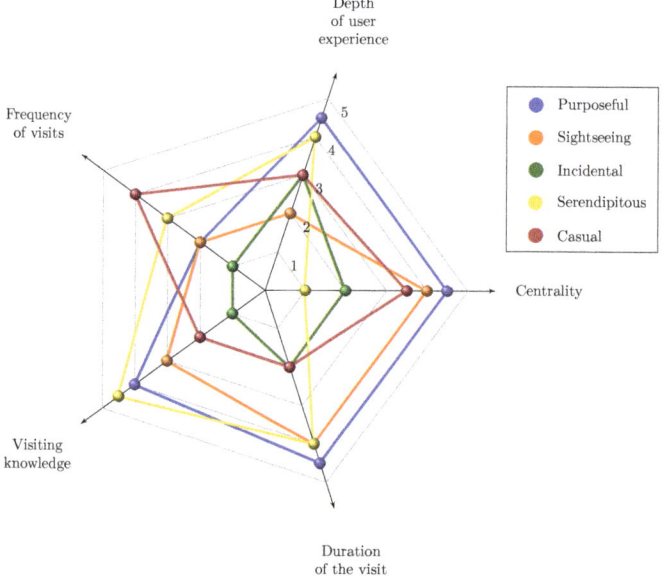

**Figure 2.** Cultural tourist Kiviat diagram.

### 3.3. Recommendation System

Having fixed the cultural user typology (Table 4 and Figure 2), it is necessary to fuse it to the cultural POI RS. In principle, the most robust RS algorithms are *model-based, collaborative filtering* (CF) *matrix factorization* (MF) techniques [22] and for this reason they have been chosen in this work. At the heart of CF MF approaches lies the interactions matrix $M$, which is also known as the ratings' matrix when explicit feedback is provided by the users (Section 2). $M$ is an $n \times m$ positive semi-definite, each row of which represent one of the $n$ users of the system (in this case, the cultural visitors) and each column of which represents one of $m$ the available items to be recommended to users (in this case, the cultural POIs). The $(i^{\text{th}}, j^{\text{th}})$ defined element of $M$ captures the interaction between visitor $i$ and POI $j$, either explicit or implicit. In reality, interaction matrices are extremely sparse, usually having less than 1% of their elements defined.

MF techniques analyze the large sparse matrix $M$ into two denser ones of lower dimensionality (Equation (1)), the $n \times f$ user feature matrix $U$ and the $f \times m$ item feature matrix $I$, so that

$$M \simeq U.I \tag{1}$$

and $f \ll n, m$. The $i^{\text{th}}$ row vector of $U$, whose dimensionality is $f$, encodes the preferences of user $i$ expressed in $M$, while, similarly, the $j^{\text{th}}$ column vector of $I$, whose dimensionality is again $f$, encodes the evaluations item $j$ has received in $M$. The extend to which unseen POI $k$ is of interest to visitor $i$ is quantified by computing the dot product of the respective vectors (Equation (2))

$$p_{i,k} = \mathbf{u}_i.\mathbf{i}_k \tag{2}$$

MF-based CF RS that recommend POIs compute Equation (2) for all unseen items around the vicinity of user $i$ and return a ranked list of the $l$ items with the largest value, which are, according to the RS, those POIs that would maximize visitor's $i$ satisfaction.

There is an abundance of techniques and approaches in the RS literature that compute the MF of Equation (1). In this work, the methodology of choice has been *LightFM* [31], for a number of reasons. Firstly, it can cope with *cold-start* recommendations; that is, it is able to recommend POIs to new users that have not any recorded interactions in matrix $M$, yet. This group of visitors is of extreme importance, as it represents cultural tourists that visit a place for the first time and they want to get accurate recommendations. The cold-start problem may also affect POIs, in the sense that a new event or exhibition might occur within a given place and therefore the RS should be able to recommended to the appropriate audience. Secondly, LightFM implements a robust MF scheme that supports both explicit and implicit user evaluations. Finally, LightFM is a *hybrid* MF algorithm, in the sense that it supports the inclusion of additional user and/or item features in the factorization process. In this case, the additional user features to be considered are those of Table 4; the extent to which each visitor to any of the five cultural tourist types discussed in Section 2.

In our adaptation of the LightFM model, the user features $\mathbf{u}_i$ are extended with user metadata in the form of the computed cultural profile $\mathbf{c}_i$ for each visitor, which is a 5-dimensional vector, one for each variable (column) of Table 4. Therefore, the extended user vector $\mathbf{q}_i = [\mathbf{u}_i, \mathbf{c}_i]$ is the concatenation of $\mathbf{u}_i$ and $\mathbf{c_u}$. System prediction for the $i, k$ pair (Equation (2)) is now given by Equation (3) below

$$p_{i,k} = f(\mathbf{q}_i.\mathbf{i}_k + b_i + b_k) \tag{3}$$

where $b_i, b_k$ are the scalar bias terms for the user and item latent vectors, respectively. $f$ is a non-linear function that smooths predictions. In our model, we have chosen the sigmoid function. The latent user and item vectors are approximated through *maximum likelihood expectation*, using asynchronous stochastic gradient descent [32].

## 4. Experiments

In this section, the experimental procedure used to evaluate the effect of the proposed approach is described in detail. Initially, the selected dataset is presented in Section 4.1, along with its peculiarities and characteristics. Then, the preprocessing steps necessary for extracting the user personas (Section 4.2) are reasoned upon.

*4.1. Dataset*

The dataset selected for the experiments is the `Flickr User-POI Visits Dataset` [33,34] (Table 5). It consists of a set of users and their visits to various POIs in eight different cities, spanning three continents. It has been derived from the currently unavailable (as of writing) `Yahoo Flickr Creative Commons 100 Million` (YFCC100M) Dataset [35]. The visits ensue from the geo-tagged and timestamped photos uploaded to the *Flickr* Image Hosting platform by its users.

**Table 5.** The Flickr User-POI Visits Dataset [33,34].

| City | Users | POIs | Visits | Photographs | Travel Sequences |
|---|---|---|---|---|---|
| Budapest | 935 | 39 | 4810 | 18,513 | 2361 |
| Delhi | 279 | 26 | 682 | 3393 | 489 |
| Edinburgh | 1454 | 29 | 7853 | 33,944 | 5028 |
| Glasgow | 601 | 29 | 2749 | 11,434 | 2227 |
| Osaka | 450 | 29 | 1372 | 7747 | 1115 |
| Perth | 159 | 25 | 920 | 3643 | 716 |
| Toronto | 1395 | 30 | 7607 | 39,419 | 6057 |
| Vienna | 1155 | 29 | 5320 | 34,515 | 3193 |

Every entry in the dataset is comprised of a *photo identifier* (photoID), a *user identifier* (userID), the *date* taken (in UNIX timestamp format), a *place identifier* (poiID), the *category* of the POI (e.g., Park, Museum, etc.), the *total number of photos* taken on this POI by all users of the dataset (poiFreq) and finally the *travel sequence number*. This number groups consecutive POI visits by the same user that differ by less than 8 h, as one travel sequence. Since on a particular visit to a POI, the visitor usually takes more than one photographs, the total number of visits (4th column of Table 5) is derived by counting the unique combinations of userID, photoID and travel sequence number. Finally, the dataset also contains the list of POIs, their name, their exact geographical coordinates, their category and the distance (in meters) in-between them.

Table 6 summarizes all 171,208 photographs in the dataset, grouped by POI category. As it might have been expected, the number of photographs is not evenly distributed in-between the categories, as certain landmarks within each city are much more likely to be visited and photographed, than others. In particular, the POI category distribution in the dataset follows a *power law*, with the four most popular categories (Historical, Cultural, Museum and Structure) accounting for more than half of the total number of photos taken.

**Table 6.** POI Categories & Classes.

| Cultural Classes | | | Non-Cultural Classes | | |
|---|---|---|---|---|---|
| Category | Photographs | Percentage | Category | Photographs | Percentage |
| Historical | 25,277 | 16.50% | Structure | 16,949 | 11.06% |
| Cultural | 23,740 | 15.50% | Sport | 7944 | 5.19% |
| Museum | 21,700 | 14.16% | Shopping | 7783 | 5.08% |
| Park | 10,062 | 6.57% | Beach | 7394 | 4.83% |
| Amusement | 7866 | 5.13% | Transport | 5032 | 3.28% |
| Entertainment | 5988 | 3.91% | Education | 3536 | 2.31% |
| Palace | 3688 | 2.41% | Zoo | 1830 | 1.19% |
| Architectural | 1845 | 1.20% | Precinct | 640 | 0.42% |
| Religious | 959 | 0.63% | | | |
| Religion | 564 | 0.37% | | | |
| Building | 401 | 0.26% | | | |
| Total | 102,100 | 66.64% | Total | 51,108 | 33.36% |

Prior to proceeding with the construction of the cultural tourist typologies, based on the presented dataset, an important decision needs to be made; which POI categories contribute to the cultural experience of a tourist and which do not. For certain categories the decision is rather straightforward; for example, visits to POIs labelled as Historical, Cultural or Museums definitely strengthen the cultural experience of the visitor. The opposite can be said for some other categories like Precinct, Transport or Shopping; these POIs can add virtually nothing to the overall cultural experience. Other categories are harder to decide upon, with the final assignment being open to debate, like Structure, Sport, Religion or Amusement. For those "intermediate" cases, the respective POIs have been examined one-by-one prior to deciding whether the category in-question is to be assigned to the Cultural or Non-cultural destination class. Table 6 displays the final members of the two classes of POI categories, with the majority of the photographs belonging in the Cultural class (102,100 or 66.64%).

*4.2. Pre-Processing*

Table 2 summarizes the 5 variables that are used to determine the cultural tourist type (Table 4 and Figure 2). Out of those variables, only the depth of the user experience cannot be determined from the dataset at hand. Therefore, for the rest of the experimental procedure (and the rest of this paper), this dimension is going to be omitted in the respective estimations and the cultural tourist type is going to be determined based on the other four; that is (i) *centrality*, (ii) *frequency of visit*, (iii) *visiting knowledge* and (iv) *duration of the visit*.

Centrality quantifies the importance of cultural sites to the visitor. The most obvious way to assess this characteristic is to count the number of distinct visits of each tourist to the various cultural places. The more sites s/he travels to, the larger the value of centrality is going to be for him/her. If the number of distinct visits per visitor is aggregated on a histogram, its shape is similar to the one of Figure 3 for Budapest. As it can bee seen, the number of visits follows a power law distribution; the overwhelming majority of tourists visit only handful of cultural sites (less than 10), with very few proceeding to discover more than 20. This is the case for all cities in the examined dataset and most likely resembles the reality in virtually every destination; the majority of tourists limit their cultural experience to just the most distinctive landmarks of the places they visit. For this reason and in an effort to smoothen the effect of the power law, the logarithm of the number of visits to cultural places has been considered for each user and it has been subsequently linearly mapped to the $[1, 5]$ range.

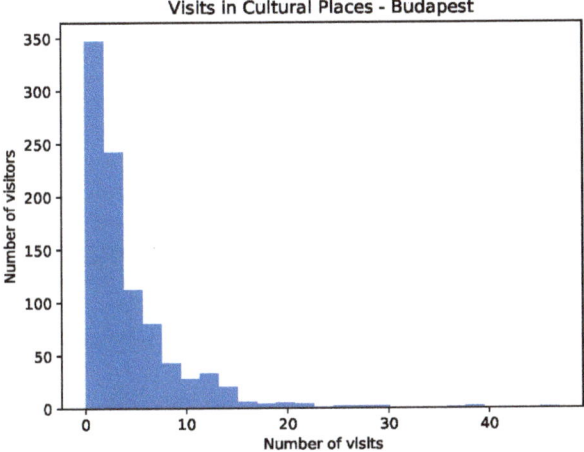

**Figure 3.** Histogram of the number of distinct visits to cultural places in Budapest.

The second variable to be considered, the frequency of the visits, is related to how often a tourist travels. Of course, users are anonymized in the dataset, represented solely by their identifier and as a result, it is impossible to determine whether they are taking photos of their hometown or of a place they are visiting. On the other hand, the timestamps of the photos do reveal when each visit took place, however, in many cases, this information is still incomplete; some photos have wrong timestamps, a few users have taken photos spanning several years, while the vast majority of them has only taken a few shots, corresponding to one or two sequences in the same year. Therefore, in this case, it has been determined that the frequency of visits is better represented by the average value of the ratio of the places visited by a user in one sequence. Figure 4 depicts the histogram of this variable for the city of Budapest, with the other cities in the dataset exhibiting a similar behavior. As it can be seen, it is also following a power law, albeit not as steep as the previous case. Most tourists visit only a couple of places in each sequence, with very few visiting more than 6. Because of the "smoothness" of this histogram, this variable has been linearly mapped to the $[1,5]$ scale.

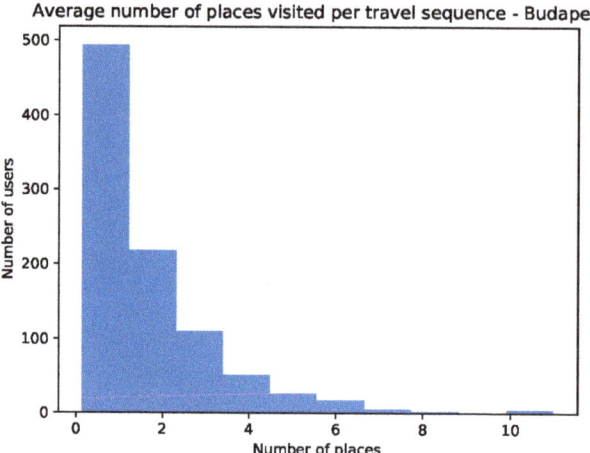

**Figure 4.** Histogram of the ratio of distinct places visited per travel sequence in Budapest.

The visiting knowledge of a place (third variable) can be estimated by the number of visits each POI receives. Cultural POIs with very few visits indicate that they are not popular or well-known attractions and therefore their visitors must have been well-informed about their existence. On the user level, his/her knowledge of the place may be considered to be proportional to the least popular cultural place s/he has visited. POI frequencies also obey a power lay distribution, with a few most popular places within each city attracting the majority of visits. Consequently, the logarithm of the POI frequency has been considered and has been subsequently linearly mapped to the $[1,5]$ scale.

The final variable to be examined is the duration of the visit. This quantity may be approximated as the time difference between the first & last photograph to be taken of a POI within a travel sequence. Based on that assumption, it is possible to compute the average duration of each user's visits, which, like the other variables discussed so far, also follows a power law distribution, with the overwhelming majority of visits lasting less than one hour. Therefore, for each user, the logarithm of his/her average visit duration is taken and is subsequently linearly mapped to the $[1,5]$ scale.

The pre-processing steps discussed so far help approximate, for each user, the values of the four variables of Table 2, that would eventually classify him/her to one of the cultural tourist typologies of Table 4. This classification may be either *hard* or *soft*; in the former case, the user is assigned to the "closest" typology, while in the latter case, a degree of membership on each typology is calculated. Both approaches have been followed in the experiments, however, the soft classification yielded better results and for this reason, it was the only one to be considered in the presented results (Section 5).

User proximity to each one of the five cultural tourist types (Table 4) has been based on euclidean similarity (Equation (4))

$$sim(\mathbf{u},\mathbf{t}) = \frac{1}{1+\sqrt{\sum_{i=1}^{4}(u_i-t_i)^2}} \quad (4)$$

where $\mathbf{u}$ is the user persona vector of the four variables discussed in this subsection and $\mathbf{t}$ is the tourist typology vector. Finally, the computed similarities of every user with the five cultural tourist typologies are normalized to unit similarity.

## 5. Results

Figures 5 and 6 summarize the results of the experimental procedure for all cities in the examined dataset. Two distinct RS have been considered; the first one is the *LightFM* [31] CF MF approach outlined in Section 3.3, which factorizes the interaction matrix of user visits to POIs. In order to study the effect of the computed user personas, the second RS is also based on *LightFM*, but the factorization scheme is hybrid in this case; the user features are augmented with the five additional personas features computed in Section 4.2, designating the extend to which each user belongs to each of the 5 pre-defined cultural tourist type categories (the source code used in the experiments is available at https://github.com/ii-aegean/user-personas-recommender). Otherwise, the rest of the parameters and hyper-parameters are the same for the two RS; the cardinality of the feature space is set to $f = 20$, the number of epochs for the factorization process is also set to 20 and the learning rate is set to 0.05. Additionally, L2 regularization is imposed on the user features, with the optimal value having been determined to be, after experimentation, $\lambda_u = 2 \times 10^{-3}$ for the cities of Vienna, Edinburgh and Toronto and $\lambda_u = 5 \times 10^{-3}$ for the rest. Finally, the test set size has been set to 20% of the total number of interactions and the results presented in Figures 5 and 6 are the averages of 10 different runs, whose statistical significance is assessed by the *Wilcoxon singed rank test* ($p_{value} < 0.01$).

System performance has been evaluated on a set of two metrics that are commonly used in offline RS evaluation [36]. Both metrics are calculated over a list of personalized recommendations returned by the system for each particular user. The first one is *precision*, which is the fraction of those items in the recommendation list that are actually of interest to the user, over all items in the list. Naturally, an ideal RS will only produce meaningful recommendations and would achieve a 100% precision. In practice and when comparing different RS algorithms, a higher precision score is an indication that the examined system adapts better to the taste of the users.

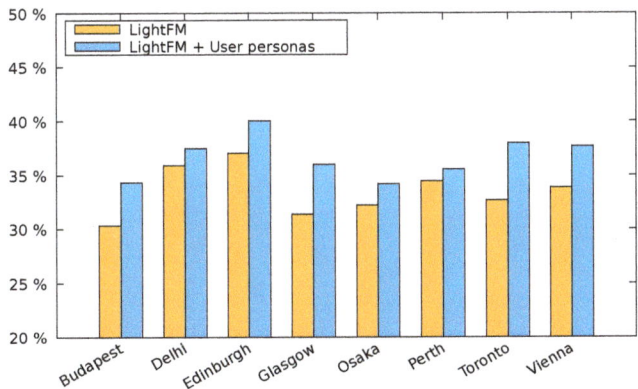

**Figure 5.** Mean Average Precision for a list of three items (MAP@3).

Figure 5 displays the *Mean Average Precision* (MAP) metric computed over a list of three recommended items. MAP designates the mean of average precision, where average precision for a list of length $l$ and for a user $u$ is defined as

$$\overline{Pr(u)} = \frac{1}{|I_u|} \sum_{i=1}^{L} Pr(i) \times rel(i)$$

$Pr(i)$ is the precision at cut-off point $i$ in the list, $I_u$ is the set of relevant items for $u$ and $rel(i)$ is equal to 1 if the $i$-th list item is relevant for $u$ and zero otherwise. The presented results indicate that the hybrid factorization scheme that takes into account the user personas produces better recommendations than the vanilla algorithm. More specifically, a performance improvement of about 3% is achieved on this metric, which the largest difference being recording in Toronto (more than 5%) and the smallest in Perth (little less than 2%). These differences are attributed to the peculiarities of the dataset (Table 5), since the userbase and the interactions in the city of Perth are among the smallest in the dataset and therefore the extracted personas information is not as rich as in the case of Toronto, which is the biggest subset of the data.

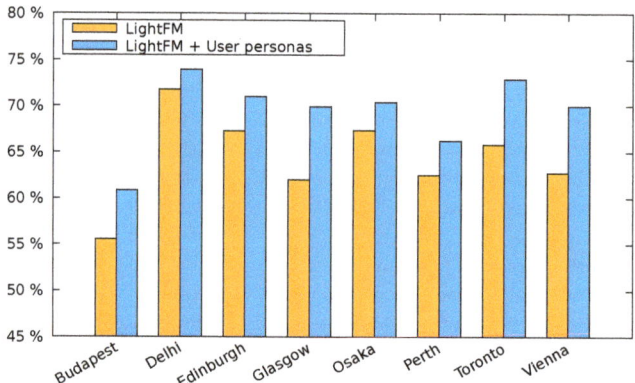

**Figure 6.** Mean Reciprocal Rank (MRR).

The second metric to be examined is the *Mean Reciprocal Rank* (MRR), which quantifies how "high" in the recommendation list lie items relevant to the user. Even when a RS is able to produce meaningful recommendations, those should appear higher in the list (e.g., fist, second, etc.). Otherwise, if the first items in the list are not relevant to the user, s/he may be frustrated by the overall experience and interaction with the system. Therefore, when a RS algorithm achieves a higher MRR score compared to another one, it actually means that it is able to place relevant recommendations (to the user) higher up in the produced list. More formally, MRR is defined as

$$MRR = \frac{1}{|T|} \sum_{l=1}^{|T|} \frac{1}{\text{rank}_l}$$

where $\text{rank}_l$ designates the position of the first relevant item for the $l$-th user in the recommendation list. The inclusion of the user personas in the factorization scheme results in relevant items being placed "higher" in the recommendation list, yielding a performance improvement in this case as well, which is 5% on average; the largest being around 8% in Toronto and the smallest being 3% in Delhi. As with the case of the previous metric, those differences are attributed to the properties of the dataset; Toronto is the biggest subset and therefore permits the creation of more complete personas profiles, while Delhi, along with Perth, are the smallest and therefore user personas are not as descriptive in those cases.

## 6. Conclusions

In this paper, a cultural tourism RS has been outlined, capable of generating personalized POI suggestions, based on an enriched cultural typology. To the best of our knowledge, the presented approach is among the first in the tourist RS domain to make extensive use of cultural user profiles and to incorporate them in the recommendation process. Cultural heritage tourists and their profiles have been examined according to the cultural typologies of McKercher, in terms of an additional three dimensions proposed in this work (visiting knowledge, duration of the visit and frequency of visits). The experimental procedure evaluated the effect of the whole approach on a reference dataset, along with its peculiarities and characteristics. Overall, this work demonstrated that, under certain assumptions, it is possible to augment the recommendation process with information pertaining to the cultural background of tourists and when doing so, the obtained recommendations are of increased quality.

The hybrid CF MF scheme that takes into account the proposed typology achieved a performance improvement over the vanilla approach, recommending meaningful POIs that are relevant to user preference. Therefore, the extra profiling information affects positively the experience of cultural tourists and induces them to learn more about other attractions and activities available in the destinations they visit. Nonetheless, the experimental procedure revealed also certain limitations. Firstly, out of the five variables, the depth of user experience cannot be easily determined. Additionally, in cases of data sparsity (e.g., as in the cities of Delhi and Perth in the examined dataset), the extracted user personas are not as descriptive as in other cases where more data are available (e.g., in Toronto).

In order to overcome the aforementioned shortcomings, a possible future research direction would be the enrichment of the user & item profile representations, by utilizing additional information sources, such as ontologies or the Semantic Web. Enriched user and item features are expected to result to a greater degree of accuracy and thus to make a more meaningful recommendations. Furthermore, in order to increase potential tourists' prior knowledge and enhance their willingness/motivation to visit a cultural attraction, popular social media applications could also be utilized in displaying an attraction's culture and heritage, prior to the actual visit.

**Author Contributions:** Conceptualization, M.K. and G.A.; methodology, M.K.; software, G.A.; validation, M.K., G.A. and G.C.; formal analysis, M.K.; investigation, G.A.; resources, G.A.; data curation, G.A.; writing—original draft preparation, M.K.; writing—review and editing, G.A.; visualization, G.A.; supervision, G.C.; project administration, G.C.; funding acquisition, G.C. All authors have read and agreed to the published version of the manuscript.

**Funding:** This research has been co-financed by the European Regional Development Fund of the European Union and Greek national funds through the Operational Program Competitiveness, Entrepreneurship and Innovation, under the call RESEARCH—CREATE—INNOVATE (project code: T1EDK-02146).

**Conflicts of Interest:** The authors declare no conflict of interest.

## Abbreviations

The following abbreviations are used in this manuscript:

| | |
|---|---|
| ANOVA | Analysis of variance |
| CF | Collaborative filtering |
| ICT | Information & Communication Technology |
| MF | Matrix Factorization |
| MAP | Mean Average Precision |
| MRR | Mean Reciprocal Rank |
| POI | Point of Interest |
| RS | Recommender Systems |
| UX | User experience |

## Appendix A. Questionnaire

The following anonymous questionnaire has been used in this research. All participants gave their consent in processing their responses for research-related tasks, in accordance to national and European data privacy regulations.

*Appendix A.1. Socio-Demographic Characteristics*

**Gender**
(i) Female (ii) Male

**Age Group**
(i) <18 (ii) 18–25 (iii) 26–35 (iv) 36–50 (v) 51–64 (vi) 65+

**Highest Degree**
(i) Primary Education (ii) Secondary Education (iii) Higher Education

**Occupation**
(i) Student (ii) Employee (iii) Self-employed (iv) Unemployed (v) Retired

**Marital Status**
(i) Married (ii) Not married (iii) Widowed (iv) Divorced

**Health condition**
(i) Good (ii) Minor impairments (iii) Significant impairments

**How familiar are you with new technologies?**
(i) Very much (ii) Little (iii) Not at all

*Appendix A.2. User Experience*

**How often do you travel to a cultural destination per year?**
(i) 1–3 times (ii) 4–6 times (iii) 7 or more times

**Are you travelling**
(i) in a group? (ii) with family? (iii) alone? (iv) with friends?

**How many different sites do you visit on average during a cultural trip?**
(i) 1–2 (ii) 3–4 (iii) 5–6 (iv) 7–8 (v) 9–10 (vi) More than 10

**What cultural sites are you interested in visiting?**
(i) Science/Technology (ii) Natural History (iii) Archeological (iv) Museum/Libraries (v) Ethnological (vi) Other

**Were you familiar with the area prior to your visit?**
(i) Familiar (ii) Somewhat familiar (iii) Not familiar at all

**How did you become aware of this museum?**
(i) Printed media (ii) Internet (iii) Friends (iv) Other

**Did you seek any information prior to visiting this museum?**
(i) Yes (ii) No

**Is this the first time visiting this museum?**
(i) Yes (ii) No

**Would you download an app for cultural destinations on a smartphone/tablet?**
(i) Yes (ii) No

**Would you be willing to pay for such an application?**
(i) Yes (ii) No

**What is the purpose of your visit?**
(i) Knowledge (ii) Socializing (iii) Entertainment (iv) Research (v) Professional (vi) Other

**How much time did you spend on this visit?**
(i) less than 1 h (ii) 1–3 h (iii) 3 h or more

**How would you characterize your visit to this place?**
(i) Boring (ii) Tiresome (iii) Inaccessible (iv) Indifferent (v) Useful (vi) Interesting (vii) Impressive (viii) Special

**Did you use your social media profiles to post material during the visit?**
(i) Yes (ii) No

**Returning home, how probable is for you to seek more information about this museum?**
(i) Highly probable (ii) Not very probable (iii) Improbable

## References

1. Pandolfo, L.; Pulina, L.; Grosso, E. A user model ontology for adaptive systems in cultural tourism domain. In *Applications of Intelligent Systems*; IOS Press: Amsterdam, The Netherlands, 2018; pp. 212–219. [CrossRef]
2. Rudan, E. The Development of Cultural Tourism in Small Historical Towns. In *Faculty of Tourism and Hospitality Management in Opatija. Biennial International Congress. Tourism & Hospitality Industry*; University of Rijeka, Faculty of Tourism & Hospitality Management: Rijeka, Croatia, 2010.
3. Di Bitonto, P.; Laterza, M.; Rossano, V.; Roselli, T. A semantic approach implemented in a system recommending resources for cultural heritage tourism. *J. e-Learn. Knowl. Soc.* 2006, 2, 97–106. [CrossRef]
4. Chen, G.; Huang, S.S. Understanding Chinese cultural tourists: Typology and profile. *J. Travel Tour. Market.* 2018, 35, 162–177. [CrossRef]
5. Özel, Ç.H.; Kozak, N. Motive Based Segmentation of the Cultural Tourism Market: A Study of Turkish Domestic Tourists. *J. Qual. Assur. Hosp. Tour.* 2012, 13, 165–186. [CrossRef]
6. McKercher, B. Towards a classification of cultural tourists. *Int. J. Tour. Res.* 2002, 4, 29–386. [CrossRef]
7. Vong, F. Application of cultural tourist typology in a gaming destination—Macao. *Curr. Issues Tour.* 2013, 19, 949–965. [CrossRef]
8. Nguyen, T.H.H.; Cheung, C. The classification of heritage tourists: A case of Hue City, Vietnam. *J. Herit. Tour.* 2013, 9, 35–50. [CrossRef]
9. Boulaalam, O.E. Design of a Tourism Recommendation System Based on User's Profile. In *Advanced Intelligent Systems for Sustainable Development (AI2SD'2019)*; Ezziyyani, M., Ed.; Springer International Publishing: Cham, Switzerland, 2020; pp. 217–223. [CrossRef]
10. Stylianou-Lambert, T. Gazing from home: Cultural tourism and art museums. Annals of Tourism Research. *J. Comput. Cult. Herit.* 2011, 38, 403–421. [CrossRef]
11. McKercher, B.; Du Cros, H. Testing a Cultural Tourism Typology. *Int. J. Tour. Res.* 2003, 5, 45–58. [CrossRef]
12. Niemczyk, A. Cultural tourists: "An attempt to classify them". *Tour. Manag. Perspect.* 2013, 5, 24–30. [CrossRef]
13. Kaufman, T.J.; Scantlebury, M. Cultural tourism and the vacation ownership industry. *J. Retail Leisure Prop.* 2007, 6, 213–220. [CrossRef]
14. Chandler, J.A.; Costello, C.A. A profile of visitors at heritage tourism destinations in East Tennessee according to Plog's lifestyle and activity level preferences model. *J. Travel Res.* 2002, 41, 161–166. [CrossRef]
15. Hausmann, A. Cultural tourism: Marketing challenges and opportunities for German cultural heritage. *Int. J. Herit. Stud.* 2007, 13, 170–184. [CrossRef]
16. de Simone, E. Non-residents' attitudes towards heritage: Exploring tourist typologies by cultural consumption. *Acta Turistica* 2012, 24, 177–208.
17. Konstantakis, M.; Aliprantis, J.; Michalakis, K.; Caridakis, G. A Methodology for Optimised Cultural User peRsonas Experience—CURE Architecture. In Proceedings of the 32nd International BCS Human Computer Interaction Conference (HCI), Belfast, Ireland, 4–6 July 2018. [CrossRef]
18. Konstantakis, M.; Aliprantis, J.; Michalakis, K.; Caridakis, G. Recommending user Experiences based on extracted cultural PErsonas for mobile ApplicaTions-REPEAT methodology. In Proceedings of the Mobile HCI 2018, 20th International Conference on Human-Computer Interaction with Mobile Devices and Services, Barcelona, Spain, 3–6 September 2018.

19. Kantaken, T.; Tikannen, I. Advertising in low and high involvement cultural tourism attractions: Four cases. *Tour. Hosp. Res.* **2006**, *6*, 99–110. [CrossRef]
20. Neuhofer, B.; Buhalis, D.; Ladkin, A. A Typology of Technology-Enhanced Tourism Experiences. *Int. J. Tour. Res.* **2014**, *16*, 340–350. [CrossRef]
21. Konstantakis, M.; Caridakis, G. Adding Culture to UX: UX Research Methodologies and Applications in Cultural Heritage. *J. Comput. Cult. Herit.* **2020**, *13*, 1–17. [CrossRef]
22. Ricci, F.; Rokach, L.; Shapira, B. *Recommender Systems Handbook*, 2nd ed.; Springer Publishing Company, Incorporated: New York, NY, USA, 2015.
23. Liu, Y.; Liu, C.; Liu, B.; Qu, M.; Xiong, H. Unified Point-of-Interest Recommendation with Temporal Interval Assessment. In Proceedings of the 22nd ACM SIGKDD International Conference on Knowledge Discovery and Data Mining, KDD '16, San Francisco, CA, USA, 13–17 August 2016; Association for Computing Machinery: New York, NY, USA, 2016; pp. 1015–1024. [CrossRef]
24. Alexandridis, G.; Chrysanthi, A.; Tsekouras, G.E.; Caridakis, G. Personalized and Content Adaptive Cultural Heritage Path Recommendation: An Application to the Gournia and undefinedatalhöyük Archaeological Sites. *User Model. User-Adapt. Interact.* **2019**, *29*, 201–238. [CrossRef]
25. Aksenov, P.; Kemperman, A.; Arentze, T. A Personalised Recommender System for Tourists on City Trips: Concepts and Implementation. In *Intelligent Interactive Multimedia Systems and Services 2016*; Pietro, G.D., Gallo, L., Howlett, R.J., Jain, L.C., Eds.; Springer International Publishing: Cham, Switzerland, 2016; pp. 525–535.
26. Cardoso, P.J.S.; Guerreiro, P.; Pereira, J.A.A.R.; Veiga, R.J.M. A Route Planner Supported on Recommender Systems Suggestions: Enhancing Visits to Cultural Heritage Places. In Proceedings of the 8th International Conference on Software Development and Technologies for Enhancing Accessibility and Fighting Info-Exclusion, DSAI 2018, Thessaloniki, Greece, 20–22 June 2018; Association for Computing Machinery: New York, NY, USA, 2018; pp. 144–151. [CrossRef]
27. Galí, N. Identifying cultural tourism: A theoretical methodological proposal. *J. Herit. Tour.* **2011**, *7*, 45–58. [CrossRef]
28. Chen, C.; Chen, F. Experience quality, perceived value, satisfaction and behavioral intentions for heritage tourists. *Tour. Manag.* **2010**, *31*, 29–35. [CrossRef]
29. Caldeira, A.M.; Kastenholz, E. Tourists' spatial behaviour in urban destinations: The effect of prior destination experience. *J. Vacat. Market.* **2018**, *24*, 247–260. [CrossRef]
30. Kang, S.; Lee, G.; Kim, J.; Park, D. Identifying the spatial structure of the tourist attraction system in South Korea using GIS and network analysis: An application of anchor-point theory. *J. Destin. Market. Manag.* **2018**, *9*, 358–370. [CrossRef]
31. Kula, M. Metadata Embeddings for User and Item Cold-start Recommendations. In Proceedings of the 2nd Workshop on New Trends on Content-Based Recommender Systems co-located with 9th ACM Conference on Recommender Systems (RecSys 2015), Vienna, Austria, 16–20 September 2015; Volume 1448; pp. 14–21.
32. Niu, F.; Recht, B.; Re, C.; Wright, S.J. HOGWILD! A Lock-Free Approach to Parallelizing Stochastic Gradient Descent. *arXiv* **2011**, arXiv:1106.5730.
33. Lim, K.H.; Chan, J.; Leckie, C.; Karunasekera, S. Personalized Tour Recommendation based on User Interests and Points of Interest Visit Durations. In Proceedings of the 24th International Joint Conference on Artificial Intelligence (IJCAI'15), Buenos Aires, Argentina, 25–31 July 2015; pp. 1778–1784.
34. Lim, K.H.; Chan, J.; Leckie, C.; Karunasekera, S. Towards Next Generation Touring: Personalized Group Tours. In Proceedings of the 26th International Conference on Automated Planning and Scheduling (ICAPS'16), London, UK, 12–17 June 2016; pp. 412–420.
35. Thomee, B.; Shamma, D.A.; Friedland, G.; Elizalde, B.; Ni, K.; Poland, D.; Borth, D.; Li, L.J. YFCC100M: The New Data in Multimedia Research. *Commun. ACM* **2016**, *59*, 64–73. [CrossRef]
36. Herlocker, J.L.; Konstan, J.A.; Terveen, L.G.; Riedl, J.T. Evaluating Collaborative Filtering Recommender Systems. *ACM Trans. Inf. Syst.* **2004**, *22*, 5–53. [CrossRef]

© 2020 by the authors. Licensee MDPI, Basel, Switzerland. This article is an open access article distributed under the terms and conditions of the Creative Commons Attribution (CC BY) license (http://creativecommons.org/licenses/by/4.0/).

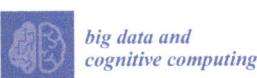

Article

# ACUX Recommender: A Mobile Recommendation System for Multi-Profile Cultural Visitors Based on Visiting Preferences Classification

Markos Konstantakis *, Yannis Christodoulou, John Aliprantis and George Caridakis

Department of Cultural Technology and Communication, Aegean University, 81100 Mytilene, Greece
* Correspondence: mkonstadakis@aegean.gr

**Abstract:** In recent years, Recommendation Systems (RSs) have gained popularity in different scientific fields through the creation of (mostly mobile) applications that deliver personalized services. A mobile recommendation system (MRS) that classifies in situ visitors according to different visiting profiles could act as a mediator between their visiting preferences and cultural content. Drawing on the above, in this paper, we propose ACUX Recommender (ACUX-R), an MRS, for recommending personalized cultural POIs to visitors based on their visiting preferences. ACUX-R experimentally employs the ACUX typology for assigning profiles to cultural visitors. ACUX-R was evaluated through a user study and a questionnaire. The evaluation conducted showed that the proposed ACUX-R satisfies cultural visitors and is capable of capturing their nonverbal visiting preferences and needs.

**Keywords:** personalization; cultural heritage; mobile tourist guide; profile classification; user interface; cultural destinations; personalized suggestions

Citation: Konstantakis, M.; Christodoulou, Y.; Aliprantis, J.; Caridakis, G. ACUX Recommender: A Mobile Recommendation System for Multi-Profile Cultural Visitors Based on Visiting Preferences Classification. *Big Data Cogn. Comput.* 2022, 6, 144. https://doi.org/10.3390/bdcc6040144

Academic Editor: Denis Helic

Received: 30 September 2022
Accepted: 25 November 2022
Published: 28 November 2022

**Publisher's Note:** MDPI stays neutral with regard to jurisdictional claims in published maps and institutional affiliations.

**Copyright:** © 2022 by the authors. Licensee MDPI, Basel, Switzerland. This article is an open access article distributed under the terms and conditions of the Creative Commons Attribution (CC BY) license (https://creativecommons.org/licenses/by/4.0/).

## 1. Introduction

During the last decades, the abundance of online data resources has encouraged the rapid spread of information, but it is also responsible for *information overload* (https://www.interaction-design.org/literature/article/information-overload-why-it-matters-and-how-to-combat-it, accessed on 10 September 2022). A Recommendation System (RS) is an advanced search tool that alleviates this overload by suggesting content that is likely to meet the preferences and needs of potential users [1,2]. RSs have gained popularity in different fields through the creation of mostly mobile applications for delivering personalized information services to the end user. In this context, research efforts have been made in the Cultural Heritage (CH) domain to identify different profiles of cultural visitors, classify them into distinct types, and exploit such classifications in order to provide personalized suggestions of potential cultural POIs (points of interest) through RSs [3–6].

In an era where the typical cultural visitor holds smartphones and uses digital technologies to facilitate their trips, they expect to receive personalized suggestions when and where they should need them. In this ubiquitous computing environment, a mobile recommendation system (MRS) can act as a *mediator* between their visiting preferences and the available cultural content, with the objective of providing useful recommendations of potential POIs [7,8]. But in order to exploit such knowledge about visitors, relevant information must be provided to the recommender. Thus, when beginning to develop an MRS, the main question would be, *"What information is required and how to elicit it?"*

A critical fact to take into account when considering what information is required as input on behalf of the cultural visitor (often termed in the bibliography as *user feedback*) is that, especially at an early phase of a visit, they may not be consciously aware of their desires and thus not be in a position to state them explicitly [9,10]. An MRS intends to make the visitor more conscious of their desires during a visit by *classifying* them according to different *visiting profiles* using a variety of criteria. For example, Walsh [11] and Özel [12] classify cultural visitors based on criteria such as personal motivation, travel behavior characteristics, or demographics. McKercher [13] classifies visitors based on *cultural centrality* (high/low), i.e., the importance of cultural motives when choosing a destination and the *depth of user experience* (deep/shallow) intended when visiting cultural content. Missaoui [3] uses a combination of contextual information (such as location and time) with content from the visitors' social media interactions in order to provide personalized suggestions. Nevertheless, there is a common agreement that the effectiveness and reliability of the classification of cultural visitors in an MRS should be based on their *visiting preferences* as the primary classification criterion [14–18].

To answer the second part of the question, a variety of user feedback elicitation techniques are used to obtain the desired information from the visitor [19]. These techniques may be *explicit* (i.e., requiring some action) or *implicit*. Explicit techniques can be further distinguished into direct (e.g., collecting information through questionnaires, ratings, or free-text comments) or indirect, i.e., engaging the visitor in activities that do not appear directly relevant to profiling (e.g., gamification). In *implicit* techniques, on the other hand, visiting preferences are automatically deduced primarily by monitoring the visitor's online activity (e.g., "checking-in" places, social network activity, or browsing history). According to Antoniou [19] and Kanoje [2], in reality, some *combination* of both techniques is highly recommended since, in this way, both the (more static) characteristics and the (more dynamic) behavioral information of the cultural visitor are retrieved and combined in a way that can eventually lead to recommendations that are closer to the visitors' *current* desires and needs. However, such an approach requires a relatively high level of visitor engagement in order to be efficient, and thus actual effectiveness cannot be guaranteed [20,21].

Drawing on the above, in this paper, we propose ACUX Recommender (ACUX-R), an MRS, for personalized recommendation of cultural POIs to visitors based on their visiting preferences. The classification of visitors implemented in ACUX-R presents the following features:

- ACUX-R experimentally employs the ACUX typology [22] for assigning profiles to cultural visitors. The ACUX typology is the outcome of *harmonization* of existing typologies of cultural visitors that base their classification on visiting preferences. As such, ACUX-R determines the visitor's profile according to their cultural preferences rather than features of the cultural content per se (e.g., popularity or cultural significance) or other non-content-related criteria such as the visitor's time availability, income level, or family obligations.
- The classification of cultural visitors implemented in ACUX-R is *multi-label*; the deduced profile of a cultural visitor may constitute some combination of the eight ACUX profiles.
- The assigned ACUX-R profile is also adjustable; ACUX-R enables users to adjust their profile at any given time, and the recommendation of POIs is automatically updated accordingly.

The rest of the paper is structured as follows. Section 2 reviews related work. Section 3 describes the proposed system. Section 4 presents the evaluation of the system. Finally, conclusions and future research points are drawn in Section 5.

## 2. Related Work

Various RSs have been developed for the CH domain with the objective of assisting cultural visitors in planning their trips. As mentioned above, a critical factor for effective recommendation is to elicit the correct information about the user. In this context, a variety of approaches for collecting user information have been developed and proposed in the relevant literature. These include *content, collaborative, knowledge, demographic,* and *hybrid* approaches [23]. Meanwhile, Burke [24] argues that content-based and knowledge-based recommendation approaches are more frequently applied in the CH domain.

Indeed, ample RSs have been developed for the CH domain, applying content-based and/or knowledge-based approaches for collecting user information. Neidhardt [21,25] presents PixMeAway, a content-based RS that provides personalized recommendations of POIs to visitors. PixMeAway combines profiles from Golberg's [26] and Gibson's [18] visitor typologies in order to present a new typology, referred to as the *seven-factor model*. First, the visitor is prompted to choose among a set of pictures of POIs that they consider appealing when thinking of vacation. Next, the pictures are mapped to the aforementioned model, and a score is calculated for each factor according to the visitor's selections in order to determine their profile. Finally, a set of POIs is recommended to the visitor based on the deduced profile.

Grün [15] introduces Go2Vienna, a knowledge-based RS that provides recommendations of POIs within the city of Vienna. Go2Vienna also classifies visitors according to the *seven-factor model*. First, the cDOTT ontology (core Domain Ontology of Travel and Tourism) is employed for measuring the similarity between visiting preferences. Then, using the Pearson correlation coefficient, the similarity between the profiles of the seven-factor model and the visiting preferences is calculated in order to determine the visitor profile and recommend an initial set of POIs. Furthermore, if the visitor is not satisfied with the recommendations, they can rate the suggested POIs by stating positive/negative feedback, which is used to refine their profiles and deliver an updated set of POIs.

PicTouRe [27] is a newer content-based version of PixmeAway which also adopts the *seven-factor model* for classifying cultural visitors. PicTouRe allows visitors to upload three to seven pictures of their choice and sort them in order of preference. Then, the system determines the visitors' profile by mapping the uploaded pictures with the seven-factor model, where each factor receives a score according to the picture's ordering. Furthermore, PicTouRe allows visitors to refine their profile using sliders that increase/decrease the percentage of each of the seven factors.

Pythia [28], City Trip Planner [29], and MyMytilene [30] follow a knowledge-based approach to collect user information, combining contextual information with visiting preferences as classification criteria.

TRIPMENTOR [31,32] is a bilingual (Greek/English) content-based MRS for Android and iOS devices, suggesting personalized routes for cultural visitors in Athens based on their visiting preferences. TRIPMENTOR is enriched with small gamification mechanisms that aim to enhance user engagement through social interaction and dynamically update the list of recommended POIs.

Regarding the collaborative approach, Herzog [33] proposes TourRec, a collaborative MRS for Android devices that recommends personalized routes to individual visitors or groups. First, TourRec determines the popularity of POIs by measuring the number of visits per POI and by matching geo-tagged photos (obtained from Flickr) with the POI's coordinates. Then, the visitor's profile is determined by combining the POI popularity, visiting preferences, and travel constraints (i.e., time limitations or the need to start/end at specific POIs). Finally, the system recommends routes of POIs that match the deduced profile. Figueredo [34] presents Find Natal, a collaborative MRS for both Android and iOS devices that recommend POIs to cultural visitors using social media photos and previous users' ratings and comments as user input information.

Moreover, various hybrid approaches have been proposed. Missaoui [3] presents LOOKER, a hybrid MRS for Android devices that delivers personalized POI recommendations to visitors, using a content-based filtering module that filters content (i.e., reviews in social posts) that the visitor has generated on social media. Then, using language models, the filtered content is converted into visiting preferences and is combined with contextual information to determine the visitor's profile. Based on the deduced profile, personalized recommendations of POIs are shown on a map or in a list, along with reviews of previous visitors. Logesh [35] introduces PCAHTRS, a personalized context-aware hybrid RS that uses contextual information, previous user reviews, and POI similarity in order to recommend POIs to cultural visitors. Finally, Meehan [36] presents VISIT, a hybrid RS that uses a combination of collaborative, content-based, and demographic approaches for classifying visitors in order to recommend POIs.

The literature review showed that, unlike ACUX-R, the great majority of RSs developed for the CH domain do not classify their users into distinct visitor profiles. Rather, the user provides the required information (usually visiting preferences, demographics, or/and contextual information), and the RSs directly suggest POIs based on that information. On the other hand, RSs that do perform user classification as an intermediate step for providing recommendations most of them classify visitors into multiple profiles (multi-label classification) and also allow them to manually fine-tune their assigned profile (as is the case with ACUX-R).

## 3. ACUX Recommender

### 3.1. ACUX-R Architecture

ACUX-R has been developed following a typical three-tier architecture, using Google's Android Studio and Flutter Software Development Kit (SDK) (see Figure 1):

- PRESENTATION tier, the GUI of ACUX-R, where the end-user (i.e., the cultural visitor) interacts with the application. The Presentation tier is responsible for collecting from the user all the information required for their classification (into one or more visitor profiles) and for displaying the generated recommendations to them. For that purpose, ACUX-R provides an icon-based interface for swift and intuitive information input/output.
- DATA tier, where all the application information is stored and managed in a Firestore Google Database (as it is compatible with Flutter SDK). This information can be distinguished into three categories:
    ○ Content data, i.e., information about the available POIs (such as name, description, location, GPS data, or images).
    ○ User data, i.e., information regarding the user's visiting preferences and assigned profile, together with other personal information (e.g., account details).
    ○ Classification data: i.e., the knowledge required for classifying (i) the visitors and (ii) the POIs available, according to visiting preferences.
- LOGIC tier, which encapsulates the logic required to perform the tasks of user classification and subsequent recommendation of POIs. Implemented in Dart (https://dart.dev/, accessed on 8 September 2022), the LOGIC tier receives and processes information from the DATA tier using API calls and returns the recommendation outcome to the PRESENTATION tier.

**Figure 1.** The ACUX-R 3-tier architecture.

### 3.2. Recommendation Algorithm

The ACUX-R algorithm consists of three stages. In the first stage, the Classification stage (Section 3.2.1), the visitor is classified under one or more ACUX profiles according to their visiting preferences. In the second stage, the Adjustment stage (Section 3.2.2), the user is allowed to manually adjust their assigned profile(s), if desired, overriding the outcome of the Classification stage. In the third and final stage, the Recommendation stage (Section 3.2.3), the set of recommended POIs is calculated according to the user's final visiting profile, and the recommended POIs are presented as pins on a map and/or in the form of a list. Table 1 presents an overview of the ACUX-R algorithm.

**Table 1.** The ACUX-R recommendation algorithm.

| | |
|---|---|
| Classification stage | User **SELECT**s icons (minimum 5) <br> **FOREACH** selected icon <br> **ASSIGN** corresponding profile to user (multi-assign) <br> **FOREACH** profile assigned (at least once) <br> **CALCULATE** score (Equation (1)) <br> **DISPLAY** ACUX-R profile (as a set of scores) |
| Adjustment stage | **IF** user **NOT** satisfied with ACUX-R profile <br> User **UPDATE**s ACUX-R profile (manually) <br> **DISPLAY** final ACUX-R profile |
| Recommendation stage | **DETERMINE** recommended POIs (Equation (2)) <br> **DISPLAY** recommended POIs |

### 3.2.1. Classification Stage

The Classification stage is the initial stage of the recommendation algorithm, where the user's visiting profile is determined based on their visiting preferences. The user selects and provides as input information a set of icons (five or more) representing their visiting preferences. For example, the icons depicted in Figure 2 (from left to right: sculptures, galleries, arts and crafts, concert halls, and graffiti) represent the Art Seeker profile.

**Figure 2.** Icons visually representing the Art Seeker profile.

According to the specification of the ACUX typology [22], the various visiting preferences that form the ACUX profiles are not necessarily matched with a single profile. As such, the icons created in ACUX-R to represent those visiting preferences (forty in total) may correspond to multiple ACUX profiles. For example, the icon galleries, which represents the preference of visitors to visit galleries, is assigned to both the Archaeologist and the Art Seeker.

Next, based on the user's selected icons, a score is calculated for each ACUX profile as follows:

$$\text{foreach } i \\ \textbf{SCORE}_i = s_i/s \times 100 \quad (1)$$

where $i$ is the ACUX profile identifier, $s_i$ is the number of selected icons per ACUX profile, $s$ is the total number of selected icons ($s \geq 5$), and **SCORE**$_i$ is the score per ACUX profile, which is a number between 1 and 100.

For example, let's assume that Visitor1 selects the icons: museums, theatres, graffiti, lakes, distilleries, farms, and temples. According to the ACUX typology [22], museums are assigned both to the Archaeologist and the Art Seeker profiles, theatres and graffiti to the Art Seeker profile, lakes and farms to the Naturalist profile, distilleries to the Gourmand profile, and temples to both the Religious Seeker and the Archaeologist profile. As a result, Visitor1 is classified under the following profiles: Archaeologist with a score of 29 (2 out of 7 icons), Naturalist also with a score of 29 (2 out of 7 icons), Art Seeker with a score of 43 (3 out of 7 icons), Gourmand with a score of 14 (1 out of 7 icons), and Religious Seeker also with a score of 14 (1 out of 7 icons).

### 3.2.2. Adjustment Stage

At the Adjustment stage, the visitor can override the results of the Classification stage and adjust their generated ACUX-R profile manually, given that they are not completely satisfied with the profiling outcome. This is a non-obligatory stage and has been implemented by providing in the GUI a set of slider controls, which enable the user to increase or decrease the generated score for each ACUX profile.

Following the same example, let us assume that Visitor1 is satisfied with the score of the Religious Seeker, Art Seeker, and Naturalist profiles but wishes to adjust the score for the Gourmand and Archaeologist profiles in order to receive more recommendations for restaurants and breweries and fewer for archaeological destinations. Consequently, Visitor1 sets the Archaeologist score to 15 and the Gourmand score to 30.

3.2.3. Recommendation Stage

The Recommendation stage is the final stage of the ACUX algorithm, where the recommended POIs are specified based on the scores assigned in the previous stages. For each ACUX profile assigned to the user (i.e., for each ACUX profile with a non-zero score), one or more POIs are recommended as follows:

$$\text{foreach i whose SCORE}_i > 0 \\ \text{DISP}_i = \text{ROUNDUP}(\text{SCORE}_i/100 \times p_i, 0) \qquad (2)$$

where $p_i$ is the total number of POIs per ACUX profile, i is the ACUX profile identifier, $\text{DISP}_i$ is the number of recommended POIs per ACUX profile, and $\text{SCORE}_i$ is the generated score per ACUX profile. The total number of recommended POIs is the sum of $\text{DISP}_i$.

Finally, drawing on the same example, the recommended POIs are presented to the user as pins on a map and also in the form of a list sorted according to the score of the Archaeologist, Art Seeker, Religious Seeker, Naturalist, and Gourmand profiles.

**4. Evaluation**

To assess the usefulness of ACUX-R in practice, we conducted a user study and an online questionnaire survey. Fifty participants of various ages, educational backgrounds, and current professions were chosen to participate in the user study, including academic staff and students from Aegean University, Android, and iOS developers, and also members of the local community (Mytilene, Lesvos). In general, the participants were regular smartphone users who enjoyed traveling and who had already visited the city of Athens or were planning to do so in the near future. Their ages ranged between 20 and 55 years.

First, the participants were asked to submit their background information, including demographic data and level of familiarity with cultural-tourism MRSs and mobile applications in general. As a next step, participants were briefly informed about ACUX-R and instructed to download and install it on their mobile devices, following online instructions (http://ii.ct.aegean.gr/acux-evaluation/, accessed on 5 September 2022). Participants were advised to work in groups or individually. Finally, a discussion was held based on the following topics:

- Level of satisfaction with the features offered by the ACUX-R
- Level of satisfaction with the recommendations provided
- GUI usability
- Quality of provided POI information
- Suggestions for improvements.

As a next step, we conducted an online questionnaire survey. Thirty-five participants installed and used ACUX-R and then filled in a questionnaire (https://tinyurl.com/yayw3853, accessed on 9 September 2022) (Appendix A), which is a part of the User Experience Questionnaire (UEQ) data analysis tool [37,38]. Both classical usability aspects (efficiency, perspicuity, dependability) and user experience aspects (originality, stimulation) were measured. Each item of the UEQ consisted of a pair of terms with opposite meanings (e.g., not understandable to understandable, inefficient to efficient). Each item was rated on a 7-point Likert scale. Thus, answers ranged from −3 (fully agree with a negative term) to

+3 (fully agree with a positive term). This analysis yielded the final questionnaire with 26 items, arranged in six scales:

- Attractiveness: Do users like ACUX-R? Is it attractive, enjoyable, or pleasing?
- Perspicuity: Is it easy to get familiar with the ACUX-R? Is it easy to learn? Is ACUX-R easy to understand and unambiguous?
- Efficiency: Can users solve their tasks without unnecessary effort? Is the interaction with ACUX-R fast and efficient
- Dependability: Do users feel in control of the interaction? Can they predict the system's behavior? Do users feel confident when working with ACUX-R?
- Stimulation: Is it exciting and motivating to use ACUX-R? Does it capture the user's attention?
- Novelty: Is ACUX-R innovative and creative?

Then, the mean values per scale for ACUX-R are compared with the existing mean values per scale for other products from a dataset provided by the UEQ data analysis tool, which contains data from 21,175 people from 468 studies concerning different products (business software, web pages, mobile apps, social networks). The overall results of the ACUX-R mean values per scale compared to the UEQ data set are depicted in Table 2 and Figure 3.

**Table 2.** ACUX-R mean values per scale compared to the UEQ dataset.

| Scale | Mean | Comparison to UEQ Data Set |
|---|---|---|
| Attractiveness | 1.96 | Excellent |
| Perspicuity | 1.81 | Good |
| Efficiency | 1.84 | Good |
| Dependability | 1.03 | Below Average |
| Stimulation | 1.19 | Above Average |
| Novelty | 1.03 | Above Average |

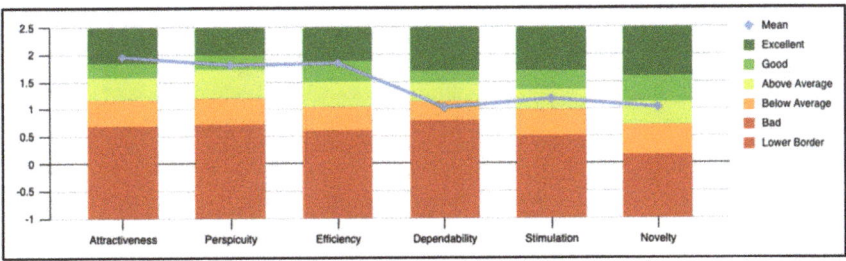

**Figure 3.** ACUX-R mean values per scale compared to the UEQ dataset.

In Table 3, the confidence interval per scale for the precision of the estimation of the scale mean is presented. The smaller the confidence interval, the higher the precision of the estimation and the reliability of the results.

**Table 3.** ACUX-R confidence intervals per scale.

| Scale | Mean | Std. Dev. | Confidence | Confidence Interval ||
|---|---|---|---|---|---|
| Attractiveness | 1.958 | 1.178 | 0.872 | 1.086 | 2.831 |
| Perspicuity | 1.813 | 1.201 | 0.890 | 0.923 | 2.702 |
| Efficiency | 1.844 | 1.260 | 0.934 | 0.910 | 2.777 |
| Dependability | 1.031 | 0.828 | 0.614 | 0.418 | 1.645 |
| Stimulation | 1.188 | 1.425 | 1.056 | 0.132 | 2.243 |
| Novelty | 1.031 | 1.333 | 0.987 | 0.044 | 2.018 |

In the user study conducted, ACUX-R was rated high in inspiration, excitement, interest, and enthusiasm. Most of the participants stated that they would like to get a diversified set of recommendations at the beginning when no further specific preferences are known to the system. Most of them stated that they chose recommendations based on the profile determined by ACUX-R, whereas only a few adjusted their profiles. Another issue discussed was that a future add-on of uploading images for profile classification could be overwhelming for most of the participants or lead to the absence of cultural features for a few of them. Moreover, most of the participants stated that even the best advice couldn't keep unexpected things from happening to cultural visitors while visiting a destination. For example, attractions may be temporarily closed due to inclement weather, and outdoor performances may be canceled. Finally, most participants appreciated the detailed information describing the ACUX profiles, which helped them understand why certain POIs had been recommended.

Regarding the online survey, the Stimulation and Novelty scales scored above average, indicating that, in general, found ACUX-R motivating and creative. Moreover, positive ratings on the Perspicuity and Efficiency scales indicate that ACUX-R usability features met or exceeded high criteria. The Dependability rating was below average, indicating that several participants experienced security and confidence difficulties. Finally, the Attractiveness scale was rated excellent, implying that the icon-based approach results in a pleasant experience.

## 5. Conclusions and Future Research

In this paper, we proposed the ACUX Recommender (ACUX-R), an MRS for personalized recommendations of cultural POIs to visitors based on their visiting preferences. The ACUX-R experimentally employs the ACUX typology for assigning profiles to cultural visitors. To assess the usefulness of ACUX-R in practice, a user study and an online questionnaire survey were conducted.

The evaluation showed that ACUX-R satisfied cultural visitors as it successfully captured their nonverbal visiting preferences and needs. Most of the participants stated that they agreed with the recommended POIs provided, whereas some adjusted their profiles.

In the future, we are planning to enhance the icon-based representation of visiting preferences with more multimedia elements, such as audio or video. Another interesting feature would be to reutilize past recommendations by recording them in order to feed them to future visitors with similar profiles. Finally, social media, gamification, and AR tools will be utilized in order to boost the visitor's motivation to visit a cultural destination, further improving the usability and effectiveness of ACUX-R.

**Author Contributions:** Conceptualization, M.K.; methodology, M.K. and Y.C.; software, J.A.; validation, M.K. and J.A.; formal analysis, M.K. and J.A.; investigation, M.K.; resources, M.K. and J.A.; data curation, M.K., Y.C. and J.A.; writing—original draft preparation, M.K.; writing—review and editing, M.K., Y.C. and G.C.; visualisation, M.K. and J.A.; supervision, G.C.; project administration, M.K.; funding acquisition, M.K. All authors have read and agreed to the published version of the manuscript.

**Funding:** This research was co-financed by the European Union and Greek national funds through the Operational Program Competitiveness, Entrepreneurship, and Innovation, under the call RESEARCH CREATE INNOVATE (project name: CAnTi, project code: MIS—5056234).

**Institutional Review Board Statement:** Not applicable.

**Informed Consent Statement:** Not applicable.

**Data Availability Statement:** Not applicable.

**Conflicts of Interest:** The authors declare no conflict of interest.

## Appendix A. UEQ Questionnaire

Please fill out the following questionnaire for the assessment of the ACUX-R. The questionnaire consists of pairs of contrasting attributes that may apply to the product. The circles between the attributes represent gradations between the opposites. You can express your agreement with the attributes by ticking the circle that most closely reflects your impression.

For example:

This response would mean that you rate the application as more attractive than unattractive.

Please decide spontaneously. Don't think too long about your decision to make sure that you convey your original impression. Sometimes you may not be completely sure about your agreement with a particular attribute, or you may find that the attribute does not apply completely to the particular product. Nevertheless, please tick a circle in every line.

It is your personal opinion that counts. Please remember: there is no wrong or right answer!

Please assess the product now by ticking one circle per line.

|   | 1 | 2 | 3 | 4 | 5 | 6 | 7 |   |   |
|---|---|---|---|---|---|---|---|---|---|
| annoying | O | O | O | O | O | O | O | enjoyable | 1 |
| not understandable | O | O | O | O | O | O | O | understandable | 2 |
| creative | O | O | O | O | O | O | O | dull | 3 |
| easy to learn | O | O | O | O | O | O | O | difficult to learn | 4 |
| valuable | O | O | O | O | O | O | O | inferior | 5 |
| boring | O | O | O | O | O | O | O | exciting | 6 |
| not interesting | O | O | O | O | O | O | O | interesting | 7 |
| unpredictable | O | O | O | O | O | O | O | predictable | 8 |
| fast | O | O | O | O | O | O | O | slow | 9 |
| inventive | O | O | O | O | O | O | O | conventional | 10 |
| obstructive | O | O | O | O | O | O | O | supportive | 11 |
| good | O | O | O | O | O | O | O | bad | 12 |
| complicated | O | O | O | O | O | O | O | easy | 13 |
| unlikable | O | O | O | O | O | O | O | pleasing | 14 |
| usual | O | O | O | O | O | O | O | leading edge | 15 |
| unpleasant | O | O | O | O | O | O | O | pleasant | 16 |
| secure | O | O | O | O | O | O | O | not secure | 17 |
| motivating | O | O | O | O | O | O | O | demotivating | 18 |
| meets expectations | O | O | O | O | O | O | O | does not meet expectations | 19 |
| inefficient | O | O | O | O | O | O | O | efficient | 20 |
| clear | O | O | O | O | O | O | O | confusing | 21 |
| impractical | O | O | O | O | O | O | O | practical | 22 |
| organized | O | O | O | O | O | O | O | cluttered | 23 |
| attractive | O | O | O | O | O | O | O | unattractive | 24 |
| friendly | O | O | O | O | O | O | O | unfriendly | 25 |
| conservative | O | O | O | O | O | O | O | innovative | 26 |

## References

1. Alexandridis, G.; Chrysanthi, A.; Tsekouras, G.E.; Caridakis, G. Personalized and Content Adaptive Cultural Heritage Path Recommendation: An Application to the Gournia and Çatalhöyük Archaeological Sites. *User Model. User Adapt. Interact.* **2019**, *29*, 201–238. [CrossRef]

2. Kanoje, S.; Girase, S.; Mukhopadhyay, D. User Profiling Trends, Techniques and Applications. *arXiv* **2015**, arXiv:1503.07474.
3. Missaoui, S.; Kassem, F.; Viviani, M.; Agostini, A.; Faiz, R.; Pasi, G. LOOKER: A Mobile, Personalized Recommender System in the Tourism Domain Based on Social Media User-Generated Content. *Pers. Ubiquitous Comput.* **2019**, *23*, 181–197. [CrossRef]
4. Nguyen, T.N.; Ricci, F. A Chat-Based Group Recommender System for Tourism. *Inf. Technol. Tour.* **2018**, *18*, 5–28. [CrossRef]
5. Christodoulou, Y.; Konstantakis, M.; Moraitou, E.; Aliprantis, J.; Caridakis, G. Personalized Artistic Tour Using Semantic Web Technologies. Available online: https://ceur-ws.org/Vol-2412/paper3.pdf (accessed on 24 November 2022).
6. Gavalas, D.; Kenteris, M. A Web-Based Pervasive Recommendation System for Mobile Tourist Guides. *Pers. Ubiquitous Comput.* **2011**, *15*, 759–770. [CrossRef]
7. Boulaalam, O.; Aghoutane, B.; Ouadghiri, D.E.; Moumen, A.; Malinine, M.L.C. Design of a Tourism Recommendation System Based on User's Profile. In *International Conference on Advanced Intelligent Systems for Sustainable Development*; Springer: Berlin/Heidelberg, Germany, 2019; pp. 217–223.
8. Aksenov, P.; Kemperman, A.; Arentze, T. A Personalised Recommender System for Tourists on City Trips: Concepts and Implementation. In *Intelligent Interactive Multimedia Systems and Services 2016*; Springer: Berlin/Heidelberg, Germany, 2016; pp. 525–535.
9. Jawaheer, G.; Weller, P.; Kostkova, P. Modeling user preferences in recommender systems: A classification framework for explicit and implicit user feedback. *ACM Trans. Interact. Intell. Syst.* **2014**, *4*, 1–26. [CrossRef]
10. Zins, A.H. Exploring Travel Information Search Behavior beyond Common Frontiers. *Inf. Technol. Tour.* **2007**, *9*, 149–164. [CrossRef]
11. Walsh, D.; Clough, P.; Foster, J. User Categories for Digital Cultural Heritage. In Proceedings of the First International Workshop on Accessing Cultural Heritage at Scale, Newark, UK, 22 June 2016; Volume 1611, pp. 3–9.
12. Çağil Hale, Ö.; Kozak, N. Motive based segmentation of the cultural tourism market: A study of Turkish domestic tourists. *J. Qual. Assur. Hosp. Tour.* **2012**, *13*, 165–186.
13. McKercher, B. Towards a Classification of Cultural Tourists. *Int. J. Tour. Res.* **2002**, *4*, 29–38. [CrossRef]
14. Vong, F. Application of cultural tourist typology in a gaming destination–Macao. *Curr. Issues Tour.* **2016**, *19*, 949–965. [CrossRef]
15. Grün, C.; Neidhardt, J.; Werthner, H. Ontology-Based Matchmaking to Provide Personalized Recommendations for Tourists. In *Information and Communication Technologies in Tourism 2017*; Schegg, R., Stangl, B., Eds.; Springer International Publishing: Cham, Switzerland, 2017; pp. 3–16.
16. Smith, M. Holistic Holidays: Tourism And The Reconciliation of Body, Mind and Spirit. *Tour. Recreat. Res.* **2003**, *28*, 103–108. [CrossRef]
17. Seaton, A.V. Tourism as Metempsychosis and Metensomatosis: The Personae of Eternal Recurrence. In *The Tourist as a Metaphor of the Social World*; CABI: Wallingford, UK, 2002; pp. 135–168.
18. Gibson, H.; Yiannakis, A. Tourist Roles: Needs and the Lifecourse. *Ann. Tour. Res.* **2002**, *29*, 358–383. [CrossRef]
19. Antoniou, A. Social Network Profiling for Cultural Heritage: Combining Data from Direct and Indirect Approaches. *Soc. Netw. Anal. Min.* **2017**, *7*, 1–11. [CrossRef]
20. Ricci, F.; Rokach, L.; Shapira, B. Introduction to Recommender Systems Handbook. In *Recommender Systems Handbook*; Springer: Berlin/Heidelberg, Germany, 2011; pp. 1–35.
21. Neidhardt, J.; Schuster, R.; Seyfang, L.; Werthner, H. Eliciting the Users' Unknown Preferences. In Proceedings of the 8th ACM Conference on Recommender Systems, Foster City, CA, USA, 6–10 October 2014; ACM: New York, NY, USA, 2014; pp. 309–312.
22. Konstantakis, M.; Christodoulou, Y.; Alexandridis, G.; Teneketzis, A.; Caridakis, G. ACUX Typology: A Harmonisation of Cultural-Visitor Typologies for Multi-Profile Classification. *Digital* **2022**, *2*, 365–378. [CrossRef]
23. Ricci, F.; Rokach, L.; Shapira, B. Recommender Systems: Introduction and Challenges. In *Recommender Systems Handbook*; Ricci, F., Rokach, L., Shapira, B., Eds.; Springer: Boston, MA, USA, 2015; pp. 1–34. [CrossRef]
24. Burke, R.; Ramezani, M. Matching Recommendation Technologies and Domains. In *Recommender Systems Handbook*; Springer: Berlin/Heidelberg, Germany, 2011; pp. 367–386.
25. Neidhardt, J.; Seyfang, L.; Schuster, R.; Werthner, H. A Picture-Based Approach to Recommender Systems. *Inf. Technol. Tour.* **2015**, *15*, 49–69. [CrossRef]
26. Goldberg, L.R. An Alternative "Description of Personality": The Big-Five Factor Structure. *J. Pers. Soc. Psychol.* **1990**, *59*, 1216. [CrossRef] [PubMed]
27. Sertkan, M.; Neidhardt, J.; Werthner, H. PicTouRe-A Picture-Based Tourism Recommender. In Proceedings of the Fourteenth ACM Conference on Recommender Systems, Virtual, 22–26 September 2020; ACM: New York, NY, USA, 2020; pp. 597–599. [CrossRef]
28. Drosatos, G.; Efraimidis, P.S.; Arampatzis, A.; Stamatelatos, G.; Athanasiadis, I.N. Pythia: A Privacy-Enhanced Personalized Contextual Suggestion System for Tourism. In Proceedings of the 2015 IEEE 39th Annual Computer Software and Applications Conference, Taichung, Taiwan, 1–5 July 2015; Volume 2, pp. 822–827.
29. Vansteenwegen, P.; Souffriau, W.; Berghe, G.V.; Van Oudheusden, D. The City Trip Planner: An Expert System for Tourists. *Expert Syst. Appl.* **2011**, *38*, 6540–6546. [CrossRef]
30. Kenteris, M.; Gavalas, D.; Economou, D. An Innovative Mobile Electronic Tourist Guide Application. *Pers. Ubiquitous Comput.* **2009**, *13*, 103–118. [CrossRef]

31. Roinioti, E.; Pandia, E.; Konstantakis, M.; Skarpelos, Y. Gamification in Tourism: A Design Framework for the TRIPMENTOR Project. *Digital* **2022**, *2*, 191–205. [CrossRef]
32. Vassilakis, C.; Poulopoulos, V.; Wallace, M.; Antoniou, A.; Lepouras, G. TripMentor Project: Scope and Challenges. In Proceedings of the CI@SMAP 2019, Larnaca, Cyprus, 9 June 2019.
33. Herzog, D.; Laß, C.; Wörndl, W. Tourrec: A Tourist Trip Recommender System for Individuals and Groups. In Proceedings of the 12th ACM Conference on Recommender Systems, Vancouver, BC, Canada, 2 October 2018; Association for Computing Machinery: New York, NY, USA, 2018; pp. 496–497.
34. Figueredo, M.; Ribeiro, J.; Cacho, N.; Thome, A.; Cacho, A.; Lopes, F.; Araujo, V. From Photos to Travel Itinerary: A Tourism Recommender System for Smart Tourism Destination. In Proceedings of the 2018 IEEE Fourth International Conference on Big Data Computing Service and Applications (BigDataService), Bamberg, Germany, 26–29 March 2018; pp. 85–92.
35. Logesh, R.; Subramaniyaswamy, V. Exploring Hybrid Recommender Systems for Personalized Travel Applications. In *Cognitive Informatics and Soft Computing*; Springer: Berlin/Heidelberg, Germany, 2019; pp. 535–544.
36. Meehan, K.; Lunney, T.; Curran, K.; McCaughey, A. Context-Aware Intelligent Recommendation System for Tourism. In Proceedings of the 2013 IEEE International Conference on Pervasive Computing and Communications Workshops (PERCOM Workshops), San Diego, CA, USA, 18–22 March 2013; pp. 328–331.
37. Laugwitz, B.; Held, T.; Schrepp, M. Construction and Evaluation of a User Experience Questionnaire. In *Symposium of the Austrian HCI and Usability Engineering Group*; Springer: Berlin/Heidelberg, Germany, 2008; pp. 63–76.
38. Schrepp, M.; Thomaschewski, J.; Hinderks, A. Construction of a Benchmark for the User Experience Questionnaire (UEQ). *Int. J. Interact. Multimed. Artif. Intell.* **2017**, *4*, 40–44. [CrossRef]

 *big data and cognitive computing*

*Article*

# Big Data Analytics for Search Engine Optimization

**Ioannis C. Drivas** [1,*], **Damianos P. Sakas** [2], **Georgios A. Giannakopoulos** [1] **and Daphne Kyriaki-Manessi** [1]

[1] Department of Archival, Library and Information Studies, Lab of Information Management, University of West Attica, Ag. Spyridonos, 12243 Egaleo, Greece; gian@uniwa.gr (G.A.G.); dkmanessi@uniwa.gr (D.K.-M.)
[2] School of Applied Economics and Social Sciences, Agricultural University of Athens, Iera Odos 75, 11855 Athens, Greece; d.sakas@aua.gr
\* Correspondence: idrivas@uniwa.gr; Tel.: +30-69-7401-6823

Received: 8 March 2020; Accepted: 30 March 2020; Published: 2 April 2020

**Abstract:** In the Big Data era, search engine optimization deals with the encapsulation of datasets that are related to website performance in terms of architecture, content curation, and user behavior, with the purpose to convert them into actionable insights and improve visibility and findability on the Web. In this respect, big data analytics expands the opportunities for developing new methodological frameworks that are composed of valid, reliable, and consistent analytics that are practically useful to develop well-informed strategies for organic traffic optimization. In this paper, a novel methodology is implemented in order to increase organic search engine visits based on the impact of multiple SEO factors. In order to achieve this purpose, the authors examined 171 cultural heritage websites and their retrieved data analytics about their performance and user experience inside them. Massive amounts of Web-based collections are included and presented by cultural heritage organizations through their websites. Subsequently, users interact with these collections, producing behavioral analytics in a variety of different data types that come from multiple devices, with high velocity, in large volumes. Nevertheless, prior research efforts indicate that these massive cultural collections are difficult to browse while expressing low visibility and findability in the semantic Web era. Against this backdrop, this paper proposes the computational development of a search engine optimization (SEO) strategy that utilizes the generated big cultural data analytics and improves the visibility of cultural heritage websites. One step further, the statistical results of the study are integrated into a predictive model that is composed of two stages. First, a fuzzy cognitive mapping process is generated as an aggregated macro-level descriptive model. Secondly, a micro-level data-driven agent-based model follows up. The purpose of the model is to predict the most effective combinations of factors that achieve enhanced visibility and organic traffic on cultural heritage organizations' websites. To this end, the study contributes to the knowledge expansion of researchers and practitioners in the big cultural analytics sector with the purpose to implement potential strategies for greater visibility and findability of cultural collections on the Web.

**Keywords:** cultural analytics; cultural data; search engine optimization; SEO strategy; SEO factors; big data; websites visibility; predictive modeling; website security; website load speed; user behavior

## 1. Introduction

Over the last 10 years, big data analytics has been called "the oil" for optimizing the digital ecosystem and, subsequently, the World Wide Web sphere. Untamed big data with enormous volume and velocity are generated regarding the interactions of users with search engines and websites and how they respectively react to the search results and the content they receive. Search engines, search results, and websites express a cause-and-effect relationship under their main purpose of existence. This purpose is related to the provision of the highest volume of information, in the best time, with the most precise results, according to the users' search terms.

In the context of the Big Data era, search engine optimization (SEO) plays a crucial role in the potential dissemination of personalized content that reflects quality. This quality is related to the curation of content and proper usability in the Web-based systems in order to cover users' information needs. SEO's main purpose is related to the provision of strategic steps to Web developers and content creators to optimize websites for higher rankings in search results and, hence, greater organic traffic that comes from search engines.

Nevertheless, despite the large volume of datasets and analytics that are produced and related to website performance and users' behavior inside them, the research field for utilizing big data analytics for strategic SEO schemas still remains in infancy. Several reasons are related with this research gap, such as symptoms of data overloading and, hence, difficulties in preprocessing, analysis, visualization, and interpretation of the outcomes. Subsequently, another drawback is related with the reduced managerial capabilities to understand the intercorrelations between the semantic Web analytics metrics and how they are aligned to SEO purposes. Another difficult point is the absence of methodological mechanisms that articulate validity, reliability, and consistency regarding the variables that are taken into consideration, with the purpose to optimize visibility of websites. Against this backdrop, this paper presents a novel methodological approach for utilizing big data analytics related to website performance and how they contribute to the SEO goal, which is an increase in organic search engine traffic percentage. We implement this methodology in the cultural heritage domain.

Cultural heritage institutions (CHIs) and their content in both the physical and digital worlds represent the social desire to preserve and cross-link the legacy of former generations in today's world, reflecting the ancestral identity of each society. Cultural institutions such as museums, galleries, libraries, and archives support the democratization of cultural heritage. They shape and reinforce the cultural and educational background of the people, while their mission is to combine the fragmented pieces of history depending on the society they belong to and serve. The information communication technologies and the Web expand the opportunities for cultural institutions to attract more stakeholders, both in physical and in online environments. This fact strengthens their scope for providing cultural knowledge to interested parties, global, national, and local communities, educating them in a quite attractive way through websites [1]. This involves a shift from traditional approaches of *keep and protect* to *experience and engage* in the era of digital humanities [2–4].

From a managerial perspective, the purpose of websites is to improve awareness, increase interest about artifacts, and holistically enhance the online visibility and findability of cultural collections. However, the nature of cultural heritage websites means that they deal with massive amounts of datasets, such as a high volume of internal webpages, links, images, and depth in user exploration and experience. This raises difficulties for managers to handle large-scale collections, increasing uncertainty about the level of visibility that cultural websites have on the Web. In this respect, it is a necessity to propose a SEO framework that utilizes generated big data analytics about CHI websites and their performance. In this way, the decision-makers in CHIs will benefit from a well-informed toolbox supportive of efforts to increase cultural content visibility on the Web.

To this end, this study unfolds in four parts. Firstly, we describe in a detailed manner the SEO factors that we assume impact the organic search engine visit percentage. After that, the methodology unfolds in three different stages. First, we summarize and validate the extracted big data analytics. Subsequently, we proceed into the development of diagnostic exploratory models that estimate the cause-and-effect relationships between the proposed factors. In the third stage of the methodology, we describe the initial steps for predictive model development and simulation for optimizing organic search engine traffic. The paper continues with the presentation and interpretation of results. Lastly, the discussion and conclusions are presented, suggesting practical managerial implications for the optimization of CHI websites in terms of performance, visibility, and findability on the Web.

## 2. The Nature of Cultural Heritage Websites

According to Wilson [5], in every cultural heritage institution (CHI), the first main purpose is the management of the cultural material they contain. The second purpose is to make that material accessible to everyone who wants to see it. Indeed, even from prior studies at the infancy phase of the Web, up to recent approaches, CHIs have utilized the opportunities of Web presence via websites in order to expand the visibility and accessibility of their cultural heritage content [2,3,6–8]. Websites under the paternity of CHIs constitute a vital online channel that improves awareness and expands capacities for visitation [7]. At the same time, it gives the advantage of presenting cultural information that is able to exceed by far that available at the physical place. Subsequently, research efforts by Voorbij [9] and Marty [10] demonstrated that the user experience across websites leads to better-prepared visitors and also to enhanced post-visit experience in terms of the meaning and interpretation they attribute to cultural collections.

However, the utilization of websites for CHIs with the purpose to optimize the visibility of their artifacts on the Web is not a straightforward and easy road. The CHI websites are constituted by massive amounts of datasets related to architectural aspects, such as the high number of webpages they contain, hundreds of images, thousands of internal and external interlinks, and so on. In this respect, prior efforts noted that the growth trend of digitizing artifacts is not sufficient or organized for the accurate retrieval of cultural information in large-scale Web-based collections. More specifically, this challenges visitors to face (a) overloading symptoms of the provided cultural heritage information [11] and/or (b) lack of cultural information due to low level of findability and visibility [12,13].

The two issues referred to above reflect the scarcity of an effective SEO approach that could be measured in a quantifying way to increase the accuracy of information retrieval from CHI websites. This statement has also been supported by a recent report by Krstic and Maslikovic. [2]. They showed that only one-third of their examined cultural institutions confirmed the utilization of analytics platforms for the evaluation and optimization of user experience during content search and navigation through digital collections. This kind of evaluation, intended to reinforce content that suffers from low levels of findability and visibility, becomes even more complex as CHI websites are characterized by the massive sizes of their content.

### 2.1. The Size of Cultural Heritage Websites

The size of cultural heritage websites can be set under the context of the Vs of big data. They contain a massive volume of cultural information integrated into unique webpages, images, and hyperlinks. At the same time, a huge number of visitors engage with the content, generating almost real-time behavioral datasets with high velocity. In terms of variety, different kinds of datasets from different smart devices are produced. This kind of data variety is related to web analytics metrics of interaction with the cultural content. Other kinds are related to unstructured datasets, such as images uploaded on social networks and text from reviews, as regards visitor opinion about cultural artifacts and their online representation [14]. Regarding the value of the produced big cultural analytics data, this is mostly related to the key point indicators that cultural institutions determine for their growth over time. For instance, the behavioral datasets generated from visitor engagement with the e-shop of the museum indicate economic value from data utilization. Similarly, the utilization of the generated datasets regarding the performance of CHI websites and their level of visibility in search engines point out societal and educational value. That is, the higher the visibility and findability, the greater the possibilities for passing on cultural heritage information to stakeholders for the improvement of their educational level.

Regardless of the type of organization, the larger it is, the greater the possibilities to utilize web data analytics strategies for potential evaluation and enhancement of its online presence [15]. However, big data analytics bring big troubles. It should be noted that the existence of a website with massive content and, thus, high volume of data production does not necessarily mean increased availability of suggestions and solutions for strategic SEO planning.

In the Big Data era, the latter assumption signals a contradictory element against prior efforts stating that "content is king" [16,17]. Controversially, the bigger the content, the harder the manipulation and the identification of technical and behavioral factors that probably influence the website's performance in terms of its visibility and findability in search engine result pages. In fact, it is practically more manageable to optimize a website that contains up to 100 webpages, rather than a website with thousands of webpages, images, and, hence, complexity in link architecture. Preliminary findings of our research indicate that CHI websites are characterized by massive size in terms of webpages, links, and images (Table 1 and Figures 1–4).

However, although prior studies have shown that the implementation of SEO strategies returns higher rankings and possibly better organic traffic [16,18,19], it remains unclear whether the size of the website affects the organic search traffic percentage, that is, the bigger the content of the website in terms of webpages, images, internal, and external links, the greater the percentage of organic search engine traffic. This implication led us to develop the first hypothesis:

**Hypothesis (H1).** *The size of cultural heritage institutional websites impacts the percentage increase of organic search engine traffic that they receive.*

**Table 1.** Descriptive statistics from the examined 171 unique cultural heritage institution websites.

| Descriptives per Unique Domain | Number of Webpages | Number of Images | Number of Internal Links | Number of External Links |
|---|---|---|---|---|
| Mean | 835.77 | 509.74 | 1502.61 | 577.5 |
| Min | 36 | 47 | 163 | 29 |
| Max | 2088 | 1368 | 2716 | 2360 |
| Std Dev | 390.53 | 302.96 | 542.49 | 461.4 |

$N = 171.$

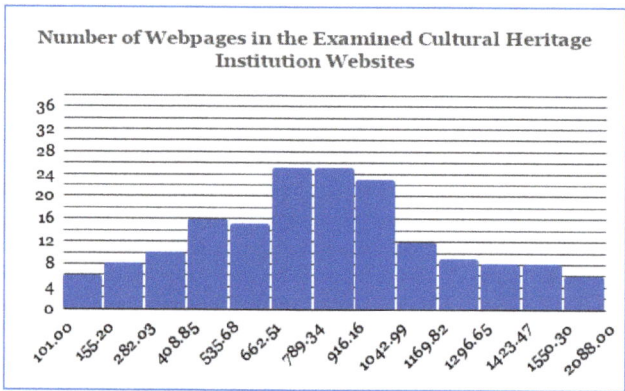

**Figure 1.** Histogram of the number of unique webpages that the examined CHI websites contain. The horizontal axis indicates the numerical amount of unique webpages that the examined websites contain. The vertical axis demonstrates how many websites contain from 101 up to 2088 unique webpages. For instance, there are 16 websites of the total 171 that ranged from 408 up to 535 unique webpages and 25 of the total 171 websites that ranged from 662 up to 789 unique webpages.

The first hypothesis and the implication that the size of a website leads to higher or lower organic search engine traffic raises a new research question. This is related with SEO technical compatibility factors, whether CHI websites follow them, and to what extent. There are prior approaches indicating that Google employs more than 250 closely guarded secret factors in its ranking algorithm [18,20]. However, quite a few studies [16,18,19,21,22] have investigated only some of them. This fact is probably linked to the until-that-time managerial inability of the retrieval of large-scale datasets regarding technical and behavioral factors that influence organic search engine traffic percentage.

Against this backdrop, big data analytics offers new opportunities in strategic SEO planning and deployment. The data gathered through application program interface (API) integration and preprocessing, result in a plurality of technical and behavioral SEO variables that probably impact the percentage variance in the organic search engine traffic of CHI websites. Based on principal component analysis, we divided these technical and behavioral variables into four additional factors: SEO Crawling, Website Loading Speed, Website Security Condition, and User Behavior.

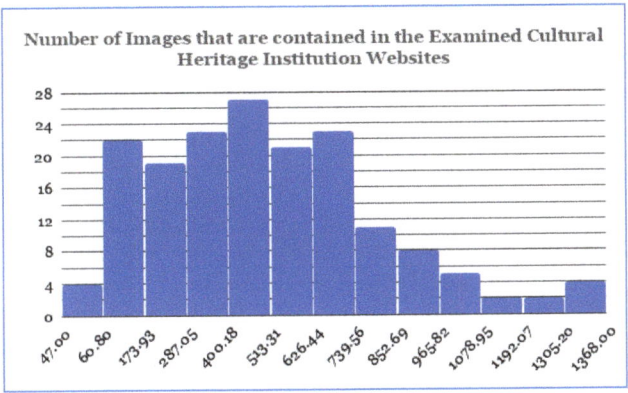

**Figure 2.** Histogram of the number of images that the examined CHI websites contain. The horizontal axis indicates the numerical amount of images that the examined websites contain. The vertical axis demonstrates how many websites contain from 47 up to 1368 images. It is noted that 408 up to 513 images represented the greatest number of websites, with a sample of 27 of the total 171 domains.

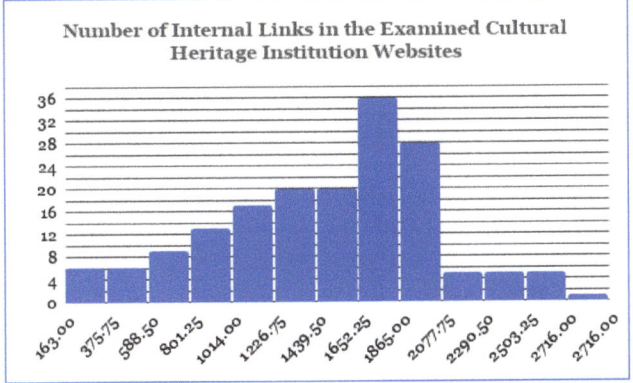

**Figure 3.** Histogram that explains the number of internal links included in the examined cultural heritage websites. Of the total, 36 websites ranged from 1652 up to 1865 internal links that allow users to navigate from one webpage to another with the purpose to provide cultural heritage content.

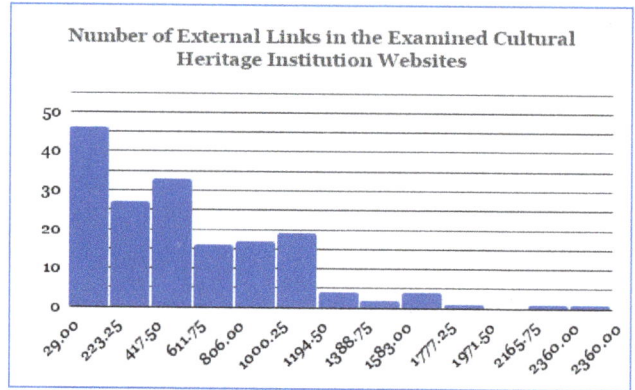

**Figure 4.** In contrast with the internal links, this histogram indicates that most of the cultural heritage institution websites do not contain a large number of external links inside their websites that allow users to navigate outside of them. Indeed, 45 of the total 171 websites ranged from 29 up to 223 external links.

*2.2. SEO Crawling*

Even from the initial approaches to identify SEO technical factors and make them comprehensible [23,24] up to the latest research implications [25–27], there are multiple de facto variables that are taken into consideration and impact the search engine rankings. These variables are related to the existence of Page Title tags [2,16,19,24,25], Meta-Descriptions [25–28], or Headings [2,23,28]. Others concentrate on aspects related to Technical Curation of Content. These are the Alt-tags on images, the prevention of duplicated page content, its re-use and repeatability, and a proper mobile scaling setup for better friendliness and adaptiveness to mobile devices [2,26,27].

Other SEO crawling variables focus on URL Diligence and their appropriate structure [25,28,29]. Link Condition, such as avoiding broken pages or setting 404 error pages for redirections [26,28], is another aspect. The Code Validity and how friendly it is to the crawlers and their indexing process is another key component. This factor investigates the availability of specific back-end files that make the crawling process more efficient, including robots.txt integration, sitemap locations, and appropriate hypertext markup language (HTML), JavaScript, and cascading style sheets (CSS) architecture [26,30–32]. These prior research efforts have demonstrated the optimization of search ranking positions.

Nevertheless, it is not yet clear whether the aforementioned factors correspond (and to what extent) to the optimization of organic search engine percent of traffic, that is, the higher the SEO technical compatibility of the websites with these variables, the higher the percentage of organic search engine traffic. Therefore, our second hypothesis is the following:

**Hypothesis (H2).** *The SEO Crawling factor impacts the percentage increase of organic search engine traffic in the websites of cultural heritage institutions.*

*2.3. Website Loading Speed*

According to Google [33], when a website improves its loading time, visitors become more engaged and their interaction with the content is increased. The number of clicks is increased and more conversions come, including sign-up forms, or purchasing products. Controversially, low loading speed could lead to reduced user–content interaction. For instance, the BBC News found that they lost up to 10% of their visitors for every additional second that their website took to load up their content [34]. On the other hand, the COOK case study as a growing business in food industry showed that, after reducing the average loading time of their website by 850 milliseconds, conversions increased by up to 7%, pages per session increased by up to 10%, and the bounce rate decreased down to 7% [33]. Indeed, slow loading speed returns almost immediate abandonments from websites, leading users to jump to other ones with better loading speed performance.

Prior studies paid attention to some key technical issues that have significant effects on website loading speed and, therefore, on a pleasant or unpleasant navigational experience for users [2,32]. Enge and colleagues indicated the negative impact on user experience as being the longer the loading time, the shorter the visit duration and, hence, the higher the bounce rate. The key technical issues are related mostly with the compression and minification of JavaScript and CSS files and the proper architecture of link redirections inside and outside the websites [22,26,29,35–37]. Therefore, it should be examined whether the compatibility of a website with loading speed time variables is associated with an enhanced organic search engine percent of traffic. That is, the higher the percentage rates of the Website Loading Speed factor, the higher the percentage increase of organic search engine traffic. Thus, our third hypothesis unfolded as follows:

**Hypothesis (H3).** *The Website Loading Speed factor impacts the percentage increase of organic search engine traffic in the websites of cultural heritage institutions.*

*2.4. Website Security Condition*

Browsers such as Chrome or Mozilla encourage web developers to follow both fundamental and advanced security policies in their websites [38,39]. In more than a few cases, cultural heritage institutions contain online shops inside their websites. This fact demands the establishment of security technologies that foster visitor convenience to explore and buy products. In addition, visitors interact with the online cultural information and sometimes submit their personal information for further services and/or potential news and updates. From a managerial point of view, the compatibility of CHI websites with security factors ensures the reputation of the cultural organizations and prevents malware and cyberattacks that will inevitably cost economic resources for rectification and recovery.

A fundamental aspect regarding the security condition of a website is related to the existence of Hypertext Transfer Protocol Secure (HTTPS) and password and contact forms secured with reCaptcha. Other website security factors are related with the hiding of server version data, avoiding in this way the indication of what software is running on the Web server. Moreover, the use of clickjack and content sniffing protection and the settlement of Multipurpose Internet Mail Extensions (MIME) to help browsers prevent content sniffing exploits are other vital factors in terms of website security condition [39].

The practical community, such as the Open Web Application Security Project (OWASP), suggests that the aforementioned variables need to be taken into serious consideration for protecting not only websites, but also cloud-based software applications [40,41]. Nevertheless, to the best of our knowledge, there is no prior clear substantiation as to whether the website security condition impacts (and to what extent) the organic search engine percent of traffic. Apparently, there are some indications about the importance of security factors in the SEO context [22,35]. However, little is known as regards the impact of security factors on the percentage increase of organic search engine traffic. In this respect, our fourth hypothesis is the following:

**Hypothesis (H4).** *The Website Security Condition factor impacts the percentage increase of Organic Search Engine Traffic in the websites of cultural heritage institutions.*

*2.5. User Behavior*

In 2012, Agarwal and colleagues introduced a semantic schema for potential personalization of content to future users based on the behavior and interactions of prior users [42]. More specifically, they proposed that the higher the engagement with the content in terms of time of interaction and depth of exploration, the greater the content for provision to potential users. Three years later, Mavridis and

Symeonidis [20] argued that search engines try to capture user interactions inside websites in order to provide feedback and optimize ranking algorithms. In the Big Data era, a necessity arises regarding the transformation of behavioral data into semantic schemas aiming at greater personalization and optimization of the World Wide Web by the people, for the people. Indeed, analytics platforms such as Google Analytics transform behavioral patterns into semantic web analytics metrics for better visualization and clear comprehension of the total user experience inside the websites.

These Web analytics metrics were previously mentioned in prior research, including Pages per Visit [19,29,32], Visit Duration [32,35,42], Total Clicks in a specified time period, and percent of immediate abandonment of the websites through the Bounce Rate metric [2,26,34,42]. All the aforementioned prior studies significantly designated these behavioral metrics as variables that numerically evaluate the interaction and experience of users inside websites. However, clear results are missing to indicate whether User Behavior inside websites impacts any forthcoming increase of the organic search engine percent of visits. That is, the greater the interaction, the higher the percentage of organic search engine traffic. Consequently, our fifth and final hypothesis is the following:

**Hypothesis (H5).** *The User Behavior factor impacts the percentage increase of organic search engine traffic in the websites of cultural heritage institutions.*

In Figure 5, we present our proposed model, depicting in this way the hypothesized relationships among the factors that probably increase the organic search engine visit percent; that is, "the higher the rates of the proposed factors, the higher the percentage of search engine visits will be". In the next section, the methodology unfolds with the purpose to answer our research questions.

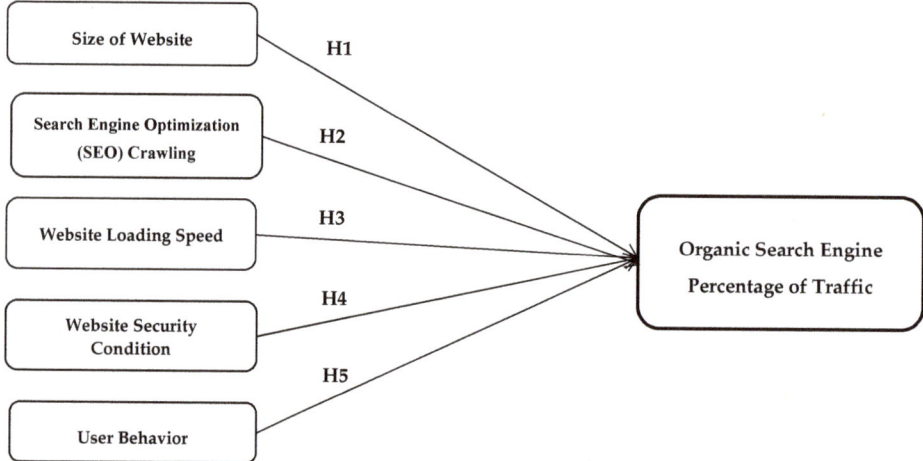

**Figure 5.** The proposed research model. Each of the proposed factors might have a different impact on the increase of the organic search engine percentage of traffic.

## 3. Methodology

The purpose of this paper is to present a novel methodology that measures and evaluates the impact of five factors, namely, the Size of Websites, SEO Crawling, Website Loading Speed, Website Security Condition, and User Behavior, on the optimization of the organic search engine percent of traffic. That is, we investigate which of these factors, and to what extent, have an impact on the number of organic visitors to CHI websites that explicitly come from search engines. In order to answer this research question, we deploy a three-stage methodology (Figure 6) composed of the following:

1. The summarization, validation, and alignment of the retrieved big data analytics with the organizations' defined key performance indicators (KPIs);
2. The development of diagnostic exploratory models that estimate the cause-and-effect relationships between the metrics;
3. The predictive model development and the process of simulation for optimization purposes.

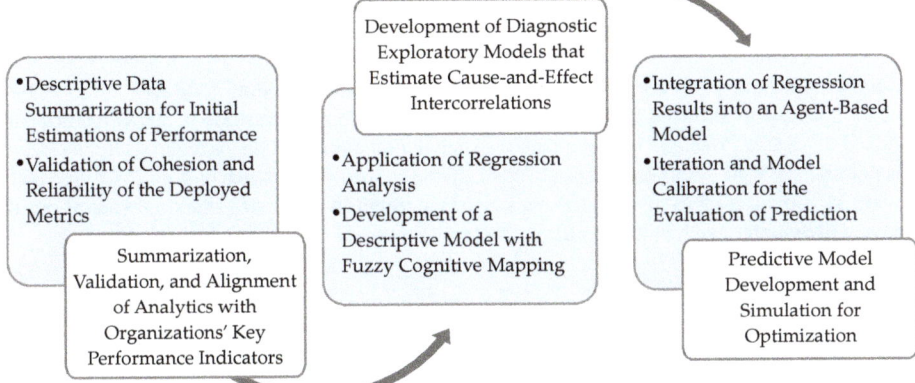

**Figure 6.** Representation of the proposed methodological approach. Each step supports the analysts and decision-makers of cultural institutions to retrieve, validate, organize, and utilize big data analytics in order to improve their online visibility and findability.

This methodological approach is able to tackle several issues derived from big data analytics utilization for optimization purposes. The first stage reflects efforts to cover drawbacks regarding managerial difficulties to utilize big data analytics in a more efficient way, while improving their veracity for further exploration. Moreover, the first stage corresponds to the process of aligning analytics metrics with the KPIs of cultural institutions and their Web presence. For example, in this study, the KPI is the increase of organic search engine traffic percent, which is aligned with all the Web metrics that are included in the five factors and probably affect the KPI itself.

The second stage gives the advantage of understanding through a quantified framework of evaluation the performance of a Web-based system and the possible intercorrelations between metrics. This gives the advantage of focusing on the critical ones while neglecting the less important. The third stage—inherited by the two previous stages—expands the opportunities to develop data-driven predictive models and simulations in all modeling steps. These models are composed with higher levels of validity and reliability and, hence, better precision of predictions.

### 3.1. Summarization, Validation, and Alignment with KPIs

In the context of big data analytics utilization, one of the most common issues is the question of whether more efficient decisions require more data or better models. This assumption returns back to the phenomena of exploring and trying to find hidden valuable gems in *big datasets* but with unfortunately *small stats*. As not all datasets are created in an equal way, we argue that neither volume of data nor better models affect the decision-making processes. Controversially, we assume that the testing process of validity, reliability, cohesion, and consistency of the extracted datasets is the first and most important thing. Besides, in the systems world, the quality of the inputs (data) always affects the outputs (models).

3.1.1. Data Sample and Preprocessing

The retrieval of big data analytics was implemented through the integration and parameterization of three different APIs. The Search Console URL API was used to retrieve data about the size of CHI websites, incorporating for exploration the number of webpages, images, and internal and external links for each of the examined 171 domains. Google Arts & Culture Database [43] was used to capture the number of websites that were investigated. An aggregated volume of 141,851 webpages, 86,788 image path files, and 254,373 internal and 97,626 external links was retrieved from all the websites.

The Checkbot API was used to encapsulate the compatibility of technical factors, namely, SEO Crawling, Website Loading Speed, and Website Security Condition. Further parameterization was applied in the API in order to explore and discover technical patterns in the HTML, JavaScript, and CSS code that were mentioned in previous research studies but not contained in the API's initial capabilities. A scale from 0 to 100 was implemented for each one of the retrieved variables as a useful managerial approach to tackle complexity in CHI website performance measurement [2,32,44,45]. In total, 9405 unique instances were retrieved for the 55 examined variables, ranging from 0% to 100%. Additionally, we utilized the Similar Web API for the retrieval of behavioral data analytics as regards Organic Search Clicks per Month, Visit Duration, Pages per Visit, and Bounce Rate for each of the 171 CHI websites that were investigated. This kind of API was also integrated in order to gather statistics about the percentage of organic search engine traffic each website receives.

3.1.2. Validation and Reliability

Consequently, statistical analysis was implemented for validation and to ensure the reliability of the extracted variables included in each factor. This was to give a clear perception of the levels of cohesion and consistency among them. Subsequently, dimension reduction was used with principal component analysis (PCA). Preliminary test analysis was performed on the first 25 percent of all examined websites (43/171) in order to ensure that there was no kind of violation of the assumption of data normality and linearity in their nature [46,47]. A second meta-analysis was performed on the full dataset to further ensure its normality and linearity.

Furthermore, Kaiser–Meyer–Olkin (KMO) testing was performed with the purpose to ensure that the retrieved datasets were suitable for principal component analysis and potential categorization [47]. The closer the value of KMO to 1, the greater the suitability of the extracted data for PCA, and vice versa. In Table 2, the examined factors are presented with reference to the factor loading for each variable, descriptive statistics, KMO, and percent of total variance explained.

Some variables with loadings below the limit of 0.500 were dropped. These are shown with a strikethrough line. Recognizing the contribution of the statistical tests to information for decision-makers, it is noted that they are applied here with the purpose of evaluating suitability for optimizing CHI website performance and organic search engine traffic percentage.

3.2. Development of Diagnostic Exploratory Models

Linear regression was implemented for the development of diagnostic exploratory models that estimate the cause-and-effect relationship between the five factors and their impact on organic search engine percent of traffic. Through this statistical approach, decision-makers will be able to understand in a clear manner the impact of each one of the proposed factors on the total change in organic search engine traffic percentage. Moreover, it is crucial to present a practical, manageable, and comprehensible methodological framework that dynamically demonstrates the intercorrelations between the factors and the defined KPIs [44,45,48]. This will also prevent the phenomenon of "*more metrics than users*" indicated by a plethora of prior approaches inside web-based systems for visualizing performance [49]. In order to achieve this, we adopted the descriptive modeling method of Fuzzy Cognitive Mapping (FCM).

FCM is used to visualize more intuitively and effectively the relationships between factors through an understandable representation of these correlations. This can be applied through the settlement of numerical weights (of +1 or −1) for each relationship of the proposed descriptive model [50]. The ease of construction and visualization, and the ease of understanding even by non-technicians, are further advantages of adopting the FCM [51]. In addition, the deployment of the FCM as a descriptive modeling method is characterized as a prerequisite step for the potential development of data-driven predictive models and simulations [51].

FCM provides a macro-level view of the examined system by aggregating and articulating the causal influence amongst the included entities [51,52]. More specifically, FCM demonstrates the correlations among the included factors and subfactors and how each one contributes to another [52].

This constitutes a process of feeding back to the administrators of CHI websites for them to understand in a manageable way the impact of each factor on increase or decrease in the organic search engine percent of traffic (Figure 7). Moreover, it should be noted that ranking algorithms change over time; hence, so do the factors that should be considered to increase or decrease organic search engine traffic. In this respect, FCM imparts flexibility in adding more factors and subfactors into the existed aggregated model, without new modifications that cause holistic restructuring of the descriptive situation within the model itself.

However, it is a commonly known fact that FCM constitutes an aggregated but stable macro-level approach, while missing individual and temporal explicitness at the micro-level without expressing system dynamic changes [53–55]. That is, in our case, each of the examined cultural heritage institution websites has its own performance over time relating to the technical factors and how users behave with the provided content. In order to predict and simulate possible optimization of the organic search engine percent of traffic while including temporal dynamic variances, agent-based modeling (ABM) is an appropriate method for predictive model development. Figure 7 illustrates the cause-and-effect relationships between the five proposed factors and the organic search engine traffic percent through the FCM method and its development via Mental Modeler cloud-based software.

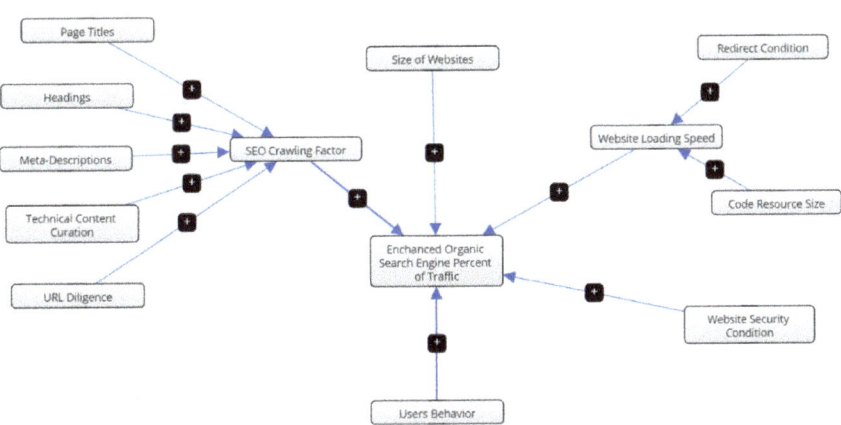

**Figure 7.** Fuzzy Cognitive Mapping integration as a descriptive, aggregated, and macro-level modeling method for representing the impacts among the examined factors on the percentage increase of Organic Search Engine Traffic.

*3.3. Predictive Model Development and Simulation for Optimization*

For the development of a predictive model and simulation run that forecasts the optimization of organic search engine traffic percent based on the impact of each factor, we proceeded with the agent-based modeling (ABM) approach. In ABM, a system is modeled as a collection of autonomous decision-making entities—the agents—while depicting relationships between them, acting via if–then rules [54,56]. The adoption of ABM as a micro-level simulation modeling strategy allows decision-makers to accomplish the following:

- Realize the full potential of the data that a cultural organization has about their online visitors and website performance. In our case, this gives a better perception of the utility of the extracted big data analytics about the performance of websites in terms of their Size, SEO Crawling, Loading Speed, and Security compatibilities. At the same time ABM expands the opportunities to utilize behavioral datasets about user engagement with the proposed content in order to provide them with even more personalized cultural information.

- Understand the organizations—in this case, each examined CHI website—from the viewpoint of not only the services that they contain, but also activities and how users interact with the services; that is, what visitors actually do inside the cultural websites, as each visitor produces different numerical values regarding time and depth of exploration.
- Exploit the flexibility that ABM gives to organizations in terms of model construction. Highlighting its practical contribution, ABM offers the opportunity for decision-makers to construct their own model. In this way, they are able to combine entities based on the prior retrieved big datasets [56,57] and their domain knowledge and experience in the management of cultural heritage institutions. This also provides complementary flexibility to the parameterization of the model and sustainability in the entities that it contains. Indeed, as SEO topics and ranking algorithms change rapidly, ABM is more flexible in adding new factors, rather than explaining the relationships of the new factors via structured differential equations [54,58].

In the next section we present the results of the study and the integration of both the descriptive and predictive models though FCM and ABM, respectively.

## 4. Results

As can be seen in Table 2, most of the variables in every factor resulted in sufficient loadings. This also indicates a sufficient extent of relevance of variables in explaining the construct of each of the proposed factors. However, there were six variables that resulted in factor loadings of less than 0.500. They are depicted in the table with a strikethrough line. We decided to exclude them from the regression analysis and their involvement as independent variables in the impact that they have on the dependent variable, namely, the organic search engine visit percent. Regarding the percent of variance explained in each factor, most of them expressed considerable variability, reaching up to 55%.

**Table 2.** Descriptives and internal validity and consistency of the examined factors and their variables.

| Factors and Items | Loading | Mean | SD | KMO | % of Variance Explained |
|---|---|---|---|---|---|
| Size of Website | | - | - | | |
| Pages | 0.758 | 834.97 | 392.97 | | |
| Images | 0.884 | 508.31 | 305.14 | 0.718 | 57.63 |
| Internal links | 0.906 | 1502.61 | 542.49 | | |
| External links | 0.609 | 577.5 | 461.4 | | |
| SEO Crawling | | 72.04 | 38.48 | | |
| Page Titles | 0.753 | 73.89 | 29.36 | | |
| Set page titles | 0.746 | 98.49 | 31.62 | 0.72 | 59.68 |
| Use optimal-length titles | 0.845 | 66.57 | 32.26 | | |
| Use unique titles | | 56.63 | 38.67 | | |
| Page Headings | | 62 | 37.65 | | |
| Set H1 headings | 0.912 | 77.64 | 32.26 | | |
| Use one H1 heading per page | 0.755 | 60.64 | 38.67 | 0.679 | 66.85 |
| Use optimal-length H1 headings | 0.883 | 73.84 | 31.97 | | |
| Use unique H1 headings | 0.702 | 36.88 | 33.45 | | |
| Page Meta-Descriptions | | 32.09 | 36.06 | | |
| Set page meta-descriptions | 0.903 | 48.32 | 40.6 | | |
| Use optimal-length meta-descriptions | 0.843 | 26.08 | 31.62 | 0.707 | 63.91 |
| Use unique meta-descriptions | 0.714 | | | | |
| | | 23.32 | 29.97 | | |

Table 2. Cont.

| Factors and Items | Loading | Mean | SD | KMO | % of Variance Explained |
|---|---|---|---|---|---|
| *Page Content Technical Curation* | | 81.26 | 31.92 | | |
| Avoid thin-content pages | 0.778 | 78.57 | 29.78 | | |
| Set image ALT text | 0.687 | 62.9 | 42.21 | 0.721 | 68.87 |
| Set mobile scaling | 0.839 | 87.61 | 30.47 | | |
| Avoid plugins | 0.727 | 98.59 | 8.25 | | |
| Avoid duplicate page content | 0.881 | 78.84 | 27.12 | | |
| *URL Diligence* | | 79.5 | 32.04 | | |
| Use short URLs | 0.795 | 83.52 | 21.47 | | |
| Avoid URL extensions | 0.753 | 80.8 | 35.64 | | |
| Avoid URL parameters | 0.665 | 76.89 | 27.71 | | |
| Avoid symbols in URLs | 0.669 | 95.41 | 16.21 | 0.679 | 59.14 |
| Set canonical URLs | 0.721 | 28.25 | 43.01 | | |
| Use lowercase URLs | 0.487 | 87.25 | 27.26 | | |
| Avoid underscores in URLs | 0.637 | 90.43 | 23.68 | | |
| Avoid deeply nested URLs | 0.288 | 94.43 | 16.09 | | |
| *Link Condition* | | 80.06 | 35.05 | | |
| Use 404 code for broken URLs | 0.847 | 85.76 | 33.39 | | |
| Avoid broken internal links | 0.663 | 73.22 | 37.92 | 0.754 | 60.02 |
| Avoid broken external links | 0.555 | 79.24 | 35.41 | | |
| Avoid broken page resources | 0.711 | 83.7 | 32.77 | | |
| *Code Validity and Crawling* | | 69.8 | 41.86 | | |
| Valid HTML | 0.762 | 30.67 | 39.66 | | |
| Valid CSS | 0.935 | 98.46 | 4.2 | | |
| Valid JavaScript | 0.712 | 99.19 | 7.72 | | |
| Avoid excessive inline JavaScript | 0.579 | 83.8 | 32.26 | 0.692 | 64.8 |
| Avoid render-blocking JavaScript | 0.701 | 18.28 | 36.88 | | |
| Avoid excessive inline CSS | 0.547 | 96.36 | 18.08 | | |
| Avoid CSS @import | 0.74 | 92.39 | 19.72 | | |
| Use of robots.txt file | 0.759 | 83.17 | 35.82 | | |
| Use of Sitemap locations | 0.874 | 25.23 | 43.24 | | |
| *Website Loading Speed* | | 79.11 | 34.61 | | |
| Code Resource Size | | 82.76 | 30.18 | | |
| Use compression | 0.816 | 78.18 | 39.08 | 0.728 | 56.11 |
| Avoid recompressing data | 0.372 | 96.83 | 15.89 | | |
| Use minification | 0.764 | 57.88 | 24.85 | | |
| Avoid inline source maps | 0.542 | 98.23 | 13.12 | | |
| *Redirect Conditions* | | 76.19 | 37.54 | | |
| Avoid internal link redirects | 0.652 | 42.49 | 45.06 | | |
| Avoid temporary redirects | 0.557 | 70.28 | 36.05 | 0.686 | 44.18 |
| Avoid redirect chains | 0.803 | 91.01 | 14.69 | | |
| Avoid meta redirects | 0.614 | 92.08 | 26.65 | | |
| Avoid resource redirects | 0.44 | 84.85 | 33.01 | | |
| *Website Security* | | 53.57 | 43.52 | | |
| Use HTTPS | 0.891 | 83.08 | 37.17 | | |
| Avoid mixed content | 0.385 | 94.26 | 17.58 | | |
| Use secure password forms | 0.584 | 92.89 | 24.81 | | |
| Use HSTS | 0.796 | 11.09 | 31.47 | | |
| Use HSTS preload | 0.621 | 2.31 | 15 | 0.781 | 64.96 |
| Use XSS protection | 0.663 | 15.83 | 36.3 | | |
| Use content sniffing protection | 0.86 | 32.66 | 41.92 | | |
| Set MIME types | 0.823 | 99.26 | 7.64 | | |
| Use clickjack protection | 0.877 | 49.33 | 49 | | |
| Hide server version data | 0.324 | 55.74 | 45.8 | | |

Table 2. Cont.

| Factors and Items | Loading | Mean | SD | KMO | % of Variance Explained |
|---|---|---|---|---|---|
| <u>User Behavior</u> | - | - | | | |
| Organic Clicks per Month | 0.968 | 266,851.00 | 71,147.00 | | |
| Visit Duration | 0.913 | 2.58 | 1.16 | 0.822 | 69.53 |
| Pages per Visit | 0.884 | 3.85 | 1.94 | | |
| Bounce Rate | 0.805 | 55.54 | 9.88 | | |
| *Organic Search Engine Percent of Traffic* | N: 171 | Min: 15.26 | Max: 89.80 | Mean: 62.76 | SD: 13.53 |

The underlines depict the factor and its items, the italics depict the sub-factors, and the strikethrough lines depict each dropped variable.

Linear regression analysis returned significant indications (Table 3). Prior preprocessing and analysis was conducted in order to exclude outliers that would possibly influence the outcomes of the prediction. We also note that no changes were observed when we used a hierarchical technique. From the results of the test, all the produced models have clear statistical significance with $p$ values less than 0.05. Nevertheless, there is a marginal exception in the factor of Website Loading Speed with a $p$ value of 0.061, greater than 0.05. In terms of $R^2$ values, the results depict alignment with prior studies stating that ranking algorithms involve a massive number of secret variables in the SEO context [20,48]. In fact, Size of Websites explained up to 30.06% of the variability of the response data around its mean; SEO Crawling, up to 17.7%; Website Loading Speed, up to 10.01%; Website Security Condition, up to 17.9%; and User Behavior, up to 29.5%.

Table 3. Regression analysis output.

| Variable | Coefficient | $R^2$ | F | $p$ Value |
|---|---|---|---|---|
| *Constant (Organic Search Engine Traffic Percent)* | 62.071 | 0.306 | 2.827 | 0.012 * |
| Size of Website | 1.060 | | | |
| Constant | 77.061 | 0.177 | 5.458 | 0.021 * |
| SEO Crawling | 2.141 | | | |
| Constant | 73.301 | 0.101 | 1.855 | 0.061 |
| Website Loading Speed | 1.115 | | | |
| Constant | 71.702 | 0.189 | 5.589 | 0.019 * |
| Website Security Condition | 1.361 | | | |
| Constant | 71.309 | 0.295 | 7.497 | 0.000 ** |
| User Behavior | 3.141 | | | |

N = 171. * and ** indicate statistical significance at the 95% and 99% levels, respectively.

Indeed, the more numerous the variables, the higher the model fit and, consequently, the $R^2$ values [59]. In other words, we defined some variables in each factor; however, all of them require further research to investigate even more variables that play a crucial role in the increase of the organic search engine traffic percent.

In terms of the first hypothesis, a significant regression equation was found with $p = 0.012$ and $R^2$ of 0.306. This means that the mean value of the organic search traffic percent is increased by 1.06% for every percentage point increase in each variable of the Size of Websites factor. For the second hypothesis, a significant regression equation was observed with $p = 0.021$ and $R^2$ of 0.177. This means that the mean value of the organic search traffic percent is increased by 2.14% for every percentage point increase in the percent of the SEO Crawling factor.

For the third hypothesis, a slightly nonsignificant regression equation was found with a marginal value of $p = 0.061$ and $R^2$ of 0.101. Even by bootstrapping of 1000 additional re-samples, there was no significant change in the $p$ value, $R^2$, or coefficients. Therefore, the mean value of the organic search traffic percent is increased by 1.11% for every percentage point increase in the Website Loading Speed factor. For the fourth hypothesis, Website Security Condition provided a significant regression equation with $p = 0.019$ and $R^2$ of 0.189. As a result, the mean value of the organic search traffic percentage is increased by 1.36% for every unit increase in the Website Security Condition factor.

For the last hypothesis, User Behavior in the examined cultural websites seems to have the highest impact on the increase in organic search engine traffic percent. More specifically, a significant regression equation was observed with $p = 0.000$ and $R^2$ of 0.295. Thus, the mean value of the organic search traffic percent is increased by 3.14% for every percentage point increase in each variable of the User Behavior factor. This constitutes an important research result. Prior research implied that search engines encapsulate user behavior in order to rank websites in their search engine result pages [20,48]. And indeed, the higher the ranking position of a website, the higher the organic search engine traffic percentage that they receive [18,19,60].

*Agent-Based Model Development*

The extracted outcomes of the regression statistics resulted in significant implications that could be incorporated into a predictive data-driven agent-based model. The purpose of ABM is to compute and represent each case individually at a micro-level view while taking into consideration temporal changes [53–55]. This is not possible through the aggregated macro-level approach of Fuzzy Cognitive Mapping.

For instance, in ABM, decision-makers are able to estimate the impact of each change in SEO performance and user behavior individually for each website. This advantage provides precise results regarding the impact that each SEO factor has for every website and also about the percentage variance of organic search traffic that the website receives. As all cultural websites differ in their content and how compatible they are with the SEO factors, it is possible to generate different data analytics, both technical and behavioral. This means that managerial staff need more or less time to rectify SEO issues and, therefore, to improve user behavior and enhance organic search traffic. In this case, ABM as a predictive modeling and simulation method gives risk-free flexibility to decision-makers. They are able to themselves define the time needed to keep up with the SEO compatibility framework and, thereafter, to improve their organic search traffic. This approach combines both managers' domain knowledge, as each cultural organization differs in its operations, and the practical insights of the data analytics results.

The first main goal of the proposed computational model is verification that the proposed methods and results can be used to optimize the organic search engine traffic percentage. The second goal is decrease of the bounce rate level as a negative indicator of the overall user behavior in the examined cultural heritage websites. In the next figure (Figure 8), we present the developed ABM, its entities, and its conditions. For model development, AnyLogic ver. 8.5.2 software was used in JAVA source code in order to compute agent behavior. We defined a specific time range of 90 days in order to predict and simulate the percentage increase of organic search engine traffic. No additional days were included as there was no other crucial percentage variance in the organic search engine and bounce rates.

The model starts in its initial stage with the possibility of entrance and visit inside the cultural heritage institution websites, an initial point that depicts fundamental aspects of the agent-based development process [54–56]. This is indicated in the first statechart, entitled "Potential Search Engine Users". The transition of users (as agents) among statecharts is computed based on the prior descriptive statistics of the study, such as min, max, mean, and mode, and the outcomes of the regression analysis. The impact level that users receive from the Size of Websites, the Website Loading Speed, and the Website Security is defined by the conditions of the Size of Websites Impact, Website Loading Speed Impact, and Website Security Impact. These three major factors and their defined conditions impact drastically on user behavior inside cultural heritage websites. However, as the regression results indicated, the Website Loading Speed factor does not impact the organic traffic percentage, so there is no kind of transition between the two statecharts. At the same time, the Size of Websites, Website

Security, and SEO Crawling factors are depicted as statecharts that impact both User Behavior and the final goal, which is positive influence of the Organic Search Engine Traffic Percentage.

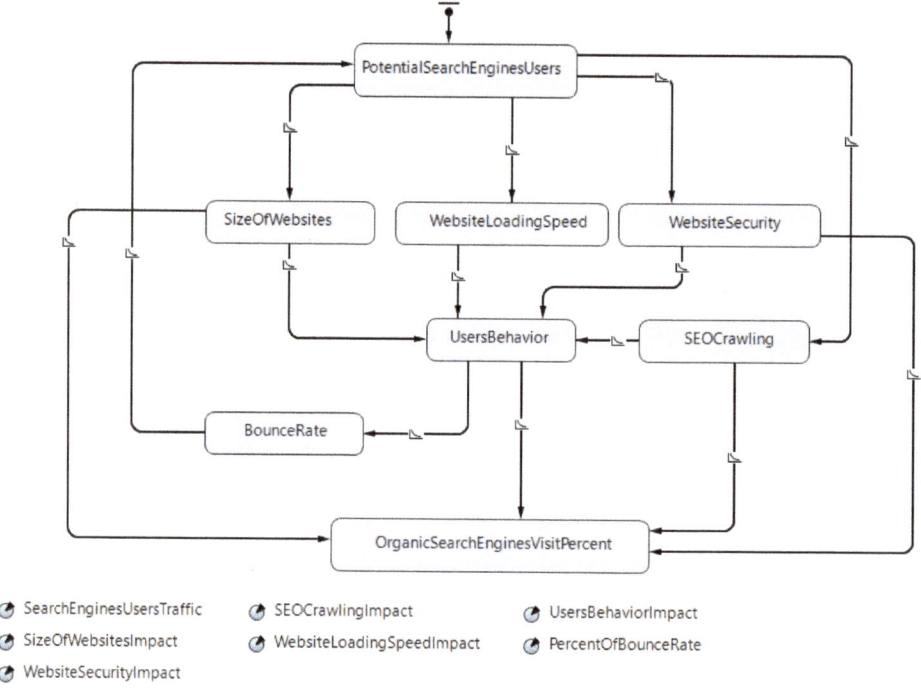

**Figure 8.** A predictive agent-based model for optimization of the organic search engine visit percentage and decrease of the bounce rate.

This kind of impact is computed through Poisson distributions, while setting up the results of the regression as lambda values ($\lambda$). The Poisson distribution was selected because our sample

(a) highlights predictive optimization in the specific time range of 90 for which the model runs;
(b) is generated by a known constant mean rate of values, most of them with the simplicity of a percentage; and,
(c) each one of the examined websites and their performance is completely independent and is not affected by the previous performances of the other websites.

Moreover, we define the consequence of low interaction rate and dissatisfied user behavior resulting in immediate abandonments via the bounce rate metric, which is illustrated through the Bounce Rate statechart and computed through the Percent of Bounce Rate condition. That is, users enter the websites, but they find insufficient content (Size of Websites), low speed of navigation (Website Loading Speed), and insufficient security in their exploration, so they leave the websites almost immediately upon their visit. In Figure 9 we present the outcomes of the predictive agent-based model.

The graph in Figure 9 represents the potential scenario of improving each of the examined factors based on the outcomes of the regression and their impact on the organic search engine traffic percentage and bounce rate level. Indeed, the model, after the initial days of the run, shows an improvement in organic search engine traffic. At the same time, a decrease and steadiness is observed in the bounce rate level without any significant sign of increase. Furthermore, it is noted that the Organic Search Engine Visit Percent does not show any further optimization after Day 50, following a straight line without any kind of fluctuation or change. This happens for two reasons. First the examined cultural websites are able to receive the rest of their visitors from paid advertising, social networks, direct traffic, email marketing campaigns, and other external websites. Secondly, it is possible for the managerial staff to cover and rectify all the SEO technical compatibility factors that are able to optimize the organic search traffic up to ~75%, as depicted in Figure 9. Therefore, new data analytics and regression results are needed in order to provide feedback, update the predictive model, and determine the potential extent of the percentage increase in organic search engine traffic.

**Figure 9.** Optimization of the organic search engine traffic percentage in a time range of 90 sequential days. The horizontal axis demonstrates the specific time range from 0 up to 90 days of the simulation run. The vertical axis depicts the percentage of organic search engine traffic.

## 5. Discussion and Future Implications

The optimization of visibility in cultural heritage websites improves the knowledge that stakeholders receive from them. More specifically, in an open and democratized way, CHI websites increase people's interest in the past and allow them to recognize how their surrounding societal context has changed over time. In this respect, the SEO strategy must be set within the prism of the overall mission of cultural heritage institutions, rather than assigning these functionalities unilaterally to technical staff. This will enhance the overall importance of SEO strategies from the support personnel to the upper management levels.

In this paper, we proposed a novel methodology that quantifies in a manageable way the impact of several factors on the organic search engine traffic percentage in CHI websites with the purpose of increasing visibility and findability. One step further, this methodology offers to the administrators of CHI websites an opportunity to convert data analytics about SEO performance into useful insights and actions for potential optimization of their visibility on the Web. Otherwise, a big data analytics framework without evaluation, analysis, interpretation, and suggestion for further improvement is completely useless [61]. Based on that, we believe that this research establishes a new SEO context of communication, as more and more big data analytics can be retrieved and interpreted, while focusing on critical factors and omitting less relevant ones in organic traffic optimization. In this respect, this methodology provides new opportunities both for managers in cultural institutions and for research on this topic.

*5.1. Managerial Implications for Cultural Heritage Institutions*

5.1.1. Implications for Optimized Website Performance and Visibility

The proposed model shows validity, reliability, and cohesion as regards the variables and factors that it contains for evaluation and, hence, optimization of organic search engine traffic. This works as a solid stepping stone for managers to adopt this methodology, evaluating the importance of each factor and focusing precisely on each one for further improvement. However, although the results of the obtained behavioral data analytics demonstrated that CHI websites receive on average up to 62.76% of their total traffic solely from search engines (Table 2), the bounce rate level was observed to reach up to 55%. This means that more than one in two visitors immediately abandon the websites after their visit.

Based on that, we suggest to marketing managers and administrators of cultural websites to focus first on usability improvement with the purpose to improve user interaction and behavior. The factor of SEO Crawling includes variables that might have crucial impacts for enhanced usability and user experience in CHI websites. The avoidance of thin or duplicated content, removal of broken links that confuse users, and proper mobile friendliness are some of these user-centered variables. Moreover, this factor includes variables that have a systemic impact on increasing search engine friendliness to crawlers. The appropriate curation of headings, titles, meta-descriptions, robots.txt, and sitemap files are some of the points that managers should focus on with the purpose to develop favorable conditions for the indexing process by search engines.

In this research, regression results show that user behavior has the highest impact among the factors that affect the percentage increase of organic search engine traffic (Table 3). Indeed, User Behavior can increase by up to 3.14% the total percentage of organic search traffic in the examined websites. Nevertheless, if the administrators do not pay greater attention to aligning their efforts firstly with the optimization of website usability, then the behavior of users and their experience will negatively affect the percentage of search engine traffic. Therefore, the managerial staff of cultural institutions must not focus only on SEO strategies that aim for ranking optimization; it is more important to improve usability for better engagement between users and content [60,62]. This will positively increase behavior and, thereafter, provide higher organic traffic percentages.

5.1.2. Utility of the Methodology

The proposed methodology not only supports managerial staff to seek an aggregated evaluation of a CHI website, it is also a flexible approach to focus on the individual performance of specific collections contained in unique webpages which unfortunately suffer from low visibility and findability on the Web. For instance, administrators could evaluate the SEO performance of specific webpages of cultural content while manipulating in a more efficient way the process of optimization in specific *parts* rather than the *whole*. This approach covers a rigorous and challenging task for cultural heritage institutions, as they have to deal with the large size of their content. Indeed, the larger the size of a web-based system, the more complex its manipulations and rectifications [12,19,45,54].

In addition, the outcomes of this methodology provide practical and educational implications for cultural institutions to avoid big data frameworks that rely more on data storage and not enough on their analysis. As the reliability of the gathered data constitutes a core value for the quality of a well-informed decision-making process [61], website analysts of cultural heritage websites should focus more on big data metrics systems that fit the following:

(a) Are aligned with their key performance indicators, such as improvement of organic search engine traffic or user engagement with the content [44,48]; and
(b) Gather reliable and veracious data that can be deployed in predictive model development and calibration [57,63].

Therefore, the proposed methodology offers the flexibility to tackle other problematic issues in the online presence of cultural heritage institutions, such as the proper utilization of analytics for social media optimization or cost-effective online paid advertising campaigns. That is, we proceed to the careful delimitation of KPIs; gather, validate, and examine the data analytics that align with the KPIs; and then develop data-driven predictive models for optimization.

5.1.3. Optimized Financing Resource Management

In the EU context, the Eurostat report of 2018 [64] depicted a low percentage of expenditures in cultural services ranging from 0.4% up to 0.8% of the GDP. Bearing in mind the reduced financial flexibility of cultural institutions and their limited available resources for the management of the cultural material that they contain, the process of search engine optimization could be a cost-effective marketing strategy.

In contrast with other digital marketing strategies that increase website visitor numbers but provide poor content curation and usability, SEO constitutes a sustainable digital marketing strategy that focuses on one of the most fundamental aspects of digital marketing: the effectiveness of the landing page. If users *land* in webpages that express usability and proper curation of content, then their experience will be better, making any kind of marketing communication strategy more effective. This constitutes a promising approach to reduce paid advertising strategies that do not eventually return the investment, due to the minimal interaction of users after visiting websites.

*5.2. Research Implications*

The dimension reduction results through principal component analysis indicated that most of these variables are suitable for providing reliable evaluations of website performance and the impact that they have on user behavior and organic search engine traffic. Notwithstanding, even if we include more than 50 variables that impact the organic search engine traffic optimization, the regression R-square values indicate the depth of search engine ranking algorithms and the multidimensionality of the variables they involve. Following the above findings, we have started further research efforts in order to explore and include more variables or factors that probably influence rankings and, hence, percentage variance in organic search engine visits. Based on this assumption, as big data mining and analytics techniques are getting more and more sophisticated and impact organizations' decision-making process in terms of marketing and promotion strategies [62], the research topic of SEO reliance in big data analytics will be discussed in a detailed manner in the future.

Regarding the predictive agent-based model development, from the initial research approaches as a computational method to describe the complexity of a system and its entities, to recent characterizations, it is referred to more as an art than as a science [56,58,65]. However, as big data analytics expand the opportunities for integrating more and more data into simulation models, the *art* is sidelined. Therefore, new research approaches are developed to overcome a lack of data and combine prior domain knowledge and analytics for logical well-informed and data-driven predictive models.

In this paper, we developed the ABM as a supportive tool that provides feedback to the managers of cultural heritage institutions regarding the impact of several factors on user behavior and organic search engine traffic percent. An abstraction level that describes the impact of each factor was developed. Nevertheless, predictive models are mostly stable in abstraction levels but unstable with larger perturbations when more conditions and entities are included. Therefore, further research is needed to evaluate predictive model efficiency through ABM when expanding the level of abstraction or integrating system dynamics approaches [66].

Furthermore, the results of the study emphasize the necessity to redefine the SEO topic. Apparently, the higher the compatibility of the SEO factors, the higher the rankings and search engine visit percentage. However, the main aim of search engines is confirmation that they provide the most qualitative content, in the highest volume, in the fastest time to their users, according to their search terms [67]. In this respect, Web developers and content creators should have practical quantified indicators in order to evaluate and optimize their website performance and content. Thus, we redefine SEO as it is not solely the process of rectification for higher search rankings. It is rather much more a *user-centric* strategy that improves the findability and visibility of information in search results and aims for integrated user experience inside websites.

**Author Contributions:** All the authors have contributed equally in this research effort in terms of the conceptualization, methodology, software, validation, formal analysis, investigation, resources, data curation, writing the original draft and writing review-editing. D.K.-M., G.A.G. and D.P.S. contributed to the supervision and project administration of this study. All authors have read and agreed to the published version of the manuscript

**Funding:** This research received no external funding.

**Acknowledgments:** Dedicated to those who fought against the covid-19, but did not make it. We heartily thank the guest editors of *Big Data Analytics in Cultural Heritage* for giving us this opportunity. We are also grateful to the Reviewers for their vital remarks. To conclude, we acknowledge the valuable technical contribution of Nikolaos Lazaridis for the provision of cutting-edge hardware helping us to work faster for this project.

**Conflicts of Interest:** The authors declare no conflict of interest.

## References

1. Di Franco, P.D.G.; Matthews, J.L.; Matlock, T. Framing the past: How virtual experience affects bodily description of artefacts. *J. Cult. Herit.* **2016**, *17*, 179–187. [CrossRef]
2. Krstić, N.; Maslikovič, D. Pain points of cultural institutions in search visibility: The case of Serbia. *Libr. Hi Tech News* **2018**, *37*, 496–512. [CrossRef]
3. Sarraf, S. A survey of museums on the web: Who uses museum websites? *Curator Mus. J.* **1999**, *42*, 231–243. [CrossRef]
4. Lykourentzou, I.; Antoniou, A. Digital innovation for cultural heritage: Lessons from the european year of cultural heritage. *SCIRES Sci. Res. Inf. Technol.* **2019**, *9*, 91–98. [CrossRef]
5. Wilson, D.M. What do we need money for? In *Money, Money, Money, and Museums*; Scottish Museums Council: Edinburgh, UK, 1991; p. 11.
6. Hume, M.; Mills, M. Building the sustainable iMuseum: Is the virtual museum leaving our museums virtually empty? *Int. J. Nonprofit Volunt. Sect. Mark.* **2011**, *16*, 275–289. [CrossRef]
7. Chiang, H.H.; Tsaih, R.H.; Han, T.S. Measurement development of service quality for museum websites displaying artifacts. In *Managing Innovation and Cultural Management in the Digital Era*; Routledge: Abingdon, UK, 2012; pp. 100–127.
8. Fantoni, S.F.; Stein, R.; Bowman, G. Exploring the relationship between visitor motivation and engagement in online museum audiences. *Museums and the Web*; San Diego, CA, USA, 11–14 April 2012. Available online: https://www.museumsandtheweb.com/mw2012/papers/exploring_the_relationship_between_visitor_mot (accessed on 2 April 2020).
9. Voorbij, H. The use of web statistics in cultural heritage institutions. *Perform. Meas. Metr.* **2010**, *11*, 266–279. [CrossRef]
10. Marty, P.F. Museum websites and museum visitors: Before and after the museum visit. *Mus. Manag. Curatorship* **2007**, *22*, 337–360. [CrossRef]
11. Ardissono, L.; Kuflik, T.; Petrelli, D. Personalization in cultural heritage: The road travelled and the one ahead. *User Model. User adapt. Interact.* **2012**, *22*, 73–99. [CrossRef]
12. Davoli, P.; Mazzoni, F.; Corradini, E. Quality assesment of cultural web sites with fuzzy operators. *J. Comput. Inf. Syst.* **2005**, *46*, 44–57. [CrossRef]
13. Schmitz, P.L.; Black, M.T. The Delphi toolkit: Enabling semantic search for museum collections. In Proceedings of the International Conference for Culture and Heritage Online, Toronto, CA, USA, 31 March 2008; Available online: http://www.archimuse.com/mw2008/papers/schmitz/schmitz.html (accessed on 2 April 2020).
14. Salah, A.A.; Manovich, L.; Salah, A.A.; Chow, J. Combining cultural analytics and networks analysis: Studying a social network site with user-generated content. *J. Broadcast. Electr. Media* **2013**, *57*, 409–426. [CrossRef]
15. Kaushik, A. *Web Analytics 2.0: The Art of Online Accountability and Science of Customer Centricity*; John Wiley & Sons: Hoboken, NJ, USA, 2009.
16. Gandour, A.; Regolini, A. Web site search engine optimization: A case study of Fragfornet. *Libr. Hi Tech News* **2011**, *28*, 6–13. [CrossRef]
17. Ryan, D.; Jones, C. *Digital Marketing: Marketing Strategies for Engaging the Digital Generation*; Kogan Page Ltd.: London, UK; Philedelphia, PA, USA, 2009.
18. Luh, C.J.; Yang, S.A.; Huang, T.L.D. Estimating Google's search engine ranking function from a search engine optimization perspective. *Online Inf. Rev.* **2016**, *40*, 239–255. [CrossRef]
19. Moreno, L.; Martinez, P. Overlapping factors in search engine optimization and web accessibility. *Online Inf. Rev.* **2013**, *37*, 564–580. [CrossRef]
20. Mavridis, T.; Symeonidis, A.L. Identifying valid search engine ranking factors in a Web 2.0 and Web 3.0 context for building efficient SEO mechanisms. *Eng. Appl. Artif. Intell.* **2015**, *41*, 75–91. [CrossRef]

21. Weideman, M.; Visser, E.B. Fusing website usability and search engine optimisation. *S. Afr. J. Inf. Manag.* **2014**, *16*, 1–9. [CrossRef]
22. Omprakash, K.S. Concept of search engine optimization in web search engine. *Int. J. Adv. Eng. Res. Stud.* **2011**, *1*, 235–237.
23. Chambers, R. Application of best practice towards improving Web site visibility to search engines: A pilot study. *S. Afr. J. Inf. Manag.* **2005**, *7*, 1.
24. Zhang, J.; Dimitroff, A. The impact of metadata implementation on webpage visibility in search engine results (Part II). *Inf. Process. Manag.* **2005**, *41*, 691–715. [CrossRef]
25. Mittal, A.; Sridaran, R. Evaluation of Websites' Performance and Search Engine Optimization: A Case Study of 10 Indian University Websites. In Proceedings of the 2019 6th International Conference on Computing for Sustainable Global Development (INDIACom), New Delhi, India, 13–15 March 2019; pp. 1227–1231.
26. Salminen, J.; Corporan, J.; Marttila, R.; Salenius, T.; Jansen, B.J. Using Machine Learning to Predict Ranking of Webpages in the Gift Industry: Factors for Search-Engine Optimization. In Proceedings of the 9th International Conference on Information Systems and Technologies, Cairo, Egypt, 24–26 March 2019; Volume 6, pp. 1–8. [CrossRef]
27. Gek, D.; Kukartsev, V.; Tynchenko, V.; Bondarev, A.; Pokushko, M.; Dalisova, N. The problem of SEO promotion for the organization's web representation. *SHS Web Conf.* **2019**, *69*, 00122. [CrossRef]
28. Khraim, H.S. The impact of search engine optimization on online advertisement: The case of companies using E-Marketing in Jordan. *Am. J. Bus. Manag.* **2015**, *4*, 76–84. [CrossRef]
29. Baye, M.R.; De los Santos, B.; Wildenbeest, M.R. Search engine optimization: What drives organic traffic to retail sites? *J. Econ. Manag. Strateg.* **2016**, *25*, 6–31. [CrossRef]
30. Shih, B.Y.; Chen, C.Y.; Chen, Z.S. Retracted: An empirical study of an internet marketing strategy for search engine optimization. *Hum. Factors Ergon. Manuf. Serv. Ind.* **2013**, *23*, 528–540. [CrossRef]
31. Dawson, A.; Hamilton, V. Optimising metadata to make high-value content more accessible to Google users. *J. Doc.* **2006**, *62*, 307–327. [CrossRef]
32. Al-Ananbeh, A.A.; Ata, B.A.; Al-Kabi, M.; Alsmadi, I. Website usability evaluation and search engine optimization for eighty Arab university websites. *Basic Sci. Eng.* **2012**, *21*, 107–122.
33. Why Performance Matters. Web Fundamentals. Available online: https://developers.google.com/web/fundamentals/performance/why-performance-matters (accessed on 4 March 2020).
34. How the BBC Builds Websites That Scale. Available online: https://developers.google.com/web/fundamentals/performance/why-performance-matters (accessed on 4 March 2020).
35. Enge, E.; Spencer, S.; Stricchiola, J.; Fishkin, R. *The Art of SEO*; O'Reilly Media, Inc.: Sevastopol, CA, USA, 2012.
36. Malaga, R.A. Worst practices in search engine optimization. *Commun. ACM* **2008**, *51*, 147–150. [CrossRef]
37. Egri, G.; Bayrak, C. The role of search engine optimization on keeping the user on the site. *Procedia Comput. Sci.* **2014**, *36*, 335–342. [CrossRef]
38. Communicating the Dangers of Non-Secure HTTP. Available online: https://blog.mozilla.org/security/2017/01/20/communicating-the-dangers-of-non-secure-http/ (accessed on 4 March 2020).
39. Why HTTPS Matters. Web Fundamentals. Available online: https://developers.google.com/web/fundamentals/security/encrypt-in-transit/why-https (accessed on 4 March 2020).
40. Modern Web Security Patterns OWASP. Available online: https://owasp.org/www-chapter-sacramento/assets/slides/20200117-modern-web-security-patterns.pdf (accessed on 4 March 2020).
41. Nigam, K.; Saxena, S.; Gupta, N. An analysis on improvement of website ranking using joomla. *IITM J. Manag. IT* **2015**, *6*, 69–72.
42. Agarwal, S.; Nishar, D.; Rubin, A.E. Providing Digital Content Based on Expected User Behavior. U.S. Patent US 8,271,413 B2, 18 September 2012.
43. Google Arts & Culture. Available online: https://artsandculture.google.com/ (accessed on 23 March 2020).
44. Saura, J.R.; Palos-Sánchez, P.; Cerdá Suárez, L.M. Understanding the digital marketing environment with KPIs and web analytics. *Future Internet* **2017**, *9*, 76. [CrossRef]
45. García, M.D.M.R.; García-Nieto, J.; Aldana-Montes, J.F. An ontology-based data integration approach for web analytics in e-commerce. *Expert Syst. Appl.* **2016**, *63*, 20–34. [CrossRef]
46. McFee, B.; Lanckriet, G.R. Metric learning to rank. In Proceedings of the 27th International Conference on Machine Learning (ICML-10), Haifa, Israel, 21–24 June 2010; pp. 775–782.

47. Dziuban, C.D.; Shirkey, E.C. When is a correlation matrix appropriate for factor analysis? Some decision rules. *Psychol. Bull.* **1974**, *81*, 358–361. [CrossRef]
48. Nakatani, K.; Chuang, T.T. A web analytics tool selection method: An analytical hierarchy process approach. *Internet Res.* **2011**, *21*, 171–186. [CrossRef]
49. Welling, R.; White, L. Web site performance measurement: Promise and reality. *Manag. Serv. Qual. Int. J.* **2006**, *16*, 654–670. [CrossRef]
50. Papageorgiou, E.I.; Salmeron, J.L. Learning fuzzy grey cognitive maps using nonlinear hebbian-based approach. *Int. J. Approx. Reason.* **2012**, *53*, 54–65. [CrossRef]
51. Glykas, M. *Fuzzy Cognitive Maps: Advances in Theory, Methodologies, Tools and Applications*; Springer Science & Business Media: Berlin/Heidelberg, Germany, 2010; Volume 247.
52. Van Vliet, M.; Kok, K.; Veldkamp, T. Linking stakeholders and modellers in scenario studies: The use of Fuzzy Cognitive Maps as a communication and learning tool. *Futures* **2010**, *42*, 1–14. [CrossRef]
53. Giabbanelli, P.J.; Gray, S.A.; Aminpour, P. Combining fuzzy cognitive maps with agent-based modeling: Frameworks and pitfalls of a powerful hybrid modeling approach to understand human-environment interactions. *Environ. Model. Softw.* **2017**, *95*, 320–325. [CrossRef]
54. An, L. Modeling human decisions in coupled human and natural systems: Review of agent-based models. *Ecol. Model.* **2012**, *229*, 25–36. [CrossRef]
55. Mehryar, S.; Sliuzas, R.; Schwarz, N.; Sharifi, A.; van Maarseveen, M. From individual Fuzzy Cognitive Maps to Agent Based Models: Modeling multi-factorial and multi-stakeholder decision-making for water scarcity. *J. Environ. Manag.* **2019**, *250*, 109482. [CrossRef]
56. Bonabeau, E. Agent-based modeling: Methods and techniques for simulating human systems. *Proc. Natl. Acad. Sci. USA* **2002**, *99* (Suppl. 3), 7280–7287. [CrossRef]
57. Kavak, H.; Padilla, J.J.; Lynch, C.J.; Diallo, S.Y. Big data, agents, and machine learning: Towards a data-driven agent-based modeling approach. In *Proceedings of the Annual Simulation Symposium*; Society for Computer Simulation International: Guildford/Surrey, UK, 2018; Volume 12, pp. 1–12. [CrossRef]
58. Barbati, M.; Bruno, G.; Genovese, A. Applications of agent-based models for optimization problems: A literature review. *Expert Syst. Appl.* **2012**, *39*, 6020–6028. [CrossRef]
59. Seber, G.A.; Lee, A.J. *Linear Regression Analysis*; John Wiley & Sons: Hoboken, NJ, USA, 2012; p. 329.
60. Rehman, K.U.; Khan, M.N.A. The foremost guidelines for achieving higher ranking in search results through search engine optimization. *Int. J. Adv. Sci. Technol.* **2013**, *52*, 101–110.
61. Ghasemaghaei, M.; Ebrahimi, S.; Hassanein, K. Data analytics competency for improving firm decision making performance. *J. Strateg. Inf. Syst.* **2018**, *27*, 101–113. [CrossRef]
62. Wedel, M.; Kannan, P.K. Marketing analytics for data-rich environments. *J. Mark.* **2016**, *80*, 97–121. [CrossRef]
63. Hair, J.F. Knowledge creation in marketing: The role of predictive analytics. *Eur. Bus. Rev.* **2007**, *19*, 303–315. [CrossRef]
64. Eurostat Statistics Explained. Total General Government Expenditure on Recreation, Culture and Religion, 2018 (% of GDP). Available online: https://ec.europa.eu/eurostat/statistics-explained/index.php?title=File:Total_general_government_expenditure_on_recreation,_culture_and_religion,_2018_(%25_of_GDP)_png (accessed on 23 March 2020).
65. Grignard, A.; Taillandier, P.; Gaudou, B.; Vo, D.A.; Huynh, N.Q.; Drogoul, A.G. 1.6: Advancing the art of complex agent-based modeling and simulation. In Proceedings of the International Conference on Principles and Practice of Multi-Agent Systems, Dunedin, New Zealand, 1–6 December 2013; pp. 117–131. [CrossRef]
66. Sarlis, A.S.; Drivas, I.C.; Sakas, D.P. Implementation and dynamic simulation modeling of search engine optimization processes. Improvement of website ranking. In *Strategic Innovative Marketing*; Springer: Cham, Switzerland, 2017; pp. 437–443. [CrossRef]
67. Drivas, I.C.; Sakas, D.P.; Reklitis, P. Improving Website Usability and Traffic Based on Users Perceptions and Suggestions—A User-Centered Digital Marketing Approach. In *International Conference on Strategic Innovative Marketing*; Springer: Cham, Switzerland, 2017; pp. 255–266. [CrossRef]

© 2020 by the authors. Licensee MDPI, Basel, Switzerland. This article is an open access article distributed under the terms and conditions of the Creative Commons Attribution (CC BY) license (http://creativecommons.org/licenses/by/4.0/).

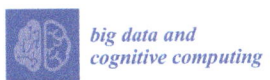 

Article

# Using Big and Open Data to Generate Content for an Educational Game to Increase Student Performance and Interest

**Irene Vargianniti [1] and Kostas Karpouzis [2],***

[1] Palladio School, 28is Oktovriou, 166 72 Vari, Greece; irene_vargianiti@hotmail.com
[2] Artificial Intelligence and Learning Systems Lab, National Technical University of Athens, 157 80 Athens, Greece
* Correspondence: kkarpou@cs.ntua.gr

Received: 25 September 2020; Accepted: 14 October 2020; Published: 22 October 2020

**Abstract:** The goal of this paper is to utilize available big and open data sets to create content for a board and a digital game and implement an educational environment to improve students' familiarity with concepts and relations in the data and, in the process, academic performance and engagement. To this end, we used Wikipedia data to generate content for a Monopoly clone called Geopoly and designed a game-based learning experiment. Our research examines whether this game had any impact on the students' performance, which is related to identifying implied ranking and grouping mechanisms in the game, whether performance is correlated with interest and whether performance differs across genders. Student performance and knowledge about the relationships contained in the data improved significantly after playing the game, while the positive correlation between student interest and performance illustrated the relationship between them. This was also verified by a digital version of the game, evaluated by the students during the COVID-19 pandemic; initial results revealed that students found the game more attractive and rewarding than a traditional geography lesson.

**Keywords:** big data; open data; game-based learning; education; geography; board games; monopoly

## 1. Introduction

### 1.1. Big Data in (and for) Education

In recent years, the abundance of online learning solutions both for children and adults has increased interest in taking advantage of the data they create. Data related to school attendance, performance, engagement and other factors are too big to handle using conventional processing techniques; in addition to this, they offer the opportunity to identify relationships and trends, which may not be otherwise evident, using data mining algorithms. As a result, the field of data analytics seems to be the most appropriate means to exploit them [1], mostly to predict student performance or interest [2], visualize information in a dashboard [3], either for school usage or for policy makers [4] or even to identify cognitive states in real-time, such as interest and fatigue [5]. In this context, ethics awareness becomes of the essence, since data mining, especially in social media, has been criticized as a channel which caters for targeted advertising and may promote dubious behavioral shifts; given that big data effectively expands the scope of educational measurement [6], it is important to educate young students about the underlying mechanics, the source of available big data (not necessarily related to education) and the means to easily collect meaningful and dependable data sets. In our work, we utilize a Game-Based Learning (GBL) approach to educate young students not only with respect to a specific school course, but also about the relationships between different entities from a Big Data set; this is also of great importance, in order to ensure that Big Data can be used and interpreted correctly [7–9].

World geography provides a handy introduction to Big Data for young students, since it incorporates diverse solitary information (e.g., Points of Interest, names of persons, etc.) and relational data, such as population and size; the latter is of major importance, since it can be used to illustrate ranking and grouping concepts between different entities (mainly countries or continents). Research shows that geographical education fosters critical thinking and increases environmental awareness [10–12]. Such skills can be cultivated by playing games, since cooperation, communication and critical thinking flourish in a playful environment, while games highly engage players and motivate the students [13–15]. Game-based learning [16] is designed to balance the content and mechanics of the game with the players' ability to transfer the concepts described in the game to the real world [17]; Prensky reports ([18]) that education and play are, indeed, interrelated. Conventional learning offers rich educational content, but little involvement, as opposed to games that sometimes promote fun, entertainment and flow, in exchange for reusable, transferable knowledge [19]. Moreover, the narrative of a game is manifested through goals and objectives that students have to accomplish in order to progress and succeed in it. Engagement is associated with learning outcomes [20–22] and motivation is considered games' fundamental elements [23]. Therefore, the game design process must be thorough, in order to engage and motivate students [24,25]. Even though literature reports quite a few examples of games having a positive effect on learning [26], this is not always the case [20]. Interest and fun can go hand in hand with learning, if we integrate educational games in the classroom, regardless of the students age group [27–30]. Today's generation have the unique opportunity to go beyond traditional means of education [31], hence, educators should use games to make learning fun and exciting but also more effective.

*1.2. Monopoly as a Serious Game*

Monopoly is one of the five most popular board games, licensed in more than 100 countries and printed in 37 languages [32]. Hasbro has produced or licensed different versions for cities, towns and regions and even for TV shows and Hollywood films. Custom-made Monopoly sets even played a role in World War II, when the British Secret Intelligence Service cooperated with the game's UK manufacturer to include genuine maps, compasses are real money, instead of the game's items, to sets delivered to prisoners via the Red Cross. Even though it is mostly considered an entertainment game, it was designed as an educational game, back in the early 20th century, by American game designer and author Elizabeth "Lizzie" Magie. Magie believed in the ideas of Henry George, an American political economist and journalist, who thought that land and natural resources should belong to the people who rent them, but never own them. Her game, called "Landlord's Game" consisted of a board with different properties, each with the distinct purchase price and rental value: in this context, the government charges tax not on profit or labor, but on the possession of land and whatever profit people can create through the investment of accumulated capital stays with them. Landlord's Game was initially rejected by one of the leading game manufacturers in the U.S. and was finally published by Parker Brothers in 1935, under the name "Monopoly" [33].

Monopoly employs several game objects and mechanics that associate them, the most prominent of which includes investing in property and re-using collected rent to build houses and hotels to increase the value of rent collected by visitors. In addition to property deeds, which correspond to street names in most Hasbro editions, players may invest in railroad stations and utility companies; as is the case with street properties, collecting more of the same kind increases the rent collected by visitors, along with the owner's chances of winning. Some of the squares in the board correspond to Chance cards, which may entail players paying taxes (players who have invested in many properties may be hurt substantially) or fund collection (redistribution of wealth) or even send players to Jail, where no rent can be collected by visitors in their properties. Chance cards, along with the use of dice that provide how many squares each player advances in each round, introduce a chance element; despite that, the dominant strategy to increase a player's chances of winning is to move early, invest in many properties and try to save funds to invest in more expensive properties, usually positioned towards the end of the boards. In general, positioning of street properties on the board implies a ranking mechanism: the price to invest in each property increases as one moves along the board and, in turn, the rent collected by visitors and, hence, the player's return on investment, increases as well [34].

*1.3. The Monopoly Game in Education*

The original properties and game mechanics included on Monopoly cater for quite a few educational uses, the most obvious of them having to do with how to save and spend money in order to invest and that investments in property may not always lead to fiscal success. There are also mechanics related to social play, with players being able to lend money to bail out their friends and prevent them from going bankrupt and leaving the game.

Another obvious use has been in the context of land and lodging development: O'Halloran and Deale [35] designed a version of Monopoly, along with the relevant teaching material, where the objective is to maximize one's asset value by developing hotels and then blocks of hotels. An interesting addition to the usual game mechanics of the original game was that, as the game was played over a semester, players had the opportunity to research the actual real estate value of each property, as well as other emerging information regarding the market, and inform their property development decisions accordingly.

In the context of accounting education, Tanner and Lindquist extended Knechel's [36] idea and used Monopoly as a business simulation for a team-based project for university students. Students would form four-person teams, form a virtual company, agree on a mutual strategy and then face other "companies" in games of 24 turns per player. After the game, the members of each company analyzed the company's transactions as a whole, set up an accounting record and used a general ledger to keep track for each type of transaction: salaries, depreciation expenses, interest expenses and tax expenses. After the evaluation of the game, authors concluded that "students' attitudes towards financial accounting and learning, mutual concern and perceived achievement were very positive at the completion of the project" [37]. Shanklin and Ehlen [38] also worked with the original idea and saw that "the use of an engaging and unusual medium early in the principles course helps students build confidence and provides positive reinforcement of understanding in a course that undergraduate business students do not always enjoy".

Besides including Monopoly in courses where its mechanics make immediate sense, the game has been used in the context of other disciplines as well. Hastunar et al. [39] designed a modified version of the game, referring to food and everyday objects, instead of properties, and to points, instead of money, to teach English to students of 7th grade in Indonesia, while Inal and Cagiltay [40] assessed Monopoly, among other games, with children aged 7 to 9, noting the "clear and immediate feedback of the game" which resulted in increased flow.

An interesting concept, not necessarily restricted to school education, is that of creating Monopoly boards from open data. Gustafsson Friberger defines data games as "as games where gameplay and/or game content is based on real-world data external to the game, and where gameplay supports the exploration of and learning from this data" [41]; in the case of open data games, most of the game content (images, text, Points of Interest, etc.) comes from sources freely available for use, such as a governmental organization, NGO or data aggregator (e.g., Google's Public Data Explorer [42] and the European Union's Open Data Portal [43]). Dissemination of open data is important, since it can provide a substantial basis for argumentation in public speaking or policy making; in the context of education, it strengthens the connection between the concepts and facts taught at school with everyday life, and empowers students to make informed decisions in their life [27]. Friberger and Togelius [44] analyzed thoroughly the different kinds of information which can be used as properties in this context, from geographic data, which is typically readily available and easy to visualize, to demographic, which can be sensitive (in terms of politics). They mention that real-time infrastructure data, such as flight information, are becoming increasingly available and may be more appealing to avid game players since it helps them relate to the actual providers of the data.

In our work, we wanted to examine whether the implied relations between entities and data contained in the game mechanics of Monopoly would help students identify the same relations between entities from a Big Data set. The subject of European geography was a straightforward choice, because it refers to a variety of numerical and reference data, typically associated with commercial versions of Monopoly. In addition to that, Monopoly entities are grouped using different colors, and ranked with respect to rent prices; we attempted to take advantage of these mechanisms to increase the students' comprehension of the relative size and population of each country and train them to identify those relations in the data. An additional game mechanic has to do with the positioning of the Monopoly entities on the board: even though in the original game there is no reference to any geographic positioning, in Geopoly the four sides of the board correspond to the region of Europe where each country resides. In order to create the required data and populate the board, we developed an automated infrastructure to retrieve data (country names, size and population, and landmarks) from Wikipedia, and create the Geopoly board respecting the grouping and ranking processes described earlier. The same approach can also be used with other Big Data sets, such as plants and animals (used in [27] in the context of a "Top Trumps" card game), where different numerical attributes (e.g., size, weight or life expectancy) or grouping elements (e.g., scientific classification, type of habitat or conservation status) may be used. As a result, we can create different versions of Monopoly to both familiarize students with concepts and relationships in Big Data sets and also follow and examine the learning objectives of the school curriculum, making it easier to integrate such a game in formal education practices.

*1.4. Research Questions*

Building upon previous research, we attempted to create an original learning environment by introducing game design and gameplay in the learning process. Our main objective was to study whether an adapted version of Monopoly integrated in the learning process would affect students' understanding of the relations contained in the game data and improve their academic performance and interest. More specifically, we wanted to identify whether:

1. the Geopoly game helps students get a better grasp of the underlying relationships contained in the data utilized to create the game content and, in the process, improves their academic performance in geography
2. there is significant difference between boys' and girls' performance
3. interest and academic performance, as measured in tests taken for a specific module or book chapter, are related
4. students find game-based learning more interesting than traditional teaching

Then, we created the following hypotheses:

**Hypothesis 1 (H1):** *Students who played the game performed better (i.e., received higher scores) than those who attended class.*

**Hypothesis 2 (H2):** *There is no significant difference in academic performance between boys and girls.*

**Hypothesis 3 (H3):** *Students who were interested in the game performed better.*

**Hypothesis 4 (H4):** *Geopoly results in increased interest in geography more than traditional teaching does.*

Taking into consideration all findings above, we wanted to further explore the impact of our game's digital version in students' interest. Due to the COVID-19 pandemic, schools were closed,

## 2. Method

*2.1. Instructional Design*

This intervention aims to introduce students in GBL practices, in the context of European geography. For this purpose, three chapters of the school textbook ("Residents and countries of Europe", "Cultural characteristics of European people" and "Monuments, sights and cultural heritage") were replaced by Geopoly.

2.1.1. Board

The four sides of the game board corresponded to regions of European (South, East, Scandinavia, North-Central), as described in the textbook, with countries bring grouped by color based on their geographical position. The country with the smallest area was placed at the first position of each group, in accordance with classic Monopoly, where the property with the smallest price and rent is placed at the right of each color group; this mechanic was meant to help students perceive the concept of relative position and size.

2.1.2. Cards

Each card (Figure 1) demonstrated the name of the country and its capital, while peninsula and island countries were marked with a special icon. Europe's main sights and monuments replaced railway stations and utility companies to help students associate them with their respective country and region.

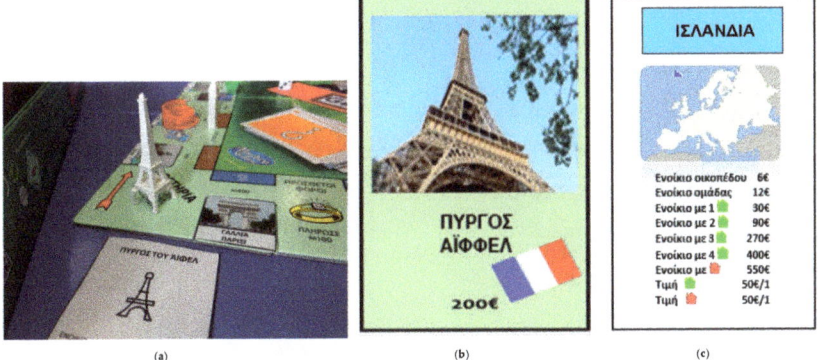

**Figure 1.** The Geopoly game board and cards from the game [45]. (**a**) The adapted game board and 3D printed player tokens; (**b**) a monument card (utility card); (**c**) a property card.

2.1.3. Tokens

In order to engage students more in the process, we asked them to design the tokens which depict Europe's famous landmarks (Colosseum, Big Ben, St Peter's Basilica, Eiffel Tower, Brandenburg's gate, windmills in the Netherlands—see Figure 2).

**Figure 2.** The 3D printed player tokens.

2.1.4. Participants

(a) Forty-three (N = 43), 6th grader students from a private elementary school aged 12 years old, participated at this intervention. Students were divided into two groups:

- experimental group (22 students played the game, which was implemented in the class)
- control group (21 students attended traditional class)

(b) Forty-seven (N = 47), 6th grader students of a private elementary school, aged 12 years old (a different sample than the main sample) played the digital game at home (due to quarantine) and evaluated it.

2.2. Procedure

2.2.1. Experimental Group

Assisted by their teacher, students chose the monuments to be modeled and then used the Thingiverse website for 3D modeling (Figure 3). All tokens were printed in a 3D printer.

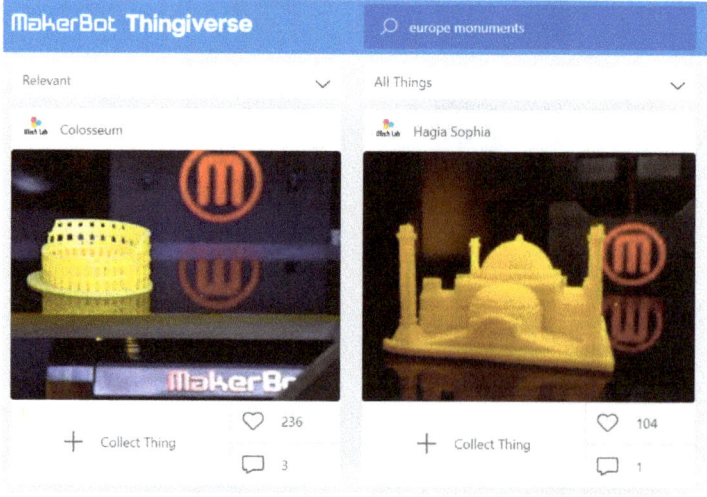

**Figure 3.** Thingiverse [46] interface to choose and download 3D models.

Following that, students were given a written test, consisting of 5 exercises aligned with the subject's (European geography) learning goals, as stated in the curriculum. Students were divided into 4 teams and played Geopoly four times. Each game lasted 40 min. In the end, for five minutes all players were discussing the game session, reflecting their strategy.

After this initial educational intervention, students were presented with a post-test assessment and filled out an Intrinsic Motivation Inventory/IMI questionnaire; IMI is a multidimensional measurement device used to assess the subjective experience of participants with respect to a specific activity, providing insight to intrinsic motivation and self-regulation [47] and has been tested for validity using CFA [48] and reliability [49]. Finally, students evaluated the game by answering a questionnaire; this process is summarized in Figure 4.

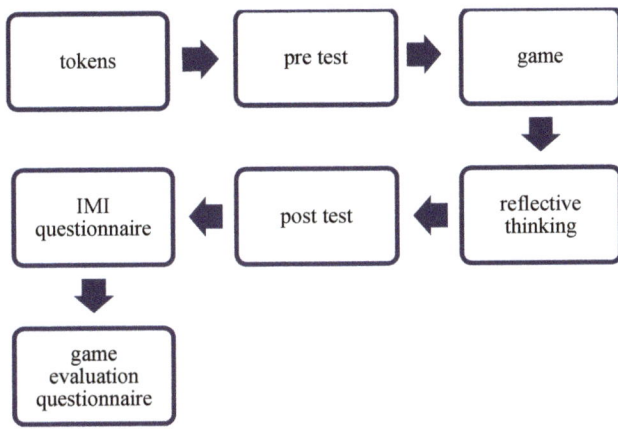

Figure 4. Experimental group's process.

2.2.2. Control Group

After filling out a pre-test questionnaire, students were taught three chapters of the school textbook, as the curriculum indicates. Finally, all control group students were tested again (post-test) and filled out the IMI and lesson evaluation questionnaires (see Figure 5).

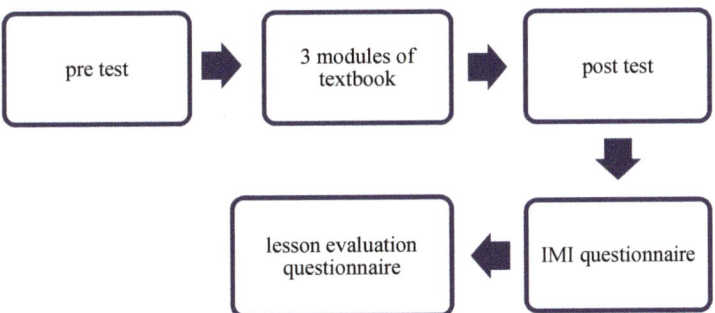

Figure 5. Control group's process.

2.3. Digital Game

We wanted to further explore Geopoly's impact on students, so after the completion of the first intervention, we designed a digital version of Geopoly, following the same principles and mechanisms as the board game. Each side of the board represented a European region, countries were grouped by color and their position represented the perception of relative position. Influenced by current affairs (COVID–19 pandemic), we replaced jail with "quarantine" and taxes with "corona bonds" to make the game more relevant to students' everyday life. Up to 7 players can play against each other or against the computer. The Digital game upholds mechanisms such as "roll dice", "buy a property", "exchange properties", which promote skills such as strategic and critical thinking.

Students played the game at home, three to four times and evaluated it by answering an online questionnaire.

### 2.4. Analysis

#### 2.4.1. Research Instruments

Pre-test: Students were tested before the first game session, in a written test, consisting of 5 closed-format exercises, relevant to European geography (ex. Choose the correct answer: One of the most prominent monument of France is (a) Colosseum, (b) Eiffel Tower, (c) Parthenon, (d) Brandenburg's Gate). Pre-test's highest score was 100 points.

Post-test: Students were tested after the last game session, in a written test, consisting of 5 closed-format exercises, relevant to European geography (ex. Choose South Europe's biggest country: (a) Greece, (b) Italy, (c) Portugal, (d) Spain). Post-test's highest score was 100 points. Both tests' scores were used to measure students' academic performance.

Post-experiment questionnaire: A five-point Likert scale questionnaire was given to students, to evaluate their experience, after they played Geopoly (ex. Did you enjoy playing Geopoly? 1. Strongly disagree, 2. Disagree, 3. Neither agree nor disagree, 4. Agree, 5. Strongly agree). We used the Cronbach α metric to test for the reliability of the chosen scale. Results ($\alpha = 0{,}813$) showed that the scale of the questionnaire is reliable (Table 1).

**Table 1.** Cronbach's alpha.

|  | N |  |
|---|---|---|
| Valid responses | 22 | 100 |
| Excluded | 0 | 0.0 |
| Total | 22 | & |
| Cronbach's alpha | Cronbach's alpha based on Standardized Items | N of items |
| 0.805 | 0.8 car | 16 |

#### 2.4.2. IMI Questionnaire

Intrinsic Motivation Inventory (IMI) is a seven-point Likert scale questionnaire [47], which was used to assess students' subjective experience. It includes nine questions in total, three for each subscale: Interest/Enjoyment; Pressure/Tension; Perceived competence.

The interest/enjoyment subscale is the self-report measure of intrinsic motivation. Perceived competence is considered to be positive predictor of intrinsic motivation as opposed to pressure/tension subscale, which is considered to be negative predictor of intrinsic motivation (ex. "While I was playing the game I was thinking about how much I enjoyed geography", scale: 1–7, 1: "not at all true", 4: "somewhat true", 7: "very true"). All participants filled out the IMI questionnaire and the data from the two questionnaires were used to measure students' interest in geography.

#### 2.4.3. Online Post-Experiment Questionnaire

A five-point Likert scale evaluation questionnaire was given to students after they played digital Geopoly to evaluate digital game.

## 3. Results

### 3.1. Performance

Overall performance: Results on the dependent variable "performance" (see Table 2) showed that both groups (control and experimental) achieved similar scores in the pre-test (~45/100).

Table 2. Performance statistics before the intervention.

| Group (Pre-Test) | N | Mean | Std. Deviation | Std. Error Mean |
|---|---|---|---|---|
| Experimental | 22 | 45.3182 | 20.61065 | 4.39420 |
| Control | 21 | 45.00 | 18.84144 | 4.11154 |

In order to check for any statistically significant difference between the scores of the two groups, we performed a parametric t-test in order to examine means' equivalence variance (see Table 3); the value of $p$ ($p = 0.958$) showed that there is no statistically significant difference in the pre-test evaluation scores.

This test was followed by a statistical check on the mean scores, which showed that performance for both groups improved. However, the scores in the experimental group were higher (Table 4). In addition, the *t*-test attested (Table 5) that the game improved students' performance.

There is a statistically significant difference between the means in the two groups ($p = 0.02 < 0.05$), which confirms our assumption that the game improved student performance.

Finally, an independent sample *t*-test for each group (Table 6 for the experimental group and Table 7 for the control group) showed the impact of the game and conventional lesson on students' academic performance.

Using Levene's test, we analyzed pre-test and post-test scores for each group. Both groups' performance was enhanced but in comparison, experimental group showed greater improvement. Hence, Geopoly did have effect on students' performance.

Gender difference: We tested for a difference between the mean score across genders (Tables 8 and 9). The significance level in the control group ($p = 0.728 > 0.05$) and the experimental group ($p = 0.574 > 0.05$) verified our null hypothesis that boys' scores do not vary from girls'. Based on Table 10, Levene's Test null hypothesis is satisfied for both cases (experimental and control) yielding that the variances are equal. Ergo, the student's t-test can be used to compare the two populations' mean (assumption for equality of means is satisfied). The *t*-test's result (Table 10) indicates that the null hypothesis is satisfied hence, the performance of the two groups displays no significant difference.

Table 3. Independent samples test (pre-test).

| | Levene's Test for Equality of Variances | | t-Test for Equality of Means | | | | | 95% Confidence Interval of the Difference | |
|---|---|---|---|---|---|---|---|---|---|
| | F | Sig. | t | df | Sig. (2-Tailed) | Mean Difference | Std. Error Difference | Lower | Upper |
| Equal variances assumed | 0.294 | 0.591 | 0.053 | 41 | 0.958 | 0.32 | 6.03 | −11.86 | 12.49 |
| Equal variances not assumed | | | 0.053 | 40.93 | 0.958 | 0.32 | 6.01 | −11.83 | 12.47 |

Table 4. Performance statistics after the intervention.

| Group (Post-Test) | N | Mean | Std. Deviation | Std. Error Mean |
|---|---|---|---|---|
| Experimental | 22 | 78.50 | 18.44 | 3.93 |
| Control | 21 | 61.00 | 15.61 | 3.41 |

Table 5. Independent samples test (post-test).

| Post-Test | Levene's Test for Equality of Variances | | t-Test for Equality of Means | | | | | 95% Confidence Interval of the Difference | |
|---|---|---|---|---|---|---|---|---|---|
| | F | Sig. | t | df | Sig. (2-Tailed) | Mean Difference | Std. Error Difference | Lower | Upper |
| Equal variances assumed | 1.375 | 0.248 | 3.351 | 41 | 0.002 | 17.500 | 5.223 | 6.95 | 28.05 |
| Equal variances not assumed | | | 3.364 | 40.439 | 0.002 | 17.500 | 5.20 | 6.99 | 28.01 |

Table 6. Independent sample t-test (pre-test–post-test) experimental group.

| Experimental Group | Levene's Test for Equality of Variances | | t-Test for Equality of Means | | | | | | |
|---|---|---|---|---|---|---|---|---|---|
| | F | Sig. | t | df | Sig. (2-Tailed) | Mean Difference | Std. Error Difference | 95% Confidence Interval of the Difference | |
| | | | | | | | | Lower | Upper |
| Equal variances assumed | 0.055 | 0.816 | −5.628 | 42 | 0.000 | −33.181 | 5.896 | −45.08 | −21.28 |
| Equal variances not assumed | | | −5.628 | 41.44 | 0.000 | −33.181 | 5.896 | −45.08 | −21.27 |

Table 7. Independent sample t-test (pre-test–post-test) control group.

| Control Group | Levene's Test for Equality of Variances | | t-Test for Equality of Means | | | | | | |
|---|---|---|---|---|---|---|---|---|---|
| | F | Sig. | t | df | Sig. (2-Tailed) | Mean Difference | Std. Error Difference | 95% Confidence Interval of the Difference | |
| | | | | | | | | Lower | Upper |
| Equal variances assumed | 0.413 | 0.524 | −2.996 | 40 | 0.0046 | −16.000 | 5.339 | −26.792 | −5.207 |
| Equal variances not assumed | | | −2.996 | 38.66 | 0.005 | −16.000 | 5.339 | −26.803 | −5.196 |

Table 8. Performance across genders.

|  | Gender | Experimental Group | | Control Group | |
| --- | --- | --- | --- | --- | --- |
|  |  | N | Mean | N | Mean |
| Pre-test | Girls | 10 | 40.1 | 8 | 44.0 |
|  | Boys | 12 | 49.6 | 13 | 45.6 |
| Post-test | Girls | 10 | 75.3 | 8 | 62.2 |
|  | Boys | 12 | 81.1 | 13 | 60.2 |

Table 9. Performance statistics per gender.

|  | Gender | Experimental Group | | Control Group | |
| --- | --- | --- | --- | --- | --- |
|  |  | N | Mean | N | Mean |
| Def | Girls | 10 | 35.2 | 8 | 18.2 |
|  | Boys | 12 | 31.5 | 13 | 14.6 |

Table 10. Statistical analysis of student performance.

| | Levene's Test for Equality of Variances | | t-test for Equality of Means | | |
| --- | --- | --- | --- | --- | --- |
| Control Group | F | Sig. | t | df | Sig. (2-Tailed) |
| Equal variances assumed | 1.632 | 0.217 | 0.352 | 19 | **0.728** |
| Equal variances not assumed | | | 0.398 | 18.992 | 0.695 |
| **Experimental Group** | | | | | |
| Equal variances assumed | 0.304 | 0.588 | 0.572 | 20 | **0.574** |
| Equal variances not assumed | | | 0.556 | 16.226 | 0.586 |

### 3.2. Interest

We wanted to examine whether Geopoly affected students' interest in geography. To this end, we used the data from the IMI questionnaire which explores intrinsic motivation and tested for correlation between interest, a positive indicator of intrinsic motivation, and academic performance. Since the variable "interest" was not distributed normally, we used Spearman's rank-correlation (see Table 11), which indicated a strong positive correlation ($\rho = 0.844$) between the two variables (academic performance and interest).

Table 11. Spearman's rank correlation.

| | | Post-Test | Interest (IMI) |
| --- | --- | --- | --- |
| Post-test | Correlation coefficient | 1.000 | 0.844 |
| | N | 22 | 22 |
| Interest (IMI) | Correlation coefficient | 0.844 | 1.000 |
| | N | 22 | 22 |

The scatter plot in Figure 6 shows a monotonic direct relationship between two variables. This correlation signifies that as students' interest increases, their performance increases as well. Anxiety and perceived competence, subscales of Intrinsic Motivation Inventory were tested but did not show any significant relation to academic performance.

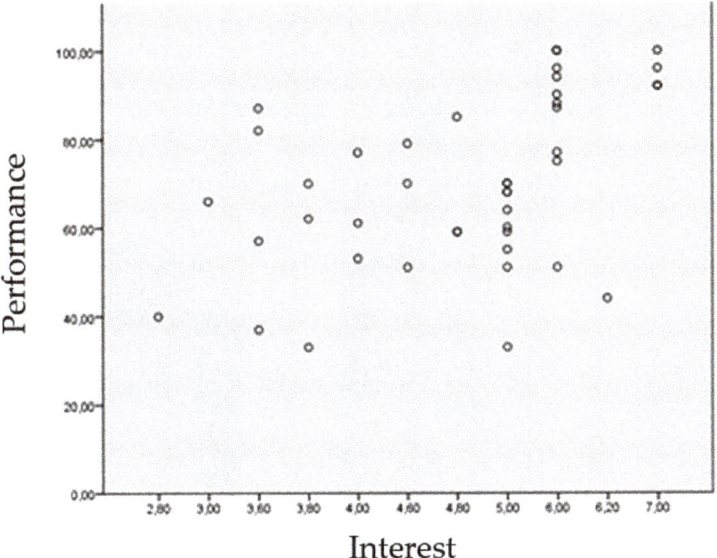

**Figure 6.** Correlation between interest and performance.

Finally, we explored whether students who played the game showed as much interest in geography as students who attended traditional class. The variable "interest" of experimental group was not normally distributed, so we used the Mann–Whitney U test to compare differences between the two groups. The test resulted in a higher average ranking (30.30) in the experimental group, compared to that of the control group (13.31), meaning that mean rank of interest is higher in the experimental group (results in Table 12).

**Table 12.** Results from the non-parametric Mann–Whitney U test.

| Group | N | Mean Rank |
|---|---|---|
| Experimental | 22 | 30.30 |
| Control | 21 | 13.31 |

As shown in Table 13, significance level ($p = 0 < 0.05$) rejects the null hypothesis for both groups and confirms that the students in the experimental group showed more interest in the subject of geography than those in the control group.

**Table 13.** Significance level Mann–Whitney's U test.

|  | Interest |
|---|---|
| Mann-Whitney U | 48.500 |
| Asymp. Sig. (2-tailed) | 0.000 |

3.2.1. Digital Game

Digital game's questionnaire results shed further light on how students' interest and strategic skills are affected by the game. Forty-seven sixth grader students (27 girls and 20 boys) played digital Geopoly. Students rated the game, evaluated their performance and compared the game to traditional method of teaching.

### 3.2.2. Motivation

At first, we wanted to know if the game had an impact on students' strategic skills.

As indicated in Figure 7, students believed that their strategy was improved, and all their moves were deliberated. By playing the game they enhanced their strategic skills.

**Figure 7.** Questionnaire results regarding students' perception of gameplay strategy improvement.

### 3.2.3. Interest

Students' answers (Figures 8–10) revealed that they found digital Geopoly really interesting and that they preferred the digital game to the traditional lesson. They would also like the game to be online and multiplayer, so they could play with their friends.

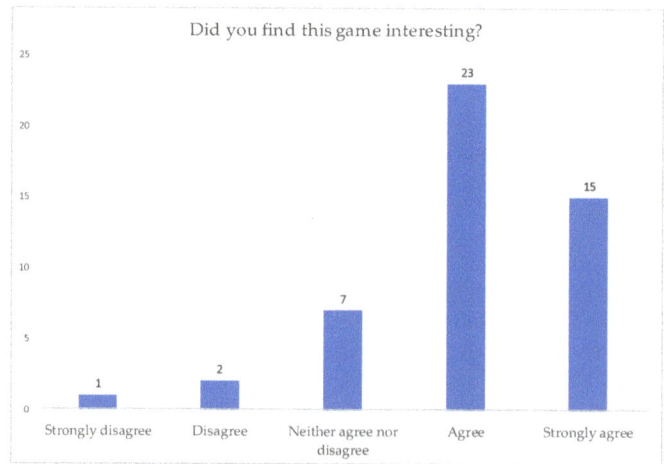

**Figure 8.** Questionnaire results regarding students' interest in the game.

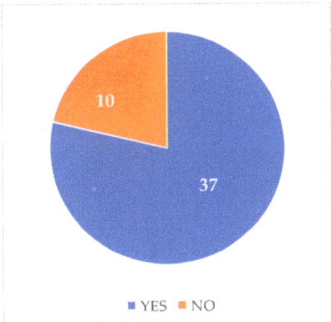

**Figure 9.** Questionnaire results on replacing the textbook with the game.

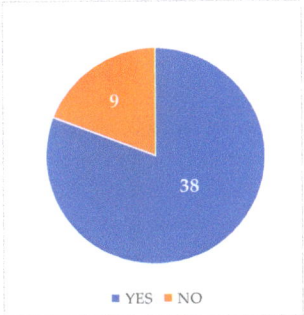

**Figure 10.** Questionnaire results on a multi-player setup for the game.

3.2.4. Academic Performance

Finally, students evaluated the impact of the game in their academic performance.

Most students believe that they gained more knowledge about Europe by playing the game (Figure 11). They also think that they met, to some extent, the learning goals of the curriculum, i.e., distinguish the four regions in which Europe is divided (Figure 12), obtain knowledge about a large number of European countries, compare their size (Figure 13) and perceive the concept of relative size.

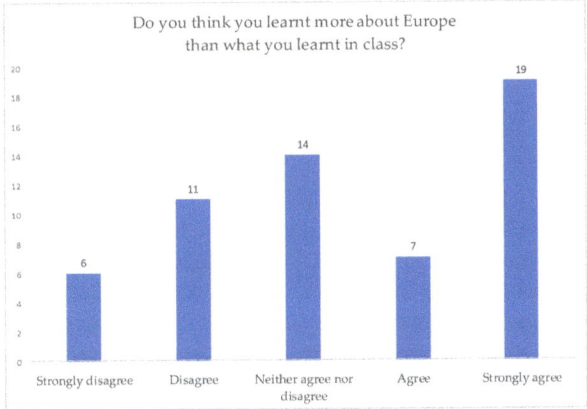

**Figure 11.** Self-reported comparison between conventional and Game-Based Learning (GBL).

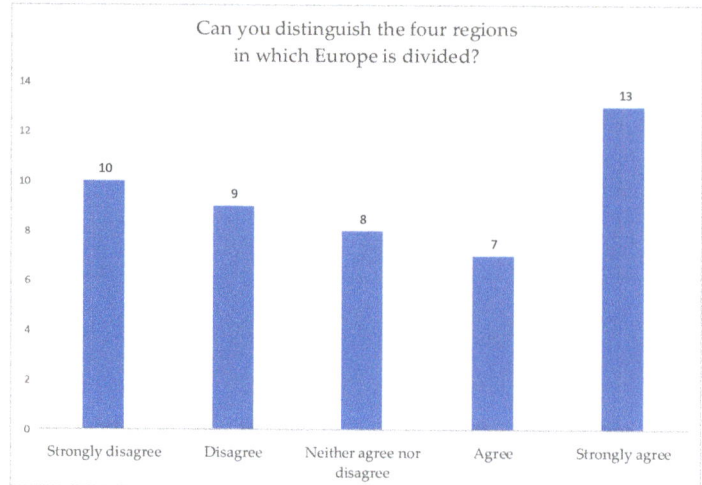

**Figure 12.** Self-reported perception of academic performance.

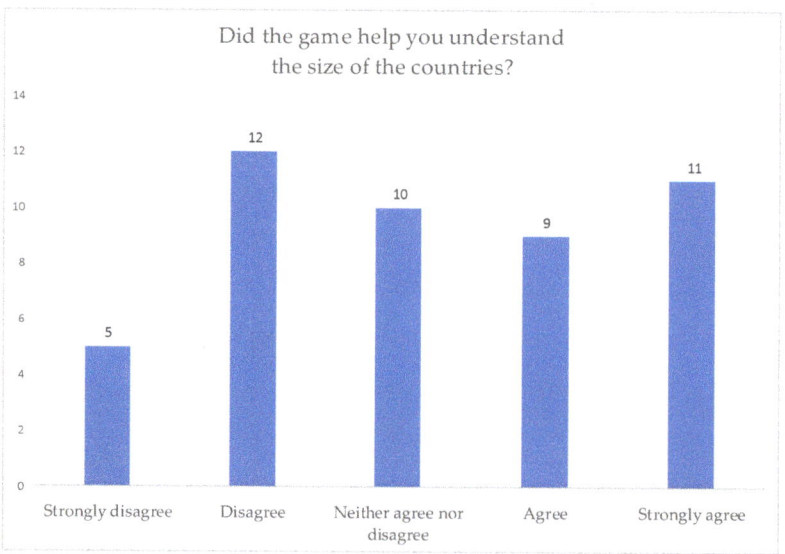

**Figure 13.** Self-reported effect on learning country size (cf. one of the core mechanics of Monopoly/Geopoly).

## 4. Discussion

This paper describes the design and implementation of a GBL study, where a board and a digital game that utilize content from Big and open Data were adapted to fit the learning objectives of a geography module. Our main objectives were to educate the students about the relationships contained in big data (ranking, grouping and spatial relations) and compare traditional learning with GBL in terms of motivation, interest and educational effectiveness. Monopoly (and Geopoly, the clone that we created for this work) utilize a grouping mechanic (group colors), a positioning mechanic (positioning countries on the four sides of the board corresponding to their position on the map), and a ranking mechanic (rent price in the original game, size and population in Geopoly); these were the actual mechanics that helped students understand the concepts contained in the data, with respect to the learning objectives, while the "pay rent" and "purchase property" mechanics were mostly related to the motivation and fun factors, fostering strategic thinking and competition.

The students' familiarization with Big Data relationships and their academic performance and interest in the game and the course were measured through respective questionnaires. Our analysis revealed that students' first contact with Big Data and GBL environments, (in physical or digital form) was successful and outmatched the traditional method of teaching. This study confirmed that the learning goals, as stated in the school curriculum, were achieved and students' academic performance improved by playing Geopoly, which effectively meant that they were able to identify the ranking, grouping and positioning relationships in the data. There has been much interest in gender differences in recent years [50], with significant results in geography-related activities [51] and STEM subjects, such as Mathematics or Physics [52]. However, our evidence suggested that there was no variation in the performance of boys and girls.

Game-based learning environments offer significant potential for increasing motivation and student engagement [53], which is related to their cognitive and emotional involvement [54–57] in the gameplay [20,58]. The digital version of the game kept students engaged and motivated all the way, which was especially difficult given that schools were closed, and strict measures were enforced during the experiment. Students made good use of their spare time at home during quarantine, as the game created a positive learning environment by bringing fun, play and learning together.

More extensive research is proposed to introduce the digital version of the board game in the educational process, so that instructors and learners become more familiar with this learning theory and integrate it in more modules by using different Big Data sets. At the same time, it would be interesting to create a more interactive, online multiplayer version of the game and adapt it so that it can be used in other subjects in which the performance of boys and girls differs greatly [52]. In general, our research emphasizes that if teachers are provided with more and better opportunities to integrate GBL in the teaching practice, this will cultivate 21st century skills [57,59], besides successfully conveying each module's learning objectives.

**Author Contributions:** Conceptualization, K.K.; methodology, I.V. and K.K.; software, K.K.; validation, I.V.; formal analysis, I.V.; Writing—Original draft preparation, I.V.; Writing—Review and editing, I.V. and K.K.; All authors have read and agreed to the published version of the manuscript.

**Funding:** This research has been co-financed by the European Union and Greek national funds through the Operational Program Competitiveness, Entrepreneurship and Innovation, under the call RESEARCH–CREATE–INNOVATE (project Mediludus, code: T2EDK- 03049).

**Conflicts of Interest:** The authors declare no conflict of interest.

## References

1. Matas-Terrón, A.; Leiva-Olivencia, J.J.; Negro-Martínez, C. Tendency to use big data in education based on its opportunities according to andalusian education students. *Soc. Sci.* **2020**, *9*, 164. [CrossRef]
2. Williamson, B. Digital education governance: Data visualization, predictive analytics, and 'real-time' policy instruments. *J. Educ. Policy* **2016**, *31*, 123–141. [CrossRef]
3. D'Aquin, M. On the use of linked open data in education: Current and future practices. In *Open Data for Education*; Springer: Cham, Switzerland, 2016; pp. 3–15.
4. West, D.M. Big data for education: Data mining, data analytics, and web dashboards. *Gov. Stud. Brook.* **2012**, *4*, 1–10.
5. Asteriadis, S.; Tzouveli, P.; Karpouzis, K.; Kollias, S. Estimation of behavioral user state based on eye gaze and head pose—Application in an e-learning environment. *Multimed. Tools Appl.* **2009**, *41*, 469–493. [CrossRef]
6. Williamson, B. *Big Data in Education: The Digital Future of Learning, Policy and Practice*; Sage: New York, NY, USA, 2017.
7. Matas-Terrón, A.; Leiva-Olivencia, J.J.; Franco-Caballero, P.D.; García-Aguilera, F.J. Validity of the "Big data tendency in education" scale as a tool helping to reach inclusive social development. *Sustainability* **2020**, *12*, 5470. [CrossRef]

8. Ruiz-Palmero, J.; Colomo-Magaña, E.; Ríos-Ariza, J.M.; Gómez-García, M. Big data in education: Perception of training advisors on its use in the educational system. *Soc. Sci.* **2020**, *9*, 53. [CrossRef]
9. Kitchin, R. The data revolution. In *Big data, Open Data, Data Infrastructures and their Consequences*; Sage: New York, NY, USA, 2014.
10. Reinfried, S.; Hertig, P. Geographical education: How human environment-society processes work. *Encycl. Life Support Syst.* **2011**, 1–48. Available online: http://www.eolss.net/sample-chapters/c01/e6-06b-46.pdf (accessed on 21 October 2020).
11. Li, Z.; Williams, M. (Eds.) *Environmental and Geographical Education for Sustainability: Cultural Contexts*; Nova Publishers: Hauppauge, NY, USA, 2006.
12. Gryl, I.; Jekel, T. Re-centring geoinformation in secondary education: Toward a spatial citizenship approach. *Cartographica* **2012**, *47*, 18–28. [CrossRef]
13. Ke, F.; Abras, T. Games for engaged learning of middle school children with special learning needs. *Br. J. Educ. Technol.* **2013**, *44*, 225–242. [CrossRef]
14. Voulgari, I.; Komis, V. Collaborative learning in massively multiplayer online games: A review of social, cognitive and motivational perspectives. In *Handbook of Research on Improving Learning and Motivation Through Educational Games: Multidisciplinary Approaches*; IGI Global: Hershey, PA, USA, 2011; pp. 370–394.
15. Yee, N. Motivations for play in online games. *CyberPsychol. Behav.* **2006**, *9*, 772–775. [CrossRef]
16. Plass, J.L.; Homer, B.D.; Kinzer, C.K. Foundations of game-based learning. *Educ. Psychol.* **2015**, *50*, 258–283. [CrossRef]
17. EdTechReview Website. What is GBL (Game–Based Learning). Available online: https://edtechreview.in/dictionary/298-what-is-game-based-learning (accessed on 28 September 2020).
18. Prensky, M.R. *From Digital Natives to Digital Wisdom: Hopeful Essays for 21st Century Learning*; Corwin Press: Thousand Oaks, CA, USA, 2012.
19. Greipl, S.; Ninaus, M.; Bauer, D.; Kiili, K.; Moeller, K. A fun-accuracy trade-off in game-based learning. In *Proceeding of the Games and Learning Alliance. GALA 2018*; Lecture Notes in Computer Science; Springer: Cham, Switzerland, 2019; Volume 11385.
20. Abdul Jabbar, A.I.; Felicia, P. Gameplay engagement and learning in game-based learning: A systematic review. *Rev. Educ. Res.* **2015**, *85*, 740–779. [CrossRef]
21. Deater-Deckard, K.; El Mallah, S.; Chang, M.; Evans, M.A.; Norton, A. Student behavioral engagement during mathematics educational video game instruction with 11–14 year olds. *Int. J. Child Comput. Interact.* **2014**, *2*, 101–108. [CrossRef]
22. Asteriadis, S.; Karpouzis, K.; Kollias, S. Feature extraction and selection for inferring user engagement in an HCI environment. In Proceedings of the International Conference on Human-Computer Interaction, San Diego, CA, USA, 19 July 2009; pp. 22–29.
23. Schunk, D.H.; Zimmerman, B.J. (Eds.) *Motivation and Self-Regulated Learning: Theory, Research, and Applications*; Routledge: Abingdon, UK, 2012.
24. Brom, C.; Šisler, V.; Slussareff, M.; Selmbacherová, T.; Hlávka, Z. You like it, you learn it: Affectivity and learning in competitive social role play gaming. *Int. J. Comput. Supported Collab. Learn.* **2016**, *11*, 313–348. [CrossRef]
25. Mavrikis, M.; Vasalou, A.; Benton, L.; Raftopoulou, C.; Symvonis, A.; Karpouzis, K.; Wilkins, D. Towards evidence-informed design principles for adaptive reading games. In Proceedings of the Extended Abstracts of the 2019 CHI Conference on Human Factors in Computing Systems, Glasgow, Scotland, UK, 2 May 2019; pp. 1–4.
26. Wouters, P.; Van Nimwegen, C.; Van Oostendorp, H.; Van Der Spek, E.D. A meta-analysis of the cognitive and motivational effects of serious games. *J. Educ. Psychol.* **2013**, *105*, 249. [CrossRef]
27. Chiotaki, D.; Karpouzis, K. Open and cultural data games for learning. *arXiv* **2020**, arXiv:2004.07521.
28. Legaki, N.Z.; Karpouzis, K.; Assimakopoulos, V. Using gamification to teach forecasting in a business school setting. In Proceedings of the GamiFIN, Levi, Finland, 8–10 April 2019; pp. 13–24.
29. Legaki, N.Z.; Xi, N.; Hamari, J.; Karpouzis, K.; Assimakopoulos, V. The effect of challenge-based gamification on learning: An experiment in the context of statistics education. *Int. J. Hum.-Comput. Stud.* **2020**, *144*, 102496. [CrossRef]

30. Chiotaki, D.; Karpouzis, K. Open and cultural data games for learning. In *Proceedings of the International Conference on the Foundations of Digital Games (FDG '20), Bugibba, Malta, 15–18 September 2020*; Association for Computing Machinery: New York, NY, USA. [CrossRef]
31. Prensky, M. Digital Game—Based Learning, The Digital Game—Based Learning Revolution, Chapter 1, Computers in Entertainment. 2001. Available online: http://www.marcprensky.com (accessed on 27 September 2020).
32. Wikipedia Contributors. Monopoly (Game). In Wikipedia, The Free Encyclopedia. Available online: https://en.wikipedia.org/w/index.php?title=Monopoly(game)&oldid=963832535 (accessed on 27 September 2020).
33. Europeana Blog. The Story of Monopoly: How Charles stole Lizzie's Idea and Made His Fortune. Available online: https://blog.europeana.eu/2019/03/the-story-of-monopoly-how-charles-stole-lizzies-idea-and-made-his-fortune/ (accessed on 18 September 2019).
34. Tao, Y.H.; Hong, W.J.; Yeh, C.R. Prototyping an online game platform through the formative design approach based on the monopoly mechanism. In *Workshop on Learning Technology for Education in Cloud (LTEC'12)*; Advances in Intelligent Systems and Computing; Uden, L., Corchado Rodríguez, E., De Paz Santana, J., De la Prieta, F., Eds.; Springer: Berlin, Germany, 2012; Volume 173. [CrossRef]
35. O'Halloran, R.; Deale, C. Designing a game based on monopoly as a learning tool for lodging development. *J. Hosp. Tour. Educ.* **2010**, *22*, 35–48.
36. Knechel, R.W. Using a Business simulation game as a substitute for a practice set. *Issues Account. Educ.* **1989**, *4*, 411–424.
37. Tanner, M.M.; Lindquist, T.M. Teaching resource using monopoly and teams-games tournaments in accounting education: A cooperative learning teaching resource. *Account. Educ.* **1998**, *7*, 139–162. [CrossRef]
38. Shanklin, S.B.; Ehlen, C.R. Using the Monopoly board game as an efficient tool in introductory financial accounting instruction. *J. Bus. Case Stud.* **2007**, *3*, 17–22. [CrossRef]
39. Hastunar, D.E.; Bharati, D.A.L.; Sutopo, D. Modifying a monopoly game for teaching written vocabulary for the seventh graders of Terang Bangsa junior high school. *Engl. Educ. J.* **2014**, *4*, 122–129.
40. Inal, Y.; Cagiltay, K. Flow experiences of children in an interactive social game environment. *Br. J. Educ. Technol.* **2007**, *38*, 455–464. [CrossRef]
41. Gustafsson Friberger, M.; Togelius, J.; Borg Cardona, A.; Ermacora, M.; Mousten, A.; Møller Jensen, M.; Tanase, V.A.; Brøndsted, U. Data games. In *Foundations of Digital Games (FDG)*; ACM Digital Library: Chania, Greece, 2013; pp. 1–8.
42. Google. Google Public Data Explorer. Available online: https://www.google.com/publicdata/directory (accessed on 1 October 2020).
43. European Union. European Union Open Data Portal. Available online: https://data.europa.eu/euodp/en/home (accessed on 1 October 2020).
44. Friberger, M.G.; Togelius, J. Generating interesting monopoly boards from open data. In Proceedings of the 2012 IEEE Conference on Computational Intelligence and Games (CIG), IEEE, Granada, Spain, 11–14 September 2012; pp. 288–295.
45. Vargianniti, I.; Karpouzis, K. Effects of game-based learning on academic performance and student interest. In *Games and Learning Alliance, Proceedings of the GALA 2019, Athens, Greece, November 27–29 2019*; Lecture Notes in Computer Science; Liapis, A., Yannakakis, G., Gentile, M., Ninaus, M., Eds.; Springer: Cham, Switzerland, 2019; Volume 11899.
46. Thingiverse.com. Digital Designs for Physical Objects. Available online: https://www.thingiverse.com (accessed on 8 October 2020).
47. Ryan, R.M.; Deci, E.L. Self-determination theory and the facilitation of intrinsic motivation, social development, and well-being. *Am. Psychol.* **2000**. [CrossRef]
48. Goudas, M.; Dermitzaki, I.; Bagiatis, K. Predictors of students' intrinsic motivation in school physical education. *Eur. J. Psychol. Educ.* **2000**, *15*, 271–280. [CrossRef]
49. Ostrow, K.S.; Heffernan, N.T. Testing the validity and reliability of intrinsic motivation inventory subscales within ASSISTments. In *Artificial Intelligence in Education, AIED 2018*; Lecture Notes in Computer Science; Penstein Rosé, C., Martínez-Maldonado, R., Hoppe, U., Luckin, R., Mavrikis, M., Porayska-Pomsta, K., McLaren, B., du Boulay, B., Eds.; Springer: Cham, Switzerland, 2018; Volume 10947. [CrossRef]
50. Kafai, Y.B.; Burke, Q. Constructionist gaming: Understanding the benefits of making games for learning. *Educ. Psychol.* **2015**, *50*, 313–334. [CrossRef]

51. Zernike, K. Girls a Distant 2nd in Geography Gap Among, U.S. Pupils. Available online: https://www.nytimes.com (accessed on 18 September 2020).
52. Kerkhoven, A.H.; Russo, P.; Land-Zandstra, A.M.; Saxena, A.; Rodenburg, F.J. Gender stereotypes in science education resources: A visual content analysis. *PLoS ONE* **2016**, *11*, 1–13. [CrossRef] [PubMed]
53. Kirby, D.; Mido, C.; Evans, E.M. Engagement states and learning from educational games. *New Dir. for Child. Adolesc. Dev.* **2013**, *139*, 21–30. [CrossRef]
54. Caridakis, C.; Karpouzis, K.; Wallace, M.; Kessous, L.; Amir, N. Multimodal user's affective state analysis in naturalistic interaction. *J. Multimodal User Interfaces* **2010**, *3*, 49–66. [CrossRef]
55. Karpouzis, K.; Yannakakis, G.N. *Emotion in Games*; Springer: Berlin, Germany, 2016.
56. Yannakakis, G.N.; Isbister, K.; Paiva, A.; Karpouzis, K. Guest editorial: Emotion in games. *IEEE Trans. Affect. Comput.* **2014**, *5*, 1–2. [CrossRef]
57. Kotsia, I.; Zafeiriou, S.; Goudelis, G.; Patras, I.; Karpouzis, K. Multimodal sensing in affective gaming. In *Emotion in Games*; Springer: Cham, Switzerland, 2016; pp. 59–84.
58. Pivec, M.; Thissen, F.; Baumann, K. Affective and emotional aspects of human-computer interaction: Emphasis on game-based and innovative learning approaches. In *The Future of Learning*; IOS Press: Amsterdam, The Netherlands, 2006; p. 312.
59. Yannakakis, G.N.; Togelius, J.; Khaled, R.; Jhala, A.; Karpouzis, K.; Paiva, A.; Vasalou, A. Siren: Towards adaptive serious games for teaching conflict resolution. In Proceedings of the ECGBL, Copenhagen, Denmark, 21 October 2010; pp. 412–417.

**Publisher's Note:** MDPI stays neutral with regard to jurisdictional claims in published maps and institutional affiliations.

© 2020 by the authors. Licensee MDPI, Basel, Switzerland. This article is an open access article distributed under the terms and conditions of the Creative Commons Attribution (CC BY) license (http://creativecommons.org/licenses/by/4.0/).

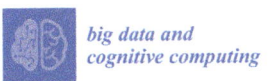

Article

# Annotation-Assisted Clustering of Player Profiles in Cultural Games: A Case for Tensor Analytics in Julia

**Georgios Drakopoulos \*, Yorghos Voutos and Phivos Mylonas**

Humanistic and Social Informatics Lab, Department of Informatics, Ionian University, 49100 Corfu, Greece; c16vout@ionio.gr (Y.V.); fmylonas@ionio.gr (P.M.)
\* Correspondence: c16drak@ionio.gr

Received: 7 October 2020; Accepted: 7 December 2020; Published: 12 December 2020

**Abstract:** Computer games play an increasingly important role in cultural heritage preservation. They keep tradition alive in the digital domain, reflect public perception about historical events, and make history, and even legends, vivid, through means such as advanced storytelling and alternative timelines. In this context, understanding the respective underlying player base is a major success factor as different game elements elicit various emotional responses across players. To this end, player profiles are often built from a combination of low- and high-level attributes. The former pertain to ordinary activity, such as collecting points or badges, whereas the latter to the outcome of strategic decisions, such as participation in in-game events such as tournaments and auctions. When available, annotations about in-game items or player activity supplement these profiles. In this article, we describe how such annotations may be integrated into different player profile clustering schemes derived from a template Simon–Ando iterative process. As a concrete example, the proposed methodology was applied to a custom benchmark dataset comprising the player base of a cultural game. The findings are interpreted in the light of Bartle taxonomy, one of the most prominent player categorization. Moreover, the clustering quality is based on intra-cluster distance and cluster compactness. Based on these results, recommendations in an affective context for maximizing engagement are proposed for the particular game player base composition.

**Keywords:** gamification; cultural gaming; cultural heritage preservation; player annotations; data enrichment; Bartle taxonomy; Simon–Ando clustering; tensor algebra; multilinear distance; Julia

**MSC:** 68T05; 68Q32; 82C32; 91E40; 92B20

## 1. Introduction

Cultural heritage preservation has been a persistent topic in most societies. Computer games can contribute by offering unhindered access to cultural content in a fun and vivid way [1]. Games promoting cultural heritage preservation rely on affective learning, namely the human ability to understand and internalize complex concepts through intense emotions and joyful activities, to successfully introduce its player base to cultural content. The latter may well include famed monuments, works of art such as paintings and films, and even anecdotal stories and myths. Each of these cultural items, material or not, cause positive or even negative sentimental reactions. It has has long been the objective of numerous private and public research initiatives to create such games [2]. The gaming industry has also been involved. One recent example is Assassin's Creed Origins which takes place in Egypt near the end of the Ptolemaic period (BC 49-44) and represents this era with great historical accuracy and making it accessible to a much greater audience.

There has been a trend towards the development of more complex, serious games, which are informed by both pedagogical and game-like, fun elements. Under this framework, the ANTIKLEIA project introduces the implementation of a specific gamified module application [3] applied on real-life content mostly collected from the Europeana repository [4]. More specifically, the interactive platform of ANTIKLEIA employs a collection of cultural content files [5] in order to be further modified by individual users, as well as groups of users, through its software components, while making them directly available to the general public. Furthermore, metadata from existing files and related collections support a cultural gamified experience, allowing large collections to be restored and managed through coordinated individual or collective efforts. This kind of (semi-)automatic enrichment can be beneficial for activating recovery, even across many languages, and adding a conceptual framework to the resources that will be accessible through its platform.

In order to keep player interest unabated, cultural games often depend on eliciting affective responses from players on two distinct levels. Low-level activity relates to simple decisions such as using in-game items. In contrast, high-level activity relies heavily on the outcome of conscious strategic decisions ranging from behavior in in-game tournaments to how game connections to the real word are exploited. Since both attributes ultimately describe player behavior from different perspectives, it makes perfect sense to combine them in player profiles. Once such profiles are created, the game player base can be better understood under Bartle taxonomy or any other player classification for that matter. To achieve that, profiles have to be clustered, as ground truth regarding player types is typically unavailable. This is essentially the principal motivation behind this work.

The primary research objective of this article is twofold. First, a template Simon–Ando iterative scheme for clustering the player profiles of a cultural game based on the Bartle player taxonomy is developed. Second, the effect of including user annotations about in-game items or player activity to the above scheme is evaluated. As a secondary objective, practical recommendations for selecting game elements based on maximizing the affective potential are given. The above were implemented in Julia and differentiate this work from previous ones. Moreover, the core of the proposed methodology will be incorporated in the aforementioned ANTIKLEIA project framework.

The remainder of this work is structured as follows. The recent scientific literature is briefly reviewed in Section 2. In Section 3, the Bartle player taxonomy and the low- and high-level attributes are presented. The proposed tensor based methodology is the focus of Section 4. The experimental setup, the results, and their analysis are given in Section 5, while the recommendations coming from this analysis are discussed in Section 6. Section 7 concludes this article by recapitulating the main findings and delineating future research directions. Tensors are represented by capital calligraphic, matrices by boldface capital, and vectors by boldface small letters. Each technical abbreviation is defined the first time it is met in the text. Finally, the notation of this article is summarized in Table 1.

**Table 1.** Notation of this article.

| Symbol | Meaning | Introduced in |
|---|---|---|
| $\triangleq$ | Definition or equality by definition | Equation (1) |
| $\{s_1, \ldots, s_n\}$ | Set with elements $s_1, \ldots, s_n$ | Equation (1) |
| $(t_1, \ldots, t_n)$ | Tuple with elements $t_1, \ldots, t_n$ | Equation (16) |
| $|S|$ | Cardinality of set or tuple $S$ | Equation (18) |
| $\times_k$ | Tensor multiplication along dimension $k$ | Equation (11) |
| $\mathbf{I}_n$ | $n \times n$ identity matrix | Equation (8) |
| $\mathbf{J}_n$ | $n \times n$ column reversal matrix | Equation (14) |

## 2. Previous Work

Games have been proven to be excellent tools for recreation and learning [6,7]. Their design is based on properties such as immersion and engagement [8]. To this end, the elements of points, leaderboard, and badges (collectively known as PBL) take advantage of the player engagement loop [9,10]. Games designed for cultural heritage preservation are explored in [11,12]. The Bartle taxonomy is examined in [13]. The mechanisms behind leaderboard operation based on personality traits are explored in [14], whereas personality patterns can be discovered through gaming [11,15].

Affective learning can be applied to gaming [12,16] in conjunction with big data [17] and machine learning (ML) techniques [18,19]. Clustering can be applied to emotional and physiological states [20]. Finally, if properly processed, voice can be a major indicator of human emotional state [21].

Tensor algebra extends linear algebra beyond two dimensions as explained in [22]. Tensor operations such as Tucker decomposition [23], Kruskal factorization [24], and higher order singular value decomposition (HOSVD) [25] naturally discover the multilinear interplay between a number of factors in the same way the singular value decomposition (SVD) can reveal linear dependencies between two vector spaces [26]. Tensor stack networks (TSNs) rely on neural network stacking in order to perform classification tasks [27], evaluate graph resiliency [28] and discover higher-order graph structures [29], and learn large vocabularies [30,31]. TSNs have also been applied to image compression as shown in [32] and in discovering geo-linguistic communities in Twitter [33]. TensorFlow is an open source low level framework for tensor operations including tensor eigenvectors and higher order SVD (HOSVD) [34,35]. Finally, in [36], a toolkit with extensive TSN functionality is described.

## 3. Players

*3.1. Bartle Taxonomy*

Bartle taxonomy describes four fundamental player types according to their objectives and how they accomplish them, the interactions with other players, and their relationship with the in-game world [13]. The four fundamental player types according to the Bartle taxonomy and potential factors behind the interest of each such type in cultural games are the following:

- **Explorers**: Every new game is a new world and they are determined to discover it. They enjoy visiting and recording every aspect of the game world, especially Easter eggs, loot boxes, cultural references, one-time items, and even game bugs. Since cultural games are frequently built around vast—and often past—worlds abounding with items, they are literally treasure houses for them.
- **Socializers**: Their gaming experience essentially comes down to intricate interaction with others and exploiting every game mechanism to achieve that. Cultural games offer an excellent chance for initiating conversations about a plethora of topics and for interaction through text chats, voice messages, and writing in in-game items such as chalk boards, portraits, mirrors, and books.
- **Achievers**: Working tirelessly towards accomplishing game objectives and ultimately achieving them, preferably first, is why they signed up. Appearing on leaderboards adds greatly to their gaming experience. Cultural games are ideal as there is a multitude of tournaments to participate in, myriad badges and one-time items to collect, and thousands of points to accumulate.
- **Killers**: As their name suggests, they seek to eliminate others, preferably accomplished players. They will relate if a game recreates military campaigns such as Cæsar's Gallic Wars (BC 58–51) or it is alternative history themed such as an open-ended American Civil War (1861–1865).

The above qualitative taxonomy can be seen from another view. This is comprised of two axes, each with two points representing the two possible options in a fundamental decision, namely:

- **Action vs. Interaction**: The degree the actions of a player are one- or two-way.
- **Environment vs. Players**: The degree a player prefers the game environment or other players.

Figure 1 shows how each player category fits in this two dimensional (2D) space set forth by the above axes. This representation contains more semantic content in comparison to a single categorical scale. According to this systematic view, there exists the following two pairs of opposite categories:

- **Achievers and socializers**: Achievers are highly competitive players since they often race against both the clock and other achievers of comparable or even superior skills to fulfill a set of objectives. On the contrary, socializers are very cooperative and seek harmonic and mutually beneficial coexistence with other players usually in a more relaxed style.

- **Killers and explorers**: Explorers aim at learning whatever is possible to be known about the game and even some more. In that sense, they are the least invasive player category as they tend to observe and not act upon the game world. On the other hand, killers do change the game world, especially if they act en masse, in numerous ways.

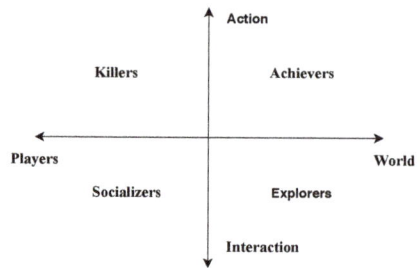

**Figure 1.** Bartle taxonomy in two dimensions (Source: Authors).

When designing game mechanics, the behavior of the player types and their expectations from the game should should be taken into consideration in order for their interest to remain unabated. Player categorization is not static. Instead, changes occur for one or more of the following reasons:

- Seeking different goals after gaining enough experience from the cultural game.
- Joining a team with a culture of explicit or implicit peer pressure.
- Cooperating with or competing against influential players or teams.

Detecting player categorization changes can be done with an LMS-like algorithm monitoring tensor gradient [37]. Such a scheme tracks separately each factor of the higher-order dynamics of the player profile. This is impossible for a matrix method, as it mixes these factors in a gradient vector.

*3.2. Player Types and Game Elements*

The relationship between the player types and certain low- and high-level game elements is critical for the cultural game success. Both element categories, taken from the literature, are shown in Table 2 and explained here. They belong to one of the three primary axes of world immersion, reward system, and engagement loop, namely affective mechanisms closely related to learning [9].

A very common player engagement system applying to all player types is the triplet of points, badges, and leaderboards (PBL). This system can be broken down to its constituent parts as follows:

- Points can be found in the overwhelming majority of games. Players learn to devise strategies for point maximization. Such is the case of arcade games where points are collected in large numbers.
- Badges indicate special achievements which may well be unique for every player. They can be seen approximately as the digital counterparts of real world military medals or sports cups.
- Leaderboards are highly advertised player rankings. A very high score hints at an alternative ending path. Thus, players finishing with a lower score were indirectly invited to play again.

Loot boxes, namely stashes with special rewards, are very common in cultural gaming. Easter eggs, namely humorous references to other games or real events, are also cases of special interest. Their use is perhaps most highlighted in the film of the universe Ready Player One [38]. Moreover, one-time items, typically available during holidays or anniversaries, increase player interest and many have been reported to be sold in both in-game and out-of-game auctions [17]. Such rewards are valuable for explorers, achievers, and conditionally for killers if they contain special equipment [16]. Writable objects such as mirrors and books are new item types where players may write something visible to others, acting thus as a local in-game chat and as a focal point for explorers and socializers.

**Table 2.** Emotions triggered by low-(upper half) and high-level (lower half) elements (Source: See text).

| Element | Explorers | Socializers | Achievers | Killers |
|---|---|---|---|---|
| Points | Neutral | Neutral | Joy | Neutral |
| Badges | Anticipation | Neutral | Anticipation | Joy |
| Leaderboards | Neutral | Anticipation | Joy | Joy |
| One-time items | Surprise | Neutral | Joy | Joy |
| Easter eggs | Joy | Neutral | Joy | Neutral |
| Loot boxes | Joy | Joy | Joy | Neutral |
| Secret rooms | Anticipation | Neutral | Joy | Neutral |
| Writable objects | Neutral | Anticipation | Neutral | Neutral |
| Cultural references | Joy | Anticipation | Neutral | Neutral |
| Interaction with players | Joy | Trust | Neutral | Anticipation |
| Interaction with NPCs | Neutral | Anticipation | Neutral | Anticipation |
| In-game tournaments | Surprise | Neutral | Surprise | Neutral |
| Cooperation in tournaments | Neutral | Joy | Neutral | Anger |
| Competition in tournaments | Neutral | Anger | Neutral | Joy |
| Alternative timelines | Anticipation | Joy | Anticipation | Anticipation |
| Crossovers | Joy | Neutral | Neutral | Neutral |
| Linear storytelling | Neutral | Neutral | Neutral | Joy |
| In media res storytelling | Joy | Neutral | Neutral | Anticipation |
| Open world | Joy | Joy | Anticipation | Joy |
| Open universe | Anticipation | Anticipation | Joy | Joy |
| Connection to physical world | Anticipation | Joy | Neutral | Neutral |

In-game events such as auctions and tournaments are also an integral part of storytelling in cultural games attracting mainly explorers, achievers, and socializers [14]. In auctions literally everything can be sold. Prime examples include classical, renaissance, or Victorian monuments, inscriptions, paintings, statues, and decorated columns, as well as handcraft objects including jewellery, vessels, books, and ordinary household belongings. Tournaments may also be held on a regular or sporadic basis. There, killers have plenty of opportunities to compete with each other and socializers to cooperate [9]. Carefully designed tournaments may well also be special cases of an inducement prize contest, benefiting ultimately the player, typically an achiever or killer, giving the prize.

In an open world, player characters are free to roam in a huge digital world, which is particularly appealing to explorers and killers [9]. An expanding world is in fact a strong motive for players not only to keep playing, but also to return once they have completed the game. Depending on its theme, a cultural game may well have secret rooms, namely bonus areas filled with rewards.

An open universe allows the plot to be expanded in a number of worlds or for a character to be developed across various game installments. Perhaps the most well-known example is the Wing Commander space opera series [39], which is famed for its original and effective immersion mechanisms. It was possible to transfer the same player character along six game installments [40,41] allowing the racking of an impressive score and resulting in a more continuous and coherent story. Such a universe is appealing to all four fundamental player types for different reasons.

Despite coming from the digital realm, a cultural game may have extensions to the outside world. This can be carried out in many ways including scanning quick response (QR) codes, taking pictures, or recording street noise. Moreover, tangible rewards such as material badges are strong motives for players, especially for achievers and explorers. More recently augmented reality (AR), virtual reality (VR), and haptic systems bridge the gap between human senses and the game world, making games even more immersive. Explorers and socializers are typically fond of this type of features [6].

The role of artificial intelligence (AI) or non-playable characters (NPCs) is instrumental in most in-game worlds. Interacting with NPCs adds ways explorers can learn about the game and well designed NPCs may well capture the attention of socializers, especially if they have advanced AI. Moreover, they may provide critical hints to achievers and serve as cannon fodder for killers.

A significant design principle is that of the uncanny valley stating that NPCs should look convincingly human in order to be realistic but not *too* human as in this case they may look disturbing [42].

Storytelling techniques are essential to the game world evolution and all elements must have a place in that story, especially since it influences all four player types [9,14]. The classical Aristotelian structure is considered appropriate when simplicity is sought or when a clear message is to be given. On the contrary, the in media res storytelling of the Homeric sagas is considered suitable for games with open ended worlds or many installments with prequels and sequels. Other techniques such as the traditional Japanese storytelling [43] may be instrumental in games with experimental or specialized mechanics. Occasionally, alternate timelines or crossovers may make a linear story more interesting.

The affective reaction of the four player categories to these elements is important for cultural game mechanics if player interest is to be stimulated. Said reaction will be examined in terms of the emotion wheel model of Figure 2. The basic emotions under this model are anger, anticipation, joy, trust, fear, surprise, sadness, disgust, and the neutral emotional state.

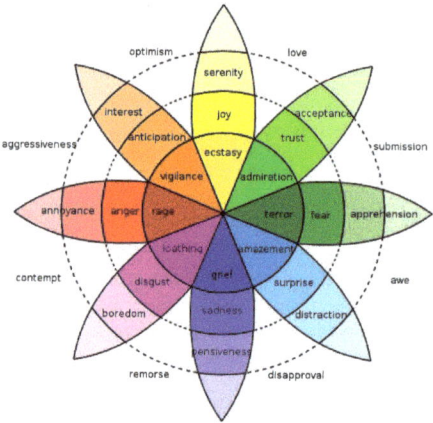

**Figure 2.** Emotion wheel (Source: Wikipedia).

Table 2 contains the emotions the most common gaming elements are most likely to trigger to the four player categories. Note that this table has been compiled under a statistical approach from reports and works (e.g., [14,16,44]). The upper half of the table has low level attributes, whereas the lower half has the high level ones. Observe the rich variability of emotional reactions.

### 3.3. Low Level Attributes

Low level attributes examined in this work pertain primarily to the way players interact with in-game items. Since they do not involve interaction with other players or with the broader in-game world, they are classified as low-level in the sense that no strategic thinking has to take place prior to or during interaction. Nonetheless, these kind of features are indicative of player psychology as they relate to unconscious and almost instinctive decisions or decisions with minor cognitive effort [6]. These features have been selected on literature recommendations [6,15,45] and are shown in Table 3.

Table 3. Elements and mnemonic names for the low-level player profile (Source: [6,15,45]).

| Element | Mnemonic | Quantile Meaning | Element | Mnemonic | Quantile Meaning |
|---|---|---|---|---|---|
| $p_L^{(i)}[1]$ | points | Points accumulated | $p_L^{(i)}[5]$ | eggs | Easter eggs found |
| $p_L^{(i)}[2]$ | badges | Badges collected | $p_L^{(i)}[6]$ | loot | Loot boxes found |
| $p_L^{(i)}[3]$ | board | Leaderboard position | $p_L^{(i)}[7]$ | rooms | Secret rooms found |
| $p_L^{(i)}[4]$ | items | One-time items collected | $p_L^{(i)}[Q_0]$ | writeable | Writable objects used |

The low-level player profile for the $i$th player is the numerical vector $\mathbf{p}_L^{(i)}$ of length $Q_0 = 8$ with the structure of Equation (1). The latter also contains symbolic names for clarity and readability in Algorithms 1 and 2. The proposed methodology can be extended to any number of attributes.

$$\mathbf{p}_L^{(i)} \triangleq \left[ p_L^{(i)}[1], \quad \ldots, \quad p_L^{(i)}[Q_0] \right]^T \in V_0^{Q_0 \times 1} \qquad (1)$$

In Equation (1), the value set $V_0$ is $\{1/5, 2/5, 3/5, 4/5, 1\}$. Because of its structure, the symbolic five star scale of Table 4 is used throughout the text to make it more legible and intuitive-friendly. To enhance legibility, symbolic names consist of only one word without any modifiers.

Table 4. Symbolic names for the numerical attribute scale (Source: Authors).

| Numerical | 1/5 | 2/5 | 3/5 | 4/5 | 1 |
|---|---|---|---|---|---|
| Symbolic | Weak | Low | Medium | High | Strong |

These symbolic values are also linearly ordered not only because they represent actual numerical values where comparisons make perfect sense, but also because of their very context they represent distinct ranking levels. Thus, for instance, Weak < High or Medium > Low are valid comparisons.

The values of $V_0$ have been chosen in order to address the following reasons:

- The large variance of players and items involved may not always lead to numerical scales.
- Ranking ensures that attribute values remain at the same scale.
- The ranking indicates how the community is going as opposed to individual player performance.
- Ranking can be applied at various stages of the game or even for different player subsets.

Notice that the number of attributes $Q_0$ in this work is the number of low-level elements found in the recent scientific literature. This number by no means limits the generality of the proposed methodology. In fact, the only actual hard constraint regarding how many attributes may be used is that the low- and high-level player profiles have the same number of components.

The distance between two low level profiles is defined as in Equation (2):

$$l\left(\mathbf{p}_L^{(i)}, \mathbf{p}_L^{(j)}\right) \triangleq l(i,j) \triangleq \exp\left(-\frac{\left\|\mathbf{p}_L^{(i)} - \mathbf{p}_L^{(j)}\right\|_2^2}{2Q_0}\right) \qquad (2)$$

*3.4. High Level Attributes*

High level game attributes pertain to player actions with higher semantic content as well as with conscious decisions. They mainly involve interaction with other players, strategic decisions, and dealing with the in-game world. As with the previous case, the high level profile of the $i$th player is a numerical vector $\mathbf{p}_H^{(i)}$ with the structure of Equation (3) and with the same length as $\mathbf{p}_L^{(i)}$:

$$\mathbf{p}_H^{(i)} \triangleq \left[ p_H^{(i)}[1], \quad \ldots, \quad p_H^{(i)}[Q_0] \right]^T \in V_0^{Q_0 \times 1} \qquad (3)$$

The components of each profile vector $\mathbf{p}_H^{(i)}$ along with the respective mnemonic names, added for enhanced readability of Algorithm 2, are shown in Table 5. Observe that the high level attributes can add more semantic context since they directly reflect decisions which require at least some cognitive effort and they can be described with annotations or a restricted vocabulary as explained in [46]. Moreover, they are indicative of the social intelligence of the players, especially in the way they choose to compete against or cooperate with each other [47]. The same quantile-based scheme of the previous case and the same five star scale are used to obtain the respective values for each player for consistency.

The similarity metric between two high level profiles is the Gaussian kernel of Equation (4):

$$h\left(\mathbf{p}_H^{(i)}, \mathbf{p}_H^{(j)}\right) \triangleq h(i,j) \triangleq \exp\left(-\frac{\left\|\mathbf{p}_H^{(i)} - \mathbf{p}_H^{(j)}\right\|_2^2}{2Q_0}\right) \tag{4}$$

Table 5. Elements and mnemonic names for the high-level player profile (Source: [7,8,14]).

| Element | Mnemonic | Quantile Meaning | Element | Mnemonic | Quantile Meaning |
|---|---|---|---|---|---|
| $p_H^{(i)}[1]$ | players | Interaction with players | $p_H^{(i)}[5]$ | competition | Tournament competition |
| $p_H^{(i)}[2]$ | npcs | Interaction with NPCs | $p_H^{(i)}[6]$ | timelines | Participation to timelines |
| $p_H^{(i)}[3]$ | tours | Tournament participation | $p_H^{(i)}[7]$ | crossovers | Participation to crossovers |
| $p_H^{(i)}[4]$ | cooperation | Tournament cooperation | $p_H^{(i)}[Q_0]$ | world | Fraction of world explored |

### 3.5. First- and Higher-Order Player Profiles

From the attributes described earlier it is possible to classify players according to the Bartle taxonomy. This is a first order player classification as it is based solely on features of a single player. Although this approach certainly has merit as is based on ground truth directly deriving from player activity, higher-order methodologies tend to systematically yield more robust player classifications as they aggregate not only local ground truth states but also information implicitly encoded in similarity matrices constructed from pairwise profile distance metrics such as those of Equations (1) and (3). Among the reasons favoring higher-order approaches are the following [14,15]:

- They rely on significantly more information regarding player profiles. As such, they can mine latent patterns, encoded for instance as profile similarities, player interactions, or player clusters.
- Higher-order methods tend to ignore the effect of outliers, typically expressed as unusual or missing attribute values. Properly designed methods can provide estimates for erroneous values.
- Most games create their own environment through rules or storytelling and players adapt to it. Thus, higher-order methodologies tend to reveal player types relative to the that environment.
- Gaming is mainly a social activity. Thus, although players have their own style, they may copy individual elements. For large player bases this leads to cluster formation over time.

The mapping of profiles to the Bartle taxonomy types will take two different forms depending whether only low-level attributes are available. This is necessitated by the form of some of the higher-order methods. When only the low-level attributes are available, Algorithm 1 applies.

Notice that in both Algorithms 1 and 2 the inequality symbols $\geq$ and $\leq$ can be applied to the symbolic values of Table 4 reserved for the profile attributes. In these cases, they are to be interpreted taking into consideration the linear order of the symbolic values. Therefore, for instance, the inequality points $\geq$ High is true when points has the values Strong or High and it is false otherwise.

Algorithm 1 relies on a number of observations about player activity as reflected in the low-level attributes. Achievers care for points and badges, which eventually will bring them to a prominent position in the leaderboard [14]. Explorers seek to find loot boxes, one-time boxes, secret rooms, or Easter eggs with the latter three being more important. This implies that explorers may well accumulate significant points in the process, so points alone cannot distinguish between these player types [14,44]. Socializers can be recognized by their extended use of writeable objects in order to communicate with other players as well as their drive to find secret rooms with the hope of finding more players there. These factors may result in an increased number of badges related to player activity [15]. Killers are less easy to define through a set of rigid rules since their objective may be simple, but in order to achieve it they frequently resort in activities which are also common in the other player types. For instance, they may seek secret rooms as socializers and explorers do, they may collect badges similar to achievers and socializers, they want one-time items as explorers do, and they share with achievers the excitement for points as well as for a prominent leaderboard position [6].

---
**Algorithm 1** Mapping of low-level attributes to Bartle taxonomy.
---
**Require:** Low-level profile as described in Equation (1).
**Ensure:** A first-order mapping to one of the four player types of the Bartle taxonomy.
1: **if** [points $\geq$ High] **and** [at least one of badges, points $\geq$ High] **then**
2:   type = achiever
3: **else if** [loot $\geq$ High] **and** [at least two of rooms, loot, eggs $\geq$ High] **then**
4:   type = explorer
5: **else if** [writeable $\geq$ High] **and** [at least one of badges, rooms $\geq$ Medium] **then**
6:   type = socializer
7: **else**
8:   type = killer
9: **end if**
10: **return** type
---

When both low- and high-level attributes are available in player profiles, then the more complex set of rules outlined in Algorithm 2 is used instead for the mapping to the Bartle taxonomy.

---
**Algorithm 2** Mapping of high-level attributes to Bartle taxonomy.
---
**Require:** High-level profiles as in Equation (3).
**Ensure:** A first-order mapping to one of the four player types of the Bartle taxonomy.
1: **if** [tours $\geq$ High] **and** [competition $\leq$ High **and** cooperation $\geq$ Weak] **then**
2:   type = achiever
3: **else if** [at least one of timelines, crossovers, world $\geq$ High] **and** [tours $\geq$ Weak **or** npcs $\geq$ Medium] **then**
4:   type = explorer
5: **else if** [at least one of players, npcs $\geq$ High] **and** [cooperation $\geq$ Medium] **then**
6:   type = socializer
7: **else**
8:   type = killer
9: **end if**
10: **return** type
---

Algorithm 2 connects high-level attributes to player types. Achievers are more likely to participate to in-game tournaments in order to accomplish game-wide objectives, possibly with the help of other players [8]. Explorers tend to investigate both the in-game world and its extensions such as crossovers and alternative timelines. In addition, they may occasionally take part in tournaments in order to find one-time boxes, loot items, or other prizes [14]. Socializers interact with other players or NPCs, and they may tend to help others in in-game events [7]. As in the previous case, killers are difficult to discern from other players as killers may join in-game events like achievers. Some killers search the game world as explorers. In addition, killers and socializers interact with other players and NPCs.

Higher-order methods may well use first-order profile classifications are starting points since the latter are obtained from ground truth data. Depending on the data representations, options include vector clustering, string matching, decision trees, or graph matching. Since here profiles are represented as numerical vectors, clustering techniques are more appropriate. In particular, iterative schemes coming from a template Simon–Ando scheme were selected and tested, as explained below.

## 4. Proposed Clustering Methodology

### 4.1. Template Simon–Ando Clustering

The algorithmic cornerstone for clustering player profiles is the Simon–Ando iterative scheme, which is based on the power method. The latter estimates the primary eigenvector $\mathbf{g}$ of a matrix $\mathbf{M} \in \mathbb{R}^{n \times n}$ through a matrix-vector computation and normalization cycle, as shown in Algorithm 3.

---
**Algorithm 3** The power method.

---
**Require:** Matrix $\mathbf{M}$ and numerical tolerance $\xi_0$
**Ensure:** The primary eigenvector $\mathbf{g}$ of $\mathbf{M}$ is computed
1: initialize vector $\mathbf{g}^{[0]}$; normalize $\mathbf{g}^{[0]} \leftarrow \mathbf{g}^{[0]} / \left\| \mathbf{g}^{[0]} \right\|_1$
2: **repeat**
3:    compute $\mathbf{g}^{[k+1]} \leftarrow \mathbf{M}\mathbf{g}^{[k]}$; normalize $\mathbf{g}^{[k+1]} \leftarrow \mathbf{g}^{[k+1]} / \left\| \mathbf{g}^{[k+1]} \right\|_1$
4: **until** $\left\| \mathbf{g}^{[k+1]} - \mathbf{g}^{[k]} \right\|_1 \leq \xi_0$
5: **return** $\mathbf{g}$

---

The main parameter of the power iteration is the initialization of vector $\mathbf{g}^{[0]}$. In the general case, initialization takes place with random elements or with information extracted from matrix $\mathbf{M}$ itself. In the former case, it is advisable that Algorithm 3 be executed many times as a random vector many not contain the direction of $\mathbf{g}$, especially when the dimension of the column space of $\mathbf{M}$ is large.

The Simon–Ando iteration is similar to the power method with one major difference: it terminates when the elements of $\mathbf{g}^{[k]}$ are clustered. To this end, a different termination criterion $\tau_0$ is necessary. Analysis of the power method indicates that it undergoes the stages described below [45,48]:

- For few iterations, the elements of $\mathbf{g}^{[k]}$ remain close to the random starting points of $\mathbf{g}^{[0]}$.
- As the iteration progresses, the elements of $\mathbf{g}^{[k]}$ move from their original positions.
- For a narrow window of iterations, the Simon–Ando phase, the elements of $\mathbf{g}^{[k]}$ are clustered.
- After the Simon–Ando phase, the elements of $\mathbf{g}^{[k]}$ are driven away from this clustering.
- The power method converges to $\mathbf{g}$ and terminates.

Algorithm 4 is the template Simon–Ando scheme from which the three iterative schemes are derived. It is a matrix free algorithm and multiplications can be seen as passing the vector $\mathbf{v}^{[k]}$ to a kernel $T[\cdot]$ and retrieving the result $\mathbf{v}^{[k+1]}$. In this work, selecting the particular form of $T[\cdot]$ uniquely determines the iterative scheme. Additionally in the template $\mathbf{v}^{[k+1]}$ is normalized by a generic norm $\|\cdot\|_H$ in a Hilbert space, but the specific norm depends on the selection of $T[\cdot]$ as well.

**Algorithm 4** The template Simon–Ando scheme.
***
**Require:** Functions of Equations (2) and (4).
**Ensure:** Players are clustered based on the basic Bartle types
1: initialize vector $\mathbf{g}^{[0]}$; normalize $\mathbf{g}^{[0]}$
2: initialize matrices $\mathbf{L}$ and $\mathbf{H}$ as in Equation (9)
3: **if** annotations are used **then**
4:   scale matrix $\mathbf{H}$ once as $\mathbf{H} \leftarrow \mathbf{HN}$
5: **end if**
6: compute kernel $T[\cdot]$ as a function of $\mathbf{L}$ and $\mathbf{H}$
7: **repeat**
8:   compute $\mathbf{g}^{k+1} \leftarrow T\left[\mathbf{g}^k\right]$; normalize $\mathbf{g}^{k+1} \leftarrow \mathbf{g}^{k+1}/\left\|\mathbf{g}^{k+1}\right\|_H$
9: **until** termination criterion $\tau_0$ is **true**
10: **return**
***

The termination criterion $\tau_0$ is a key component of Algorithm 4 since it determines clustering quality. The critical requirement for $\tau_0$ is to detect the Simon–Ando phase before it is over. One way to achieve this is to compute the elementwise harmonic mean of the second order difference between three successive versions $\mathbf{g}^{[k-1]}$, $\mathbf{g}^{[k]}$, and $\mathbf{g}^{[k+1]}$ as shown in Equation (5), assuming their length is $n$:

$$\tau_0[k] \triangleq \frac{n}{\sum_{j=1}^{n} \frac{2}{\left|\mathbf{g}^{[k+1]}[j] - 2\mathbf{g}^{[k]}[j] + \mathbf{g}^{[k-1]}[j]\right|}} \geq \eta_0 \tag{5}$$

The harmonic mean has been selected in this work for the following reasons:

- **Robustness**: The harmonic mean in sharp contrast to the geometric mean is immune to erroneous values close to zero or to outliers in general.
- **Reliability**: For stochastic input, even for a relatively few observations and for a wide array of distributions, the harmonic mean converges to its true value.

To understand why the eingenstructure of $\mathbf{M}$ appears in the Simon–Ando clustering, consider the following: Let $\mathbf{g}[i]$ be a fixed element of $\mathbf{g}$. For the very small number of iterations of the Simon–Ando phase, the multiplication with $\mathbf{M}$ should at most perturb the clustering of the elements of $\mathbf{g}$. By construction, the elements of the former are weighted linear combinations of the elements of the latter, as shown in Equation (6). It follows then that for each of the $n$ elements of $\mathbf{g}^{[k]}$ it holds that:

$$\mathbf{g}^{[k+1]}[i] = \sum_{j=1}^{n} \mathbf{M}[i,j]\mathbf{g}^{[k]}[j], \quad 1 \leq i \leq n \tag{6}$$

If some $\mathbf{g}^{[k]}[j]$ does not appear in (6), namely it is zero, then it can be added into both sides. Then, by stacking the $n$ equations and casting them in an equivalent matrix notation leads to Equation (7):

$$\begin{bmatrix} \mathbf{g}^{[k+1]}[1] \\ \mathbf{g}^{[k+1]}[2] \\ \vdots \\ \mathbf{g}^{[k+1]}[n] \end{bmatrix} = \begin{bmatrix} \mathbf{M}[1,1] & \mathbf{M}[1,2] & \cdots & \mathbf{M}[1,n] \\ \mathbf{M}[2,1] & \mathbf{M}[2,2] & \cdots & \mathbf{M}[2,n] \\ \vdots & \vdots & \ddots & \vdots \\ \mathbf{M}[n,1] & \mathbf{M}[n,2] & \cdots & \mathbf{M}[n,n] \end{bmatrix} \begin{bmatrix} \mathbf{g}^{[k]}[1] \\ \mathbf{g}^{[k]}[2] \\ \vdots \\ \mathbf{g}^{[k]}[n] \end{bmatrix} \tag{7}$$

Under the assumption that for two successive steps in the clustering phase of the Simon–Ando $\mathbf{g}^{[k+1]} \approx \mathbf{g}^{[k]}$ Equation (7) can be cast as a linear equation or as an eigenvalue problem as in (8):

$$\mathbf{g}^{[k]} = \mathbf{A}\mathbf{g}^{[k]} \Leftrightarrow (\mathbf{A} - \mathbf{I}_n)\mathbf{g}^{[k]} = \mathbf{0} \tag{8}$$

Matrices **L** and **H** in (9) contain the low- and high-level attribute distance metrics, respectively, as:

$$\mathbf{L} \triangleq \begin{bmatrix} 1 & l(1,2) & \dots & l(1,P_0) \\ l(2,1) & 1 & \dots & l(2,P_0) \\ \vdots & \vdots & \ddots & \vdots \\ l(P_0,1) & l(P_0,2) & \dots & 1 \end{bmatrix} \qquad \mathbf{H} \triangleq \begin{bmatrix} 1 & h(1,2) & \dots & h(1,P_0) \\ h(2,1) & 1 & \dots & h(2,P_0) \\ \vdots & \vdots & \ddots & \vdots \\ h(P_0,1) & h(P_0,2) & \dots & 1 \end{bmatrix} \qquad (9)$$

In Equation (9), $P_0$ is the total number of players. Because of the form of the Gaussian kernel both distance matrices **L** and **H** are symmetric and their diagonal elements equal one.

The user annotation weight matrix **N** is defined elementwise as in Equation (10). It is based on the annotations of Table 6. As a sign of the pairwise joint player activity between players $i$ and $j$, the harmonic mean of the ratio of the annotation references to either player for the three annotation categories of Table 6 to the respective maximum is computed. This choice yields a real symmetric **N**.

$$\mathbf{N}[i,j] \triangleq \min\left[\mu_0, \frac{3}{\frac{\sum_{k=1}^{P_0}\left(f_k^1+f_k^2\right)}{\left(f_i^1+f_j^1\right)+\left(f_i^2+f_j^2\right)} + \frac{\sum_{k=1}^{P_0} f_k^3}{f_i^3+f_j^3} + \frac{\sum_{k=1}^{P_0}\left(f_k^4+f_k^5\right)}{\left(f_i^4+f_j^4\right)+\left(f_i^5+f_j^5\right)}}\right] \qquad 1 \leq i,j \leq P_0 \quad (10)$$

Table 6. Annotations description (Source: See text).

| Annotation | Symbol | Category | Meaning |
|---|---|---|---|
| Player | $a_1$ | Interaction | A player has interacted with another (not in tournament) |
| NPC | $a_2$ | Interaction | A player has interacted with an NPC (not in tournament) |
| Timelines | $a_3$ | Game world | A player participates to an in-game alternative timeline |
| Cooperation | $a_4$ | Tournament activity | A player has cooperated with another player |
| Competition | $a_5$ | Tournament activity | A player has competed against another player |

In the above equation, $f_i^k$ is the frequency of annotation $a_k$ regarding player $i$ in the dataset and $\mu_0$ is a small positive constant. The rationale behind the selection of the particular weight of Equation (10) is that joint player activity should be high when they are of the same type since they have similar objectives and in-game behavior. Additionally, this choice allows the separate treatment of different annotation categories. Notice that annotations $a^4$ and $a^5$ refer to opposing behaviors, namely cooperation and competition in tournaments. In this case, for most players, either one of the frequencies $f_i^4$ and $f_i^5$ will be high but not both. Of course both can be down as well. There are many ways of selecting the constant $\mu_0$. Since it represents the minimum amount of player interaction in the game, here it was set to be the minimum non-zero value of Equation (10).

The scheme named *matrix* is derived from the Simon–Ando template by selecting the kernel $T[\cdot]$ to be matrix **L** and the scheme named *comb* is the half-sum of matrices **L** and **H**. Therefore, the former iteration relies only only on low- level player attributes, whereas the latter exploits both low- and high-level ones. If the matrix **N** is used, then it multiplies **H** from right once before iteration starts. This is called scheme *comb-a* (see Table 7 for an overview of the clustering methods).

Table 7. Overview of iterative clustering schemes (Source: Authors).

| Method | Kernel | Explicit | Attributes | Annotations |
|---|---|---|---|---|
| matrix | Matrix | Yes | Low | No |
| comb | Matrix | Yes | Low+High | No |
| comb-a | Matrix | Yes | Low+High | Yes |
| tensor | Tensor | No | Low+High | No |
| tensor-a | Tensor | No | Low+High | Yes |

### 4.2. Tensor-Based Clustering

Tensors allow similarity metrics modeling simultaneous linear dependencies between sets of variables. Although from a programming perspective a tensor is a multidimensional array indexed by an array of $p$ integers, where $p$ is the tensor order, the formal tensor definition is the following:

**Definition 1.** *A pth order tensor $\mathcal{T}$, where $p \in \mathbb{Z}^*$, is a linear mapping coupling $p$ non necessarily distinct vector spaces $\mathbb{S}_k$, $1 \leq k \leq p$. If $\mathbb{S}_k = \mathbb{R}^{I_k}$, then $\mathcal{T} \in \mathbb{R}^{I_1 \times \ldots \times I_p}$.*

Tensor multiplication along the $k$th dimension $\mathcal{G} = \mathcal{X} \times_k \mathcal{Y}$ between tensors $\mathcal{X}$ of order $p$ and $\mathcal{Y}$ of order $q$ can occur if both tensors have the same number of entries $I_k$ in the $k$th dimension.

**Definition 2** (Tensor multiplication). *The multiplication of $\mathcal{X}$ and $\mathcal{Y}$ along the $k$th dimension is defined as:*

$$(\mathcal{X} \times_k \mathcal{Y})[i_1, \ldots i_p, j_1, \ldots j_{k-1}, j_{k+1}, \ldots j_q] \triangleq \sum_{i_k=1}^{I_k} \mathcal{X}[i_1, \ldots, i_k, \ldots, i_p] \mathcal{Y}[j_1, \ldots, i_k, \ldots, j_q] \quad (11)$$

Observe that, as a special case, a tensor-vector product $\mathcal{X} \times_k \mathbf{v}$ along the $k$th dimension where $\mathcal{X} \in \mathbb{R}^{I_1 \times \ldots \times I_p}$ is a $p$th order tensor and $\mathbf{v} \in \mathbb{R}^{I_k}$ is a vector is defined elementwise as:

$$(\mathcal{X} \times_k \mathbf{v})[i_1, \ldots, i_{k-1}, i_{k+1}, \ldots, i_p] \triangleq \sum_{i_k=1}^{I_k} \mathcal{X}[i_1, \ldots, i_k, \ldots, i_p] \mathbf{v}[i_k] \quad (12)$$

The result is a tensor of order $p - 1$. Therefore, for a third order tensor the result is a matrix.

**Definition 3** (Frobenius norm). *The Frobenius norm of a pth order tensor $\mathcal{X} \in \mathbb{R}^{I_1 \times \ldots \times I_p}$ is:*

$$\|\mathcal{X}\|_F \triangleq \left( \sum_{i_1=1}^{I_1} \ldots \sum_{i_p=1}^{I_p} \mathcal{X}[i_1, \ldots, i_p]^2 \right)^{\frac{1}{2}} \quad (13)$$

Given the above, the iterations named *tensor* and *tensor-a* in the experiments are built around the third-order tensor $\mathcal{T} \in \mathbb{P}_\mathcal{V} \times \mathbb{P}_\mathcal{V} \times \mathbb{L}_\mathcal{V}$, where $L_0$ is the available level of attributes, namely two in this case. If more levels were available, then the proposed approach could be extended to use them by adding one layer per level. This demonstrates the generality as well as the simplicity of this particular method. Notice that each level of $\mathcal{T}$ is a proper matrix by itself. The geometric insight for it can be seen as stacking matrices **L** and **H** along the third dimension, as shown in Figure 3.

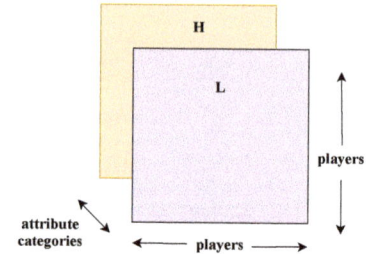

**Figure 3.** Tensor structure (Source: Authors).

The computation part of the iteration loop has the block form of Equation (14). When the annotation weight matrix **N** is used, **H** is multiplied from the right by it once during initialization.

$$\mathbf{H} = \mathbf{HN}, \quad \mathbf{G}^{[0]} \triangleq \begin{bmatrix} \mathbf{g}_L^{[0]} & \mathbf{g}_H^{[0]} \end{bmatrix}, \quad \mathbf{Y}^{[k+1]} \triangleq \mathcal{T} \times_1 \mathbf{G}^{[k]}, \quad \mathbf{G}^{[k+1]} \triangleq \mathbf{J}_2 \mathbf{Y}^{[k+1]} \quad (14)$$

The above iteration is based on running the low- and high-level cluster schemes separately and then combining them. An optional weight deriving from annotations for the high-level attributes can be added. The iteration steps of the computation part of the loop of Algorithm 4 are as follows:

- The two cluster schemes for $\mathbf{g}_L^{[0]}$ and $\mathbf{g}_H^{[0]}$ are initialized with random entries.
- If user annotations are used, then **H** is multiplied by **N** once during initialization.
- Tensor $\mathcal{T}$ multiplies matrix $\mathbf{G}^{[k]}$, essentially filtering $\mathbf{g}_L^{[k]}$ and $\mathbf{g}_H^{[k]}$ through **L** and **H**, respectively.
- At the next step, the two columns of matrix $\mathbf{Y}^{[k+1]}$ are swapped through matrix $\mathbf{J}_2$.

In this case, the kernel $T[\cdot]$ of Algorithm 4 is an implicit function of **L**, **H**, and $\mathbf{J}_2$. Moreover, at the end of the computation part of the loop, normalization is done with the Frobenius norm, which is valid since matrices are tensors of order two. This happens as now iterations are about matrices.

Table 7 offers an overview of the iterative clustering schemes deriving from the template of Algorithm 4. It is based on applicable standard criteria for classifying iterative schemes [37].

## 5. Results

### 5.1. Setup

Table 8 shows the experimental setup for evaluating the proposed methodology. It contains those parameters indirectly influencing clustering, but they have to be manually inserted by the developer.

**Table 8.** Experimental setup (Source: Authors).

| Parameter | Value | Parameter | Value |
| --- | --- | --- | --- |
| Number of attributes $Q_0$ | 8 | Attribute groups $P_0$ | 2 (low and high) |
| Maximum vector size | 1 MB | Processor | Intel Core i5 3210M @ 1.6 GHz |
| Maximum matrix size | 8 MB | Main memory size | 16 GB |
| Maximum tensor size | 16 MB | L1/L2/L3 cache size | 1/3/4 MB |
| Raw dataset rows $L_0$ | 175 K | Processed dataset rows $L_0'$ | 64 K |
| Number of annotators $N_0$ | 8617 | Annotation options $E_0$ | 11 |
| Number of players $P_0$ | 1024 | Termination threshold $\eta_0$ | 0.2 |
| Number of runs $R_0$ | 1000 | Maximum number of iterations $\eta_1$ | 1024 |

The experiments are designed to answer the following questions:

- **First vs. higher order:** These tests examine the clustering quality achieved by the first-order mappings of Algorithms 1 and 2 compared to that of the higher-order iterative clustering methods. Recall that the latter aggregate local ground truth to reveal global properties.

- **Tensor vs. matrix:** From the iteration template of Algorithm 4, matrix- and tensor-based clustering schemes are derived as outlined in Table 7. The objective is to determine whether switching to the latter can offer an advantage concerning player clustering ignoring annotations.
- **Effect of annotations:** These experiments aim at evaluating the effect of user annotations. To this end, the methods relying on user annotations to obtain weights for the high-level attributes are compared against their counterparts without these weights.

*5.2. Dataset Synopsis*

The dataset serving as benchmark to test the proposed methodology as well as the effect of user annotations was obtained from Kaggle. It comprises of $L_0$ rows pertaining to an anonymized fantasy-style cultural game involving a number of late Roman and medieval historical elements including gladiatorial style combats, castle building, and knight quests, with jousting tournaments being one of the main in-game events. These rows had the following fields:

- **Annotator:** The user creating the annotation. This field is independent of the player(s) involved in the activity. As such, it was ignored as it did not contribute information to the experiments.
- **Timestamp:** Automatically generated date and time of the annotation in ISO 8601 format. This field was also ignored as it was not relevant to the analysis conducted here.
- **Category:** It is one of the possible categories: Interaction of a player with a player or with an NPC, presence of a player in the alternative timelines, and interaction with players in a tournament.
- **Subject:** The player who does or initiates an action, as described in the respective field. To keep annotations simple, even in multiplayer events only elementary actions were recorded.
- **Object:** The player or NPC who is the target of the action, where applicable. It has the same format with the previous field but its semantics are much different from an analysis perspective.
- **Action:** Although there are many actions, here stand out the cooperation and the competition in tournaments and the participation to timelines. Everything else is listed as generic interaction.

The above annotations come from $N_0$ distinct players, they refer to the in-game events, and they were drawn from a restricted list with a total of $E_0$ options. The latter means that annotating users had to choose only from a pre-specified set of annotations intended for the game designers to understand how certain game elements were understood by the player base. Therefore, there were no missing or erroneous values in the various fields of the dataset and the semantics were well defined. Observe that the number of annotators is significantly larger than the number of players the annotations are about. A possible explanation is that annotators chose to provide information about players with considerable in-game activity. Additionally, the relatively small number and format of options $E_0$ in the annotations list made them easy to remember, therefore making easy their creation. In turn, this is an important incentive for creating a large number of them over a short amount of time.

Table 6 has the meaning of each user annotation as well as the category it belongs to. It resulted from processing the raw dataset and extracting player as well as action information. The latter was the grouping factor for the processed $L'_0$ rows in order to form the annotations categories $a_1$ to $a_5$.

Table 9 contains the distribution of each of the five categories in the resulting dataset. Observe that this distribution is rather balanced, therefore greatly facilitating analysis. Notice there is only one category probability, namely that of generic interaction, is much larger than the other ones.

**Table 9.** Category distribution in the processed dataset (Source: Authors)

| Player | NPC | Timelines | Cooperation | Competition |
|---|---|---|---|---|
| 24.25% | 19.5% | 18.25% | 20% | 18% |

*5.3. Number of Iterations and Floating Point Operations*

The primary figure of merit for each iterative algorithm is the number of iterations. Table 10 presents for the methodologies of Table 7 the number of iterations required to achieve the same level of convergence $\eta_0$. Since the starting point is random, the number of iterations is a stochastic quantity. Therefore, for each scheme was run $R_0$ and the mean and variance were computed. Moreover, as an additional safeguard, a maximum of $\eta_1$ iterations was included.

Table 10. Iterations for each method (Source: Authors).

|  | Matrix | Comb | Comb-a | Tensor | Tensor-a |
|---|---|---|---|---|---|
| mean | 262.6178 | 234.1333 | 224.3334 | 205.9500 | 193.0333 |
| var | 44.1445 | 42.1133 | 42.4467 | 41.3345 | 40.9987 |

The termination criterion $\tau_0$ used to achieve the number of iterations of the above figure was that of Equation (5) with a parameter of $\eta_0$ selected, as shown in Table 8. This value is low enough to achieve convergence without allowing the power method proceeding too far. From the results in Table 10, the following can be inferred about the number of iterations for each of the clustering schemes:

- The matrix based methods systematically yield a higher number of iterations. Thus, their convergence to the same level is slower compared to the tensor based ones.
- The annotation based methods achieve systematically lower number of iterations from their counterparts. This is a clear indication that they contribute to the overall clustering quality.
- The combination of tensor representation with the user annotations resulted in the lowest number of iterations. Therefore, they contribute individually to mining knowledge from the dataset.

Table 11 has the average number of floating point operations (flops) for each method. Again, since the clustering schemes are stochastic, the procedure of the previous case was applied.

Table 11. Flops for each method (Source: Authors).

|  | Matrix | Comb | Comb-a | Tensor | Tensor-a |
|---|---|---|---|---|---|
| mean | 414.867 | 409.556 | 407.332 | 397.403 | 394.309 |
| var | 37.497 | 38.683 | 40.803 | 40.6711 | 38.445 |

From the results in Table 11, the following conclusions can be drawn regarding the scaling:

- The tensor based methods achieve a somewhat lower number of flops although they contain more expensive operations of linear algebra. This can be attributed to the lower number of iterations.
- The cost for incorporating annotations is negligible, as can be seen from the entries for flops. Thus, it pays off to have them in the scheme as part of the mining strategy.

*5.4. Cluster Distance*

As ground truth is unavailable for the processed dataset, the following quality metrics were used. They rely solely on the results of the experiments and do not require tuning or hyperparameters.

- The average inter-cluster $\bar{d}$ distance of Equation (16)
- The maximum inter-cluster $d^*$ distance of Equation (17)
- The average intra-cluster distance $\bar{D}$ of Equation (19)

Table 12 shows the normalized values of $\bar{d}$, $d^*$, and $\bar{D}$ for each clustering scheme. The reason for this is that a relative indicator of clustering quality sheds more light to the performance of each algorithm. Each clustering scheme was normalized to its respective minimum.

Table 12. Clustering metrics for each scheme (Source: Authors).

|  | Matrix | Comb | Comb-a | Tensor | Tensor-a |
|---|---|---|---|---|---|
| $\bar{d}$ | 1 | 1.2276 | 1.9937 | 2.2816 | 3.0145 |
| $d^*$ | 1 | 1.3333 | 2.4423 | 2.8497 | 3.9973 |
| $\bar{D}$ | 2.8936 | 2.3444 | 2.0025 | 1.1215 | 1 |

Let $C_i$ and $C_j$ be the $i$th and $j$th cluster and $C_0$ the total number of available clusters. Then,

$$d_{i,j} \triangleq \frac{1}{|C_i||C_j|} \sum_{\mathbf{w} \in C_i} \sum_{\mathbf{w}' \in C_j} d(\mathbf{w}, \mathbf{w}') \qquad (15)$$

In (15), $|C_i|$ and $|C_j|$ are the number of data points of clusters $C_i$ and $C_j$. Then,

$$\bar{d} \triangleq \frac{1}{\binom{C_0}{2}} \sum_{(i,j)} d_{i,j} = \frac{2}{C_0(C_0-1)} \sum_{(i,j)} d_{i,j} \qquad (16)$$

Along a similar line of reasoning, $d^*$ is the maximum over all pairwise distances $d_{i,j}$:

$$d^* \triangleq \max\left[d_{i,j}\right] \qquad (17)$$

Another figure of merit is how compact clusters are. This is measured by the average distance $\bar{D}$ between any two points in a cluster. The intra-cluster distance $D_i$ for $C_i$ is defined as in Equation (18):

$$D_i \triangleq \frac{1}{|C_j|(|C_j|-1)} \sum_{(\mathbf{w},\mathbf{w}')} d(\mathbf{w}, \mathbf{w}') \qquad (18)$$

Metric $\bar{D}$ is obtained by averaging the intra-cluster distances as in Equation (19):

$$\bar{D} \triangleq \frac{1}{C_0} \sum_{i=1}^{C_0} D_i \qquad (19)$$

From the entries of Table 12, the following observations can be made:

- The tensor based methods consistently result in better separated clusters both in the average distance case and in the maximum distance as indicated respectively by the high values of $\bar{d}$ and $d^*$. This means that bounds between clusters contains fewer data points and are more clear.
- The tensor based methods yield more compact clusters compared to the matrix based ones, as indicated by the low values of $\bar{D}$. This complements the findings for $\bar{d}$ and $d^*$, as more distant clusters "push" the same number of data points to smaller regions, resulting in higher density.
- Both the above hold even more when the annotation-based methods are compared against their counterparts. This is a clear indication that the inclusion of user annotations improves the overall clustering process. Combined with the tensor representation, this is even more enhanced.

### 5.5. Player Type Distribution

Once profile clustering is complete, two player type distributions are of interest:

- **First-order distributions**: It is the player type distribution as obtained by Algorithms 1 and 2. Therefore, the mapping from the player profile to the Bartle taxonomy is based on the former.
- **Higher-order distributions**: Once a clustering scheme is complete, clusters are formed, profiles are mapped as before, and then each player receives the majority type of the respective cluster.

From the entries of Table 13, the following can be said:

- All methods yield approximately the same percentage for achievers. This also almost holds for socializers. This is an indication these player categories may have distinct behavior which can be almost directly translated to both low- and high-level attributes.
- The first-order distributions and the *matrix* method give a very high number for killers which is inconsistent with the very low number obtained from the remaining methods. A possible explanation is they tend to treat as killers every profile not fulfilling the criteria for the other types.

- The tensor-based methods yield almost identical distributions. This may be an indication that despite the different starting points they both eventually converge to the same distribution exploiting higher order patterns with annotations accelerating this convergence.
- The above is also true but to a lesser extent for the results from the *comb* and the *comb-a* iterative schemes. This can be attributed to the fact that annotations help the clustering process but do not suffice by themselves to uncover all the patterns in the processed dataset.

Table 13. Player type distributions (Source: Authors).

|  | Algo. 1 | Algo. 2 | Matrix | Comb | Comb-a | Tensor | Tensor-a |
|---|---|---|---|---|---|---|---|
| Achievers | 33.6666% | 32.7500% | 25.7500% | 36.7500% | 33.3334% | 36.2534% | 36.5000% |
| Explorers | 11.5000% | 32.5000% | 30.3334% | 37.1250% | 34.6666% | 32.7066% | 32.5000% |
| Socializers | 18.5000% | 8.500% | 21.2500% | 23.2500% | 25.2500% | 26.0400% | 24.3366% |
| Killers | 26.3334% | 26.2500% | 22.6666% | 2.875% | 6.7500% | 5.0000% | 6.6634% |

*5.6. Discussion*

The results obtained earlier agree with these reported elsewhere in the recent scientific bibliography. In particular, the combination of low- and high-level player attributes to improve player experience has been proposed [19]. Moreover, in [14], it is maintained that players can easier fit the Bartle taxonomy when their collective behavior is taken into consideration. The need for an advanced player clustering scheme is highlighted in [17]. Tensor clustering fulfills these requirements.

Based on the experiment results the inclusion of user annotations to the clustering scheme seem to make a difference both in clustering quality and in scalability. In addition, it should be highlighted that the tensor representation for player profiles and the user annotations are two different factors contributing in their own way to clustering. The results presented here are consistent with the findings of Yang et al. [49] where high quality labeling rules for reducing annotation cost were derived by crowdsourcing. In [50], these rules are augmented with ones mined with ML. Large-scale data annotation is indispensable for other type of games including serious games [51]. Annotations have also been proposed as a supplementary mechanism for understanding player actions in affective games [52]. To this end, games intended for cultural preservation may well benefit from including a dedicated module designed for collecting and processing them such as the one described in [53]. Since human activity patterns are to be extracted from gaming activity, it makes perfect sense that mining algorithms may rely on human assistance, even a partial one like annotations.

Regarding the role of user annotations in general, if they are utilized properly, they can be instrumental in the disambiguation of player activity [52]. As such, they can significantly boost the performance of mining algorithms by providing the initial information and ontological structure they can start from. The primary reasons for this happening are listed below [17]:

- Humans can almost immediately understand both the complex semantics inherent in player actions and the possible ultimate objectives of other players, especially in the context of the game.
- Moreover, dedicated or even casual players can draw on considerable information from their respective gaming experience in order to interpret the actions of other players.

As a specific example for the above, we plan to incorporate the strategy proposed in this work within the gamification module of the ANTIKLEIA project in order to exploit the user annotations. Through a suite of open markup technologies, such as the extensible markup language (XML), the resource description framework (RDF), and JavaScript Object Notation (JSON), as well as open protocols such as *Dublin core*, annotations can be driven as ground truth data from the dedicated user interface (UI) component to the data management one. Meta-data have been known to boost the performance of mining algorithms in terms of accuracy and robustness [54].

In this framework, Figure 4 depicts how annotations fit in the software architecture of ANTIKLEIA. Once the raw annotations are extracted, they are first locally stored as JSON documents. The underlying storage could very well be a document database, such as MongoDB, but a relational database is suitable as well. Then, the following analysis takes place in parallel:

- Annotations, as explained above, are driven to the data mining algorithms for interpreting the actions of the players. In turn, this leads to a better understanding of the player base.
- Annotations are also analyzed in terms of the players who gave them. This gives insight into the segment of players who are willing to improve the game, participating thus in a deeper level.
- The value of the available cultural objects for the player base is estimated through analytics based on the annotations. This is an important cultural preservation function.

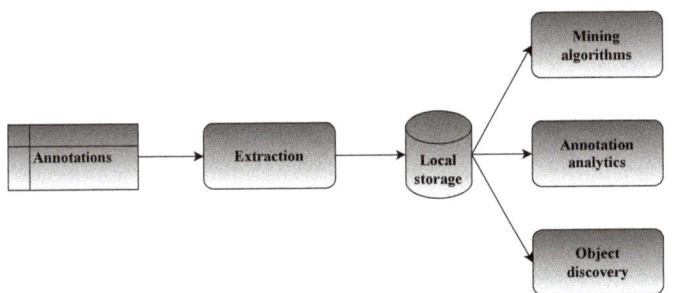

**Figure 4.** Annotations and the architecture of project ANTIKLEIA (Source: Authors).

Besides game designers, the above analytics may be of use to cultural enthusiasts, cultural professionals, and independent developers alike, as further described in the ANTIKLEIA use cases [3]. User annotations can even contribute to the data-driven construction of massive ontologies for cultural items [55]. The latter can reveal how the player base sees these items based on diverse criteria that clearly go beyond the scope of the present work.

## 6. Recommendations

With knowledge of the particular player base composition certain recommendations can be stated for game designers and practitioners with the explicit aim of keeping player interest unabated from an affective perspective. It is a long running tenet of the gaming industry that a successful game should be played more than once [11]. Several criteria for this purpose have been proposed in the literature with engagement, replayability, and immersion being among them [14,20]. The strategy in this work will be to maximize engagement, which will be achieved based on the following data:

- Table 2 will serve as a guide for the relationship between game elements and the basic emotions they elicit across player types. However, this is only a statistical approach.
- The last column of Table 13, namely the results of clustering with the *tensor-a* methodology, will be considered as the true player base distribution.

The analysis will be based on two complementary factors. First, emphasis will be placed on those gaming elements which attract the majority of player types. Conversely, elements eliciting negative emotions to the majority of players will be in general ignored. To this end, the following analysis will be used: Each basic emotion of Figure 2 is assigned the value ±1 depending on its polarity, whereas the neutral state is assigned the value zero. For each element, the score of Equation (20) is computed:

$$\sigma_i \triangleq \sum_t e_{i,t} p_t \qquad (20)$$

In Equation (20), $e_{i,t}$ is the statistical emotional response of players of category $t$ to the $i$th game element, while $t$ ranges over the four player types. Given the above, Table 14 is generated for the elements used in the low- and high-level player profiles in Tables 3 and 5, respectively. This analysis can be conducted for the remaining elements of Table 2 or any other game elements for that matter.

Table 14. Scores for the game elements (Source: Authors).

| Element | Score | Element | Score | Element | Score | Element | Score |
|---|---|---|---|---|---|---|---|
| Points | 0.3650 | Eggs | 0.6900 | Players | 0.6350 | Competition | −0.1766 |
| Badges | 0.7567 | Boxes | 0.9333 | NPCs | 0.3100 | Alternative | 1 |
| Leaderboards | 0.6750 | Rooms | 0.6900 | Tournaments | 0.6900 | Crossovers | 0.3250 |
| One-time | 0.7567 | Writable | 0.24333 | Cooperation | 0.1766 | World | 1 |

Given the values of Table 14, for the specific player base, priority should be given to widening the in-game world, creating alternative timelines, and including loot boxes. In addition, tournaments should be cooperative instead of competitive. On the contrary, writeable objects and the inclusion of more NPCs will offer little to the in-game experience as they attract only a small number of players.

## 7. Conclusions and Future Work

Games in the digital era promote cultural heritage by relying on several affective capabilities. This article has a twofold focus. First, a template Simon–Ando iterative scheme is developed for clustering player profiles consisting of attributes with affective content. Certain schemes deriving from this template are evaluated based on inter- and intra-clustering distances as well as on the number of iterations and the number of floating point operations required. The former are indicators of clustering quality, while the latter of scalability. The results are interpreted in light of the Bartle taxonomy. Understanding the player base in this way can lead to recommendations about placing emphasis on specific game elements. Second, the role of user annotations on clustering is evaluated by deriving versions using weight matrices based on them. Experiment results clearly show that in every case the inclusion of user annotations had a distinct positive effect.

Concerning future research directions, the algorithmic aspect of the proposed methodology can be improved by examining alternative combinations of attributes and tensors utilizing them. Moreover, the stability properties as well as its complexity should be carefully evaluated through extensive simulations. Another possible research direction lies in constructing more datasets from diverse player audience. This will lead to better evaluation of alternative player clustering methodologies.

**Author Contributions:** G.D. did the coding and developed the algorithmic strategy; Y.V. contributed to the algorithmic approach and did the bibliographic search; and P.M. provided guidance and oversight. All authors have read and agreed to the published version of the manuscript.

**Funding:** This research was co-financed by the European Union and Greek national funds through the Competitiveness, Entrepreneurship and Innovation Operational Programme, under the Call "Research-Create-Innovate"; project title: "Development of technologies and methods for cultural inventory data interoperability—ANTIKLEIA"; project code: T1EDK-01728; MIS code: 5030954.

**Conflicts of Interest:** The authors declare no conflict of interest.

## References

1. Squire, K. Cultural framing of computer/video games. *Game Stud.* **2002**, *2*, 1–13.
2. Mortara, M.; Catalano, C.E.; Bellotti, F.; Fiucci, G.; Houry-Panchetti, M.; Petridis, P. Learning cultural heritage by serious games. *J. Cult. Herit.* **2014**, *15*, 318–325. [CrossRef]
3. ANTIKLEIA Greek Web Site. Available online: https://www.antikleia.gr (accessed on 20 November 2020).
4. Europeana Web Site. Available online: https://www.europeana.eu/en (accessed on 20 November 2020).
5. ANTIKLEIA Web Site. Available online: http://antikleia.website/ (accessed on 20 November 2020).
6. Lumsden, J.; Edwards, E.A.; Lawrence, N.S.; Coyle, D.; Munafò, M.R. Gamification of cognitive assessment and cognitive training: A systematic review of applications and efficacy. *JMIR Ser. Games* **2016**, *4*, e11. [CrossRef] [PubMed]

7. Lister, M. Gamification: The effect on student motivation and performance at the post-secondary level. *Issues Trends Educ. Technol.* **2015**, *3*, 112–120. [CrossRef]
8. Streukens, S.; van Riel, A.; Novikova, D.; Leroi-Werelds, S. Boosting customer engagement through gamification: A customer engagement marketing approach. In *Handbook of Research on Customer Engagement*; Edward Elgar Publishing: London, UK, 2019.
9. Landers, R.N.; Bauer, K.N.; Callan, R.C. Gamification of task performance with leaderboards: A goal setting experiment. *Comput. Hum. Behav.* **2017**, *71*, 508–515. [CrossRef]
10. Huang, B.; Hew, K.F. Do points, badges and leaderboard increase learning and activity: A quasi-experiment on the effects of gamification. In Proceedings of the 23rd International Conference on Computers in Education, Ishikawa, Japan, 30 November–4 December 2015; pp. 275–280.
11. Seaborn, K.; Fels, D.I. Gamification in theory and action: A survey. *Int. J. Hum.-Comput. Stud.* **2015**, *74*, 14–31. [CrossRef]
12. Triantoro, T.; Gopal, R.; Benbunan-Fich, R.; Lang, G. Would you like to play? A comparison of a gamified survey with a traditional online survey method. *Int. J. Inf. Manag.* **2019**, *49*, 242–252. [CrossRef]
13. Menéndez, H.D.; Vindel, R.; Camacho, D. Combining time series and clustering to extract gamer profile evolution. In *International Conference on Computational Collective Intelligence*; Springer: Heidelberg, Germany, 2014; pp. 262–271.
14. Jia, Y.; Liu, Y.; Yu, X.; Voida, S. Designing leaderboards for gamification: Perceived differences based on user ranking, application domain, and personality traits. In Proceedings of the Conference on Human Factors in Computing Systems, Denver, CO, USA, 6–11 May 2017; pp. 1949–1960.
15. Codish, D.; Ravid, G. Detecting playfulness in educational gamification through behavior patterns. *IBM J. Res. Dev.* **2015**, *59*, 1–6. [CrossRef]
16. Conejo, F. Loyalty 3.0: How to revolutionize customer and employee engagement with big data and gamification. *J. Consum. Mark.* **2014**, *31*, 86–87.
17. Kim, B. The Popularity of Gamification in the Mobile and Social Era. *Libr. Technol. Rep.* **2015**, *51*, 5–9.
18. Kyriazidou, I.; Drakopoulos, G.; Kanavos, A.; Makris, C.; Mylonas, P. Towards Predicting Mentions to Verified Twitter Accounts: Building Prediction Models over MongoDB with keras. In *WEBIST*; ScitePress: Setubal, Portugal, 2019; pp. 25–33.
19. Tekofsky, S.; Van Den Herik, J.; Spronck, P.; Plaat, A. PsyOps: Personality assessment through gaming behavior. In Proceedings of the International Conference on the Foundations of Digital Games, SASDG, Crete, Greece, 14–17 May 2013.
20. Yang, W.; Rifqi, M.; Marsala, C.; Pinna, A. Physiological-based emotion detection and recognition in a video game context. In Proceedings of the IJCNN, Rio de Janeiro, Brazil, 8–13 July 2018; pp. 1–8.
21. Drakopoulos, G.; Pikrammenos, G.; Spyrou, E.D.; Perantonis, S.J. Emotion Recognition from Speech: A Survey. In Proceedings of the 2014 International Conference on Circuits, Systems, Communication and Information Technology Applications (CSCITA), Mumbai, India, 4–5 April 2019; pp. 432–439.
22. De Lathauwer, L. Signal Processing Based on Multilinear Algebra. Ph.D. Thesis, KU Leuven, Leuven, Belgium, 1997.
23. De Lathauwer, L.; De Moor, B. From matrix to tensor: Multilinear algebra and signal processing. In *Institute of Mathematics and Its Applications Conference Series*; Oxford University Press: Oxford, MA, USA, 1998; Volume 67, pp. 1–16.
24. Papalexakis, E.E.; Pelechrinis, K.; Faloutsos, C. Spotting misbehaviors in location-based social networks using tensors. In Proceedings of the WWW 14: 23rd International World Wide Web Conference, Seoul, Korea, 7–11 April 2014; pp. 551–552. [CrossRef]
25. Papalexakis, E.E.; Faloutsos, C. Fast efficient and scalable core consistency diagnostic for the PARAFAC decomposition for big sparse tensors. In Proceedings of the ICASSP 2015, Brisbane, Australia, 19–24 April 2015; pp. 5441–5445.
26. Alexopoulos, A.; Drakopoulos, G.; Kanavos, A.; Mylonas, P.; Vonitsanos, G. Two-Step Classification with SVD Preprocessing of Distributed Massive Datasets in Apache Spark. *Algorithms* **2020**, *13*, 71. [CrossRef]
27. Bao, Y.T.; Chien, J.T. Tensor classification network. In *MLSP*; IEEE: Piscataway, NJ, USA, 2015; pp. 1–6.
28. Drakopoulos, G.; Mylonas, P. Evaluating graph resilience with tensor stack networks: A keras implementation. *Neural Comput. Appl.* **2020**, *32*, 4161–4176. [CrossRef]

29. Benson, A.R.; Gleich, D.F.; Leskovec, J. Tensor spectral clustering for partitioning higher-order network structures. In *ICDM*; SIAM: New Delhi, India, 2015; pp. 118–126.
30. Yu, D.; Deng, L.; Seide, F. The deep tensor neural network with applications to large vocabulary speech recognition. *IEEE Trans. Audio Speech Lang. Process.* **2012**, *21*, 388–396. [CrossRef]
31. Yu, D.; Deng, L.; Seide, F. Large vocabulary speech recognition using deep tensor neural networks. In Proceedings of the INTERSPEECH 2012 ISCA's 13th Annual Conference, Portland, OR, USA, 9–13 September 2012.
32. Ma, J.; Liu, X.Y.; Shou, Z.; Yuan, X. Deep tensor admm-net for snapshot compressive imaging. In Proceedings of the 2019 IEEE/CVF International Conference on Computer Vision (ICCV), Seoul, Korea, 27 October–2 November 2019; pp. 10223–10232.
33. Drakopoulos, G.; Stathopoulou, F.; Kanavos, A.; Paraskevas, M.; Tzimas, G.; Mylonas, P.; Iliadis, L. A genetic algorithm for spatiosocial tensor clustering: Exploiting TensorFlow potential. *Evol. Syst.* **2019**. [CrossRef]
34. Abadi, M.; Barham, P.; Chen, J.; Chen, Z.; Davis, A.; Dean, J.; Devin, M.; Ghemawat, S.; Irving, G.; Isard, M.; et al. TensorFlow: A system for large-scale machine learning. In *OSDI'16*; USENIX Association: Berkeley, CA, USA, 2016; pp. 265–283.
35. Abadi, M. TensorFlow: Learning functions at scale. In *SIGPLAN International Conference on Functional Programming*; ACM: New York, NY, USA, 2016; pp. 1–8.
36. Palzer, D.; Hutchinson, B. The tensor deep stacking network toolkit. In *IJCNN*; IEEE: Piscataway, NJ, USA, 2015; pp. 1–5.
37. Drakopoulos, G.; Mylonas, P.; Sioutas, S. A Case of Adaptive Nonlinear System Identification with Third Order Tensors in TensorFlow. In *INISTA*; IEEE: Piscataway, NJ, USA, 2019; pp. 1–6. [CrossRef]
38. imdb. Ready Player One. Available online: imdb.com/title/tt16777720 (accessed on 28 September 2020).
39. Star Citizen. Wing Commander I 25th Anniversary Gameplay Video. Available online: https://www.youtube.com/watch?v=ADrl5uWckJw (accessed on 28 September 2020).
40. imdb. Wing Commander. Available online: imdb.com/title/tt0245563 (accessed on 28 September 2020).
41. WC CIC. Wing Commander. Available online: www.wcnews.com (accessed on 28 September 2020).
42. Mori, M.; MacDorman, K.F.; Kageki, N. The uncanny valley [from the field]. *IEEE Robot. Autom. Mag.* **2012**, *19*, 98–100. [CrossRef]
43. Bryan, J.I. Japanese Story-Telling. *Lotus Mag.* **1914**, *5*, 407–412.
44. Chou, Y.k. *Actionable Gamification: Beyond Points, Badges, and Leaderboards*; Packt Publishing Ltd.: Birmingham, UK, 2019.
45. Levin, S.A. The architecture of robustness. In *Global Challenges, Governance, and Complexity*; Edward Elgar Publishing: Cheltenham, UK, 2019.
46. Vallet, D.; Fernandez, M.; Castells, P.; Mylonas, P.; Avrithis, Y. A contextual personalization approach based on ontological knowledge. *Contexts Ontol. Theory Pract. Appl.* **2006**, *2006*, 35.
47. Diplaris, S.; Sonnenbichler, A.; Kaczanowski, T.; Mylonas, P.; Scherp, A.; Janik, M.; Papadopoulos, S.; Ovelgoenne, M.; Kompatsiaris, Y. Emerging, collective intelligence for personal, organisational and social use. In *Next Generation Data Technologies for Collective Computational Intelligence*; Springer: Berlin, Germany, 2011; pp. 527–573.
48. Hartfiel, D. Proof of the Simon-Ando theorem. *Proc. Am. Math. Soc.* **1996**, *124*, 67–74. [CrossRef]
49. Yang, J.; Fan, J.; Wei, Z.; Li, G.; Liu, T.; Du, X. Cost-effective data annotation using game-based crowdsourcing. *PVLDB* **2018**, *12*, 57–70. [CrossRef]
50. Yang, J.; Fan, J.; Wei, Z.; Li, G.; Liu, T.; Du, X. A game-based framework for crowdsourced data labeling. *VLDB J.* **2020**, *29*, 1311–1336. [CrossRef]
51. Seneviratne, L.; Izquierdo, E. An interactive framework for image annotation through gaming. In Proceedings of the International Conference on Multimedia Information Retrieval, Philadelphia, PA, USA, 29–31 March 2010; pp. 517–526.
52. Yannakakis, G.N.; Paiva, A. Emotion in games. In *Handbook on Affective Computing*; Springer: Berlin/Heidelberg, Germany, 2014; pp. 459–471.
53. Liu, T.; Yang, J.; Fan, J.; Wei, Z.; Li, G.; Du, X. CrowdGame: A Game-Based Crowdsourcing System for Cost-Effective Data Labeling. In Proceedings of the International Conference on Management of Data, Amsterdam, The Netherlands, 30 June–5 July 2019; pp. 1957–1960.

54. Voutos, Y.; Drakopoulos, G.; Mylonas, P. Metadata-enriched Discovery of Aspect Similarities Between Cultural Objects. In *SMAP*; IEEE: Piscataway, NJ, USA, 2020. [CrossRef]
55. Drakopoulos, G.; Voutos, Y.; Mylonas, P. Recent Advances On Ontology Similarity Metrics: A Survey. In *SEEDA-CECNSM*; IEEE: Piscataway, NJ, USA, 2020. [CrossRef]

**Publisher's Note:** MDPI stays neutral with regard to jurisdictional claims in published maps and institutional affiliations.

© 2020 by the authors. Licensee MDPI, Basel, Switzerland. This article is an open access article distributed under the terms and conditions of the Creative Commons Attribution (CC BY) license (http://creativecommons.org/licenses/by/4.0/).

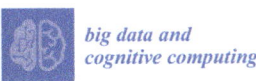

*Article*

# Networks and Stories. Analyzing the Transmission of the Feminist Intangible Cultural Heritage on Twitter

Jordi Morales-i-Gras *, Julen Orbegozo-Terradillos, Ainara Larrondo-Ureta and Simón Peña-Fernández

Journalism Department, University of the Basque Country, 48940 Leioa, Spain; julen.orbegozo@ehu.eus (J.O.-T.); ainara.larrondo@ehu.eus (A.L.-U.); simon.pena@ehu.eus (S.P.-F.)
* Correspondence: info@jordimorales.com

**Abstract:** Internet social media is a key space in which the memorial resources of social movements, including the stories and knowledge of previous generations, are organised, disseminated, and reinterpreted. This is especially important for movements such as feminism, which places great emphasis on the transmission of an intangible cultural legacy between its different generations or waves, which are conformed through these cultural transmissions. In this sense, several authors have highlighted the importance of social media and hashtivism in shaping the fourth wave of feminism that has been taking place in recent years (e.g., #metoo). The aim of this article is to present to the scientific community a hybrid methodological proposal for the network and content analysis of audiences and their interactions on Twitter: we will do so by describing and evaluating the results of different research we have carried out in the field of feminist hashtivism. Structural analysis methods such as social network analysis have demonstrated their capacity to be applied to the analysis of social media interactions as a mixed methodology, that is, both quantitative and qualitative. This article shows the potential of a specific methodological process that combines inductive and inferential reasoning with hypothetico-deductive approaches. By applying the methodology developed in the case studies included in the article, it is shown that these two modes of reasoning work best when they are used together.

**Keywords:** feminism; hashtivism; Twitter; social network analysis; Machine Learning

**Citation:** Morales-i-Gras, J.; Orbegozo-Terradillos, J.; Larrondo-Ureta, A.; Peña-Fernández, S. Networks and Stories. Analyzing the Transmission of the Feminist Intangible Cultural Heritage on Twitter. *Big Data Cogn. Comput.* **2021**, *5*, 69. https://doi.org/10.3390/bdcc5040069

Academic Editors: Manolis Wallace, Vassilis Poulopoulos, Angeliki Antoniou and Martín López-Nores

Received: 18 October 2021
Accepted: 17 November 2021
Published: 24 November 2021

**Publisher's Note:** MDPI stays neutral with regard to jurisdictional claims in published maps and institutional affiliations.

**Copyright:** © 2021 by the authors. Licensee MDPI, Basel, Switzerland. This article is an open access article distributed under the terms and conditions of the Creative Commons Attribution (CC BY) license (https://creativecommons.org/licenses/by/4.0/).

## 1. Introduction

This article is part of a broader research project dedicated to the analysis of social movements through digital conversations in social networks, taking as a reference certain public controversies of high impact in the online and offline public debate. Our methodological proposal is framed within the new research currents within the Sociology of Communication [1], which employ the digital footprint that millions of Internet users leave at the disposal of the scientific community through their interactions and actions. It is therefore a matter of using massive data and processing them through certain methodological processes to obtain information that helps the scientific community to describe and put into their interpretative context the social phenomena that take place around us, with the aim of better understanding the dynamics and changes in the logics of collective action. It is also a matter of understanding the consequences of these dynamics in the shaping of social movements, necessarily anchored in their own immaterial cultural heritage, and projecting themselves towards a future that each generation defines based on its own aspirations.

In this context, this methodological proposal offers a research perspective to the scientific community interested in social movements, the logics of collective action, contemporary public debate, and deliberative processes, among others. It does so, moreover, using the big data provided by a microblogging network such as Twitter, and with a method that not only describes, but also explains, interprets, and helps to understand how and why social networks are used and what effects and what social and democratic transformations they promote.

Social media are, after all, conversation tools of our society in the contemporary digital context and, as Castillo [2] argues, examining the conversation tools of a culture is an excellent way to understand it, and to understand its links with the past and with the future. The social media that have emerged alongside the web 2.0 have created spaces for communication and citizen participation that foster cooperation and mutual aid [3]. Those media are one of the main open mechanisms of public conversation, fundamental for the creation of the public agenda and deserving of in crescendo attention from the scientific community. Information technologies have given rise to what authors such as Dery [4], Joyanes [5] or Lévy [6] have baptized as "cyberculture" or "culture of connectivity" [7]. There is no doubt that the expansion of the main online platforms such as Facebook, Twitter, Flickr, Youtube, or Wikipedia reinforce the idea that contemporary society is facing a constantly evolving technocultural ecosystem and a phase of sociability that has online interaction as one of its main exponents. In such an ecosystem, meanings are permanently negotiated and reconsidered in a multilateral situation in which different generations participate and in which they reinterpret and construct themselves.

The methodological proposal contained in this article to observe and analyze public debate through digital network conversations reinforces the scientific production on the phenomenon that the sociologist Javier Toret calls the "connected multitude". This is defined as "the ability to connect, group and synchronize, through technological and communicative devices, and around objectives, the brains and bodies of a large number of subjects in sequences of time, space, emotions, behaviors and languages" [8] (p. 23). According to Toret, this would be one of the many structural conditions in the Network Society [9]. The connected crowd, then, emerges in the new paradigm of Mass Self-Communication [10] in the Network Society and as one of the main characteristics of what researchers such as Melucci [11], Candón-Mena [12] and Romero [13] call "New Social Movements". In this context, the demonstrations against the World Trade Organization summit in Seattle (1999), the Black Lives Matter movement, the Arab Spring, the Spanish 15-M, the movements fighting for degrowth or the feminist movements that are re-emerging in the new political, social, and communicative context.

In this organizational context, the concept of a "social network" ceases to be a metaphor and becomes pure metonymy, and therefore, all those that understand that the relationship between agents is the minimum unit of social analysis emerge as privileged perspectives of analysis: we will see that Social Network Analysis –or simply, SNA— is particularly fertile in these contexts. Activist networks or networks of social movements, sometimes defined with uncomfortably cybernetic references, are bundles of interactions, communicative and action spaces where experiences of struggle and self-organization are shared, where a certain reflexivity lives and a shared sense of protests is built through current and virtual dialogues with past generations that embody the different stages or waves of the movements themselves, thus managing their immaterial cultural heritage. Beyond a social morphology, networks have become a model for emergent forms of politics [14] (p. 92). In our opinion, this also applies to the politics of collective memory and of the intangible cultural heritages of political and social movements.

In this article we take this metonymic conception of social movements as social networks as our starting point. We intend, firstly, to present the main characteristics of the research with which our epistemology is connected, and secondly, to detail the methodological proposal that we have articulated in other research and make it available to the scientific community for discussion and improvement.

We are going to present a methodological proposal designed for the study of massive conversations in social media, through which to generate knowledge about a particular object of study, which is hashtag feminism and its importance for the configuration of the so-called fourth wave of feminism, understanding such a process of self-definition as an exercise of transmission and management of an immaterial cultural heritage [15]. At the heart of the proposal lies the will to contribute to the necessary hybridization between perspectives linked to Computer Science and Social Science, between Data Engineering and content analysis, between quantitative and qualitative analysis techniques, and between inductive and hypothetico-deductive reasoning. We strongly believe, and we will try to argue, that such hybrid approaches are today more necessary than ever.

In this article we will focus on the following issues:

- We will argue the generational importance of hashtag feminism and the fourth feminist wave, and we will especially focus on explaining why working with Twitter data gives us access to a privileged vantage point from which to observe the dynamics of self-definition of the movement itself that are taking place during these same years.
- We will outline the main characteristics of big data as a socio-technical paradigm and highlight the opportunities it offers to social scientists who approach it with a hybrid analytical perspective: mathematically and technically solvent as well as phenomenologically grounded;
- We will also discuss the universe of technical opportunities and the legal limits we face when we want to work with massive data from social media to understand the dynamics that occur in them;
- We will present a particular methodological proposal based on Network Analysis and Machine Learning techniques. We will argue in favor of the implementation of a series of unsupervised algorithms to provide analytical context to big data, and then we will defend the articulation of Data Engineering techniques to facilitate further analysis;
- We will present four different investigations that we have already developed in the framework of the broad project that also gives rise to this article with a more methodological orientation. In these four investigations we have deployed the methodology we present, giving epistemological priority to the analysis of the context by means of inductive logics, without renouncing causal reasoning and hypothetico-deductive logic;
- Finally, we will elaborate a series of concluding reflections.

## 2. Objectives

### 2.1. Analyzing the Shaping of the Current Feminist Wave through Twitter

The aim of this article is double. On the one hand, we want to bring to the table a specific methodology for the analysis of Twitter conversations that can be applied to the study of the shaping of the contemporary feminist movement. This involves the assumption, in line with Deborah Withers' work on the politics of transmission of the feminist intangible cultural heritage in the digital age [15] (p. 5), that each feminist generation defines and generates itself through practices that involve the transmission of an intangible cultural heritage that connects and enables dialogue between generations. This is precisely what a metaphor as beautiful as that of the "waves" tells us when characterizing such generations. On the other hand, we would also like to present a series of empirical works that we have developed and reflect on them in these same keys of transmission of a feminist intangible cultural heritage.

This methodological proposal focuses especially on the most well-known microblogging platform at a global level, which is Twitter. This is so, among other reasons, because Twitter is the source of information that best allows segmenting users, discovering how citizens participate in the political debate and how they are grouped by ideological affinity [16]. Likewise, Twitter has become a consolidated medium for communicating issues related to politics, having since its birth in 2006 a growing importance in political contexts and having been used by virtually all actors interacting in the public-political space [17]. Five years after its creation in 2006, Rodríguez and Ureña [18] already pointed out Twitter as the social network that had acquired the greatest relevance among the political and journalistic class. For Piscitelli [19] (p. 15) at that time it also constituted "one of the most powerful communication mechanisms in history".

Subsequently, from various scientific perspectives authors such as Pariser [20], Page [21], Carr [22], Marwick [23], or Fuchs [24] lowered the most encouraging expectations around the use of social networks and social or political mobilization. As summarized by Giraldo-

Luque, Fernández-García, and Pérez-Arce [25] in their research on the mobilization that emerged around the hashtag #Niunamenos, Twitter is a means of dissemination and a space for expression around certain public controversies, but its scope for building consensus scenarios or transforming preconceived imaginaries is limited.

That said, Twitter has also been defined during its decade of existence as a space for social interaction, dialectical exchange, and as a sphere of deliberation in which much of the activism of social movements and contemporary social mobilization is [26–28]. In fact, this social network has aroused great interest in the academic community in recent years due to the specific type of conversation that takes place on it. Twitter is undoubtedly the most popular network for discussing political issues and current news, and has had a great impact on all the political and social mobilizations that have taken place in the world in recent years: from the Arab Spring to the Black Lives Matter movement that emerged during the pandemic following the spread of the COVID-19 virus in the U.S. For this reason, social and political movements have been a privileged object of analysis through Twitter data and SNA techniques.

In this sense, the scientific field attaches particular importance to the observation of the changing communication paradigm to further elucidate the dichotomy between the dichotomy of social media and their social function. To this end, big data from social media interaction is an immense source of information with great potential to explain social processes from multidisciplinary perspectives such as sociology, communication, or politics.

In the specific case of feminism, we believe that the analysis of conversations established on Twitter allows us to understand several dynamics that are established for the transmission of the feminist intangible cultural heritage, and even for the conformation of the "waves" that characterize the extension and temporal evolution of the movement. Several authors have already pointed out the importance of feminist hashtivism in shaping the fourth wave [28–30]. In this regard, over the past few years many studies have proliferated around the #metoo movement and its aftershocks beyond the initial scandals linked to the Hollywood film industry [31–34]. In our view, all these analyses and meta-analyses pivot around a series of generational phenomena that are intimately linked to the transmission of the feminist intangible cultural heritage, and even, to the controversies that can develop between generations of activists.

### 2.2. Related Works

The perspective we will develop in the following section is certainly innovative. However, it should also be acknowledged that we are also underpinned by a growing scholarly interest in social movements on Twitter, and more specifically, in feminism on Twitter. Several authors have already contributed to framing fourth-wave feminism as a connected or networked feminism, which was internationally raised by the strength of protests such as #MeToo [34,35]. There has also been a strong recent interest in the particularity of Spanish feminism on Twitter [36–38], which is the subject of several of the papers that follow.

A trend that has advanced in parallel to the academic interest in feminism is the interest in the social consequences of artificial intelligence. Here, a small yet increasingly important number of feminist articles around the concept of algorithmic injustice, data justice or data feminism are noteworthy [39,40]. In addition to this, there is a small group of research with which, in addition to sharing an object of study such as fourth-wave feminism on Twitter, we have important methodological links. This is research that uses Social Network Analysis to investigate relationships and discourse [41,42]. Undoubtedly, our methodological proposal should be considered within this general paradigm.

## 3. Methodology
### 3.1. Big Data and Interpretative Perspectives

The kind of challenges that have shaped the big data paradigm have largely been technical and technological challenges. In his famous 2001 article—in which big data is not yet referred to as such—technologist Doug Laney [43] mentioned the three "Vs" (i.e., volume, velocity, and variety) that would become crucial in the field of data management over the next few years. All of Laney's Vs referred to different technical aspects of data storage and processing infrastructures. Later, other authors [44–46] would go on to add more Vs to characterize the paradigm, such as "variety", "veracity", "validity", "volatility", "virtuality", or "visualization". It is at this point that the concept of "value" is presented as central, associated with the notion that data needs to be interpreted to generate return, whether economic or otherwise.

The predictions of some overconfident observers during the first decade of the 21st century invited us to think of a "post-analytical" world [47]. Instead, if anything has become clear over the last 20 years in reference to big data, it is that the analysis and interpretation of such data is a key aspect that can compromise the most sophisticated of automatic processing systems. Over the last few years, dozens of cases have come to light in which systems based on heavily automated massive data—many of them based on "black box" algorithms such as neural networks—have given rise to socially unacceptable situations. Among these situations or perverse effects, algorithms that reinforce human cognitive biases giving rise to echo chambers [48] or bubble filters [20], algorithms that discriminate socially vulnerable collectives [49,50] or, even, chatbots that acquire racist behaviors through community "training" [51] stand out.

Nowadays, large amounts of data flow through new channels becoming a valuable source of information [52]. At the same time, as evidenced by all the cases mentioned above, the most important and socially transcendent challenges faced by the big data paradigm are those related to the analysis and interpretation of data, and not so much to the technical capacity for its storage and processing. Such is the case that some of the most authoritative voices in the world of Artificial Intelligence [53] have already urged the community to abandon the use of black box algorithms (e.g., deep neural networks). These experts propose to redesign systems based on simpler and more transparent algorithms (e.g., regression or decision trees) that facilitate analytical and interpretative work.

This epistemological shift that is taking place among researchers and practitioners of big data, artificial intelligence, and data mining in general [54], represents a great opportunity for social scientists, and for communication scientists. The big data paradigm relies on enormously diverse data sources: hence the V for "variety". Leaving aside exceptional sources such as genomic and biomedical data, meteorological, and environmental data, and some of the data from industry and mining, most big data is social, or has a large social component (e.g., financial, banking, GPS mobility, urban sensor, web browsing, e-commerce, or credit card consumption data). Among them, data from the so-called social media are particularly voluminous, as they come from a wide variety of user-platform and user-user interactions within the different platforms (e.g., posts, mentions, likes, swipes, or shares).

Social media data is a sociotechnological by-product generated jointly by platforms and users from the systematic recording of a series of interactions [55]. Therefore, given its interactive and relational nature, the most abundant data in social media is that which is easily computable as a matrix of relationships (e.g., mentions between users, friendship or follower relationships between users, or relationships established between users and content). This gives great centrality to structural analysis methods [56] such as Social Network Analysis (SNA). With a somewhat smaller but equally important presence, social media also includes data of an attributional nature (e.g., metadata associated with a post or a user). Unlike relational data, attributive data tend to be used in prediction and classification models using Machine Learning (ML) techniques [57].

It is around these two types of techniques (i.e., SNA and ML), that most social media data mining studies are framed, often combining aspects of both. These techniques are usually labeled as "quantitative" because of their mathematical and computational orientation. According to the view defended in this article, this is a more than questionable label, rooted in a dichotomy that is debatable to say the least (i.e., the difference between qualitative and quantitative perspectives). SNA has demonstrated on multiple and diverse occasions its ability to be applied as a mixed methodology [58,59]; on the other hand, ML is increasingly used as a supporting method in qualitative analyses, especially with data from social media [60,61].

In our view, both SNA and ML challenge the tension artificially established in Social Science between quantitative and qualitative techniques, inviting us to overcome this dichotomy. These techniques put on the table the need to articulate analytical strategies that combine the mathematical and computational rigor typical of quantitative approaches with the interpretative skills that characterize qualitative analysis. The type of perspective that we have tried to develop in the research reported in this article is intended to be a contribution to this way of understanding Social Science and big data.

### 3.2. Social Media as Relational and Textual Big Data Sources: Possibilities and Legal Limits

Twitter is the social media with the most open data policy to date, compared to other platforms such as Facebook or Instagram. Twitter has a free API (Application Programing Interface) that allows data retrieval with a maximum of seven days of retroactivity, and allows, according to the information provided by the company on its website, real-time data capture, provided that no more than 1% of the platform's global traffic is captured.

The data that the standard, free Twitter API can retrieve is quite extensive: tweets and retweets published, relationships between users, and even their metadata (e.g., their biography, number of followers or number of followers). As reported by the company itself, the standard API does not return 100% of the tweets issued, but it does return "the most important ones" since its API "is oriented towards relevance and not completeness" [62]. As such, the data we can retrieve from the free API represents an indeterminate portion of the total that, in principle, reflects the totality of the conversation very well. Twitter raises the possibility of acquiring 100% of the data and greater retroactivity in its payment plans.

Derived from these conditions of opportunity and the relational nature of the data that can be retrieved from the Twitter API, studies on Twitter using SNA techniques have proliferated during the second decade of the 21st century [63,64]. In this sense, as indicated above, social, and political movements have been a central object of analysis using Twitter data and SNA techniques.

It is possible to distinguish three different strategies of analysis through the conversations and digital interactions of this type of movements and other expressions of collective action developed on Twitter: (1) mention networks, (2) semantic networks, and (3) following relationship networks. All three types derive from a series of decisions that researchers make about the type of data to be represented in the graphs, and about the representation strategy itself. Likewise, the three types of analysis raise different possibilities to be transferred to the methodological processes applied to data captured in other social networks.

The first type consists of the analysis of dynamic relationships, formalized in networks of mentions, retweets, or replies between users [65–68]. This type of networks tends to be conceptualized as directed (i.e., the edges of the network have direction, they are emitted by a node and received by another node) and weighted (i.e., the edges of the network have weights, being able to represent a relationship of one or several mentions), due to the type of relationship they represent.

In general, these are networks with very low densities (i.e., most of the nodes in the network are not directly linked) and with very high "Modularity" figures obtained using the Louvain algorithm [69] (i.e., the communities reflect very strong intra-group association patterns, and very weak inter-group association patterns), which we will see in detail later. Because of the type of data represented, this analysis can only be carried out on Twitter or other platforms where the mention-type relationship plays an analogous role: Mastodon, Gab, or Slack. This type of analysis is not directly transferable to networks such as Facebook or Instagram. On Facebook pages, it is normal to respond to the messages posted, and there is no analogous element to the retweet that is traceable between pages. On Instagram, people like rather than comment, and likes are not provided by the API at the level of each user.

Semantic networks, as a second line of research, have been explored in a complementary or alternative way to Topic Modeling algorithms [70–72]. Word networks tend to be conceptualized in an undirected and weighted way. That means that it is assumed, as a rule, that two words will co-occur symmetrically, or that they will be symmetrically linked, and also, that the number of times two words co-occur in a discourse is usually a relevant factor in the analysis.

The morphological characteristics of semantic networks are highly variable since they can represent different types of discourse with very different levels of lexical diversity. It is very common for semantic networks to be the result of a series of data processing operations using Natural Language Programming techniques, such as the segmentation or "tokenization" of a text (i.e., its division into words, sentences or paragraphs), the filtering of stopwords (i.e., the removal of particles that do not provide relevant information, such as articles, adverbs, or conjunctions) or "lemmatization" (i.e., the transformation of the words of a text into their canonical form, according to a pre-designed dictionary). In contrast to the previous case, this type of analysis is extremely versatile and transferable to any textual data source: social media, written and digital press, blogs, books, or scientific articles, among other cases of analysis.

Relationships between words, between sentences or between documents can be studied through SNA, which has yielded very good results in recent research [73]. To this end, several types of networks can be synthesized according to analytical needs: networks of words according to the number of times they appear together, networks of documents according to the number of words they share, networks of hashtags according to the frequency with which users have used them in their posts, and so on.

In any case, the most common approach to this type of analytical problems has been through heuristic rule processes from the fields of Natural Language Programming [74] or in combination with ML models [75], which usually imply a significant improvement in the predictive or classificatory capacity of such models. Due to the great complexity of the human language, black box analysis techniques such as embeds or embeddings have proliferated during the last few years [76]. These are deep neural networks which, as we have already seen, provide very good results in exchange for a great opacity in the internal processes of the algorithms. These technologies enjoy enormous popularity among computational scientists faced with problems such as word prediction in search engines or automatic text translation.

Finally, it is worth highlighting the third type of analysis, most likely the least employed, which is the one that consists of observing networks of established relationships and their effects or consequences [77,78]. The networks synthesized from the relationships established between social media users will be directed or undirected, depending on the platform (e.g., on Twitter they will be directed, since one user can follow another without being followed back by the other; whereas on Facebook or LinkedIn they should be undirected, since if there is no agreement between two users, they will not be "friends" or "contacts" on these networks), and, typically, they will be unweighted (i.e., it is not possible to follow anyone more than once on Twitter, nor to be friends with someone more than once on Facebook or LinkedIn).

In this type of analysis, a distinction can be made between egonets and socionets, which are fundamental categories of the SNA [79]. The first type of networks (i.e., egonets), in the context of social media, are those that reflect the links between a user's followers or friends. The second type (i.e., socionets) represents the relationships established between a group of nodes, without any of them constituting the center of the network. In the second case, the population of the network will have been designed according to some criterion external to the network itself (e.g., the network of relationships among the students of a course or among the journalists of a media outlet). The formal characteristics of the network will depend on the criteria according to which they have been constituted, although they will tend to be denser than the networks of mentions because of transitivity and homophily characteristic of personal networks: it is to be expected that someone's friends will end up knowing each other and establishing friendship as well [80]. Likewise, the Modularity figures derived from the Louvain algorithm will tend to be lower than for mention networks.

Twitter allows synthesizing egonets and socionets by retrieving data from its standard API. The other powerful networks, such as Facebook or LinkedIn, allowed egonets with their standard API before the Cambridge Analytica scandal [81]. Currently, these networks no longer provide these data, although they can be achieved through web scraping or web scraping techniques (i.e., techniques for the automatic extraction of data available on websites and social networks), increasingly popular, being used for a myriad of data mining operations (e.g., robots for indexing web content, flight, hotel, or insurance comparators, or for automatic alert systems). However, their legal basis is still somewhat unclear [82].

Web scraping can be implemented with completely legal tools, but its use may contravene the regulations of the social media platforms or websites from which the data is extracted. As a rule, therefore, these are operations that cannot be implemented by a logged-in user, but which the social media company will not be able to prevent if they occur from a non-logged-in user, since nothing that a social media platform makes available to a non-logged-in surfer can contravene the provisions of the data protection laws operating in the territories in which the platform operates. Although this is a swampy terrain with many issues, the type of judicial decisions that have been made over the last few years are favorable to web scraping of information available to non-logged-in users [83].

Following this doctrine, and if we stick to data that can be accessed by a non-logged-in user, web scraping is a very good alternative to API data access for research aimed at synthesizing semantic networks, or some hybrid models, such as networks between users and words, or between users and hashtags. One way or another, it will always be possible to apply web scraping techniques to obtain semantic data from social media, as well as from other sites on the Internet. In this way, the analyst will be able to rely on complete datasets rather than an indeterminate portion of the total and will have a greater temporal margin and retroactivity. However, web scraping is not feasible for research that focuses on the mention relationships between users of the major social media platforms, let alone their follower or friendship relationships. Obtaining this data is technically feasible, but it is necessary to violate the social media regulations, and in many cases, also the data protection laws in force in each territory.

## 4. Results

*4.1. Network Analysis and Machine Learning as Assistants for the Interpretation of Dynamics in Virtual Networks*

We have previously emphasized the need to articulate analytical and interpretative perspectives to overcome the artificial distinction between quantitative and qualitative analysis that has characterized social science in recent decades. The big data paradigm –and more specifically, techniques such as SNA and ML— exposes the obsolescence of this way of segmenting scientists based on their skill repertoires, while pointing to the need to generate new hybrid methodological frameworks that allow for simultaneous mathematical and phenomenological analyses.

In our opinion, one of the most effective ways to analyze and interpret the dynamics of virtual networks is to articulate SNA and content analysis techniques, through the development of workflows more typical of Data Engineering. This involves taking as a starting point the mention-type interactions (i.e., nominations of one user by another) on the social network Twitter, in the context of a series of digital conversations related to issues of public and political debate, and then synthesizing networks or graphs from them (i.e., Figure 1). Thus, in the resulting massive graphs, each point or node represents a user of the Twitter social network (e.g., a personal account, a company, a media outlet, a political party, etc.) and each line represents an established mention from one user to another (e.g., a retweet, a reply, or a direct allusion). These are therefore directed and weighted networks, to which a series of algorithms are applied to generate value from the data.

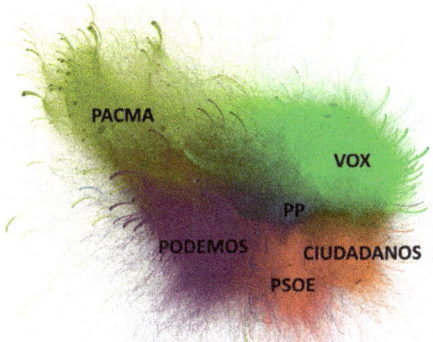 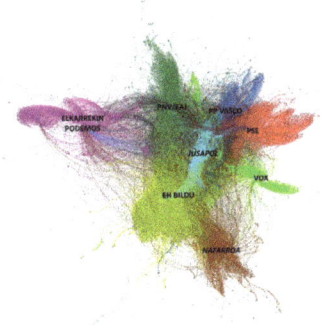

**Figure 1.** Network of mentions to political parties on Twitter during an electoral campaign (April 2019, Spain) in two different spheres of influence. Source: Own elaboration with Gephi software.

One of the most useful Machine Learning algorithms for a perspective such as the one detailed in this paper is the Louvain algorithm for community identification in massive graphs [69]. It is an unsupervised learning algorithm that performs a series of operations on the data in a recursive manner and allows the identification of clusters or sets of nodes that make up specific communities within a network. The process by which the Louvain algorithm identifies communities consists of randomly grouping nodes, and permanently evaluating the gain or loss of Modularity (i.e., a metric that evaluates the overall quality of the community partition of a network, comparing it with a randomly constituted network of equal size) [84] implementing only those groupings that result in gains in this metric (i.e., optimizing the quality of the community partition).

The output of the Louvain algorithm consists of a set of communities (i.e., a community partition) and a Modularity figure that allows us to evaluate its mathematical relevance. According to the creator of the Modularity metric, Mark Newman [84], values between 0.3 and 1.0 indicate a good quality of the community partition of a Network (i.e., it is assumed that the network is significantly different from the one that could have been constituted by chance). Despite their obvious similarities, modularity should not be confused with a hypothetical validation metric such as the "$p$-value" used in inferential statistics for the acceptance or rejection of the null hypothesis. Modularity is not used by the Louvain algorithm as a metric for hypothetical validation, but as an internal optimization mechanism. In other words, the algorithm is oriented to obtain the best possible Modularity figure. This feature, far from being a problem, is what allows the researcher to work with categories based on empirical data. This is a great example of how unsupervised algorithms facilitate qualitative readings of massive quantitative data.

In community identification, being an unsupervised process, the role of the analyst is not to train the algorithm to identify one or another type of groups, but to interpret the results of a node clustering process based on the patterns that the algorithm itself is able to identify in the data autonomously. Common SNA software (e.g., Gephi or Pajek) allows the analyst to establish community partitions at different resolutions [85], thus being able to choose between identifying more smaller groups or fewer larger groups. Thus, when it comes to analyzing social movements such as feminism itself, this type of approach allows conceptualizing the complexity of social identity (i.e., the diversity of identifications available in the Self and its hierarchical structure) and intergroup relations in a privileged way and allows social analysts to move away from essentialist and reductionist conceptualizations [86].

In this analytical model, the cluster is the element that provides the context for the analysis of the rest of the data: the leaders in the network and its contents. Regarding the analysis of the leaders of a network (e.g., the most mentioned users, the most active in mentioning third parties, the best intermediaries, the ones that can most easily reach any other, etc.), it will be relevant to use metrics such as the input degree (i.e., the number of edges received by a node), the output degree (i.e., the number of outgoing edges) or the betweenness centrality degree (i.e., the number of shortest paths between pairs of nodes in a network that have to pass through each node). On the other hand, for content analysis, lists of tweets and lists of hashtags are elaborated by clusters, by means of Data Engineering strategies of crossing and combining data sources (i.e., Figure 2).

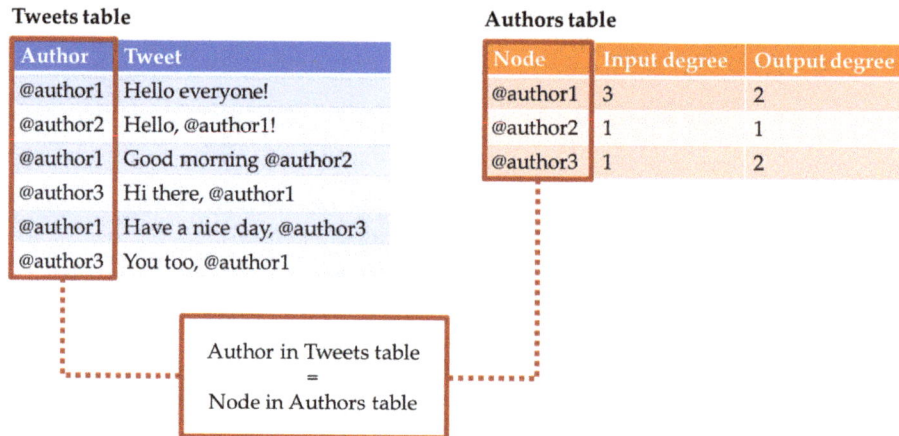

**Figure 2.** Example of combining data from two different tables. Source: Own elaboration with Power Point.

The next step in this proposal is to use certain Business Intelligence software such as Tableau, PowerBi, Google Data Studio, or Grafana to carry out the cross-referencing of data. All this without neglecting the desirability of also being able to count on SQL and NoSQL database technologies that allow to establish links between databases with different degrees of structuring, depending on specific categories, and to subsequently represent the combined fields in tables or graphs. Using this type of tools, it is possible to generate dashboards with linked visualizations that allow interactive navigation: selecting each cluster and visualizing its properties based on the indicators and key variables for each case of analysis. This type of approach therefore requires analytical profiles that are also familiar with some fundamental operations of Data Engineering, such as value transformation or table joining.

*4.2. Combining Induction and Deduction to Understand the Current Feminist Wave*

Social media constitute a sort of public sphere in which different social movements deploy their strategies and define themselves through practices that involve the transmission of an immaterial legacy [15]. In the case of feminism, this has been recurrently expressed through the metaphor of "waves," about which several authors suggest that we are currently facing the fourth [87]. The role of hashtivism and, very particularly that which has been developed on Twitter, is becoming very important in the self-definition of fourth wave feminism, a constructor of new political subjects that pivot around particular campaigns or hashtags [88]. The fourth wave of feminism thus dialogues with analogical activists who have endowed them with a whole tradition of struggle and a not inconsiderable set of small victories that, taken together, have improved the living conditions of women in different parts of the world. It is precisely this dialogue, sometimes explicit and sometimes implicit, in which the practices of intangible cultural heritage transmission and political self-definition of fourth-wave feminism materialize. It is this dialogue that we wish to analyze here.

The guidelines and steps described above can be applied in various investigations to approach the object of study from different perspectives, depending on the research objectives. We will now look at four practical applications of the described methodology applied to the analysis of fourth-wave feminism and feminist hashtivism. In them, we start from a perspective that develops from a type of inductive and inferential reasoning that seeks theoretical synthesis from the observation of cases (i.e., Figure 3). We will also see how this type of approach is used in a complementary way with hypothetico-deductive approaches that seek the opposite: the validation of theories and hypotheses based on the observation of cases. In fact, by putting these practical and real examples on the table, it is argued that these two modes of reasoning work best when used together, and this is precisely one of the main strengths of the method of analysis described.

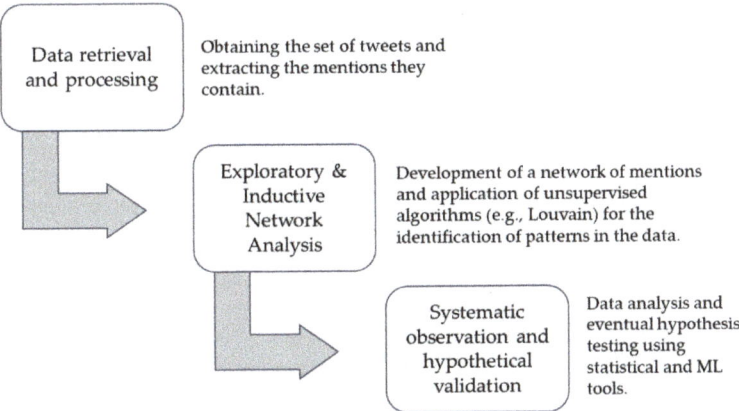

**Figure 3.** General workflow for the proposed methodology. Source: Own elaboration with Power Point.

In methodological terms, we argue that attributing epistemological priority to contextual analysis using unsupervised algorithms and an inducive logic (e.g., detecting communities with the Louvain algorithm) is an efficient strategy to overcome part of the most common problems in the analysis of massive social media data, such as, for example, uninformative and/or spurious sentiment analysis [89].

Below we cite four case studies of research published in scientific journals that employ this method and apply it to the observation of phenomena related to one of the most significant contemporary mobilizing currents such as feminisms and their presence in the online public debate. All these investigations are part of the general project whose methodological documentation we are carrying out in these pages. It is a project dedicated to the analysis of different conversations and controversies that occupy fourth wave feminism in the Spanish, Spanish-speaking and, eventually, also international sphere. All of them have in common, therefore, being investigations thought and executed from the same epistemological and methodological mentality, and furthermore, the fact of dealing with an object of study linked to the practices, transmitters of the intangible cultural heritage of feminism.

### 4.2.1. Feminisms Outraged at Justice

The reaction of Spanish-speaking feminism on Twitter to the controversial sentence against the members of "la manada"—a group of men who raped a woman at a local festival—is analyzed in this article using SNA techniques [90]. The sentence in question condemned the rapists for harassment, but not for rape, despite recognizing the materiality of the crime, also acquitting them of the crimes of recording the rape with a cell phone and robbery with intimidation.

Following network analysis and community identification, the five most disseminated tweets in each community are identified, along with their most prominent leaders by input degree (i.e., the most mentioned). From the content analysis, a total of three "macro-narratives" are identified around the Spanish judicial system, raised by the reaction to the sentence on Twitter. Two of these "macro narratives" projected a very negative evaluation of the Spanish judicial system, while the third narrative was one of defense of the system and, simultaneously, of criticism towards the feminist movement.

In this research it was possible to identify a series of practices strongly linked to the construction of the political subject of fourth-wave feminism, as well as a series of practices of identification and differentiation with respect to older generations and to the historical feminist movement.

4.2.2. Digital Prospects of the Contemporary Feminist Movement for Dialogue and International Mobilization

An analysis is carried out based on the analysis of the conversation in Spanish and English around the 2018 international day against violence against women on Twitter [88]. The most shared contents of each cluster of the network, both messages and images, are inspected and the levels of intercommunity homophily (i.e., to what extent nodes tend to establish links with those who are part of the same group or with those who are part of the other group) [91] are examined.

Overall, the nuances between Latin feminist activisms (i.e., generally more contentious) and Anglo-Saxon ones (i.e., more liberal and based on the support of individual cases) and the absence of shared transnational and translinguistic narratives are observed, which leads researchers to problematize the usefulness of feminist hashtivism, at least, as far as its international coordination is concerned.

The results of this research open the door to consider the plurality of forms in which fourth-wave feminism materializes, as well as the different links established with the legacy of feminist activists of previous waves and the transmission of their immaterial cultural heritage.

4.2.3. Feminist Hashtag Activism in Spain

An analysis is made of the contents of the clusters during the digital conversation that arose because of the sentence of "la manada" in April 2018 and continued for a few months, through a series of hashtags in solidarity with the victim [92]. On this occasion, attention is paid to the tone of their messages, and an interesting correlation is detected between those clusters with higher Input Degree Centralization (i.e., to what extent the reception of mentions is centralized or decentralized in the network) [93] and a greater banality in the contents (e.g., memes and other viral contents) and, in turn, between those clusters more decentralized in the reception of mentions and a greater seriousness, formality and anchorage with the historical feminist movement in the contents disseminated and the codes used.

In addition, a link is established between an external variable to the network (i.e., the degree of politicization of the users, according to the number of politicians' accounts followed) and the belonging to a cluster of high or low input degree Centralization by means of a Machine Learning algorithm: a logistic regression that achieved a predictive capacity with an accuracy of 67.4%. In other words, it is inferred that the number of followed politician accounts is a very good predictor for the mode of political participation on Twitter.

This study invites us to consider the diversity of modes of participation and belonging to fourth-wave feminism, as well as the diversity of forms of linkage (i.e., stronger, or weaker, more conscious, or more unconscious) with previous generations and with the feminist immaterial cultural heritage.

4.2.4. Influence of Gender in Electoral Debates in Spain

The type and tone of the most shared messages in different clusters are identified, with the occasion of two televised electoral debates (April 2019 General Elections in Spain), which were starred entirely by men (#ElDebateDecisivo) and the other entirely by women (#L6Neldebate) [94].

It is observed, through the analysis of the most shared tweets in each cluster, and the strategy of identifying the nodes present in the female debate in the clusters of the male one, that the type of users who participate in the conversation of both debates do so with more serious codes, while those who participate only in the male one made use of banal and humorous resources more frequently.

In line with the findings of the previous article, in this one we can observe a certain alignment between the modes of articulation of the more self-conscious feminist hashtivism with the feminist agenda of political parties, while a greater alignment of spontaneous and depoliticized feminism with the irreverent and sometimes banal standards of virtual conversations.

## 5. Conclusions with Discussion

Social networks such as Twitter are a constant object of analysis by the various disciplines of social science, among which we highlight in this paper the discipline that focuses on the analysis of mass communication, transformed into mass interpersonal communication [95]. This field has evidenced an indisputable transformation that alters the traditional theoretical-methodological foundations of research on communicative production and reception. One of the main evidences of such an evolution would be the growth in the use of systematic and standardized data techniques in empirical works, as well as the tendency to put the research effort into the discursive and dialogic dimension of communication [96].

After presenting a specific workflow, which we believe is also replicable and applicable to many analytical objects, we have presented four different investigations around the same theoretical object. With variations, in the four investigations we have proceeded with the download of data from the Twitter API, with Network Analysis applied to the mention relationships between Twitter users, with community identification based on the network of mentions, and with the visualization of each community through a data modelling and visualization strategy. Not surprisingly, each investigation has led to a separate set of results. At the aggregate level, however, what we have seen is the usefulness of the methodology.

Our intention here has been to expose a replicable methodology for the generation of knowledge in massive data environments that require hybrid analytical perspectives and skills that can articulate rigorous mathematical analysis and relevant phenomenological interpretations. Our object of study has been fourth-wave feminism, and more specifically, we have focused on some reflections on the processes of transmission of the feminist intangible cultural heritage that take place on Twitter, in the thread of massive conversations, often chaotic, which nevertheless vertebrate and emplace the contemporary self-definition of the movement, always in dialogue with its recent and not so recent past, as well as projecting into the future. To this end, a series of specific analytical procedures have been defined to study the processes of communication on Twitter.

The distinctiveness of this methodological procedure consists not only in the use of analysis techniques and tools that are not very common in the social-scientific field, although increasingly so, but also in deploying a type of strategy that makes it possible to combine quantitative and qualitative analysis, as well as hypothetico-deductive and inductive perspectives. The paradigm of big data and the techniques associated with the computational sciences to which we have referred—SNA and ML—make it possible, to a large extent, to overcome old technical, methodological, and even epistemological dichotomies or, at least, place us before new scenarios that provoke new metaphors and ways of looking at the classic objects of study of the social and communication sciences. These analyses not only serve to characterize the most recent research in communication 2.0, but also shape an analytical proposal based on the virtues of Twitter to weave individual messages with collective dialogic capacity around certain conversations or hashtags, this being a logic closely linked to feminist hashtivism, fourth-wave feminism, and the processes of transmission of immaterial cultural heritages in digital environments.

In any case, neither the proposed methodology nor the research we have used as an example obviate the existence of critical positions on the potential of the digital medium, on hashtivism in general, and on feminist hashtivism. We understand that, in addition, many of these critiques—traditionally established from the academy and from the feminist activism of previous generations—not only imply a form of real dialogue between feminists, but also imply in themselves practices of transmission of the immaterial cultural heritage: a transmission that never takes place in a linear and unidirectional way, but that necessarily passes through the self-constructive and creative filter of each generation or wave. Similarly, the proposals collected present not only the benefits, but also the methodological limitations of research on Twitter [97] based on the restrictions of the data collected, the bias of representation when making general assumptions and other problems, derived, for example, from the language of use of the users.

**Author Contributions:** Conceptualization, J.M.-i.-G. and J.O.-T.; methodology, J.M.-i.-G.; software, J.M.-i.-G.; validation, A.L.-U., J.O.-T. and S.P.-F.; formal analysis, A.L.-U.; investigation, J.O.-T.; resources, S.P.-F.; data curation, J.M.-i.-G.; writing—original draft preparation, J.M.-i.-G.; writing—review and editing, J.O.-T., A.L.-U. and S.P.-F.; visualization, J.M.-i.-G.; supervision, J.O.-T. and J.M.-i.-G.; funding acquisition, A.L.-U. and S.P.-F. All authors have read and agreed to the published version of the manuscript.

**Funding:** This research was funded by Basque Government grant number IT-1112.

**Institutional Review Board Statement:** Not applicable.

**Informed Consent Statement:** Written informed consent was not obtained due to Twitter API access policies.

**Data Availability Statement:** Data available upon request.

**Conflicts of Interest:** The authors declare no conflict of interest.

## References

1. Fernández-Ferández, M.; Tardivo, V. La sociología de la Comunicación y la Mass Coomunication Research: Tradición y actualidad. *Espac. Abierto Cuad. Venez. Sociol.* **2016**, *25*, 133–142.
2. Castillo, A. *Neologismos y Sociedad del Conocimiento*; Ariel: Barcelona, Spain, 2007.
3. García-Estévez, N. La convergencia activista en Hong Kong: Del ciberactivismo de 'Occupy Central' al hacktivismo de 'Operación Hong Kong'. In *Move.Net: Actas del I Congreso Internacional Move.Net Sobre Movimientos Sociales y TIC (139–156)*; Grupo Interdisciplinario de Estudios en Comunicación, Política y Cambio Social de la Universidad de Sevilla: Seville, Spain, 2015.
4. Dery, M. *Velocidad de Escape. La Cibercultura en el Final del Siglo*; Siruela: Madrid, Spain, 1998.
5. Joyanes, L. *Cibersociedad, los Retos Sociales Ante un Nuevo Mundo Digital*; McGraw-Hill: Madrid, Spain, 1997.
6. Lévy, P. *Cibercultura. La Cultura de la Sociedad Digital*; Anthropos: Mexico City, Mexico, 2007.
7. Van Dijck, J. *La Cultura de la Conectividad. Una Historia Crítica de las Redes Sociales*; Siglo Veintiuno Editores: Buenos Aires, Argentina, 2016.
8. Toret, J. *Tecnopolítica: La Potencia de las Multitudes Conectadas. El Sistema Red 15M, un Nuevo Paradigma de la Política Distribuida*; IN3 Working Paper Series; Universitat Oberta de Catalunya: Barcelona, Spain, 2013.
9. Castells, M. Comunicación, poder y contrapoder en la sociedad red (I). Los medios y la política. *Telos* **2008**, *74*, 1–19.
10. Castells, M. *Comunicación y Poder*; Alianza Editorial: Madrid, Spain, 2009.
11. Melucci, A. *Acción Colectiva, Vida Cotidiana y Democracia*; Centro de Estudios Sociológicos: Mexico City, Mexico, 1999.
12. Candón-Mena, J.I. *Internet en Movimiento: Nuevos Movimientos Sociales y Nuevos Medios en la Sociedad de la Información*; Universidad Complutense de Madrid, Servicio de Publicaciones: Madrid, Spain, 2011.
13. Romero, U.P.M. *Movimientos Sociales y la Autocomunicación de Masas. Una Revisión del Movimiento 15-M*; Colegio San Luis: San Luis Potosí, Mexico, 2012.
14. Rovira-Sancho, G. Movimientos Sociales y Comunicación: La Red Como Paradigma. *Anàlisi: Quad. Comun. Cult.* **2012**, *45*, 91–104.

15. Withers, D. *Feminism, Digital Culture and the Politics of Transmission: Theory, Practice and Cultural Heritage*; Rowman & Littlefield: Lanham, MA, USA, 2015.
16. Congosto, M.L.; Fernández, M.; Moro Egido, E. Twitter y Política: Información, Opinión y ¿Predicción? *Cuad. Comun. Evoca* **2011**, *4*, 11–16.
17. Campos-Domínguez, E. Twitter y la comunicación política. *El Prof. Inf.* **2017**, *26*, 785–793. [CrossRef]
18. Rodríguez, R.; Ureña, D. Diez razones para el uso de Twitter como herramienta en la comunicación política y electoral. *Comun. Plur.* **2011**, *5*, 89–116.
19. Piscitelli, A. Prólogo: Twitter, la revolución y los enfoques ni-ni. In *Mundo Twitter: Una Guía Para Comprender y Dominar la Plataforma que Cambió la Red*; Orihuela, J.L., Ed.; Alienta: Barcelona, Spain, 2011; pp. 15–20.
20. Pariser, E. *The Filter Bubble: What the Internet Is Hiding from You*; Penguin: London, UK, 2011.
21. Page, R. The linguistics of self-branding and micro-celebrity in Twitter: The role of hashtags. *Discourse Commun.* **2012**, *6*, 181–201. [CrossRef]
22. Carr, D. Hashtag Activism and Its Limits. *The New York Times*, 25 March 2012.
23. Marwick, A. *Status Update: Celebrity, Publicity, and Branding in the Social Media Age*; Yale University Press: New Haven, CT, USA, 2013.
24. Fuchs, C. *Social Media. A Critical Introduction*; Sage: Thousand Oaks, CA, USA, 2014.
25. Giraldo-Luque, S.; Fernández-García, N.; Pérez-Arce, J.C. La centralidad temática de la movilización #NiUnaMenos en Twitter. *El Prof. Inf.* **2018**, *27*, 1–226.
26. Anduiza, E.; Cristancho, C.; Sabucedo, J.M. Mobilization through online social networks: The political protest of the indignados in Spain. *Inf. Commun. Soc.* **2014**, *17*, 750–764. [CrossRef]
27. Bennett, W.L.; Segerberg, A. The logic of connective action: Digital media and the personalization of contentious politics. *Inf. Commun. Soc.* **2012**, *15*, 739–768. [CrossRef]
28. Dixon, K. Feminist online identity: Analyzing the presence of hashtag feminism. *J. Arts Humanit.* **2014**, *3*, 34–40.
29. Zimmerman, T. #Intersectionality: The Fourth Wave Feminist Twitter Community. *Atlantis Crit. Stud. Gend. Cult. Soc. Justice* **2017**, *38*, 54–70.
30. Shiva, N.; Nosrat Kharazmi, Z. The fourth wave of feminism and the lack of social realism in cyberspace. *J. Cyberspace Stud.* **2019**, *3*, 129–146.
31. Mendes, K.; Ringrose, J.; Keller, J. #MeToo and the promise and pitfalls of challenging rape culture through digital feminist activism. *Eur. J. Women's Stud.* **2018**, *25*, 236–246.
32. Worthington, N. Celebrity-bashing or# MeToo contribution? New York Times Online readers debate the boundaries of hashtag feminism. *Commun. Rev.* **2020**, *23*, 46–65.
33. Zhou, Q.; Qiu, H. Predicting online feminist engagement after MeToo: A study combining resource mobilization and integrative social identity paradigms. *Chin. J. Commun.* **2020**, *13*, 351–369. [CrossRef]
34. Clark-Parsons, R. I see you, I believe you, I stand with you:# MeToo and the performance of networked feminist visibility. *Fem. Media Stud.* **2021**, *21*, 362–380.
35. Thelwall, M. International Women's Day 2009–2020 on Twitter: Postfeminist or Fourth Wave Feminism? *SSRN* **2021**, 3846542. [CrossRef]
36. Sanchez-Duarte, J.M.; Fernandez-Romero, D. Feminist sub-activism and digital collective repertoires: Cyberfeminist practices on Twitter. *El Prof. Inf.* **2017**, *26*, 894–902.
37. Navarro, C.; Coromina, Ò. Discussion and mediation of social outrage on Twitter: The reaction to the judicial sentence of "La Manada". *Commun. Soc.* **2020**, *33*, 93–106. [CrossRef]
38. Idoiaga-Mondragon, N.; Berasategi-Sancho, N.; Beloki-Arizti, N.; Belasko-Txertudi, M. #8M women's strikes in Spain: Following the unprecedented social mobilization through twitter. *J. Gend. Stud.* **2021**, 1–16. [CrossRef]
39. Birhane, A. Algorithmic injustice: A relational ethics approach. *Patterns* **2021**, *2*, 100205. [CrossRef]
40. Graham, S.S.; Hopkins, H.R. AI for Social Justice: New Methodological Horizons in Technical Communication. *Tech. Commun. Q.* **2021**, 1–14. [CrossRef]
41. Kuo, R. Racial justice activist hashtags: Counterpublics and discourse circulation. *New Media Soc.* **2018**, *20*, 495–514. [CrossRef]
42. Almazor, M.G.; Canteli, M.J.P.; de la Cal Barredo, M.L. New approaches to the propagation of the antifeminist backlash on Twitter. *Investig. Fem.* **2020**, *11*, 221–237. [CrossRef]
43. Laney, D. 3D data management: Controlling data volume, velocity and variety. *META Group Res. Note* **2001**, *6*, 1.
44. Khan, M.A.; Uddin, M.F.; Gupta, N. Seven V's of Big Data understanding Big Data to extract value. In Proceedings of the 2014 Zone 1 Conference of the American Society for Engineering Education, Bridgeport, CT, USA, 3–5 April 2014; pp. 1–5.
45. Oguntimilehin, A.; Ademola, O. A Review of Big Data Management, Benefits and Challenges. *J. Emerg. Trends Comput. Inf. Sci.* **2014**, *5*, 433–438.
46. Patgiri, R.; Ahmed, A. Big data: The v's of the game changer paradigm. In Proceedings of the IEEE 18th International Conference on High Performance Computing and Communications, Sydney, Australia, 12–14 December 2016; pp. 17–24.
47. Anderson, C. The end of theory: The data deluge makes the scientific method obsolete. *Wired Mag.* **2008**, *16*, 16–17.
48. DiFonzo, N. The Echo-Chamber Effect. *The New York Times*, 22 April 2011.
49. Sweeney, L. Discrimination in online ad delivery. *Queue* **2013**, *11*, 10–29. [CrossRef]

50. Datta, A.; Tschantz, M.C.; Datta, A. Automated experiments on ad privacy settings: A tale of opacity, choice, and discrimination. *Proc. Priv. Enhancing Technol.* **2015**, *1*, 92–112. [CrossRef]
51. Metz, R. Why Microsoft Accidently Unleashed a Neo-Nazi Sexbot. Available online: https://www.technologyreview.com/2016/03/24/161424/why-microsoft-accidentally-unleashed-a-neo-nazi-sexbot/ (accessed on 23 November 2021).
52. Arcila-Calderón, C.; Barbosa-Caro, E.; Cabezuelo-Lorenzo, F. Técnicas big data: Análisis de textos a gran escala para la investigación científica y periodística. *El Prof. Inf.* **2016**, *25*, 623–631. [CrossRef]
53. Campolo, A.; Sanfilippo, M.; Whittaker, M.; Crawford, K. *AI Now 2017 Report*; AI Now Institute at New York University: New York, NY, USA, 2017.
54. Edizel, B.; Bonchi, F.; Hajian, S.; Panisson, A.; Tassa, T. FaiRecSys: Mitigating algorithmic bias in recommender systems. *Int. J. Data Sci. Anal.* **2020**, *9*, 197–213. [CrossRef]
55. Morales-i-Gras, J. *Datos Masivos y Minería de Datos Sociales, Conceptos y Herramientas Básicas*; Fundació Universitat Oberta de Catalunya: Barcelona, Spain, 2020.
56. Garcia-Alsina, M. *Big Data: Gestión y Explotación de Grandes Volúmenes de Datos*; Editorial UOC-El Profesional de la Información: Barcelona, Spain, 2017.
57. Morales-i-Gras, J. *Minería de Datos de los Social Media, Técnicas Para el Análisis de Datos Masivos*; Fundació Universitat Oberta de Catalunya: Barcelona, Spain, 2020.
58. Crossley, N. The social world of the network. Combining qualitative and quantitative elements in social network analysis. *Sociologica* **2010**, *4*. [CrossRef]
59. Edwards, G. *Mixed-Method Approaches to Social Network Analysis*; Routledge: Abingdon-on-Thames, UK, 2010.
60. Karamshuk, D.; Shaw, F.; Brownlie, J.; Sastry, N. Bridging big data and qualitative methods in the social sciences: A case study of Twitter responses to high profile deaths by suicide. *Online Soc. Netw. Media* **2017**, *1*, 33–43. [CrossRef]
61. Chen, N.C.; Drouhard, M.; Kocielnik, R.; Suh, J.; Aragon, C.R. Using machine learning to support qualitative coding in social science: Shifting the focus to ambiguity. *ACM Trans. Interact. Intell. Syst.* **2018**, *8*, 1–20. [CrossRef]
62. Twitter. *Standard Search—Twitter Developers*; Twitter Developers: San Francisco, CA, USA, 2018.
63. Ediger, D.; Jiang, K.; Riedy, J.; Bader, D.A.; Corley, C.; Farber, R.; Reynolds, W.N. Massive social network analysis: Mining Twitter for social good. In Proceedings of the 39th International Conference on Parallel Processing Workshops, San Diego, CA, USA, 13–16 September 2010; pp. 583–593.
64. Chatfield, A.; Brajawidagda, U. Twitter tsunami early warning network: A social network analysis of Twitter information flows. In Proceedings of the 23rd Australasian Conference on Information Systems, Melbourne, Australia, 3–5 December 2012; Volume 56.
65. Tremayne, M. Anatomy of protest in the digital era: A network analysis of Twitter and Occupy Wall Street. *Soc. Mov. Stud.* **2014**, *13*, 110–126. [CrossRef]
66. Congosto, M.L. Elecciones Europeas 2014: Viralidad de los mensajes en Twitter. *Redes Rev. Hisp. Para Análisis Redes Soc.* **2015**, *26*, 23–52.
67. Del Fresno García, M.; Daly, A.J.; Supovitz, J. Desvelando climas de opinión por medio del Social Media Mining y Análisis de Redes Sociales en Twitter. El caso de los Common Core State Standards. *Redes Rev. Hisp. Para Análisis Redes Soc.* **2015**, *26*, 53–75.
68. Morales-i-Gras, J. Desenredando las identidades soberanistas vasca y catalana: Un Análisis de Redes Sociales de las etiquetas de Twitter# BasquesDecide y #Up4Freedom. *Pap. CEIC Int. J. Collect. Identity Res.* **2015**, *2*, 1–37.
69. Blondel, V.D.; Guillaume, J.L.; Lambiotte, R.; Lefebvre, E. Fast Unfolding of Communities in Large Networks. *J. Stat. Mech. Theory Exp.* **2008**, *2008*, 10. [CrossRef]
70. Zhao, Y. Analysing Twitter data with text mining and social network analysis. In Proceedings of the 11th Australasian Data Mining and Analytics Conference, Camberra, Australia, 13–15 November 2013; Volume 146.
71. Gualda, E.; Borrero, J.D. La 'Spanish Revolution' en Twitter (2): Redes de hashtags (#) y actores individuales y colectivos respecto a los desahucios en España. *Redes Rev. Hisp. Para Análisis Redes Soc.* **2015**, *26*, 1–22.
72. Himelboim, I.; Smith, M.A.; Rainie, L.; Shneiderman, B.; Espina, C. Classifying Twitter topic-networks using social network analysis. *Soc. Media Soc.* **2017**, *3*, 2056305117691545. [CrossRef]
73. Gerlach, M.; Peixoto, T.P.; Altmann, E.G. A network approach to topic models. *Sci. Adv.* **2018**, *4*. [CrossRef] [PubMed]
74. Bird, S.; Klein, E.; Loper, E. *Natural Language Processing with Python: Analyzing Text with the Natural Language Toolkit*; O'Reilly Media Inc.: London, UK, 2009.
75. Ray, P.; Chakrabarti, A. A mixed approach of deep learning method and rule-based method to improve aspect level sentiment analysis. *Appl. Comput. Inform.* **2019**. [CrossRef]
76. Mikolov, T.; Chen, K.; Corrado, G.; Dean, J. Efficient estimation of word representations in vector space. *arXiv* **2013**, arXiv:1301.3781.
77. Myers, S.A.; Sharma, A.; Gupta, P.; Lin, J. Information network or social network? The structure of the Twitter follow graph. In Proceedings of the 23rd International Conference on World Wide Web, Seoul, Korea, 7–11 April 2014; pp. 493–498.
78. Grandjean, M. A social network analysis of Twitter: Mapping the digital humanities community. *Cogent Arts Humanit.* **2016**, *3*, 1171458. [CrossRef]
79. Lozares-Colina, C. La teoría de redes sociales. *Pap. Rev. Sociol.* **1996**, *48*, 103–126.
80. Louch, H. Personal network integration: Transitivity and homophily in strong-tie relations. *Soc. Netw.* **2000**, *22*, 45–64. [CrossRef]

81. Isaak, J.; Hanna, M.J. User data privacy: Facebook, Cambridge Analytica, and privacy protection. *Computer* **2018**, *51*, 56–59. [CrossRef]
82. Lykousas, N.; Patsakis, C. Large-scale analysis of grooming in modern social networks. *arXiv* **2020**, arXiv:2004.08205. [CrossRef]
83. Boulanger, M. Scraping the Bottom of the Barrel: Why It Is No Surprise That Data Scrapers Can Have Access to Public Profiles on LinkedIn. *Sci. Technol. Law Rev.* **2018**, *21*, 77.
84. Newman, M.E. Modularity and community structure in networks. *Proc. Natl. Acad. Sci. USA* **2006**, *103*, 8577–8582. [CrossRef]
85. Lambiotte, R.; Delvenne, J.C.; Barahona, M. Laplacian dynamics and multiscale modular structure in networks. *arXiv* **2008**, arXiv:0812.1770.
86. Morales-i-Gras, J. Soberanías Enredadas: Una Perspectiva Reticular, Constructural y Agéntica Hacia los Relatos Soberanistas Vasco y Catalán Contemporáneos en Twitter. Ph.D. Dissertation, Universidad del País Vasco-Euskal Herriko Unibertsitatea, Leioa, Spain, 2017.
87. Munro, E. Feminism: A fourth wave? *Political Insight* **2013**, *4*, 22–25. [CrossRef]
88. Larrondo Ureta, A.; Orbegozo Terradillos, J.; Morales i Gras, J. Digital Prospects of the Contemporary Feminist Movement for Dialogue and International Mobilization: A Case Study of the 25 November Twitter Conversation. *Soc. Sci.* **2021**, *10*, 84. [CrossRef]
89. Gaspar, R.; Pedro, C.; Panagiotopoulos, P.; Seibt, B. Beyond positive or negative: Qualitative sentiment analysis of social media reactions to unexpected stressful events. *Comput. Hum. Behav.* **2016**, *56*, 179–191. [CrossRef]
90. Orbegozo-Terradillos, J.; Morales-i-Gras, J.; Larrondo, A. Feminismos indignados ante la justicia: La conversación digital en el caso de La Manada. *IC Rev. Científica Inf. Comun.* **2019**, *16*, 249–283.
91. Krackhardt, D.; Stern, R.N. Informal networks and organizational crises: An experimental simulation. *Soc. Psychol. Q.* **1988**, *51*, 123–140. [CrossRef]
92. Larrondo, A.; Morales-i-Gras, J.; Orbegozo-Terradillos, J. Feminist hashtag activism in Spain: Measuring the degree of politicisation of online discourse on #YoSíTeCreo, #HermanaYoSíTeCreo, #Cuéntalo y #NoEstásSola. *Commun. Soc.* **2019**, *32*, 207–221.
93. Freeman, L.C. Centrality in social networks conceptual clarification. *Soc. Netw.* **1978**, *1*, 215–239. [CrossRef]
94. Orbegozo-Terradillos, J.; Larrondo-Ureta, A.; Morales-i-Gras, J. Influencia del género en los debates electorales en España: Análisis de la audiencia social en #ElDebateDecisivo y# L6Neldebate. *El Prof. Inf.* **2020**, *29*, 12.
95. Noguera, J.M. *Redes y Periodismo. Cuando las Noticias se Socializan*; Editorial UOC: Barcelona, Spain, 2012.
96. Martínez-Nicolás, M.; Sapera-Lapiedra, E.; Carrasco-Campos, A. La investigación sobre comunicación en España en los últimos 25 años (1990–2014). Objetos de estudio y métodos aplicados en los trabajos publicados en revistas españolas especializadas. *Empiria Rev. Metodol. Cienc. Soc.* **2019**, *42*, 37–69. [CrossRef]
97. Ruiz-Soler, J. Twitter research for social scientists: A brief introduction to the benefits, limitations and tools for analysing Twitter data. *Dígitos* **2017**, *3*, 17–31.

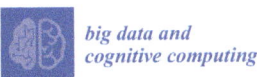

*Article*

# Digital Technologies and the Role of Data in Cultural Heritage: The Past, the Present, and the Future

Vassilis Poulopoulos *,† and Manolis Wallace †

Knowledge and Uncertainty Research Laboratory, University of the Peloponnese, 221 31 Tripolis, Greece; wallace@uop.gr
* Correspondence: vacilos@uop.gr; Tel.: +30-6972-700-533
† These authors contributed equally to this work.

**Abstract:** Is culture considered to be our past, our roots, ancient ruins, or an old piece of art? Culture is all the factors that define who we are, how we act and interact in our world, in our daily activities, in our personal and public relations, in our life. Culture is all the things we are not obliged to do. However, today, we live in a mixed environment, an environment that is a combination of "offline" and the online, digital world. In this mixed environment, it is technology that defines our behaviour, technology that unites people in a large world, that finally, defines a status of "monoculture". In this article, we examine the role of technology, and especially big data, in relation to the culture. We present the advances that led to paradigm shifts in the research area of cultural informatics, and forecast the future of culture as will be defined in this mixed world.

**Keywords:** big data; culture; cultural informatics; museum informatics; mixed environment; social media

## 1. Introduction

We live in an era that is defined by technology and its advances. Every aspect of our everyday life includes a kind of a machine. The type of machine that Turing and Von Neumann described [1,2], where people explicitly or implicitly provide inputs which a machine processes and then outputs results. Explicitly, in the cases where people are aware of the information shared, information that is intentionally provided to any kind of machine in order to fulfill a job; implicitly in any other case, in which technology collects information in order to "predict" and aim towards a better world. However, when it comes to culture, to the past that defines who we are today, and how we will progress for the rest of our lives, then it is based upon every single person's selections, on how to respond to technology; we define—or should define—the way, and not technology or algorithms.

Technology and culture is not a novel combination. More than 50 years ago, people in the humanities, primarily in museums, were seeking for technological assistance [3,4]. Simple databases were the beginning of the need for a technological presence in cultural institutions [5]. While the technology was emerging, the technologically unexploited area of museum informatics was gaining attention. Museum informatics was the "beginning"; it was the noble area that technology could explore. A first 'touch' between technology and humanities; actually a large part of humanities.

As technology was advancing, it was not only cultural spaces that attracted the attention of innovation. Culture is spread all around us; new types of culture were defined, and as this kept happening, technology was finding a new area of application. The simple—yet advanced for its age—research on databases and cultural spaces started to shift with the domination of the world wide web. It was the time that the Internet started to seem an ideal space for virtual museum tours and multimedia presentations [6]. Despite the fact that the humanities declined to follow the pace of technological advances, technology still remained present in several aspects of culture. Virtual reality, augmented reality, social media, 3D

---

**Citation:** Poulopoulos, V.; Wallace, M. Digital Technologies and the Role of Data in Cultural Heritage: The Past, the Present, and the Future. *Big Data Cogn. Comput.* **2022**, *6*, 73. https://doi.org/10.3390/bdcc6030073

**Academic Editor:** Fabrizio Marozzo

Received: 4 May 2022
Accepted: 28 June 2022
Published: 4 July 2022

**Publisher's Note:** MDPI stays neutral with regard to jurisdictional claims in published maps and institutional affiliations.

**Copyright:** © 2022 by the authors. Licensee MDPI, Basel, Switzerland. This article is an open access article distributed under the terms and conditions of the Creative Commons Attribution (CC BY) license (https://creativecommons.org/licenses/by/4.0/).

representations, aerial photos (scanning), personalization, mesh networking, IoT, and automated guidance, and more technological advances will define the next two decades.

Today, we should be thinking of modern culture, everyday culture, and "online" culture. That is, because, over the years, our perspective towards culture is changing. It is not only technology that makes us change, but it is the medium (technology) that led to a more universal environment, in which we are eventually forced to live. People are, more than ever, closer to new cultures, behaviours, religions, socio-economical approaches, music, art, movies and more. One could claim that the internet has generated a new type of culture, though, it seems to be very flat.

People tend to use technology in order to overcome problems, to do their job faster, but at the end of the day, they remain out of time. The amount of data generated and targeted towards people is such that they are unable to process them, to give them the period of time data deserve (and people deserve). Technology is the solution to problems, but was provided to the people without any guidelines; ending up as a means of a universal monoculture generation.

Technology today is capable of uniting the whole world. We are able to "travel" to places that we would not be able to in our real life. We can talk, discuss, learn, and exchange culture with people from the other side of the Earth. However, the ease of access generates the problem of huge amounts of information that no human being is able to process; at least in real time. We live the era of big data and culture. Technology is the medium to communicate and spread culture; cultural organizations need to define their presence in this world, and people should be able to "survive" in this world without losing their roots. As such, we need to review the position of technology in culture, especially when it comes as a massive stream expressed through big data.

In this manuscript, we examine the effect of technology on culture, how the advances of technology emerged and altered the way culture is accessed by a broader audience, the way culture is presented, recorded, and spread. In parallel, we envisage a future of culture spread among people and discuss how cultural related organizations should adapt their processes in this future. The next section presents technology in culture from its very beginning, until today and the connection to data. It is also focused on big data, projects related to culture, as well as the role of social media. We present a view of what is expected from the combination of technology and culture in the future. Finally, the discussion on technology and culture is presented.

## 2. Technology in Culture

The advances of technology are vast. Many of them are directly or indirectly related to culture in any of its forms. A great deal of research is being conducted on the combination of technology and culture, having many different perspectives. Researchers tend to support that there is a two-way relationship between technology and culture [7–10]. Of course, they are precise, as civilizations that dominated parts of the world in history are directly related to advanced technologies for their era. As mentioned, a large number of efforts examine the connection and the effect between culture and technology [11–14]. Furthermore, it is obvious that culture and arts were part of the past civilizations that managed to have their "basic problems" solved; and in order to do so technology must had been very advanced, at least for their era.

In the modern world we need to narrow down the relation of technology to culture, only to what is related to computers and the internet. It is this kind of technology that altered the way we got used to face culture and react to it.

### 2.1. The First Steps

The first recorded efforts in the modern world can be found in the 1970s. R.G. Chenball discussed museum cataloguing in the 'Computer Age' [5], while J.D. Wilcock tried to establish the role of the computer in archaeology [15]. It is obvious that researchers were trying to interconnect advances in technology with culture and, as a first step, several efforts were focused primarily on museum cataloguing [16] or even systems to classify any man-made object (e.g., nomenclature [17,18]). Still, the problem is close to the one we face today, there was no common language for the standardization of the systems and processes. As D.C. Stam [19] states in 1989, "the already reaching 20 years of research on museum informatics had not ended up with a common standard". So, a first generation of cooperation between culture and technology in the modern world is directly related to databases.

*2.2. The Internet*

Not very far from this first approach, technology started entering several different areas of the humanities and affecting culture. With the internet era rising, the relation between culture and technology started its path on the Net. Cultural informatics became more extrovert, a number of conferences started focusing on technology and culture (museums) and a shift has started by considering the interaction with the visitor as an equally important factor. D. Bearman, editor of 'Archives and Museums Informatics', was a pioneer in the field with numerous research on the issue of hypermedia and interactivity, as well as the presence on the web [6,20,21]. We are entering an era of technology where a huge number of changes are happening. The wide adaptation of the Internet and emerging technologies, such as digitization, object visualization, 3D representations, Virtual Reality, Augmented and Enhanced Reality, Artificial Intelligence, Semantic Representations, and Ontology Specification are only some of the factors that affect cultural informatics. People do not hesitate to adopt the Internet, and cultural informatics has to follow [22,23]. W. Schweibenz examines both the perspective of the Internet as a knowledge-base and as a communication system [24]. He is also referring to the cultural spaces as the "virtual museum". The term is not something novel for the museums [25]. Many years after his first approach on the "virtual museum" he still thinks that museums are standing still. He states: "The idea of becoming virtual might not be a pleasant one for some museums, but this development is inevitable because of the increasing digitisation of cultural heritage and the demand to make collections more accessible" [26]. It is obvious that it is a matter of accessibility. The stakes for the museums are clear: either they follow the river or they remain a sterile space.

*2.3. Virtual Worlds*

The changes in museums and cultural spaces are huge. The first decade of the 21st century is almost monopolized with Virtual and Augmented Reality in the museums [27–34]. This "differentiated reality" can be found in several forms, named Virtual, Augmented, Mixed, or Extended (referred to as XR from now on). It all refers to "photorealistic representations of places, people and sites that do not exist, never existed, or may not be easily experienced" [28]. In parallel, it is possible to provide a lot of data (information) and enable interactions. The most extraordinary about this technology seems to be the "immersion", which is the "illusion of being in the projected (author note: idealized) world, in such a way that makes you believe that you are really there", that leads to the assumption that it may offer a "better than real life" experience [28].

The facts about virtual, mixed, and augmented reality are simple. The visitor can have an alternative enhanced experience, either it is on-site or online (remote) as well. Moreover, XR takes advantage of the digitization of objects, places, and cites, a procedure that was and is already underway, but possibly not utilized. Virtual exhibitions can be multiple instead of the single exhibition that is formed by the original objects. It is a matter of fact, that only a small amount of the objects that a museum owns are exposed to public. XR may provide information about "hidden" objects and artefacts as well. A survey at the end of the decade proves that the steps being taken are numerous [35].

Virtual Reality and Augmented Reality have never lost their glamour till today. In fact, research on the field is such that the number of XR solutions for museums is huge [36–41]. The idea of XR in museums does not change from its very early roots: enhancing the visitor's experience. Throughout the years, research includes several different factors, either related to personalized content (better applied to AR), differentiated environments (worlds) in which the user navigates, presentation of different objects, representation of the past and rebuilding ancient ruins (e.g., Ancient Olympia (https://inculture.microsoft.com/arts/ancient-olympia-common-grounds/, accessed on 27 June 2022—Digitally preserving and restoring Ancient Olympia as it stood over 2000 years ago) and more. We have already been informed that the future of one of the most well-known social media platforms will emerge in virtual reality. We are talking about Meta from Facebook (Meta—https://about.facebook.com/meta/, accessed on 27 June 2022 which is referred to as "...the next evolution of social connection".

### 2.4. Metadata

Another important aspect of museum informatics is related to information representation. As digitization is continuous and unstoppable there is a strong need of a common "language" for data recording. Ontologies try to provide a solution to this issue. The CIDOC conceptual reference model provides a generic solution [42], while, other conceptual models proposed are not that widespread. The CIDOC CRM represents an "ontology" for cultural heritage information, i.e., it describes in a formal language the explicit and implicit concepts and relations relevant to the documentation of cultural heritage. On the other hand, one can find a large number of protocols that are constructed in order to describe cultural related objects. However, when one deals with information recording there is a strong need to define metadata that accompany such a kind of object. According to [43], four aspects of the cultural data have to be discussed and taken under consideration when dealing with metadata of museum and cultural objects. These are:

- Data structure standards;
- Data content standards;
- Data value standards;
- Data format/exchange standards.

For each of the aforementioned sections, there is a set of information that accompanies and provides useful information. The important part of this analysis is not only the fact that technology is hugely affecting the way that cultural information is recorded, but the fact that we are facing a completely differentiated analysis of the approach of database creation; and this is because we are facing an occasion where the audience does not have a technological background—instead the audience is related to humanities—but still the effort of technology adoption is great.

Talking about metadata, there is a strong need to realize their importance for the multi-level analysis of data deriving from cultural objects. Metadata are information related to an object and provide answers to questions that can be considered "additional information". For example, trying to "explain" or "understand" a piece of art from an artist, our work could be made easier if we new when and where he was born, not to mention their personal and family status or socio-economic conditions. This (add-on) information is the medium to interpret parts of the work, as well as make connections with the past, the present, and the future of the artist, and ours. So metadata are the information carrier that demolishes any barriers that block the universality of culture.

The actual part related to metadata is the numerous efforts worldwide to record information about objects, thus creating large sets of scattered databases. Within these grounds, Europeana holds the largest artefact database in Europe, trying in parallel for two aspects [44]. First of all, empower the recording of cultural related information and secondly, establishing a prototype so that the information is not only "saved" and "preserved" digitally but also be portable and readable; ultimately, accessible to everyone.

### 2.5. Content Digitization

Apart from the information that is related to an object's metadata we should also stand on the digitization part. Although metadata can be considered the information carrier for an object's digital existence, the digitization is the part that holds the actual "image".

Applying only to tangible cultural heritage the power of images is such that digitization is considered to be one of the major branches of the research related to cultural informatics, having a great impact on the combination of technology and culture [45].

Talking about digitization, one can consider that taking a picture of an artefact is sufficient to talk about digitization. This is not very far from being true apart from the fact that the digitization process is also a process that has specific standards and protocols. The European Commission has once more invested a large number of projects related to digital cultural heritage focusing on the digitisation processes. https://digital-strategy.ec.europa.eu/en/policies/cultural-heritage, accessed on 27 June 2022. Projects like VHH (Visual History of the Holocaust—https://www.vhh-project.eu/, accessed on 27 June 2022) which is an innovation action that focuses on the digital curation and preservation of film records relating to the discovery of Nazi concentration camps and other atrocity sites, or such as GRAVITATE (Geometric reconstruction and novel semantic reunification of cultural heritage objects, https://cordis.europa.eu/project/id/665155, accessed on 27 June 2022 and Scan4Reco (Multimodal scanning of cultural heritage assets for their multilayered digitization and preventive conservation via spatiotemporal 4D reconstruction and 3D printing, https://scan4reco.iti.gr/, accessed on 27 June 2022) put the research efforts on the cultural objects and the procedures for preservation and digitization.

Although these efforts are considered to be "modern" the need for digitization started together with the efforts of information recording and it started the decade of the worldwide web expansion. Reproducing the words from [46] back in 1996 we understand the level of innovation at that time. Mannoni states when analysing the organisation, publishing and distributing large collections of materials online: "We used Kodak photo CD technology for digitalization and CERN World-Wide Web technology for the HTTP daemon linked to a WAIS research engine to query the database". It was—once more—"the Internet", the need for online presentation, publishing and sharing of our history and culture that brought digitization to an advanced level. Other efforts refer to practices and techniques for digitization [47,48], till reaching the point where the procedures for digitization include 3D, photogrammetry, and point clouds [49–61], making the digitization process reach very high levels of representation fidelity.

The digitization procedure provides a "picture" of the cultural objects. However, technology has emerged and digitization procedure together with artificial intelligence and 3D technologies can be used to restore [62], redesign, and regenerate objects. The possibility for rapid prototyping of such objects inspired and intrigued research [63–65].

However, digitization and publishing on the Internet generates a number of side issues especially related to copyrights which remains a field of huge discussion till nowadays [66–70].

*2.6. Adaptation on People*

In the last decade, we have witnessed a paradigm shift that is directly related to data generation and culture spread. Culture in the modern world, from the perspective of a museum, has gone through many different stages. Starting from the object-centric approach, to the museum-centric, leading today to people-centric approaches.

Having all of the world in their pockets, or more precisely in their hands, people are the centre for some cultural informatics approaches. Customization, personalization, personality of the people are only some of the "keywords" that lead to this change of stance towards people [71–73]. The museum is not just an information carrier, the object is not only a masterpiece, the work from curators and guides is not only static, but we are designing experiences and their maximization, brain stimulation, immersion of different levels, and total adaptation to the needs of the visitors. The efforts being made are based upon the existing technologies (XR, Digitized material, metadata, web), but they are tailor-made for each user. A whole new generation of application related to museums and cultural spaces is born, including user personalization, adaptive content, custom storytelling even procedures in order to combine physical with digital narratives. Apart from the aforementioned, the research works presented in [74–76]. are typical examples of research approaches targeting on the connection of user profiles with the museum visit.

Personalization becomes a matter with the evolution of the web in the early 2000s, where user generated content begins to be large enough to enable users to be producers of information. It is the time when web personlization is established as part of a museum's online presence as well [77]. P. F. Marty, a pioneer in museum informatics does not stop to mention the personalization as an important factor in a user's experience [78]. Many cases start to appear in several museums around the world [79], while the parallel rise of online games makes it possible to create personalized experiences in the online virtual worlds, such as Second Life [80]. As we approach the present, a combination of technologies occur for the personalization, including visitors' personal devices, as well storytelling and narratives [81–84].

Machine learning, especially through artificial intelligence has played important roles in the scope of adding algorithmic approaches to the process of interconnecting people with culture. An extensive survey on machine learning for cultural heritage has recently been presented by Fiorucci et al. [85]. They conclude, however, "in most cases that ML is applied to culture, it is a 'black box' for the research community" and that it is usually focused on "visual or textual features". In parallel, despite the fact that CH data are created so as to be publicly available for everyone, still, only some of the large cultural organizations enable access to large sets of data.

*2.7. Projects Related to Culture and Technology*

Europe has performed enormous steps towards supporting the interconnection of culture and technology. A huge amount of funding has been and keeps being invested in cultural informatics and cultural heritage. Europeana (Europeana, Discover inspiring European Cultural Heritage, https://www.europeana.eu, accessed on 27 June 2022) is a main axe in founding a place of common grounds. A place to define a common language, to dig for our roots, to search for interconnections. According to its website, Europeana "provides cultural heritage enthusiasts, professionals, teachers, and researchers with digital access to European cultural heritage material". This is performed in order "to inspire and inform fresh perspectives and open conversations about our history and culture". This is achieved with the support of the European countries' local authorities that force digitization procedures to follow the model defined by Europeana for the metadata description (Europeana Data Model (Europeana Data Model, https://pro.europeana.eu/page/edm-documentation, accessed on 27 June 2022). An equally important project is CLARIAH [86,87] which is established by the merge of projects CLARIN [88] and DARIA [89]. DARIAH project "develops, maintains and operates an infrastructure in support of ICT-based research practices and sustains researchers in using them to build, analyse, and interpret digital resources", while CLARIN project "creates and maintains an infrastructure to support the sharing, use and sustainability of language data and tools for research in the humanities and social sciences". It is obvious that they both serve similar roles within the research field of humanities and supporting IT tools. This is the reason they were merged into CLARIAH project, which scope is to "provide researchers with access to large collections of digital data and to innovative and user-friendly applications for the processing of these data" (https://www.clariah.nl/about-clariah, accessed on 27 June 2022).

Apart from Europeana, that leads the way to digitization and access to culture and cultural heritage, an important procedure in order to interconnect with our roots, during the last two decades, a large number of research projects have been funded in order to tackle problems in the field of cultural informatics. The efforts being made in order to create a bridge between informatics and humanities are enormous. Starting from simple steps mainly in museums in order to offer a better experience to the visitor, or attract more people, leading to complex AR systems, technology remains a powerful tool for both "front-end" and "back-end" activities as well.

The ARCHES project scope was to help people in environments where inclusion is an important issue. People with difficulties or differences was the main target in order to associate with perception, cognition, communication, and memory (Project ID: 693229). The project outcomes include recognition of data on how people interact with cultural related incentives. CROSSCULT intends to target the understanding of European common history, which is achieved by providing advanced experiences and entertainment through social learning [90]. Within the scope of this project, a number of factors, including analysis of large data, were researched [91].

GRAVITATE (GRAVITATE: Discovering relationships between artefacts using 3D and semantic data. EU H2020 REFLECTIVE project) focuses on geometric reconstruction. Apart from that it researches novel ways of displays (e.g., virtual or tangible) in order to present and communicate relationships of past societies.

Virtual museums and "emotive storytelling" is the main research outcome of EMOTIVE project. Supporting the creation of virtual spaces, especially for the creative industries, is the main objective and it is achieved by defining and researching new tools and methodologies [92]. In this case, the project acts as a medium of good practices for content generation in the online world. PLUGGY supports citizens in shaping cultural heritage and being shaped by it. Amongst its goals is to look at new approaches of presenting cultural resources, and new ways of experiencing them [93].

Another important project trying to support virtual museums is ViMM. It focuses on supporting the world's leading public and private sector organisations, using high-quality technical approaches [94]. Although ArchAIDE aims to serve mainly archaeologists, it also has a number of outcomes related to visualization that can help the access to archaeological heritage. It actually deals with large scale data in archaeology [95].

The fact that Europe keeps changing, and people that live or inhabit in it, or deal with the digital world are largely unaware of the heritage is the main targte of Rices project [96]. Digital heritage in a mixed environment, as well as identifying the differentiation between cultures in Europe, is the main objective of CulturalBase social platform (CulturalBase EU project, https://culturalbase.eu, accessed on 27 June 2022). The INVENT project (INVENT EU project, https://inventculture.eu/, accessed on 27 June 2022) sets out the identification of the social and cultural prerequisites in order to achieve the key aspects of the New EU Agenda for Culture. CHIEF project (Chief Project—Cultural Heritage and Identities of Europe's Future, https://cordis.europa.eu/project/id/770464, accessed on 27 June 2022 is also concerned about the EU agenda related to cultural heritage and identity. Understanding the new environment in which creative and cultural industries will work, and how the spread of the Internet and digital technologies will impact this industry is the main focus of inDICEs (inDICEs EU Project—https://indices-culture.eu/, accessed on 27 June 2022). Empowering policy-makers and decision-makers in these sectors is a main purpose.

UNCHARTED (UNCHARTED EU Project—Understanding, Capturing and Fostering the Societal Value of Culture, https://uncharted-culture.eu/, accessed on 27 June 2022) aims to identify, contextualize, understand, measure, and analyse the emergence and conformation of the values of culture from an interdisciplinary, collaborative, and pluralistic perspective. SPICE project aims to promote citizen curation of cultural heritage by providing a set of state-of-the-art tools so that people can share their own interpretations of culture and engage with a diverse range of perspectives [97]. CultureLabs investigates and proposes the use of digital services and tools for facilitating the access to Cultural Heritage through tailor-made novel experiences, creative reuse, enrichment, and co-creation [98]. CREARCH is a project the intends to show to the public the development and building of shared values and common heritage as a result of trading or migrations within Europe. It is based on digital storytelling based on visual, digital, and transmedia performances [99]. Advanced methods in cultural heritage digitization is the scope of the VAST project. It achieves that with the provision of methods, techniques, and tools in order to support collaboration in studying, to enable annotation in digitization procedures and to examine significant moments of European culture/history [100]. The projects mentioned are only some of the numerous projects related to arts, culture, cultural heritage, and their connection to cultural informatics or technology in general. Table 1 has a collection of all the aforementioned projects followed by their main focus.

**Table 1.** List of projects related to culture.

| Project | Start Year | Focus |
|---|---|---|
| ARCHES | 2016 | Inclusive Culture |
| CrossCult | 2016 | Reflective Societies |
| Gravitate | 2015 | 3D Modelling |
| EMOTIVE | 2016 | Virtual Museum |
| PLUGGY | 2016 | Social Platform |
| ViMM | 2016 | Virtual Museum |
| ArchAIDE | 2016 | Technology to Support Archaeology |
| CulturalBase | 2015 | Social Platform |
| Riches | 2013 | Engage with heritage in the digital world |
| INVENT | 2020 | Inclusive Cultural Policies |
| CHIEF | 2018 | Cultural Literacy |
| UNCHARTED | 2020 | Societal Value of Culture |
| inDICE | 2020 | Impact of Digitization |
| SPICE | 2020 | Collaborative Approach to CH |
| CultureLabs | 2018 | Participatory Approaches |
| CREARCH | 2019 | Archives through storytelling |
| VAST | 2020 | Digital Assets & Advanced Digitization |

*2.8. Big Data and Cultural Heritage*

The new "trends" in technology usually affect the research branches that are attached to it, and so, cultural heritage is examined from the perspective of big data. Big data usually derive from social media, online gaming, data lakes, logs, or frameworks that either generate or use large portions of data. For example, the authors in [101], examine cultural recommender systems in order to enhance user profiling. Talking of (user profiling), the tender on social media is a culture that includes user personas. The authors in [102] analyse how the data from the medium itself can possibly help upon building on this cultural trend of personas. Another interesting sector of culture and cultural heritage is games. The authors in [103] explain an algorithm for user clustering in cultural games. Intangible cultural heritage and the analysis on social media is the main theme of [104]. Specifically, the authors analyse the Transmission of the Feminist Intangible Cultural Heritage on Twitter. The perspective of multi-faceted analytics in the cultural heritage domain is researched in [105]. The authors present a data lake that offers both fundamental and advanced user and data/knowledge management functionality for big cultural data management.

However, one should think, why is big data examined as a different perspective. It is in fact the way that technology emerged and the interconnection of technology with humanities in this case brings to light huge amounts of data and their usage. Therefore, technologically we live in the era of big data, but theoretical sciences (e.g., cultural sociology) generate theories without technical background. A connection between the interdisciplinary field of both is thoroughly described by Bail [106]. In his research work, he tries to narrow the gap between theoretical sciences and technological advances, both related to data. He applies big data algorithms in order to extract information based on cultural sociology theories but concludes to big challenges, which can be summed up by the lack of metadata.

Many recent works try to tackle problems related to culture, cultural heritage, and cultural informatics from the perspective of big data [107–113]. The real question is why issues that keep existing in cultural informatics for years, are now being investigated from this perspective. The answer is quite simple. Like when the "Internet" offered a novel approach and paradigm shift to the museums presence, the same change is happening today with the trending term "Big Data". People, worldwide, are directly connected to each other using the Internet, while the ability of them to be both consumers and producers of data gives birth to the term Big Data. The museums and cultural institutions should be present in this shift, either by applying algorithms and technological advances related to big data or by becoming part of the big data stream. It is inevitable that the role of social media in this change is significant.

*2.9. The Role of Social Media*

As we may observe, the advances of technology towards the role of data and their value affect directly fields like culture. In fact, if we dig deeper, we will realize that it was the social media that forced this change, this paradigm shift. However, what do social media have to do with culture. Prensky is the one that mentioned the terms digital natives vs digital immigrants in order to separate the generations of people who were born with technology in their hands versus people that faced technology sometime in their lives [114]. Despite the fact that Prensky mentioned the term considering the educational system, it is the part of technology that has to do with our everyday culture that leads the way. It all comes down to social media and how people react, discuss, share, behave, and express their inner culture, digital religion, economy, and culture. Understanding culture in social media, popular and celebrity culture, participatory culture, creator culture [115–120] are only some of the different angles from which to explore the influence of social media on people. What has changed with social media is not only that people have turned into prosumers on the web, but they also have the feeling of knowledge sharing that can turn everyone into an "influencer" with "followers"; of course, this feeling alters the "culture" of people. The aforementioned need to be considered when trying to analyse the future of culture in the online world, as the power of the medium—transferred to people—can possible guide the advances in technology.

## 3. The Future of Culture in the Online World

The future of culture in the online world is a matter that has concerned the research community for decades. It is not an issue or a problem that we came up with today and have to find a solution. On the contrary, culture and cultural heritage management remains in the discussion of how we should deal with it in each era and its modern world. Every time, this issue has to be tackled by trying to foresee what is the factors that lead both the research part, the advances that affect the research, as well as the issues that are related to the audience.

*3.1. The Role of the EC*

As already mentioned, a large number of European projects have been conducted over recent decades, having as their main topic culture, cultural heritage, a combination of humanities and technology, and so on. Actually, behind this huge funding on behalf of the EU, there is a strategic plan concerning culture and cultural heritage. There are two ways to examine the strategy of the EU towards culture. The first one is to directly analyse the strategic framework and the second one—the indirect—is to analyse the axes of funding for cultural related projects for the upcoming period. As it is expected, the first one will be based on more generic pillars, while the second one will specialize on what is expected to be the future of research and innovation.

According to the strategic framework of the EC (https://culture.ec.europa.eu/policies/strategic-framework-for-the-eus-cultural-policy (accessed on 5 June 2022)) for the period 2019–2024 there are six political priorities that affect the key themes of European cultural cooperation.

- A European Green Deal;
- A Europe fit for the digital age;
- An economy that works for people;
- A stronger Europe in the world;

- Promoting the European way of life;
- A new push for the European democracy.

All these political approaches for the future of Europe define the agenda for culture by introducing three strategic areas.

- Social;
- Economic;
- External.

These very generic areas are further analysed into work plans, coming to the actual vision for the needs of CH and its future. These include:

- Sustainability in CH;
- Cohesion and well-being;
- Ecosystem supporting artists and professionals;
- Gender equality;
- International cultural relations;
- Culture as a driver for sustainable development.

By analysing the funding tenders of the Pillar II (https://ec.europa.eu/info/research-and-innovation/funding/funding-opportunities/funding-programmes-and-open-calls/horizon-europe/cluster-2-culture-creativity-and-inclusive-society_en (accessed on 5 June 2022)) it is possible to recognize how these work plans will be supported and implemented. It is obvious that EC recognizing issues related to governance and democracy. As such, a proportion of funding is based on protection and nurturing of democracies, as well as reshaping them. The second part is directly related to cultural heritage and includes green technologies, new ways for sustainability in museums and cultural institutions, advanced technologies for preservation and enhancement of CH. Furthermore, connection and engagement with stakeholders is considered to be an important factor while a number of innovative research is based on the changing trends of technology and future. The latter includes support in a changing world of work and protections; key drivers for inequality trends; skills and early school problems; new technologies in education; public policies for well-being and sustainable development; spatial mobility; gender and social, economic, and cultural empowerment; and development of skills matched to needs. It is obvious that the EC is focusing on the problems that concern more and more people, not only in the EU but worldwide. The role of technology to achieve the aforementioned work plans should be crucial. Technology is the medium to resolve these issues in a more efficient way.

Despite the fact that the EC strategic plan seems to be focus on people and communities, there is a strong need of analysis of the peoples' trends towards culture and technology in order to recognize which should be the best approach towards approaching the issues raised.

### 3.2. An Institutional Approach

The European Commission leads the research based on political key themes and approaches. It is important to analyse the issue of culture and technology from an institutional approach. This approach is considered to be closer to the stakeholders, as well as the daily trends of people in the changing world. An interesting report published in 2016 by New Media Consortium [121] tries to predict the technological changes in the museum. The reality that is described through challenges, trends and technology developments envisages a future of museums that are very much related to technology. The challenges have to do with effective digital strategies, and improvement of the digital literacy of museum professionals. It is obvious that the report believes the strong attachment of culture to technology, such that professionals (mainly with a humanities background) need to adapt to technology. It furthermore states that some challenges may seem impossible to tackle, such as privacy and knowledge obsolescence. Finally, difficulties that are reported and should be taken under great consideration is the accessibility for disabled people and the measurement of the new technologies' impact.

The approach is accompanied with the technology trends that could help improvise the challenges. These include focus on mobile (content and applications), personalization, and participatory experiences, as well as data analytics as part of the museum operations.

All the aforementioned deal with a large amount of data within a museum or culture generally. However, the aforementioned also introduces another axis which is the universality of the "system"; this related to cultural heritage and cultural informatics when it comes to people-centric approaches. Data cannot be encountered as an autonomous piece of information or as part of a small collection of objects. Nowadays, culture is universal, people are able to communicate and exchange information fast and universally. This is the reason the report focuses on long-term trends, such as collaboration between institutions and new roles for museum professionals. At the end of the day, culture belongs to people, not only the ones that are able to access a museum exhibition (on-site or online). The situation today is such that the visitor-centric model has to be re-introduced.

In parallel, it is important to recognize what is the strategic plan of the universal cultural institutions. For example, the Smithsonian Institution (https://www.si.edu/sites/default/files/about/smithsonian-2022-strategic-plan.pdf (accessed on 5 June 2022)) has clear goals for the future of culture: engage, inspire, and impact. These goals are fulfilled by having a digital-first strategy (mainly focused on mobile-first), understanding the 21st century audiences, driving visionary interdisciplinary research, preserving natural and cultural heritage, providing a more efficient administrative infrastructure, and by looking out-of-the-box on a global level.

Another important institute, the Getty Institute having as its core mission: "...working internationally to further the appreciation and preservation of the world's cultural heritage for the enrichment and use of present and future generations", has as its strategic plan to put the focus on:

- Society's role in conservation decisions;
- Respect for diverse cultural values;
- Research;
- Education;
- Exploration;
- Sustainable solutions;
- Communication;
- Inclusiveness;
- Continuous learning and renewal.

These axes are absolutely aligned to the strategic plan of the EC, as well as with the report from NMC and the Smithsonian Institute. We should not forget to mention the two large initiatives by the technology giants Microsoft and Google, the first one with its initiative called AI for Cultural Heritage (https://www.microsoft.com/en-us/ai/ai-for-cultural-heritage (accessed on 5 June 2022)) and the second one with its platform called "Arts and Culture", launched 11 years ago, which intends to incorporate high-end technological advances to arts and culture in order to provide unique experiences to people around the globe (https://artsandculture.google.com/ accessed on 5 June 2022).

It is inevitable that there is a huge turn to a model that puts humans in the centre. In fact, today, the audience is broader than ever, including the whole universe. The multi-culture of the Internet, the capability to be in any place in the world at any time, and sharing and receiving information has eliminated any barriers, physical or not, that could limit cultural exchange. Additionally, despite the fact that this sounds like an ultimate wish, in contrary it leads to devastating results. The speed with which information is shared and transferred is such that any piece of information has a very short period of life. This short period of life is catastrophic for any kind of culture on the medium. This is because it does not let people think, realize, and absorb any kind of information. What can be done in order to encounter this problem is a matter to be discussed. Firstly, the research has to put its focus on this issue and perform detailed interdisciplinary research in two axes: The first one, an horizontal axis, needs to examine the spread of culture across the world, while the second one, a vertical axis needs to focus on the locality of culture.

### 3.3. Horizontal Analysis

The horizontal analysis can also be thought as an holistic analysis, whose scope is to examine how the culture is spread from country to country, how it is transformed and how it is identified. It is the culture of the online world, the world where information is transferred in high volumes and speeds, such that people are unable to observe it and understand it. In order to understand culture in the online world, there is a need to define it and analyse it. The types of culture that derive from the online world, usually, are expressed by each times trends. However, in fact, the trends are constantly changing, creating the belief of the ephemeral. Talking of which, it seems like a cultural trend of our era is to get used to the ephemeral.

This horizontal analysis is missing from the approach and it seems to be a prerequisite in order to recognize the culture as a whole.

### 3.4. Vertical Analysis

The vertical analysis, also known as the analysis of the natives, has as its scope the recognition of the connections of the fast changing online culture to each area's culture of the past. Each individual person is defined by his or her past. On these grounds, there is a strong need to empower and highlight the connections of what is considered as modern culture to the inner culture of each individual. This analysis will help people understand that their roots, their own definition, have a part in the globalized world. In addition, it is the mix of cultures that helps the evolution and, as such, we need to know our roots and how they are connected to our present and the stimulation of our reflections by the objects (real or digital) that we come across daily.

### 3.5. Technology as the Key to Unlock the Future of Our Culture

As technology advances more and more, and as the expectations of people become higher and higher, culture needs special attention and treatment. It seems that the limitations deriving from lockdown due to COVID-19 put pressure on cultural organizations to modernize their procedures in order to provide better experiences for people.

Although 15 years ago we were introduced to the "virtuous circle" as the noble procedure that has to be followed in order to achieve maximization of experience using a combination of online and on-site tools [122], the situation today has changed significantly. What we believe is the future of culture on the web relies on three factors:

- Recognize the types of culture of our era;
- Interconnect the different cultural categories;
- Intervene to the cultural circles in order to create a "virtuous spiral".

First of all, as part of every era there is a strong need to recognize the different types of culture. Either we are talking about "high culture" or subculture and "trash", there is a need to identify the culture and connect it with socio-economic conditions. The new medium (internet) has changed the way we produce culture in speeds that is impossible to follow. The digital natives [114] live and create in a different cultural environment, while digital immigrants deny this change leading to a wider generation gap. The different types of culture synthesize our lives, either online or offline, and the sooner we understand it, the sooner we will decode it. In this procedure, technology can play an important role as most types of novel culture is produced digitally or at least a digital medium is used for their transfer and spread. Every new generation needs to segregate, usually carrying a culture of the past, integrating into it a new "feature". However, in the era that we live in, it seems that there is a total denial and renunciation of any past type of culture, which proved to be catastrophic in the past. Technology is the medium to help us recognize and record all the new types of culture in order to understand the future and shape it. It is obvious that we have the underlying technology; the variety of the research projects' approach is the proof.

It is also obvious that we have the willing; the strategic plans from the EC are clear both from a political and socio-culture perspective. Finally, the cultural institutions' approach.

Secondly, it is important to recognize the monoculture of the web, the straight line that does not have ups and downs and does not have something to offer to an individual (educational, social, psychological, etc.). The speed of information, the constantly changing trends and the nihilism of everything does not enable a person to get accustomed to a type of culture, leading to incomplete personalities or personalities without any interest. In this case, we need technology to stand by people and create interconnections with the past. What we are is our roots, and how we behave is our culture. The indifferent culture of the online world will create indifferent generations. Technology can play the role of the culture carrier and connector. All kinds of emerging technologies, especially those with high levels of immersion, are a perfect example of the connection of the cutting-edge technological features (which produce the higher stimulation to the new generations) with the culture of the past. This, of course, means that the cultural spaces and organizations need to enter the technological era, produce digitized objects and tons of metadata so that technology can play its role. Now it becomes clear, that technology together with understanding all new types of culture-online included-will become a carrier of information in order to interconnect the future of culture to the past.

Third, and most important, we believe that we live in the era of the "virtuous spiral" (Figure 1). Although the virtuous circle is a procedure that always leads to the same spot, it remains a two-dimensional shape. The Internet proved to be the medium that actually connected all the world in a common culture. It is the place to expose common roots and common paths together with the differentiation of the individual. Through the virtual spiral, each individual remains in a state of continuous acquisition of new incentives in order to explore cultures so that a person can shape its character. In fact, the ultimate goal is a multi-spiral shape with each spiral emerging, while, in parallel, connecting to each other in a never-ending shaping of the personality. The spiral includes the steps of:

- Searching;
- Growing expectations;
- Visiting (either online or on-site, or any other form);
- Shaping reflections;
- Sharing of information.

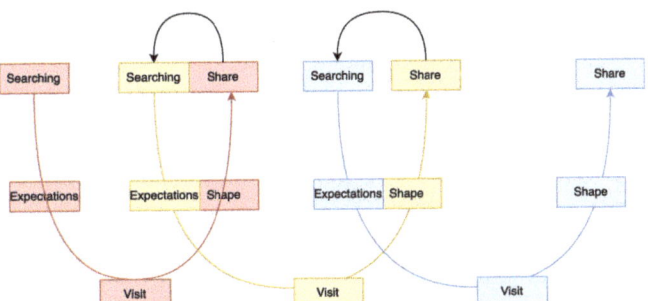

**Figure 1.** Virtuous spiral.

Analysing the steps, the part of sharing of information is the one leads to the results of searching for another, creating in this way the never-ending spiral. On this occasion, there is a strong need to understand that, despite the fact the on-site visiting of cultural objects may be considered as the ultimate experience, the direct contact with the object could not be considered as indispensable in our era. On the contrary, the experience can be acquired with the help of technology. In other cases, which are more frequent as time passes, the "object" does not exist to be exhibited in a real environment but has solely digital form (e.g., NFTs).

The fourth and fifth steps reveal the importance of "crowdsourcing" for our common grounds. On this occasion, crowdsourcing stands for shaping and sharing. It is obvious that culture flourishes with the exchange of information. Although people tend to become prosumers, technology can provide the essential tools to record the shaping of reflections for every time someone has a contact with a cultural related object (online or offline); this is the important information that has to be shared across the huge network that interconnects all people, the Internet. The spiral closes with the fact that a person's searches for information is someone else's sharing of information.

The role of data in the shaping of the proposed model is critical. We live in an era in which people are bombarded with big data deriving from the Internet. People are either of a state of connected (awake) and disconnected (sleeping), and during their connection they are interacting with information that is largely related to culture. In this notion, the amount of data that are formed, the role of the advances of technology, the contribution of the projects in order to end up in this status, reveals a strong need for a reformation of the way we think of a user-centric model in culture. The main condition of the proposed model is a united model for culture under a common infrastructure. Additionally, while the Internet provides the infrastructure, large steps are still needed by the cultural organizations in order to shape a universal model to confront the universality of culture.

## 4. Discussion

The expansion of the web that lead to culture spread across the globe in little time changes the way we face our multi-cultural universe. In fact, we are entering a mixed culture world in which people are changing their cultural approaches very quickly and directly. The "direct" part is the desired one, but the factor of speed (fast) is not. On these grounds, the cultural exchanges cannot be possibly understood and if absorbed there is no clear evidence or awareness of the habits or behaviors.

This world is shaped by the changes and advances in technology. Despite the fact that technology analysis leads to a large number of different approaches, nowadays it is obvious that everything is lead by data. We described the different aspects of data in cultural informatics. Starting from the large paradigm shift of the Internet, progressing the Virtual World, the analysis of data and metadata, as well as the digitization (i.e., the production of digital assets—data). Furthermore, we discussed the algorithmic approaches and the adaption of the visitors, and described a number of important EU funded projects related to culture and technology. Finally, we described big data and the role of social media in the shaping of today's culture.

Talking about the future of culture in the "connected world", we examined the strategic plan of the EC, as well as the approaches from institutions. It is obvious that all of them believe that culture must play an important role in the connected world. We need to redefine our view of people in cultural informatics and follow strategic plans that involve everyone as a unity and as a whole in a museum's procedures.

It seems that the term "big data" will follow several aspects of our lives and culture is not to be excluded. The trends to be followed should include a universal approach with free, open, connected data, collaboration between institutions and definition of new, important roles within the procedures of a museum.

As per the user perspective, the universal character of our future, leads as to a model that keeps "spinning" around culture; culture all over the world. Each one becomes the consumer of cultural experiences, and producer of reflections, feelings, and information for herself and everyone else. We believe in a novel culture approach by defining the spiral of culture. Technology can help us identify culture and create never-ending connected experiences.

In conclusion, we believe that the sector of cultural informatics should put the focus on the universal, holistic, data driven, user-centric approach. The approach is affecting all technologies used to create experiences for visitors, either on-site or online. The "traditional museum" remains a unique experience, but visitors demand multi-level interaction, and technology is the medium to achieve it.

**Author Contributions:** The authors have contributed equally to this work. All authors have read and agreed to the published version of the manuscript.

**Funding:** This research received no external funding.

**Conflicts of Interest:** The authors declare no conflict of interest.

## Abbreviations

The following abbreviations are used in this manuscript:

| | |
|---|---|
| NFT | Non-fungible tokens |
| CI | Cultural Informatics |
| VR | Virtual Reality |
| AR | Augmented Reality |
| ER | Enhanced Reality |
| XR | Extended Reality |
| MR | Mixed Reality |
| ML | Machine Learning |
| AI | Artificial Intelligence |
| CH | Cultural Heritage |
| EU | European Union |
| EC | European Commission |
| NMC | New Media Consortium |

## References

1. Shannon, C.E. A universal Turing machine with two internal states. *Autom. Stud.* **1956**, *34*, 157–165.
2. Burks, A.W.; Goldstine, H.H.; Von Neumann, J. *Preliminary Discussion of the Logical Design of an Electronic Computer Instrument*; Technical Report; Institute for Advanced Study: Princeton, NJ, USA, 1946.
3. Chenhall, R.G. Computer use in museums today. *Mus. Int.* **1978**, *30*, 139–145. [CrossRef]
4. Ellin, E. An international survey of museum computer activity. *Comput. Humanit.* **1968**, *3*, 65–86. [CrossRef]
5. Chenhall, R.G. *Museum Cataloging in the Computer Age*; American Association for State and Local History: Nashville, TN, USA, 1975.
6. Bearman, D.; Trant, J. Interactivity comes of age: Museums and the World Wide Web. *Mus. Int.* **1999**, *51*, 20–24. [CrossRef]
7. Cuomo, S. *Technology and Culture in Greek and Roman Antiquity*; Cambridge University Press: Cambridge, UK, 2007.
8. Gordon, R.B.; Killick, D.J. Adaptation of technology to culture and environment: Bloomery iron smelting in America and Africa. *Technol. Cult.* **1993**, *34*, 243–270. [CrossRef]
9. Misa, T.J. *Leonardo to the Internet: Technology and Culture from the Renaissance to the Present*; JHU Press: Baltimore, MD, USA, 2011.
10. Jones, P.M. *Industrial Enlightenment: Science, Technology and Culture in Birmingham and the West Midlands, 1760–1820*; Manchester University Press: Manchester, UK, 2017.
11. Gallivan, M.; Srite, M. Information technology and culture: Identifying fragmentary and holistic perspectives of culture. *Inf. Organ.* **2005**, *15*, 295–338. [CrossRef]
12. Hughes, T.P.; Hughes, T.P. *Human-Built World: How to Think about Technology and Culture*; University of Chicago Press: Chicago, IL, USA, 2004.
13. Murphie, A.; Potts, J. *Culture and Technology*; Macmillan International Higher Education: London, UK, 2017.
14. Bell, D.; Hollows, J. *Science, Technology and Culture*; McGraw-Hill Education: London, UK, 2005.
15. Wilcock, J.D. A General Survey of Computer Applications in Archaeology. Computer Applications in Archaeology, Science and Archaeology, no. 9. 1973. Available online: https://bibliographie.uni-tuebingen.de/xmlui/bitstream/handle/10900/61764/02_Wilcock_CAA_1973.pdf?sequence=2 (accessed on 27 June 2022).
16. Bierbaum, E.G. Records and access: Museum registration and library cataloging. *Cat. Classif. Q.* **1988**, *9*, 97–111. [CrossRef]
17. Chenhall, R.G.; Blackaby, J.R.; Greeno, P. *The Revised Nomenclature for Museum Cataloging: A Revised and Expanded Version of Robert G. Chenhal l's System for Classifying Man-Made Objects*; AltaMira Press: Lanham, MD, USA, 1989.
18. Bourcier, P.; Rogers, R. *Nomenclature 3.0 for Museum Cataloging*; Rowman & Littlefield: Lanham, MD, USA, 2010.
19. Stam, D.C. The quest for a code, or a brief history of the computerized cataloging of art objects. *Art Doc. J. Art Libr. Soc. N. Am.* **1989**, *8*, 7–15. [CrossRef]
20. Bearman, D. Interactive and Hypermedia in Museums. In Proceedings of the ICHIM—International Conference on Hypermedia & Interactivity in Museums, Pittsburgh, PA, USA, 14–16 October 1991; pp. 1–6.

21. Bearman, D. Museum strategies for success on the Internet. In Proceedings of the Conference on Museums and the Internet, London, UK, 10 May 1995; Volume 10.
22. Donovan, K. The best of intentions: Public access, the Web and the evolution of museum automation. In Proceedings of the Museums and the Web, Los Angeles, CA, USA, 16–19 March 1997; Volume 97, pp. 127–134.
23. Taylor, J.H.; Ryan, J. Museums and Galleries on the Internet. *Internet Res.* **1995**, *5*, 80–88. [CrossRef]
24. Schweibenz, W. The "Virtual Museum": New Perspectives For Museums to Present Objects and Information Using the Internet as a Knowledge Base and Communication System. *Isi* **1998**, *34*, 185–200.
25. Tsichritzis, D.; Gibbs, S.J. Virtual Museums and Virtual Realities. In Proceedings of the ICHIM—International Conference on Hypermedia & Interactivity in Museums, Pittsburgh, PA, USA, 14–16 October 1991; pp. 17–25.
26. Schweibenz, W. Virtual museums. *Dev. Virtual Mus. ICOM News Mag.* **2004**, *3*, 3.
27. Lepouras, G.; Vassilakis, C. Virtual museums for all: Employing game technology for edutainment. *Virtual Real.* **2004**, *8*, 96–106. [CrossRef]
28. Roussou, M. Immersive interactive virtual reality in the museum. In Proceedings of the TiLE (Trends in Leisure Entertainment), London, UK, May 2001. Available online: https://www.researchgate.net/profile/Maria-Roussou-2/publication/2861971_Immersive_Interactive_Virtual_Reality_in_the_Museum/links/0c9605192924ee109d000000/Immersive-Interactive-Virtual-Reality-in-the-Museum.pdf (accessed on 27 June 2022).
29. Hirose, M. Virtual reality technology and museum exhibit. *Int. J. Virtual Real.* **2006**, *5*, 31–36. [CrossRef]
30. Walczak, K.; Cellary, W.; White, M. Virtual museum exbibitions. *Computer* **2006**, *39*, 93–95. [CrossRef]
31. Wojciechowski, R.; Walczak, K.; White, M.; Cellary, W. Building virtual and augmented reality museum exhibitions. In Proceedings of the Ninth International Conference on 3D Web Technology, Monterey, CA, USA, 5–8 April 2004; pp. 135–144.
32. Pletinckx, D.; Callebaut, D.; Killebrew, A.E.; Silberman, N.A. Virtual-reality heritage presentation at Ename. *IEEE MultiMedia* **2000**, *7*, 45–48. [CrossRef]
33. Miyashita, T.; Meier, P.; Tachikawa, T.; Orlic, S.; Eble, T.; Scholz, V.; Gapel, A.; Gerl, O.; Arnaudov, S.; Lieberknecht, S. An augmented reality museum guide. In Proceedings of the 2008 7th IEEE/ACM International Symposium on Mixed and Augmented Reality, Cambridge, UK, 15–18 September 2008; pp. 103–106.
34. Bonis, B.; Stamos, J.; Vosinakis, S.; Andreou, I.; Panayiotopoulos, T. A platform for virtual museums with personalized content. *Multimed. Tools Appl.* **2009**, *42*, 139–159. [CrossRef]
35. Styliani, S.; Fotis, L.; Kostas, K.; Petros, P. Virtual museums, a survey and some issues for consideration. *J. Cult. Herit.* **2009**, *10*, 520–528. [CrossRef]
36. Lee, H.; Jung, T.H.; tom Dieck, M.C.; Chung, N. Experiencing immersive virtual reality in museums. *Inf. Manag.* **2020**, *57*, 103229. [CrossRef]
37. Shehade, M.; Stylianou-Lambert, T. Virtual reality in museums: Exploring the experiences of museum professionals. *Appl. Sci.* **2020**, *10*, 4031. [CrossRef]
38. Carrozzino, M.; Bergamasco, M. Beyond virtual museums: Experiencing immersive virtual reality in real museums. *J. Cult. Herit.* **2010**, *11*, 452–458. [CrossRef]
39. Parker, E.; Saker, M. Art museums and the incorporation of virtual reality: Examining the impact of VR on spatial and social norms. *Convergence* **2020**, *26*, 1159–1173. [CrossRef]
40. Barbieri, L.; Bruno, F.; Muzzupappa, M. User-centered design of a virtual reality exhibit for archaeological museums. *Int. J. Interact. Des. Manuf. (IJIDeM)* **2018**, *12*, 561–571. [CrossRef]
41. Keil, J.; Pujol, L.; Roussou, M.; Engelke, T.; Schmitt, M.; Bockholt, U.; Eleftheratou, S. A digital look at physical museum exhibits: Designing personalized stories with handheld Augmented Reality in museums. In Proceedings of the 2013 Digital Heritage International Congress (DigitalHeritage), Marseille, France, 28 October–1 November 2013; Volume 2, pp. 685–688.
42. Doerr, M. The CIDOC conceptual reference module: An ontological approach to semantic interoperability of metadata. *AI Mag.* **2003**, *24*, 75.
43. Baca, M.; Coburn, E.; Hubbard, S. Metadata and museum information. In *Museum Informatics*; Routledge: London, UK, 2012; pp. 123–144.
44. Purday, J. Think culture: Europeana. eu from concept to construction. *Bibliothek* **2009**, *33*, 170–180. [CrossRef]
45. Nelson, G.; Ellis, S. The history and impact of digitization and digital data mobilization on biodiversity research. *Philos. Trans. R. Soc. B* **2019**, *374*, 20170391. [CrossRef]
46. Mannoni, B. Bringing museums online. *Commun. ACM* **1996**, *39*, 100–105. [CrossRef]
47. Liu, Y.Q. Best practices, standards and techniques for digitizing library materials: A snapshot of library digitization practices in the USA. *Online Inf. Rev.* **2004**, *28*, 338–345.
48. Cotter, G.A. The digitization of museum specimens: Much is at stake as museums worldwide work to put their collections and data online. *Scientist* **2004**, *18*, 8–9.
49. Arias, P.; Herraez, J.; Lorenzo, H.; Ordonez, C. Control of structural problems in cultural heritage monuments using close-range photogrammetry and computer methods. *Comput. Struct.* **2005**, *83*, 1754–1766. [CrossRef]
50. Yastikli, N. Documentation of cultural heritage using digital photogrammetry and laser scanning. *J. Cult. Herit.* **2007**, *8*, 423–427. [CrossRef]

51. Grussenmeyer, P.; Landes, T.; Voegtle, T.; Ringle, K. Comparison methods of terrestrial laser scanning, photogrammetry and tacheometry data for recording of cultural heritage buildings. *Int. Arch. Photogramm. Remote Sens. Spat. Inf. Sci.* **2008**, *37*, 213–218.
52. Tucci, G.; Cini, D.; Nobile, A. Effective 3D digitization of archaeological artifacts for interactive virtual museum. *Int. Arch. Photogramm. Remote Sens. Spat. Inf. Sci.* **2011**, *38*, 413–420. [CrossRef]
53. Gonizzi Barsanti, S. 3D digitization of museum content within the 3dicons project. *ISPRS Ann. Photogramm. Remote Sens. Spat. Inf. Sci.* **2013**, *II-5/W1*, 151–156. [CrossRef]
54. Mathys, A.; Brecko, J.; Semal, P. Comparing 3D digitizing technologies: What are the differences? In Proceedings of the 2013 Digital Heritage International Congress (DigitalHeritage), Marseille, France, 28 October–1 November 2013; Volume 1, pp. 201–204.
55. Sportun, S. The future landscape of 3D in museums. In *The Multisensory Museum: Cross-Disciplinary Perspectives on Touch, Sound, Smell, Memory, and Space*; Rowman & Littlefield: Lanham, MD, USA, 2014; pp. 331–340.
56. Guidi, G.; Gonizzi Barsanti, S.; Micoli, L.L.; Russo, M. Massive 3D digitization of museum contents. In *Built Heritage: Monitoring Conservation Management*; Springer: Cham, Switzerland, 2015; pp. 335–346.
57. Singh, G. CultLab3D: Digitizing cultural heritage. *IEEE Comput. Graph. Appl.* **2014**, *34*, 4–5. [CrossRef]
58. Tommasi, C.; Achille, C.; Fassi, F. From point cloud to BIM: A modelling challange in the cultural heritage field. *Int. Arch. Photogramm. Remote. Sens. Spat. Inf. Sci.* **2016**, *41*, 429–436. [CrossRef]
59. Rahaman, H.; Champion, E. To 3D or not 3D: Choosing a photogrammetry workflow for cultural heritage groups. *Heritage* **2019**, *2*, 1835–1851. [CrossRef]
60. Grilli, E.; Farella, E.; Torresani, A.; Remondino, F. Geometric feature analysis for the classification of cultural heritage point clouds. In Proceedings of the 27th CIPA International Symposium "Documenting the past for a better future", Ávila, Spain, 1–5 September 2019; Volume 42, pp. 541–548.
61. Pierdicca, R.; Paolanti, M.; Matrone, F.; Martini, M.; Morbidoni, C.; Malinverni, E.S.; Frontoni, E.; Lingua, A.M. Point cloud semantic segmentation using a deep learning framework for cultural heritage. *Remote Sens.* **2020**, *12*, 1005. [CrossRef]
62. Bombini, A.; Anderlini, L.; Giaocmini, F.; Ruberto, C.; Taccetti, F. The AIRES-CH Project: Artificial Intelligence for Digital REStoration of Cultural Heritages Using Nuclear Imaging and Multidimensional Adversarial Neural Networks. In Proceedings of the International Conference on Image Analysis and Processing, Lecce, Italy, 23–27 May 2022; pp. 685–700.
63. Balletti, C.; Ballarin, M.; Guerra, F. 3D printing: State of the art and future perspectives. *J. Cult. Herit.* **2017**, *26*, 172–182. [CrossRef]
64. Ballarin, M.; Balletti, C.; Vernier, P. Replicas in cultural heritage: 3D printing and the museum experience. *Int. Arch. Photogramm. Remote Sens. Spat. Inf. Sci.* **2018**, *42*, 55–62. [CrossRef]
65. Muenster, S. Digital 3D Technologies for Humanities Research and Education: An Overview. *Appl. Sci.* **2022**, *12*, 2426. [CrossRef]
66. Milone, K.L. Dithering over digitization: International copyright and licensing agreements between museums, artists, and new media publishers. *Ind. Int. Comp. Law Rev.* **1994**, *5*, 393. [CrossRef]
67. Appel, S. Copyright, digitization of images, and art museums: Cyberspace and other new frontiers. *UCLA Entertain. Law Rev.* **1998**, *6*, 149. [CrossRef]
68. Appel, S.E. The copyright wars at the digital frontier: Which side are art museums on? *J. Arts Manag. Law Soc.* **1999**, *29*, 205–238. [CrossRef]
69. Pessach, G. Museums, digitization and copyright law: Taking stock and looking ahead. *J. Int. Media Entertain. Law* **2006**, *1*, 253.
70. Garvin, K.M. Reclaiming Our Domain: Digitization of Museum Collections and Copyright Overreach. *IDEA* **2018**, *59*, 455.
71. Kosmopoulos, D.; Styliaras, G. A survey on developing personalized content services in museums. *Pervasive Mob. Comput.* **2018**, *47*, 54–77. [CrossRef]
72. Kontogiannis, S.; Kokkonis, G.; Kazanidis, I.; Dossis, M.; Valsamidis, S. Cultural IoT Framework Focusing on Interactive and Personalized Museum Sightseeing. In *Towards Cognitive IoT Networks*; Springer: Cham, Switzerland, 2020; pp. 151–181.
73. Thakur, N.; Han, C.Y. Indoor Localization for Personalized Ambient Assisted Living of Multiple Users in Multi-Floor Smart Environments. *Big Data Cogn. Comput.* **2021**, *5*, 42. [CrossRef]
74. Vassilakis, C.; Antoniou, A.; Lepouras, G.; Poulopoulos, V.; Wallace, M.; Bampatzia, S.; Bourlakos, I. Stimulation of reflection and discussion in museum visits through the use of social media. *Soc. Netw. Anal. Min.* **2017**, *7*, 40. [CrossRef]
75. Antoniou, A.; Lepouras, G. Modeling visitors' profiles: A study to investigate adaptation aspects for museum learning technologies. *J. Comput. Cult. Herit. (JOCCH)* **2010**, *3*, 1–19. [CrossRef]
76. Naudet, Y.; Lykourentzou, I.; Tobias, E.; Antoniou, A.; Rompa, J.; Lepouras, G. Gaming and cognitive profiles for recommendations in museums. In Proceedings of the 2013 8th International Workshop on Semantic and Social Media Adaptation and Personalization, Bayonne, France, 12–13 December 2013; pp. 67–72.
77. Bowen, J.P.; Filippini-Fantoni, S. Personalization and the web from a museum perspective. In *Museums and the Web 2004*; Archives & Museum Informatics: Toronto, ON, Canada, 2004; Volume 4.
78. Marty, P.F. Museum informatics. In *Encyclopedia of Library and Information Sciences*; CRC Press: Boca Raton, FL, USA, 2010; pp. 3717–3725.
79. Aroyo, L.; Brussee, R.; Rutledge, L.; Gorgels, P.; Stash, N.; Wang, Y. *Personalized Museum Experience: The Rijksmuseum Use Case*; Archives & Museum Informatics: Toronto, ON, Canada, 2007.
80. Oberlander, J.; Karakatsiotis, G.; Isard, A.; Androutsopoulos, I.I. Building an adaptive museum gallery in Second Life. In *Museums and the Web 2007: Proceedings*; Archives & Museum Informatics: Toronto, ON, Canada, 2008.

81. Kuflik, T.; Kay, J.; Kummerfeld, B. Lifelong personalized museum experiences. In Proceedings of the Pervasive User Modeling and Personalization (PUMP'10), Big Island, HI, USA, 20 June 2010; pp. 9–16.
82. Roussou, M.; Katifori, A. Flow, staging, wayfinding, personalization: Evaluating user experience with mobile museum narratives. *Multimodal Technol. Interact.* **2018**, *2*, 32. [CrossRef]
83. Christodoulou, Y.; Konstantakis, M.; Moraitou, E.; Aliprantis, J.; Caridakis, G. Personalized Cultural Tours using Semantic Web Technologies. In Proceedings of the SMAP2019 Workshop, Larnaca, Cyprus, 9–10 June 2019; pp. 9–10.
84. Komianos, V.; Oikonomou, K. Adaptive exhibition topologies for personalized virtual museums. *IOP Conf. Ser. Mater. Sci. Eng.* **2018**, *364*, 012011. [CrossRef]
85. Fiorucci, M.; Khoroshiltseva, M.; Pontil, M.; Traviglia, A.; Del Bue, A.; James, S. Machine learning for cultural heritage: A survey. *Pattern Recognit. Lett.* **2020**, *133*, 102–108. [CrossRef]
86. Buddenbohm, S.; de Jong, M.; Minel, J.L.; Moranville, Y. Find research data repositories for the humanities-the data deposit recommendation service. *Int. J. Digit. Humanit.* **2021**, *1*, 343–362. [CrossRef]
87. Buddenbohm, S.; Eckart, T. *Merging Subject-Specific Searches of CLARIN and DARIAH in CLARIAH-DE: Challenges of Technical Integration*; Funded by the German Federal Ministry of Education and Research; Funding Reference Number 01UG1910 A to I; German Federal Ministry of Education and Research: Bonn, Germany, 2021. [CrossRef]
88. Krauwer, S.; Hinrichs, E. The CLARIN research infrastructure: Resources and tools for e-humanities scholars. In Proceedings of the Ninth International Conference on Language Resources and Evaluation (LREC-2014), Reykjavik, Iceland, 26–31 May 2014; pp. 1525–1531.
89. Blümm, M.; Schmunk, S. Digital Research Infrastructures: DARIAH. In *3D Research Challenges in Cultural Heritage II*; Springer: Cham, Switzerland, 2016; pp. 62–73.
90. Antoniou, A.; Lopez-Nores, M.; Yannick, N.; Solano, G.; Jones, C.; Vassilakaki, E.; Padfield, J. Empowering reuse of digital cultural heritage in context-aware crosscuts of European history. In Proceedings of the Workshop on Cultural Informatics co-located with the EUROMED International Conference on Digital Heritage 2018 (EUROMED 2018), Nicosia, Cyprus, 3 November 2018; pp. 1–10.
91. Poulopoulos, V.; Vassilakis, C.; Antoniou, A.; Lepouras, G.; Theodoropoulos, A.; Wallace, M. The Personality of the Influencers, the Characteristics of Qualitative Discussions and Their Analysis for Recommendations to Cultural Institutions. *Heritage* **2018**, *1*, 239–253. [CrossRef]
92. Katifori, A.; Roussou, M.; Perry, S.; Drettakis, G.; Vizcay, S.; Philip, J. The EMOTIVE Project-Emotive Virtual Cultural Experiences through Personalized Storytelling. In Proceedings of the CIRA@EuroMed, Nicosia, Cyprus, 3 November 2018; pp. 11–20.
93. Lim, V.; Frangakis, N.; Tanco, L.M.; Picinali, L. PLUGGY: A pluggable social platform for cultural heritage awareness and participation. In *Advances in Digital Cultural Heritage*; Springer: Cham, Switzerland, 2018; pp. 117–129.
94. Ioannides, M.; Davies, R. ViMM-Virtual Multimodal Museum: A manifesto and roadmap for Europe's digital cultural heritage. In Proceedings of the 2018 International Conference on Intelligent Systems (IS), Funchal, Portugal, 25–27 September 2018; pp. 343–350.
95. Anichini, F.; Gattiglia, G. Big archaeological data. The ArchAIDE project approach. In *The Data Way to Science*, Associazione Consorzio GARR: Rome, Italy, 2018; pp. 22–25.
96. Sabiescu, A.; Charatzopoulou, K. The museum as ecosystem and museums in learning ecosystems. In *Museum Experience Design*; Springer: Cham, Switzerland, 2018; pp. 325–345.
97. Daga, E.; Asprino, L.; Damiano, R.; Daquino, M.; Agudo, B.D.; Gangemi, A.; Kuflik, T.; Lieto, A.; Maguire, M.; Marras, A.M.; et al. Integrating citizen experiences in cultural heritage archives: Requirements, state of the art, and challenges. *ACM J. Comput. Cult. Herit. (JOCCH)* **2022**, *15*, 1–35. [CrossRef]
98. Kaldeli, E.; Tsakou, G.; Giglitto, D.; Cesaroni, F.; Tzouvaras, V.; Stamou, G. CultureLabs: Cultural heritage and digital technology at the service of social innovation. In Proceedings of the CEUR Workshop Proceedings, Larnaca, Cyprus, 9 June 2019; Volume 2412, p. 9.
99. Xepapadakou, A.; Papalexiou, E. Creating a Contemporary Performing Arts Archive. In Proceedings of the Archives—Borders, Identities, Reflections: International Conference, Online, 25–26 March 2021.
100. Castano, S.; Ferrara, A.; Montanelli, S.; Periti, F. From digital to computational humanities: The VAST project vision. In Proceedings of the Italian Symposium on Advanced Database Systems, Pizzo Calabro, Italy, 5–9 September 2021; Volume 2994, pp. 24–35.
101. Konstantakis, M.; Alexandridis, G.; Caridakis, G. A personalized heritage-oriented recommender system based on extended cultural tourist typologies. *Big Data Cogn. Comput.* **2020**, *4*, 12. [CrossRef]
102. Spiliotopoulos, D.; Margaris, D.; Vassilakis, C. Data-assisted persona construction using social media data. *Big Data Cogn. Comput.* **2020**, *4*, 21. [CrossRef]
103. Drakopoulos, G.; Voutos, Y.; Mylonas, P. Annotation-assisted clustering of player profiles in cultural games: A case for tensor analytics in Julia. *Big Data Cogn. Comput.* **2020**, *4*, 39. [CrossRef]
104. Morales-i Gras, J.; Orbegozo-Terradillos, J.; Larrondo-Ureta, A.; Peña-Fernández, S. Networks and Stories. Analyzing the Transmission of the Feminist Intangible Cultural Heritage on Twitter. *Big Data Cogn. Comput.* **2021**, *5*, 69. [CrossRef]
105. Deligiannis, K.; Raftopoulou, P.; Tryfonopoulos, C.; Platis, N.; Vassilakis, C. Hydria: An online data lake for multi-faceted analytics in the cultural heritage domain. *Big Data Cogn. Comput.* **2020**, *4*, 7. [CrossRef]

106. Bail, C.A. The cultural environment: Measuring culture with big data. *Theory Soc.* **2014**, *43*, 465–482. [CrossRef]
107. Amato, F.; Moscato, V.; Picariello, A.; Colace, F.; Santo, M.D.; Schreiber, F.A.; Tanca, L. Big data meets digital cultural heritage: Design and implementation of scrabs, a smart context-aware browsing assistant for cultural environments. *J. Comput. Cult. Herit.* **2017**, *10*, 1–23. [CrossRef]
108. Shi, M.; Zhu, W.; Yang, H.; Li, C. Applying semantic web and big data techniques to construct a balance model referring to stakeholders of tourism intangible cultural heritage. *Int. J. Comput. Appl. Technol.* **2016**, *54*, 192–200. [CrossRef]
109. Li, P.; Shi, Z.; Ding, Y.; Zhao, L.; Ma, Z.; Xiao, H.; Li, H. Analysis of the Temporal and Spatial Characteristics of Material Cultural Heritage Driven by Big Data—Take Museum Relics as an Example. *Information* **2021**, *12*, 153. [CrossRef]
110. Zhao, M.; Wu, X.; Liao, H.T.; Liu, Y. Exploring research fronts and topics of Big Data and Artificial Intelligence application for cultural heritage and museum research. *IOP Conf. Ser.: Mater. Sci. Eng.* **2020**, *806*, 012036. [CrossRef]
111. Levin, N.; Ali, S.; Crandall, D.; Kark, S. World Heritage in danger: Big data and remote sensing can help protect sites in conflict zones. *Glob. Environ. Change* **2019**, *55*, 97–104. [CrossRef]
112. Alexakis, E.; Kapassa, E.; Touloupou, M.; Kyriazis, D.; Georgopoulos, A.; Moropoulou, A. Innovative methodology for personalized 3D representation and big data management in cultural heritage. In Proceedings of the International Conference on Transdisciplinary Multispectral Modeling and Cooperation for the Preservation of Cultural Heritage, Athens, Greece, 10–13 October 2018; pp. 69–77.
113. Dimoulas, C.A. Cultural Heritage Storytelling, Engagement and Management in the Era of Big Data and the Semantic Web. *Sustainability* **2022**, *14*, 812. [CrossRef]
114. Prensky, M. Digital natives, digital immigrants part 2: Do they really think differently? *On Horizon* **2001**, *9*, 1–6. [CrossRef]
115. Cheong, P.H.; Fischer-Nielsen, P.; Gelfgren, S.; Ess, C. *Digital Religion, Social Media and Culture: Perspectives, Practices, and Futures*; Peter Lang: New York, NY, USA, 2012.
116. Fuchs, C. *Culture and Economy in the Age of Social Media*; Routledge: London, UK, 2015.
117. Kozinets, R.V.; Dolbec, P.Y.; Earley, A. Netnographic analysis: Understanding culture through social media data. *SAGE Handbook of Qualitative Data Analysis*; SAGE Publications Ltd.: New York, NY, USA, 2014; pp. 262–275.
118. Burns, K.S. *Celeb 2.0: How Social Media Foster Our Fascination with Popular Culture*; ABC-CLIO: Santa Barbara, CA, USA, 2009.
119. Giaccardi, E. *Heritage and Social Media: Understanding Heritage in a Participatory Culture*; Routledge: London, UK, 2012.
120. Baym, N.K. *Creator Culture: An Introduction to Global Social Media Entertainment*; NYU Press: New York, NY, USA, 2021.
121. Freeman, A.; Adams Becker, S.; Cummins, M.; McKelroy, E.; Giesinger, C.; Yuhnke, B. *NMC Horizon Report: 2016 Museum Edition*; The New Media Consortium: Austin, TX, USA, 2016.
122. Barry, A. Creating a virtuous circle between a museum's on-line and physical spaces. In Proceedings of the Museums and the Web, Albuquerque, NM, USA, 22–25 March 2006; pp. 22–25.

MDPI
St. Alban-Anlage 66
4052 Basel
Switzerland
Tel. +41 61 683 77 34
Fax +41 61 302 89 18
www.mdpi.com

*Big Data and Cognitive Computing* Editorial Office
E-mail: bdcc@mdpi.com
www.mdpi.com/journal/bdcc

www.ingramcontent.com/pod-product-compliance
Lightning Source LLC
LaVergne TN
LVHW070736100526
838202LV00013B/1250